School of Classical Dance

The textbook
of the Vaganova
Choreographic School,
Leningrad, USSR

Including the current eight-
year syllabus, a sample senior
lesson, and additional material
specially written for this edition
by Vera Kostrovitskaya

School of Classical Dance

Vera Kostrovitskaya
Alexei Pisarev

Authorized translation by John Barker

DANCE BOOKS
Cecil Court London

Edited by
Natalia Roslavleva and Vladislav Kostin

© 1995 Dance Books

First published 1978

This edition published 1995 by
Dance Books Ltd
15 Cecil Court
London WC2N 4EZ

ISBN 1 85273 044 7

Printed in the UK by
Hartnolls Ltd
Bodmin, Cornwall

A CIP catalogue record for this book
is available from the British Library

Contents

Développé Balancé (Quick) 118
Développé Balancé Taking the Leg Around
  a Quarter or a Half of a Circle and
  Quickly Returning It (d'ici-delá) 119
Développé Tombé 120
Battements Divisés en Quarts 122

III. Rond de Jambe

Rond de Jambe par Terre 125
Rond de Jambe par Terre en Tour-
  nant 129
Rond de Jambe en l'Air 129
Grand Rond de Jambe Jeté 133

IV. Port de Bras

The Basic Forms of the Academic Ports de
  Bras 137

V. Temps Lié

Temps Lié with a Bend of the Body 147
Temps Lié par Terre with a Tour 149
Temps Lié at 90° 150
Temps Lié at 90° with a Tour 152
Temps Lié at 90° with a Tour from Grand
  Plié 153

VI. The Poses of Classic Ballet

The Initial Study of the Poses Croisées 155
The Initial Study of the Poses Effacées 156
The Basic Big Poses Croisées 157

VII. Connecting and Auxiliary Movements

VIII. Jumps

XI. Turning Movements Used in Adagio

XII. Pointe Work

A Sample Lesson for the Senior Class

First Year Class

Second Year Class

Third Year Class

Fourth Year Class

Foreword

Vera Kostrovitskaya is one of the closest disciples of Agrippina Vaganova, entrusted by the great master to be her assistant. For many years senior teacher of the Vaganova Academic Choreographic School in Leningrad, Vera Kostrovitskaya is one of the leading figures in the development of the method of teaching classical dance, as it is now adopted for all the state schools of the Soviet Union.

It gives me great pleasure to introduce this book, wherein the very substance of classical dance and the method of its teaching is presented in great detail.

The first half of the book (sections I-VII) had been written by the late Alexei Pisarev, pupil of the renowned Vladimir Ponomaryov and for many years teacher of the Vaganova School and the Kirov Ballet company classes. After his untimely death Kostrovitskaya took upon herself the task of editing the sections written by him, giving them their final form.

In the book each movement is presented in each of its forms, beginning with the simplest and leading to the more complicated and perfect ones. Kostrovitskaya firmly supports this principle in her teaching, considering that this is the best way for the study of classical dance as it produces the best result.

It goes without saying that this principle evolved out of the general advance of the teaching method of Soviet ballet. It is based on a unified pedagogical system, practised by all Soviet teachers of classical dance, whether they work in Moscow, Leningrad, Tashkent or Ulan-Udeh.

It has been brought about by the great advance made by Soviet professional performing arts, including that of ballet.

One should not identify the Russian method as taught by Nikolai Legat and other teachers of his generation with the present Soviet method of ballet education, though the second is, of course, a progressive development of the first. The principles of the Russian School, the experience of its best teachers have been scientifically analysed, furthered and codified.

This process had been taking place for some years, starting in the 1920s when Vaganova began working out her method on a group of talented pupils. In teaching them she taught herself, and grew to be the leading figure in the great constructive work conducted by all the staff of the school that now bears her name.

Publication of Vaganova's *Basic Principles of Classical Ballet* in 1934 signified a new period in Soviet ballet instruction. Professor Vaganova unified the experience of generations and offered a clear and concise system of an infallible way of teaching and performing the entire "alphabet" of classical dance. She never denied the dependence of teaching on contemporary practice and, had she lived today, would have introduced innumerable changes into her system of training.

Therefore the present system as used and worked out by special "method departments" of the leading Soviet schools cannot really be called "the Vaganova method", though this great professor had a lot to do with its origin and development.

On the basis of the joint experience of the Leningrad and Moscow schools new syllabi had been worked out by 1961 — exactly ten years after Vaganova's death. These are based on an eight-year course of study, including all the material taught formerly in nine years. Since ballet is the art of the young, and it takes approximately ten years of professional experience to mature a real artist, it was deemed expedient to graduate dancers at an earlier age. By 1967 this syllabus was finally perfected, officially adopted and printed for the use of all Soviet ballet schools. It is included as an appendix to this book, translated by John Barker.

In 1969, Vera Kostrovitskaya was personally asked to work out a syllabus for a six-year course of study (so-called "experimental class"), starting at twelve, rather than at ten years of age. This syllabus is worked out so that the entire eight-year course is accelerated and passed in six years. The idea behind it was to give talented boys and girls, who had missed the required age of entrance, a chance to study and prove their worth. In the case of the really gifted ones this method invariably produced excellent results, and we could name some very prominent Bolshoi and Kirov dancers who had studied only in the "experimental" classes.

Incidentally, these syllabi are also methodological guides, for they contain minute details as to when, how and what to teach in each of the eight or six years.

Aside from these brief instructions, there are various other forms of keeping teachers all over the country posted on the latest developments. Most important are regular teachers' courses organised by the Moscow Academic Choreographic School.

Publication of reliable textbooks is an important part of this work. Such are *The ABC of Classical Dance* by Nadezhda Bazarova and Varvara Mei (1964), Vera Kostrovitskaya's and Alexei Pisarev's *The School of Classical Dance* (1968), Kostrovitskaya's *Temps Lié* (1958) and *100 Lessons in Classical Dance* (1972), *Partnering* by Nikolai Serebrennikov (1969), that great professor of male dancing Nikolai Tarasov's *Classical Dance* (1971), awarded posthumously a State Prize in arts for 1975, *et alia*, not to forget the valuable textbooks on character dance that is also taught according to a definite syllabus and method. These books have greatly simplified the spreading of correct methods of teaching, expanding the available methodological material.

Among them Kostrovitskaya's work attracts special attention by the extremely lucid manner of presentation. Of course, the book had been written for Soviet professional teachers and presumes that the reader is well versed in such prerequisites as co-ordination of the head, neck and arm movements, knows all the poses and positions by heart and does not have to be reminded about the essentials of the Vaganova theory concerning mastery of the entire body, which, in its turn, is determined by the control of the dancer's lower back.

But the English-language edition, as translated and prepared by John Barker, has taken these points into consideration.

Vera Kostrovitskaya, at the request of the translator, who is also well versed in the Vaganova method, has written some additional paragraphs to make such possible misunderstandings clear to the Western teacher.

The English-language edition, with these valuable additions, has acquired therefore a new quality.

In closing, I would like to emphasise that the improvement of the method of teaching, supported by the experience of numerous teachers, many of whom have now benefited from a higher pedagogical education, is ever continuing.

Kostrovitskaya's investment has enriched in no small measure this furthering of the Soviet method of teaching classical ballet.

Natalia Roslavleva,
Candidate of Arts

Moscow

From the author

In the Leningrad Choreographic School named after A. Y. Vaganova, much fruitful work is being done, perfecting the teaching method as a process for mastering the technique of dance. The programme for the study of classical dance has been continually re-examined and broadened.

My generation of ballet teachers is obliged to Vaganova and to her amazing teaching method. Still, Vaganova often expressed the thought that there was a necessity for compiling a textbook that would be broader and more detailed than her *Basic Principles of Classical Ballet,* and that would set down the development of technical execution and the whole method of teaching classical dance. The authors of this book have taken upon themselves the task of providing this.

The textbook has twelve sections. Section I covers the basic concepts: the meaning of the barre and centre exercise, the meaning of adagio and allegro; Section II deals with all forms of battement; Section III discusses ronds de jambe; Section IV treats of port de bras; Section V treats temps lié; Section VI describes the basic poses of classical dance; Section VII covers connecting and auxiliary movements; Section VIII takes up all the jumps; Section IX describes beats; Section X deals with tours on the floor and in the air; Section XI explains turning movements in adagio; Section XII covers the pointe work.

The first part of the book (Sections I-VII) is the work of the late A. A. Pisarev, a teacher of the choreographic school. The second part (Sections VIII-XII) was written by me.

In its structure, the book is similar to Vaganova's *Basic Principles of Classical Ballet,* which defines the form of the Russian classical dance; the movements are grouped by their basic genres, the technique of execution is described, etc.

But in contrast to A. Y. Vaganova's book, in which the movements are described mainly in their final form, as well as in contrast to the recent book by N. P. Bazarova and V. P. Mei, *The ABC of Classical Dance,* which covers the programme of the first three years of training, this textbook describes the evolution of each movement from its simplest to its final, most complex, form, as well as different versions of each movement.

The book thus includes the method of teaching classical dance for the entire eight-year course of training in the choreographic school, for men's as well as women's classes, since the development of the method of classical dance brings the system of teaching in women's and men's classes to mutual enrichment and even almost to full community. Thus, the series of methods for the execution of jumps used in the men's class (for example, the short spring-board-like rebound from the floor) has been adopted today by teachers of the women's classes; and to the men's classes have come, from the women's class, the sequence of movements and the sequence of the exercise at the barre and in the centre of the room (as being the most logical and useful for the muscles), the construction of the adagio combinations, and the co-ordination of the movements.

All the movements are described here with their musical counts and are supplied with a detailed explanation of the method of their execution. Beginning with the section on allegro, at the end of the description of each movement, an example of a combination with the given pas is offered.

For the execution of most of the movements that have been described in this book, stability (aplomb) is essential.

"The centre of balance is in the spine," A. Y. Vaganova said in her book, *Basic Principles of Classical Ballet.*

Defining this in more detail, it should be added that, for the stability of the body, the one most important thing is the gradual development of the small but very strong muscles in the small of the back, approximately in the area of the fifth vertebra.

Precisely this part of the back (with lowered shoulders and shoulder blades) must be felt by the dancer as if tightened and pulled upwards.

While in the first year it is not recommended that the small of the back be pulled up too strongly (for this can lead to an undesirable "caving in" of the back), in the following years, a well-developed back not only helps to provide stability in the poses and in tours on the floor and in the air, but makes possible a thorough mastery of the movements of the body as well. For the complicated work of the torso which consists of harmonious transitions from one pose to another, small inclinations and bends in the adagio, in the barre and centre exercise, in allegro, and in the movements on pointe, furthers a more complete mastery of the whole complex of dance movements and, consequently, permits the development of technique and a high artistic quality of execution.

But, by the words "development of technique", we do not imply work only on swift chaînés, a great number of fouettés, or the like. For it is possible to speak of a real technique of execution only when the body, arms, and head of the dancer become the means by which the language of dance is expressed and are responsive to every emotion.

The basic as well as the principal goal of the preparation of the ballet artist is the maximum development in him of his capacities to embody concrete theatrical images.

In connection with this, it is necessary to mention also the great importance of the development of the quality of "danciness", the elements of which are first absorbed in the elementary years, when even the simplest port de bras must be done expressively, intelligently, and unmechanically. For a dry

execution of port de bras in the various poses at the beginning
can leave a bad mark, and dry up the student for years to come.

Even in the first year, in the barre and centre exercise, when
the hands slightly open on the upbeat with a turn of the head,
before raising the arms to a position, there already is laid one
element of the development of future "danciness".

In the second year, battements tendus are sometimes done
with a port de bras (that is, with a gradual raising and lowering
of the arms accompanied by turns of the head and eyes), and
this also trains for a "danced" co-ordination of movements. At
this stage, battements frappés, ronds de jambe en l'air, etc.,
done in the number necessary for the development of the
strength of the legs, finish in the small poses croisées, effacées,
and écartées.

And in intermediate and advanced years, of course, the goals
of a "danced" co-ordination are considerably broadened.

It is necessary, however, to approach the development of
"danciness" carefully, with a sense of moderation, a feeling for
the limits of correct form and a clear and methodical
foundation, so that in no case do false "danciness" and empty
posing conceal a weak execution.

In speaking of the arms, it is necessary to emphasise
especially their double role in classical dance.

On the one hand, the arms, like the body, are one of the main
elements of the expressiveness of dance; but, on the other
hand, they actively *help* in dance, assist in providing stability in
the poses, provide force for all tours and other turning
movements on two legs and on one. Furthermore, the arms
play a special role in the execution of the big jumps, where, by
energetically helping in the take-off from the floor and the
suspension in the air, they simultaneously preserve and
emphasise the design of the pose.

In the big jumps (with the legs at a height of 90°), the arms
will usually be in full positions in the big poses. But, in small
jumps, the arms are held at a half-height (in half positions) in

the small poses, which creates an entirely different design for the dance, emphasising the difference between the big and small pas.

Furthermore, there must be a constant careful attention to the arms during the whole lesson, beginning with the barre exercise.

These general remarks on the holding of the lower back and the use of the arms, which I have written for the English edition of this book, should make it easier for the foreign ballet teacher to perceive at once a number of important principles that are fundamental to the Soviet method of teaching classical dance.

For I should like to hope that this work will do its modest bit in the pursuit of the general improvement of the teaching of classical dance throughout the world. With this in mind, I dedicate my work, with great respect and love, to the memory of Professor Agrippina Vaganova.

Vera Kostrovitskaya,
Merited Art Worker
of the Byelorussian SSR

Illustrations

Attitude en profile

Pas soubresaut
Grand jeté en attitude effacé

Grand jeté in 2nd arabesque

Attitude effacé épaulée

Variant of pose 1st arabesque
Pas soubresaut

Brisé dessus-dessous

1st arabesque penché (supported by one hand on the waist)

Pose écartée derrière (supported by one hand)

Arabesque (supported by one hand on the shoulder)

Grand sissonne in 1st arabesque

Introduction

The Sequence and Significance
of the Daily Exercise

Training in classical dance is begun with the barre and centre exercise.*

This many-faceted daily exercise developes the muscles of the legs, their turn-out, extension, and plié, as well as the organisation of the body, arms, and head, and the co-ordination of movements. As a result of daily training, the body acquires a pulled-up character, and stability is achieved. The future ballet artist accustoms himself to the proper distribution of body weight over both or over one of his legs.

The daily exercise begins at the barre and then, as the movements are mastered, is taken to the centre of the room. The adagio and the allegro work follow the centre exercise. The good habits acquired by the students in the exercise must be maintained by daily practice based on strict methodological rules.

The work load during the lesson should be distributed evenly among all the exercises. If the teacher finds it necessary, for example, to increase the amount of repetition of a certain movement, then he should shorten the following exercise, since all physical overwork is harmful and leads to a weakening of the musculature and ligaments. As a result of this, the legs may easily be damaged.

---

* In the Russian school, the entire series of movements practised at the barre is referred to as the "barre exercise"; similarly, the "centre exercise" and "pointe exercise".

The sequence of the exercise must not be haphazard. Depending on the degree of difficulty, the teacher must consider a useful and logical combination of movements and not join them in combinations merely for the sake of design.

In the first year, the barre and centre exercise is done on the whole foot (i.e., not on demi-pointe).

In the second year, a rise to demi-pointe is added to certain of the exercises at the barre, in which case, the first half of the exercise is done on the whole foot and the second half on demi-pointe. Later on, it will be done completely on demi-pointe.

In the third and following years, the barre and centre exercise (with the exception of pliés and ronds de jambe par terre) is done completely on demi-pointe. The small and the big adagios are also executed with the maximum use of a rise to demi-pointe.

In the elementary classes, a rise to low demi-pointe ($^1/_4$ pointe) is recommended, for this gives the greatest possibility of preserving the turn-out, which as yet is insufficiently developed and strengthened. This excludes, of course, the préparations for tours and tours sur le cou-de-pied, which are always done on high demi-pointe ($^3/_4$ pointe).

In the intermediate and advanced classes, the barre and centre exercise and the adagio may be done on high demi-pointe, in which case the turn-out of the legs must be carefully watched. Students with little turn-out must use the rise to high demi-pointe in the most disciplined and careful way.

On high demi-pointe, it is considerably more difficult to preserve the turn-out of the supporting leg; but, in training, it is necessary to introduce it, since the Achilles tendon, calf, buttocks, and thigh muscles are more actively included in the work; the arch of the foot is more strongly developed and strengthened, and the leg acquires a beautiful and finished line in the big poses, tours, pirouettes, tours chaînés, and other movements.

The Barre Exercise

First exercise. Plié in all the positions. In this exercise, the body, arms, and head all take part. The muscles and ligaments of the legs are stretched and contracted in calm, slow movements. The dancer's body is in this way prepared ("warmed-up") for the more complicated movements to follow.

Second exercise. Battement tendu combined with battement tendu jeté, in which the legs and feet are trained to work in a turned-out position, actively brings into play all the groups of small and big muscles. These are basic movements that strengthen the legs and feet.

Battement tendu jeté is organically linked with battement tendu, and therefore is done immediately after it. The tempo of execution is twice that of battement tendu.

Third exercise. Rond de jambe par terre (which, in the intermediate and advanced classes, is joined with grand rond de jambe jeté) should follow battement tendu.

Grand rond de jambe jeté is a complicated continuation of rond de jambe par terre and is done with an energetic throw of the leg to 90°.

Both of these movements, the most effective in the whole barre exercise, fulfil a common (but different, according to the degree of complexity) function—the development of the rotary mobility of the hip joint, on which the extent of the turn-out of the legs depends.

At the end of the rond de jambe combination, a port de bras is done, which prepares the body and arms for the following exercises in which they will more widely and more actively participate, since the movements become more complicated and tours and turning movements are brought in.

Fourth exercise. Battement fondu. This is the first movement in which the supporting foot is raised to demi-pointe, preparing it for later, more strenuous work.

Fondu produces a soft plié and the elasticity necessary for

jumps. One can compare this movement with the stretching and the controlled shortening of a taut rubber band.

Battement fondu is joined by frappé and double frappé, which are done sharply and energetically. This trains the muscles and tendons to switch quickly from soft, legato movements to sharp, staccato ones.

Fifth exercise. Rond de jambe en l'air develops the mobility of the knee joint and the strength and elasticity of its ligaments.

These circular movements of the lower leg in the air at a height of 45° can be combined with tours sur le cou-de-pied and petits battements sur le cou-de-pied, in which case a switch of the work of the muscles and ligaments also will occur.

It is recommended that rond de jambe en l'air be practised at 90° as well, for this produces strength of the thigh and prepares the leg for prolonged work with a turned-out thigh at this height.

Sixth exercise. Petit battement sur le cou-de-pied produces quick, free control of the lower part of the leg (from the knee to the toe) with a turned-out and immobile thigh. Tours sur le cou-de-pied and half or whole turns of the body toward or away from the barre may be combined with petit battement sur le cou-de-pied.

Seventh exercise. Battement développé. This is the most difficult movement of the barre exercise. It is done at 90° and higher and demands a thorough preparation.

Développé produces extension and the strength of the thigh, which helps to hold the working leg at its maximum height. It also prepares the body for the complicated adagio in the centre of the room and for jumps, where a strong thigh is necessary for the push from the floor and the soft demi-plié on landing.

Eighth exercise (which concludes the barre exercise). Grand battement tendu jeté. This promotes extension more actively than développé, for the big, energetic throwing out of the leg develops the elasticity of the muscles and tendons of the inside of the thigh and increases the mobility of the hip joint—the two main factors in the acquirement of extension.

This sequence of the barre exercise was not carelessly determined but is the result of a long course of development, with teachers introducing many changes and additions. Furthermore, it is the basis for instruction at the Leningrad Choreographic School today.

Reviewing the barre exercise, we see that each exercise introduces into the working of the muscles and the ankle, hip and knee joints something new: a rise to demi-pointe is introduced, the combinations become more complicated, and, in the sequence of movements, the tempo is speeded up (for example, rond de jambe en l'air, petit battement sur le cou-de-pied, etc., are at first done in quarter notes, then in eighths, and finally in sixteenths).

In the barre exercise, a great load also falls on the supporting leg, which must be strongly stretched and turned out, taking onto itself the weight of the entire body.

With the exception of those movements, in which the combination demands an inclination, twist, or turn of the torso, the body is in a vertical and pulled-up position in all the exercises.

In the movements of the arms through the positions, and in the poses, softness is produced; but the organisation of the arms and the securing of the correct form occurs mainly in 2nd position.

All possible inclinations and turns of the head accompany all the movements of the exercise, beginning with the first exercise at the barre.

The Centre Exercise

The exercise in the centre of the room has the same significance and development as the barre exercise, and its sequence is basically the same. However, it is considerably more difficult to preserve the turn-out of the legs and the stability of the body (especially on demi-pointe) without the help of the barre. The basic conditions for the mastery of stability are the correct distribution of the centre of weight of the pulled-up body over both legs or over one, level hips, and, especially, a pulled-up and turned-out thigh of the working leg.

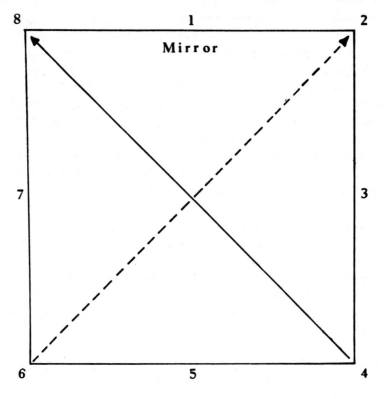

The points of the room

Working in front of the mirror, the student must not con-centrate on any one part of the body. Instead, he must take in with his eyes the entire body, watching for correct form and the position of the legs. And besides the visual perception, there must also be a *physical sensation* of the body as a whole, of its assembled and pulled-up character.

In the first year, the centre exercise proceeds in a strictly programmed sequence and is done in full.

In the second year, it has the same sequence as the barre exercise, but relevés lents and the simplest développés are added to pliés in all the positions.

In the third year, demi-rond de jambe développé and the big poses are added to pliés in all the positions.

From the fourth year on, before the centre exercise, it is recommended that a small and uncomplicated adagio (not more than eight measures of 4/4) be done, joining it in combination with battements tendus and jetés, and finishing it with small tours sur le cou-de-pied.

In the intermediate and advanced classes, the number of exercises may be cut because some movements can be combined. The enchaînements then become more complicated and varied.

Battements tendus, jetés, fondus, and grands battements may be considered the basic movements of the centre exercise and must be done every day.

Ronds de jambe par terre, ronds de jambe en l'air, battements frappés, doubles frappés, and petits battements sur le cou-de-pied may be combined with the basic movements.

Adagio

A dance phrase consisting of various kinds of développé, relevés lents, slow turns in the poses (tours lents), port de bras, all possible kinds of renversé, grand fouetté, tours sur le cou-de-pied, and tours in the big poses, is customarily called an adagio.

The movements of adagio are learned gradually. In the elementary classes, for example, the adagio consists of the simplest forms of relevé lent to 90°, développé, and port de bras, done at a slow tempo and on the whole foot.

In the intermediate classes, the adagio is complicated by tours lents in the big poses, prolonged stability on demi-pointe in the poses at 90°, the préparations for tours and tours in the big poses, tours sur le cou-de-pied, transfers from one pose to another, etc.

The tempo of this adagio is slightly faster than that in the elementary classes.

In the advanced classes, the concept of adagio takes on a relative character, since it can be done not only at a moderate tempo, but also faster, and is distinguished in its construction from the intermediate adagio by the inclusion of more turning movements, tours, renversés, fouettés, and even several jumps. This is no longer a "typical" adagio, for the accelerated tempo and its dynamic quality bring it nearer to allegro and, in fact, prepare the body for the pas allegro.

The importance of the adagio cannot be overestimated. It combines a series of movements into one harmonious whole, strengthens the movements of classical dance, and developes their correct form.

If, in the elementary and intermediate classes, the adagio develops stability, habits of a free and easy control of the body in the transitions from pose to pose, and smooth, expressive movements of the arms, then, in the advanced classes, the use of technically difficult movements in adagio, which are done, as a rule, on demi-pointe, and their complex, various linking, sums up a thorough technical preparation.

In masculine dance on the stage, adagio as a dance form is not encountered; but its study is equally necessary in both men's and women's classes, because it is inseparably linked with jumps, primarily with the big jumps, and gives them correct form.

Of all the sections of the lesson, the adagio includes the greatest quantity of heterogeneous movements and presents a special difficulty in correct musical and choreographic construction. The small adagio is built on a musical phrase of no less than four measures of 4/4—or eight or twelve measures. The big adagio is built on a phrase of from twelve to sixteen measures. Precise meter, rhythm, tempo, and the observance of metrical squareness are necessary for the construction of the adagio.

Strong movements such as tours in the big poses, grand fouettés, renversés, tours sur le cou-de-pied, and a series of other movements that must be included in adagio begin on the strong beats of the measure, that is, for example, on the first or third quarter of a four-beat measure. If the above movements fall on the weak beats of the measure (the second and fourth quarters), they disturb the unity of the musical and choreographic construction.

On the weak beats fall, mainly, the linking and auxiliary movements, the pas de bourrée, all kinds of passé, etc.

Allegro

The jumps are the most difficult part of the lesson. Everything that is produced by the barre and centre exercise and the adagio is directly linked with jumps and in many ways fosters their development. But special attention must be given to the jumps themselves.

A jump depends on the strength of the leg muscles, the elasticity and strength of the ligaments of the foot and knee, a developed Achilles tendon, the strength of the toes, and, especially, the strength of the thigh. The most important thing is to be able, at the moment of pushing away from the floor in plié, to preserve the simultaneity of the throwing out of the working leg and the pushing off from the floor with the heel, instep, and toes of the supporting leg, to pull up the body (which increases the height of the jump), to provide help with the arms, and to feel the assembly—the "gathered-togetherness"—of the whole body, not only before the jump, but at the moment of the jump, and at its conclusion in demi-plié as well.

In the first year, jumps are not studied until the organisation of the body, the turn-out of the legs, the elasticity of plié, etc., are sufficiently developed through practice of the barre and centre exercise.

Jumps in 1st, 2nd, and 5th positions (temps levés) facing the barre are learned first. Later on, changements de pieds, échappés, assemblés, jetés, etc., follow. Each new jump is studied facing the barre for no more than two weeks of daily lessons, after which it is practised in the centre of the room.

In all classes, the first jump combination must consist of little jumps from two feet to two feet, which will prepare the legs and feet for the more difficult small jumps onto one leg. The transition from little jumps to big ones must be gradual, uncomplicated big jumps being combined with small ones.

After that, the technically difficult big jumps may follow: saut de basque, cabriole, etc. (and, in advanced men's classes, these are complicated with beats, double turns, and tours en l'air). Then combinations of small jumps with beats are done.

The tempo of the jumping exercises is set by the teacher according to the demands of the study programme for the given class and, naturally, will be different in elementary, intermediate, and advanced classes. All new jumps are learned first at a slow tempo, then the tempo is speeded up as mastery of the movement is acquired.

The tempo set for a jump combination is preserved until the end of the phrase, even if the combination consists of different kinds of little and big jumps. Musical design plays an important role here, since it must underscore the diverse character of the jumps.

I. Basic Concepts

The Positions of the Feet

The five turned-out positions of the feet are fundamental to the execution of the movements of classical dance.

1st position. The feet are turned-out with the toes to the side in one straight line, and the heels touch.

2nd position. The feet are also turned-out in a straight line, but the heels are separated by the distance of about a foot.

3rd position. The turned-out feet are one in front of the other, the heel of one foot tightly adjoining the middle of the other foot.

4th position. The turned-out feet are parallel and opposite one another at the distance of about a foot. The toes of one foot are opposite the heel of the other.

5th position. The feet are turned-out, one in front of the other, and tightly adjoin each other. The toe of one foot must be in alignment with the heel of the other.

The Study of the Positions of the Feet

1. *Facing the barre.* The initial study of the positions of the feet takes place facing the barre for approximately two weeks of daily lessons.

    Stand facing the barre and place the feet with the heels together, the toes slightly (but not completely) turned-out. The leg muscles are taut, the knees stretched. The hands are on top of the barre, opposite the shoulders. They do not clasp the barre, but lie easily on it, the fingers adjoining one another. The thumb, joined to the remaining fingers, also lies on top of the barre. The elbows are held easily in a low position and are slightly in front of the body, opposite the hands. The head is held erect, the eyes directed forward. The body is erect, with the stomach tightly pulled up, the buttocks muscles pulled up and tense, the shoulders lowered, and the thorax open. The shoulder blades must not be pulled together, but should be held in a relaxed condition.

Having prepared the correct position of the whole body, move to 1st position: without moving the heel or lifting the foot from the floor, rotate the right foot to a turned-out position; then turn out the left foot, so that the feet form a straight line. The centre of the body's weight is distributed evenly on both feet.

The leg that is in motion and free from the weight of the body is called the working leg, and the leg that bears the weight of the body at the moment of movement is called the supporting leg. The supporting leg may be immobile or may itself be in motion (as in battement fondu, for example).

Now, going from 1st position to 2nd, take the right—the working-leg, stretching the instep and toes, to the side in a straight line, at the same time transferring the centre of the body's weight onto the left, supporting, leg, which at the moment of movement remains immobile and turned out. With the lowering of the heel of the working foot onto the floor in 2nd position, the body's weight is again distributed evenly on both legs. The hands slide a little along the barre to maintain the position opposite the shoulders.

To go to 3rd position, stretch the instep and toes of the right foot, transferring the centre of the body's weight back onto the left leg. Then, moving the hands slightly along the barre, to keep them opposite the shoulders, the working foot moves, in a straight line, in front of the supporting foot. Having placed the foot in 3rd position (the heel of one foot tightly pressed against the centre of the other foot), transfer the centre of the body's weight evenly onto both feet.

After the mastery of 3rd position, 5th position is learned (also facing the barre). To move from 3rd position to 5th, transfer the centre of the body's weight onto the left, supporting, leg, and take the right, working, foot, with a stretched instep and toes, forward, so that the toe of the working foot is opposite the heel of the supporting foot. Then the working foot returns to the supporting foot and is placed in 5th position. The body's weight is distributed evenly on both feet.

Having done 1st, 2nd, 3rd, and 5th positions facing the barre with the right foot, repeat them with the left. Fourth position is learned last, since it is the most difficult. The study of 4th position is begun after 1st, 2nd, 3rd, and 5th positions have been mastered facing the barre. Still later, the students will continue their study of the five positions of the feet standing sideways to the barre, holding it with one hand.

Having acquainted the students with the positions and with the changing of the feet in the positions, the musical accompaniment is introduced. The tempo is slow. Stand in each position for four measures of 4/4, eight measures of 2/4, or sixteen measures of 3/4 (later on, the same number of measures will be required for pliés in all the positions). The changing of the foot to the next position takes place on an introductory measure of 4/4 in the following manner: on the first quarter, the foot, with the stretched instep and toes, is taken in the required direction; on the second quarter, it is held stretched; on the third quarter, it is placed in the position; and on the fourth quarter, the position is maintained.

Later on, during pliés, the changing of the foot from position to position is done in an unbroken fashion. The taking of the working foot to the side and its return to the initial position take place on the last eighth of the 4/4 measure, thus maintaining intact the musical and choreographic phrase.

After the mastery of the positions of the feet, preparatory position and the positions of the arms are learned. And later on, the movements of the feet through the positions are accompanied by movements of the arms.

2. *With one hand on the barre.* The study of the positions of the feet continues standing sideways to the barre. The students start with their left hand on the barre, lightly holding it with the fingers (the thumb clasps the barre from below, the other fingers from above). The elbow of the curved left arm is held easily in a low position and is slightly in front of the body. The right arm remains in preparatory position. The head is turned toward the right shoulder. The feet, starting with the inside, open to 1st position one after another.

The musical time is 4/4. A préparation (that is, preparatory movements of the arm and head, described more fully on page 59.) precedes the study of the positions of the feet and the transitions from one position to another and takes one measure of introductory music in the following manner: On the first and second quarters, the arm is raised to 1st position; and on the third and fourth quarters, it opens to 2nd position. Then, at the beginning of the musical phrase, taking the whole of the first measure, the arm is lowered from 2nd position to preparatory position. The movement is executed two times in all. Then the working leg is taken to 2nd position.

During the changing of the position of the feet, the arm remains in 2nd position, the head turned to the side of the arm that is in 2nd position, with the eyes directed at the hand. Following this, 2nd, 3rd, 4th, and 5th positions are studied, also accompanied by movements of the arm and head.

The drawing of the working leg out along the floor to the side, the lowering of the heel in 2nd position, and the changing of the centre of the body's weight onto the supporting foot during the change from 1st to 2nd position and from 2nd to 3rd position are the same as during the study of the positions of the feet facing the barre.

Going from 3rd position to 4th, it is necessary first to transfer the weight of the body onto the left leg, and then take the right leg forward, stretching the instep and toes. The toe of the working foot must be opposite the heel of the supporting foot. As the heel is lowered to the floor, the toes are drawn back and the right foot assumes a turned-out position parallel to the left foot. At the moment of turning out the foot, the upper part of the working leg (the thigh) moves a little closer to the supporting leg. And during the lowering of the heel to the floor, the body moves forward so that its weight is distributed equally onto both legs.

The turned-out 3rd position is studied only in the first year. Later on, it is dropped, since it is not used in classical dance. When 3rd position is excluded, the change of the foot to 4th position at the barre and in the centre of the room goes from 2nd position: stretching the instep and toes of the working leg, transfer the body's weight onto the supporting leg; the working foot, without taking the toe from the floor, moves forward in an arc and is put in 4th position.

Going from 4th to 5th position, transfer the weight of the body onto the left leg, and stretch the instep and toes of the right foot, freely moving the toe forward. The right foot then moves to the left foot (the foot gradually taking on a turned-out position) and is placed in 5th position.

At the end of the exercise (on the final measure of 4/4), the arm is lowered to preparatory position. Having done the exercise with the right leg, turn toward the barre to the other side and repeat it with the left.

General Remarks. The feet, having been placed in a position, must bear the body's weight evenly, without a preponderance of weight over the big or the little toe.

During the changing of the feet and the standing in the positions, it is necessary to maintain the correct position of the whole body—the arms, body, and head. The foot should be ¹₋d out with a turned-out heel, without lifting the toe from the floor, and with the whole leg turned out from the hip joint.

On taking the working foot to a new position, the heel must not immediately be raised from the floor: first the heel should be pressed lightly on the floor, but this pressure must not prevent the free sliding of the foot along the surface of the floor. In the beginning of the movement, the whole foot slides, then the instep and toes are gradually stretched.

On the return of the working leg to the supporting leg, the toe slides without coming off the floor. Then the instep is softly lowered, the heel comes down, and the whole foot, lightly touching the floor, finishes the sliding movement.

The Positions of the Arms

In classical dance, an enormous role belongs to the placement of the arms. In fact, the arms are a basic means of expression for the ballet dancer. They give a finished design to the various poses. Furthermore, the arms must help in the execution of the dance movements, especially turns on the floor and in the air and the difficult jumps, where they actively aid the body and legs.

By the placement of the arms we mean the manner of

holding them in a definite form, at a definite height, in the basic positions as well as in the other forms that are accepted in classical dance.

The training of the arms is begun with preparatory position and the three basic positions. In academic work, study of preparatory position is obligatory, for from it the arms begin the movement to all the other positions.

Preparatory position. The arms are lowered in front of the body and at no point come in contact with it. The elbows are to the side, slightly bent, the arms forming an oval. The hands and fingers are curved with the palms facing up. The hands almost touch each other, the distance between them being approximately the width of two fingers. The fingers are lightly held together with the thumb directed toward the middle finger (which is moved somewhat forward), without, however, actually touching it.

The shoulders, in preparatory position as well as in all other positions, are lowered. They must not be moved forward, backward, or raised.

Some ballet masters and teachers distinguish seven positions of the arms. We feel, however, that the three positions accepted at the Leningrad Choreographic School are sufficient to develop the basic directions of the arms and successfully fulfil the task of their organisation. First position gives the direction of the arms to the front; second position, the direction to the side; third position, the direction upward. There is no reason to consider the other ways of holding the arms as positions in themselves, since they consist of combinations of the three basic positions and are learned without special designation, by the visual demonstration of the teacher.

1st position. The arms are raised in front of the body on a level with the diaphragm, slightly bent in the elbows and wrist, forming an oval, as in preparatory position. The palms are turned towards oneself. The elbows and fingers are level. The shoulders are lowered. The hands are near each other, the distance between the fingers and their arrangement being the same as in preparatory position.

The accepted height for 1st position of the arms at the level of the diaphragm is not arbitrary. At such a height, the arms can support the body well, owing to the tension of the muscles of the upper part of the arm (from the shoulder to the elbow); this is particularly important for pirouettes, tours en l'air, tours chaînés, and many other movements where the arms are fixed in 1st position during the tour. In the big jumps, 1st position is a kind of springboard before the opening of the arms to another position, and helps to pull up the body at the moment of take-off. If the arms are raised higher than the accepted level, they cannot help the body, and lose their activity. A slight deviation from the level of the arms in 1st position is allowed only when lowering them, never when raising them. Moreover, the accepted height of the arms in 1st position allows the chest area to be exposed, which is important from an esthetic point of view.

2nd position. The arms are open to the side at the height of the shoulders. The shoulders, elbows, and hands are on one level. The elbows are turned back, the line of the arms forming an arc, and the palms are turned to the audience. The arrangement of the fingers is the same as in preparatory position and in 1st position. The arms should be a little in front of the shoulders.

During the barre and centre exercise, one must carefully observe the correct positions of the arms, the level of which is maintained by the muscles of the shoulders and the upper part of the arms. They should not be taken behind the shoulders, and the shoulders must not be raised.

The arms, raised to the level of the shoulders, maintain a horizontal position. If they are raised higher, the shoulders will inevitably be raised. If the shoulders are held in place but the hands are raised above their level, it will be impossible to preserve the correct line, for the elbows will be too low. If the hands are lowered somewhat below the level of the shoulders, they may not destroy the correct line, but they will seem lethargic.

3rd position. The arms are raised and form an oval above the head. The hands are near each other, as in preparatory position and 1st position. The palms are turned downward. The arrangement of the fingers is as before. The teacher must watch that the elbows do not go forward and that the hands are not lowered.

The arms must not be directly *over* the head, and it is even more inadmissible for them to go *behind* the head. Instead, they should be slightly *in front* of the head. This is especially important for men, since, in taking the arms back, the developed shoulder muscles will bulge and create an impression of raised shoulders. Furthermore, when seen in profile, the face should not be covered by the arms.

The correctness of the arms in 3rd position can be checked in the following manner: without raising the head, look upward; if the little fingers are visible, 3rd position is correctly placed. If all the fingers are visible, the arms must be taken slightly back. If the little fingers are not visible, the arms have gone too far back. Such a check should be conducted until the students possess the habit of correctly fixing the arms in 3rd position by means of the mirror and the physical sensation.

The other positions of the arms. Besides the three positions enumerated, in academic as well as stage work there are intermediate positions of the arms called half-positions. For example, there is the position between preparatory position and 1st position (approximately at waist level) to the front and to the side, and the position between 2nd and 3rd positions, in which the arms may be either curved or outstretched.

The position of the arms in arabesques is completely different from the basic arm positions or the position of the arms in the poses, for the arms do not make a curved line. In arabesques, both arms are freely extended without tension. The palms are turned down, and the hands and fingers continue the straight line of the arms. The fingers are arranged together, the thumb near the middle finger. Such a position of the arms is maintained in other poses as well, for example, in attitude allongée.

Changing the Arms from One Position to Another

The study of the positions of the arms takes place in the centre of the room in the following order: from preparatory position, the arms are raised to 1st position, then go to 3rd, and, opening, are lowered to 2nd, after which the movement ends in the initial position. Such a sequence is the most logical for the study of the positions in movement.

Elementary study takes place at a slow tempo, with a pause in each position. If the execution is done in 3/4 time, then, on the first measure, the arms are raised to 1st position, and on the second measure they are held in that position, etc.

The hands play an important role in the development of softness and expressiveness of the arms. They make the arms come alive and "speak". In the raising and lowering of the arms, in transitions to a position or a half-position, and in various combinations, the movement begins with the hands. The movement of the hands must be especially active in the opening of the arms through 1st position to 2nd and from 3rd position to 2nd; in these movements, the oval line is somewhat straightened, which makes the arms more expressive.

Students must be carefully trained in the transitions of the arms from 3rd to 2nd position, and from 2nd position to preparatory position. One must watch that during the opening of the arms from 3rd to 2nd position, the hands do not turn their palms up, but gradually open the palms to the audience. In this, the elbows should not be lowered, but maintain the level line of the curved arms.

When lowering the arms from 2nd position to preparatory position, the arms are slightly raised, with the hands simultaneously cast slightly upward, so that the palms are turned down. The oval line is slightly straightened. During the lowering of the arms, the hands fall a little behind and, during the movement, gradually curve the line. This turning and falling behind of the hands during the lowering and raising of the arms can be done only when movement through the positions is well mastered.

The academic raising of the arms to 2nd position takes place through 1st position. The raising of the arms to 3rd position can take place from 1st or 2nd position. The lowering of the arms from 3rd position to preparatory position takes place through 2nd position. From 3rd position to 2nd, the arms can be lowered directly, or may also pass through 1st position.

The Participation of the Arms in the Daily Exercise

In a static position or in a jump, at the moment the pose is fixed in the air, the arms must maintain the clarity of the line. In the movement of one or both arms, it is necessary to see that, at times when they are in front of the torso or the head, they do not go behind the central line of the entire figure.

In the barre exercise, the arms, as a rule, maintain a static position: one in 2nd position, the other on the barre. Second position is the most comfortable and useful one in which to work, therefore it is used as the basic position at the barre (especially in elementary classes). And, in the execution of those exercises in the centre of the room that are done on demi-pointe, the arms, opened in 2nd position, help to maintain balance.

Many exercises at the barre and in the centre begin with a preliminary opening of the arms to a position (most often to 2nd) or to combined positions. This is the preparation for the exercise, that is, the préparation.

To begin with, the arm is raised to 1st position, then the leg, from the initial position (1st or 5th), simultaneously with the arm, opens to 2nd position. In the préparation for certain exercises (rond de jambe par terre, for example), the arm and leg begin the movement together.

In the first half of the first year, the préparation at the barre is done on the introductory measure of 4/4 in the following manner: on the first and second quarters, the arm is raised to 1st position; on the third and fourth quarters, it is brought to 2nd position. In the centre, both arms are raised in the same manner simultaneously..

In the second half of the first year and in the following years, one or both arms are raised to the required position before the exercise on a two-count introduction played with chords. As the arms are raised to 1st position, the head (which, by this time, begins all of the barre exercises turned toward the outside shoulder) turns straight forward and the eyes accompany the hand (later on, the head will slightly incline toward the shoulder opposite the raised arm). Then, together with the movement of the arm, the head turns to the side of the arm opening to 2nd position, the eyes accompanying the hand.

At the end of the exercise, the arms are lowered to preparatory position on the final measure of 4/4 (in advanced classes, on two final chords).

In certain of the exercises at the barre and in the centre (for example, in battement développé and fondu), one or both arms can begin the movement simultaneously with the legs at the beginning of the musical phrase and finish it simultaneously with them at the end of the phrase. This develops co-ordination of the arms with the legs.

The Head and Face

The position of the head and the expression of the face have a great importance in dance. Without the various inclinations and turns of the head no pose has a finished look. The expressiveness of the face and eyes inspires the pose.

The positions of the head, its inclinations and turns, are

studied from the first year. Head movements are introduced gradually, first in the préparation (during the opening of the arms to 2nd position), then in grand plié, in épaulement, and in the study of port de bras and the poses.

During the exercise, students often, from tension and the physical exertion, strain their neck or bite their lips. Convulsive twitchings of the face muscles may appear. These defects should be eliminated quickly so that they do not become a habit and interfere later on.

Épaulement

In classical ballet, various positions of the body itself are encountered: the body may directly face the audience or the mirror (en face), be 1/8 of a turn away from the audience (épaulement), have the back to the audience, or be in profile to the audience. However, those most widely used in ballet are the positions en face and with épaulement.

Épaulement is a term for the position of the body after it has made in eighth of a turn away from the audience, and it is closely linked with the concepts croisé and effacé.

Croisé (French, "crossed") indicates a position of the body turned in such a way that it produces a crossing of lines from the point of view of the audience.

Effacé (French, "effaced") indicates a position of the body turned in such a way as to be without crossed lines from the point of view of the audience.

Thus, for example, if in 5th position the right foot is in front, with the body turned 1/8 of a turn to the left, the right shoulder forward and the head to the right, this is the épaulement croisé. If, without changing the position of the shoulders or the head, the right foot is placed in 5th position back, the crossing of the lines is lost and the body assumes the pose épaulement effacé.

The concepts of croisé and effacé are the basis for all of the small and big poses of classical dance.

In the first year, épaulement is introduced in the second half of the year in the centre exercise, first in plié in 3rd, 4th, and 5th positions, then in the study of the poses, port de bras, and temps lié.

Stability (Aplomb)

Stability is one of the basic elements of classical dance. The stance of the body in the poses and in exercises on the whole foot, on demi-pointe, and on pointe, on both legs and on one, must be assured and steady, without movement of the supporting leg and without hopping on it.

To maintain prolonged stability on demi-pointe and on pointe on one leg in a fixed pose is difficult. And it is still more difficult not to lose the stability of a pose after landing on one foot from a big jump with a turn in the air, or in tours and pirouettes.

The development of stability is begun in the first year, with the training of the legs and the body in the barre exercise, through which the student acquires the ability to distribute the centre of the body's weight evenly on one or both legs. Generally speaking, for stability, the posture of the body must be vertical, without an inclination forward or back or a sagging in the waist; the back is erect and the buttocks muscles are tensed. The waist is strengthened by the tension of the lower back muscles. However, in no case should the student attempt to hold the back by joining the shoulder blades, for this inevitably weakens the pulled-up character of the lower torso.

The basis of stability lies in the preservation of the vertical axis, which passes through the middle of the head and body to the ball of the supporting foot when one is standing on demi-pointe, and in front of the heels when one is standing on the whole foot.

To attain stability in those cases where a bend of the body to the side or back or an inclination forward is required, the centre weight must be over the supporting leg, through which passes the vertical axis of the body. Equilibrium is maintained by the correct distribution of the body's weight on either side of this axis in combination with a pulled-up lower back and thighs. A secure, turned-out position of the thigh of the working leg and the turn-out of the supporting leg also aids in the achievement of stability.

The Concepts en Dehors and en Dedans

Rotary movements of the leg in a circle, or turns of the body on the floor or in the air around its vertical axis on one or on both legs, either traveling or in place, are defined by the concepts en dehors (outward) and en dedans (inward).

Students are first acquainted with these concepts in the study of rond de jambe par terre, where the working leg from 1st position moves forward and in an arc to the side and back, closing the semi-circle in 1st position—that is, it describes an "outward" semicircle from front to back, "away" from the supporting leg (a rond de jambe en dehors). The movement of the leg to the back and in an arc to the side and forward, describing an "inward" semicircle, "toward" the supporting leg, is a rond de jambe en dedans.

Having thus learned, in rond de jambe par terre, the movement of the leg in a circular movement en dehors and en dedans, it is much easier for the student to orient himself to these two concepts when learning other turning movements and tours. A turn en dehors is a turn "away" from the supporting leg (to the right, if one is standing on the left foot); a turn en dedans is a turn "toward" the supporting leg (to the left, if one is standing on the left foot). The concepts en dehors and en dedans, therefore, underlie the definition of all turning movements of the leg and the body in an outward or inward direction.

Plié

Demi-plié (a half-bending of the knees) and grand plié (a deep, complete bending of the knees) develop the Achilles tendon and the knee and ankle ligaments, the elasticity and strength of which play an important role in classical ballet. In pliés, especially grands pliés, the back should actively participate in the movement by maintaining an erect (that is to say, vertical) position, which makes possible the development and strengthening of the muscles of the lower back.

Demi-plié is a constant companion of jumps, for every jump begins and ends with an elastic and controlled demi-plié. Therefore, it must be given special attention, not only when it is first executed at the barre in the five positions, but also in the various combinations of movements.

General Remarks. The study of plié is begun in the first year with demi-plié in the various positions of the feet, facing the barre. Fourth position (as when learning the positions of the feet) is not included until later, when the students are doing demi-plié holding onto the barre with one hand.

The study of grand plié is begun later, for it demands organised,* turned-out, and sufficiently strong legs, and an organised and secure back. These qualities are formed during the study of the positions of the feet, demi-plié, battement tendu, and the other movements executed on the floor. Only after this is it possible to go on to the study of grand plié.

In demi-plié and grand plié, special attention should be paid to the turned-out position of the legs, otherwise the Achilles tendon will not be fully included in the work and will not receive the necessary development. The centre of the body's

---

*   By the "organisation" of a part of the body we mean its deliberate and conscious arrangement, not only in itself but also in its relationship to the adjacent parts, so that it will function in the movements of classical ballet with the greatest possible efficiency.

weight must be distributed evenly on both feet. There should be no rolling over onto the inner side of the foot or resting of the weight on the big toe. The body must be erect and pulled up, the back held without caving in, and the buttocks muscles tensed (especially in the execution of plié in 2nd position). The muscles of the legs are also tense, the knees turned-out to the utmost and, during the plié, directed outward, in alignment with the feet.

The bending and straightening of the knees is smooth, without jerks, and having reached the lowest point, one must not pause, or "sit" in plié, but begin to rise immediately, so as not to interrupt the movement.

In the first year, demi-plié and grand plié are studied as separate exercises and are done twice in each position. Later on, two demi-pliés followed by a single grand plié in each position begin the daily exercise.

In the following years, the quantity of pliés is cut by half, because movements are added to the barre and centre exercise that are related to plié (such as fondu and soutenu); a superfluous number of pliés weakens the ligaments of the leg. It is recommended that, in daily lessons and throughout the whole course of study, only one set of pliés at the barre be done. On one day, they will be practised with the right side to the barre and on the next day, with the left side, etc. Such an alternation will produce an even development of both legs.

Demi-Plié. In demi-plié, the heels do not leave the floor. The resulting stretch develops the Achilles tendon and produces the correct position for the take-off in jumps, where the push from the floor is done with the heels. In practising demi-plié, the arm opens beforehand to 2nd position.

In the very beginning of the training (in the first half of the first year), demi-plié is done in two measures of 4/4 and at a slow tempo. During the first measure, the knees bend; during the second, they straighten. In the second half-year, demi-plié is done in one measure of 4/4. On the first and second quarters, the plié is done, and, on the third and fourth quarters, the legs are straightened. In the following years, it is also executed in one measure of 4/4, but the tempo is somewhat faster.

Grand Plié. In the grand plié in 2nd position, the heels do not come off the floor. However, in grand plié in the other positions, the heels should remain on the floor as long as possible, that is, until the deep bend of the knees forces them to rise involuntarily, and then, during the straightening of the legs, they should be lowered to the floor as soon as possible, but without accelerating the tempo of the straightening. Both heels must come off the floor and return to the floor simultaneously. For the entire duration of the plié, the utmost turn-out of the thighs and the feet must be maintained.

In the plié in 4th position, the centre of the body's weight must be distributed correctly between the feet and the plié done equally on both legs.

In the first half-year, grand plié is studied at a slow tempo in two measures of 4/4; during the first measure, the plié is done, during the second, the straightening. In the second half-year, it may be done in one measure of 4/4, but the slow tempo is maintained. And in the subsequent elementary years (second and third), grand plié is still done at a slow tempo in one measure of 4/4. In the intermediate and advanced classes, it is also executed in one measure, but the tempo is somewhat faster.

Demi-plié and grand plié can also be combined with each other or with other movements, and can be done in one measure of 2/4.

Grand plié demands co-ordination of the movements of the legs, arms, and head, and the active participation of the body. Before beginning pliés at the barre, the arm opens through 1st position to 2nd (the préparation). During the plié, the arm is lowered from 2nd position to preparatory position, passing near the knee but without touching it, and then is raised to 1st position before opening to 2nd. The movement of the arm is smooth and absolutely co-ordinated with the movement of the legs, beginning and ending simultaneously with the beginning and endind of the plié. This exact distribution of the entire movement on the musical counts develops co ordination.

In lowering the arm (especially in plié in 4th and 5th positions), it is necessary to watch that the shoulder does not move forward.

Before beginning the plié, the head is turned to the side of the arm that is opened to 2nd position and the eyes are directed toward the hand. During the movement of the arm to preparatory position, the eyes accompany its movement, and, in doing so, the head is slightly lowered and, without turning, slightly inclines toward the shoulder that is opposite the working arm. Then, as the arm is raised to 1st position, the head is raised and turned to follow the arm as it opens to 2nd position, the eyes still directed toward the hand.

Plié in the Centre of the Room. In the centre exercise, demi-plié and grand plié in all the positions are studied at first en face, both arms opening to 2nd position on the préparation. Later, the 3rd, 4th, and 5th positions are done with épaulement and only the 1st and 2nd positions are en face. Demi-plié and grand plié in 4th position in the centre of the room can be done croisé or effacé.

In the beginning of the study of plié in 4th position in the centre, it is recommended that the arms be held without changing their position: one arm (that which is opposite the leg in front) in 1st position, the other in 2nd. This will help to keep the body erect and to prevent it from bending sideways. Later on, when the correct position of the body and shoulders is secured, the usual arm movements for plié in the other positions can be added.

5*

Relevé

In ballet terminology, *relevé* (French, "raised") has a double meaning: it can mean a rise to demi-pointe or pointe on two legs or on one, or it can mean the raising of the stretched leg to a different height in any direction. Relevé, in either sense, is done from all positions.

Relevé, a Rise to Demi-Pointe or Pointe. In the first year, the rise to demi-pointe is initially studied facing the barre, with the help of special exercises: first on stretched legs, then with demi-plié on two legs and on one (plié-relevé). During the rise to demi-pointe on one leg, the fully stretched foot of the other leg is in the position sur le cou-de-pied devant or derriére (in front or in back).

Relevé, a Raising of the Working Leg. The study of this relevé, the raising of the stretched leg to 90°, precedes the study of développé at the barre and in the centre of the room.

Relevé is done in all directions—to the front, to the side, and to the back—at first in one direction at a time with each leg separately, then with one leg in the different directions. During the study of the big poses at 90°, it is useful to begin with the practice of relevé lent (see below, p. 68) and only afterward go on to the study of développé.

Having raised the leg to a height of 90° by means of relevé, it is further possible to bend it in the knee, executing a passé at 90°, and take it to the pose attitude croisée or attitude effacée, etc.

The raising of the working leg can be done with the supporting leg stretched or in plié.

Relevé Lent. Relevé lent is done in the following manner: from 1st or from 5th position, the working leg, stretching the instep and toes, is drawn out, as in battement tendu, in any direction and then is slowly raised to 90°, after which it is just as slowly lowered to the initial position, with the foot sliding along the floor to 1st or 5th, according to the rules for battement tendu.

The sequence of study is the same as for développé.

II. Battements

The drawing out of the working leg in one or another direction and its return to the supporting leg is, in choreographic terminology, called a battement.

This drawing out of the leg can be from a stretched position or from a bent to a stretched position, and the return of the leg can be to either a stretched or a bent position.

Each kind of battement has its own form and its own name.

Battement Tendu Simple

Battement tendu simple (*tendu*, from the French, "stretched") is done from 1st or 5th position, forward, to the side, and backward; the musical time is 4/4 or 2/4.

In the beginning, it is studied at a slow tempo, each element separately, and with a pause after each part. The opening and closing of the stretched leg is later done in a connected manner. In the final form of battement tendu, the accent of the movement falls on the moment of the return of the foot to 1st or 5th position. During the movement, the thigh of the working leg must be turned out and pulled up in the hip joint, and the hips must be held level.

At first, battement tendu is studied facing the barre in 1st position with a drawing out of the right leg to the side, and is repeated in this direction from four to eight times. It is then done with the left leg. The turned-out position of the leg to the side gives the beginner the clearest notion of turn-out and is easier to master than the position in front or in back. Later on, the exercise is studied forward, alternating the legs, and backward in the same manner.

In 5th position, battement tendu is done in the same order (at first to the side, then forward and backward). And, in the study of battement tendu with one hand on the barre, as well as in the centre, the sequence of execution remains the same and is practised first in 1st position, then in 5th.

Later on, these directions are put together in one combination and are done in the generally accepted sequence: forward, to the side, backward, and to the side (i.e., en croix).

After battement tendu has been learned in this sequence, the directions can be varied in numerous other ways.

Battement tendu from 1st position with one hand on the barre. Stand in 1st position and, for the préparation, open the right arm through 1st position to 2nd.

a) Battement tendu forward. Without permitting the toe to leave the floor, the right foot is drawn forward, completely stretching the instep and toes. The toe goes directly forward from its initial point in 1st position to a 4th position opposite 1st position. The centre of the body's weight is transferred onto the supporting leg, while the working foot lightly moves along the surface of the floor. The heel must be strongly moved forward in order to maintain the turned-out position of the foot.

The return of the working leg to 1st position begins with movement from the toe: still holding the heel forward, the toe is drawn back, the foot gradually bending in the instep, and returns to a turned-out 1st position.

b) Battement tendu to the side. The working foot is drawn along a straight line out from the supporting leg. For the preservation of the turn-out, the heel is held forward and the toe kept back. On returning the foot to 1st position, the turn-out must also be carefully maintained.

c) Battement tendu backward. The foot is drawn out to the back, beginning the movement from the toe and holding the leg in its most turned-out position during the movement of the foot along the floor. The toe goes straight back from its initial point in 1st position to 4th position opposite 1st. Regardless of the direction, the centre of the body's weight must always remain over the supporting leg.

On returning the leg to 1st position, the movement is begun from the heel, leaving the toe well drawn back. This gives the foot the necessary turn-out.

Battement tendu from 5th position. The leg is drawn forward, with the toe opposite the heel of the supporting leg, to a 4th position opposite 5th. To the side, the foot is drawn out with the toe in alignment with the supporting leg, the toe opposite its heel. Backward, the leg goes out in the same way as it did forward, the toe of the working leg opposite the heel of the supporting leg.

In doing battement tendu from 5th position, it is necessary to carefully watch that the knee remains stretched during the drawing out and bringing in of the working leg to 5th position front from the directions forward and to the side. The tightness of the knee during the drawing out and bringing in of the leg to 5th position back from the directions backward and to the side is achieved with considerably more ease. To maintain the turned-out position of the foot, the working leg follows the same rules as for battement tendu in 1st position: while drawing the leg forward, the heel should be actively moved forward, and, on returning the leg to the initial position, one should lead the movement with the toe, drawing it quickly in to the heel of the supporting leg, so that the heel and toe of the working leg simultaneously make contact with the foot of the supporting leg. In the closing of the leg from 2nd position to 5th back, the heel of the working leg moves along the foot of the supporting leg, ultimately pressing tightly against the toe of the supporting foot. In the movement backward, the toe of the working foot is actively drawn out, and on closing the leg in 5th position back, one should lead the movement with the heel, more quickly bringing it in to the toe of the supporting leg, so that the heel and toe of the working leg simultaneously make contact with the foot of the supporting leg.

General Remarks. In the drawing out of the leg forward, sliding the toe along the floor, at the final point one must be sure to remain in contact with the floor with the big toe. In the bringing of the leg in to 1st or 5th position, the heel must not be lowered, but must be held forward and high; the foot, bending, slides in, the contact of the big toe with the floor being gradually transferred to the entire sole of the foot.

In the drawing out of the leg backward, sliding the toe along the floor, the contact with the floor gradually transfers to the big toe; in the closing of the leg to 1st or 5th position, the heel is not raised, but remains lowered; the foot, bending in the instep, slides in, the contact with the floor being gradually transferred from the big toe to the entire sole of the foot.

In drawing the foot out to the side, only the big toe must finally touch the floor.

Study Sequence

1. In eight quarters. 2/4 time. On the first measure, the leg is drawn out; on the second, the position is held; on the third, it returns to 1st or 5th position; and, on the fourth, the position is held.
2. In four quarters. 2/4 time. On the first quarter of the first measure, the leg is drawn out; on the second, the position is held. On the first quarter of the second measure, the leg returns to 1st or 5th position; and, on the second, the position is held.
3. In two quarters. 2/4 time. On the first quarter of the first measure, the leg is drawn out; on the second, it returns to 1st or 5th position. On the first quarter of the second measure, the leg is drawn out; and, on the second, it returns to 1st or 5th position, etc.

4. Final form, in one quarter. 2/4 time. On the upbeat (an introductory eighth note), the working leg is drawn out; on the first eighth of the first measure, it returns to 1st or 5th position; on the second eighth of the measure, the leg is drawn out again; and, on the third eighth, it returns to 1st or 5th position, etc.

Thus, in its final form, in 2/4 time, two battements tendus are done in one measure.

In the beginning, battement tendu is done four times in each of the three directions, later, eight times in each direction.

Battement Tendu with Demi-Plié

Battement tendu with demi-plié consists of a battement tendu simple and a demi-plié. The initial position is either 1st or 5th.

The working leg is drawn out forward, to the side, or backward according to the rules for battement tendu (during which the supporting leg remains tautly stretched) and then returns to the initial position. In conclusion, demi-plié on both legs.

During the repetition of the battement, the supporting leg is stretched, then demi-plié is again done on both legs, etc.

The movement of the legs must be co-ordinated: the stretching and bending (in demi-plié) of the working and the supporting leg takes place at the same time.

Study Sequence

1. In eight quarters. 2/4 time. On the first quarter of the first measure, the working leg is drawn out from the initial position (1st or 5th) in the required direction; on the second, it is held tautly stretched. On the first quarter of the second measure, it is brought back to 1st or 5th position; on the second, it holds this position. On the third measure, demi-plié; and on the fourth measure, come up from demi-plié. This is usually done twice in each direction, en croix.

2. In four quarters. 4/4 time. The working leg is drawn out on the first quarter of the upbeat and held for the second quarter. Then, on the first and second quarters of the first measure, it is brought back to the initial position simultaneously with a demi-plié on both legs. On the third quarter, simultaneously rise from demi-plié and draw out the leg in the required direction. On the fourth quarter, pause in the extended position, etc.

3. Final form, in two quarters. 2/4 time. In the second and third years, the tempo of execution is somewhat accelerated. One battement tendu with demi-plié is done in one measure of 2/4 time in the following manner: on the upbeat of one quarter, the working leg is drawn out in the required direction; on the first quarter of the first measure, the leg is brought back to the initial position simultaneously with a demi-plié; on the first eighth of the second quarter, rise from demi-plié and simultaneously draw out the leg in the required direction; on the second eighth, a pause is sustained in this position, etc.

General Remarks. In its final form, the accent must fall on the closing in demi-plié, with the movement beginning on the upbeat (analogous to battement tendu simple). In the second year and particularly the beginning of the third year, battement tendu with demi-plié is often done in various uncomplicated combinations with battement simple. For example, one battement tendu with demi-plié and two battements simples, executed in two measures of 2/4, done en croix, are divided musically in the following manner: on the upbeat, the working leg is drawn out forward; on the first quarter of the first measure, it is returned to the initial position with a demi-plié; on the second quarter, it is drawn forward again, straightening from the demi-plié; this is followed by a pause in the extended position; then, on the first quarter of the second measure, the first battement tendu simple is done; on the second quarter, the second battement tendu simple is done; then the whole sequence is repeated to the side, backward, and to the side again.

Double Battement Tendu

Double battement tendu is a variation of battement tendu simple. After the leg is drawn out, the heel is lowered to the floor in 2nd position (or, more rarely, in 4th position) and the instep is stretched again before closing in 1st or 5th position. Double battement tendu can be done with one, two, three, or more lowerings of the heel to the floor. At the moment the heel is lowered, the muscles remain tense, the instep maintains resiliency, and the centre of the body's weight remains on the supporting leg.

The execution of double battement tendu, especially with many lowerings of the heel, promotes the development of the foot, strengthens the ligaments, and increases the elasticity of the Achilles tendon, the instep, and the toes.

Double battement tendu, like battement tendu simple, is studied in the beginning at a slow tempo, in 4/4 or 2/4 time. The accent of the movement falls on the lowering of the heel to the floor. In 2/4 time, the leg is drawn out to the side (or to 4th position, forward or backward) on the upbeat; on the first quarter, the heel is lowered to the floor, between the first and second quarter (i.e., on the second eighth of the measure), the instep is stretched (the foot touching the floor only with the toe); on the second quarter, the leg returns to the initial position.

Doubles battements tendus are often combined with battements tendus simples.

Example. Do four battements tendus simples to the side, closing in 5th position, in two measures of 2/4. On the last eighth of the second measure, draw the leg out to 2nd position. On the first eighth of the third measure, lower the heel to the floor and stretch the instep. On the second and third eighths, do the same thing. On the fourth eighth, pause, holding the foot out with a stretched instep and toes. On the fourth measure, repeat all the movements of the previous measure. Then repeat the combination from the beginning.

Doubles battements tendus, like battements tendus simples and battements tendus with demi-plié, can also be done in the poses at the barre and in the centre of the room. The changes from one pose to another develop co-ordination of the movements of the legs, arms, head, and body.

Example of a combination at the barre. 2/4 time. On the first measure, with the right leg, do two battements tendus simples forward, closing in 5th position. On the second measure, in the same direction, do battement tendu with demi-plié in 5th position. On the last eighth of the measure, straightening from demi-plié, draw the working leg forward effacé with a stretched instep and toes, raising the right arm to 3rd position; the head inclines toward the left shoulder, and the eyes are directed upward at the hand. On the third measure, do two battements tendus simples to 5th position in the pose effacée devant. On the fourth measure, battement tendu with demi-plié in 5th position in the same pose. On the last eighth, coming up from demi-plié, draw the working leg back écarté (on the floor); and turn the head to the left. On the fifth measure, do two battements tendus simples to 5th position in the pose écartée derrière (finishing the first battement by bringing the working foot to 5th position back, the second to 5th position front). On the sixth measure, do a battement tendu with demi-plié in the pose écartée derrière, closing the leg in 5th position back. On the last eighth of the measure, coming up from demi-plié, draw the leg out to 2nd position with a stretched instep and toes, and, at the same time, turn en face, lowering the arm to 2nd position. On the seventh measure, do a double battement tendu to 2nd position and close the leg in 5th position front. On the eighth measure, repeat the double battement and close the leg in 5th position back.

Then repeat the whole combination in the opposite direction, with the pose effacée derrière (or 2nd arabesque) and the pose écartée devant.

Battement Tendu en Tournant

All battements tendus can be done in the centre of the room en tournant with an eighth or a quarter turn, drawing the leg out forward (when turning en dehors), backward (when turning en dedans), or to the side (when turning either en dehors or en dedans).

Battement Tendu Simple Forward en Tournant, with an Eighth of a Turn en Dehors. Stand in 5th position en face, right foot front, the arms opened to 2nd position.

2/4 time. On the upbeat, the working leg is drawn forward to point 2 of the classroom plan (see page 44); and, at the same time, the body turns to face that same point. On the first quarter, the leg returns to 5th position. On the second eighth of the first quarter, the leg is drawn forward to point 3, together with a turn of the body. On the second quarter, the leg returns to 5th position. Then the movement is continued in exactly the same way to points 4, 5, 6, 7, 8, and 1. The exercise is finished when a complete turn has been done.

In elementary study, at least two battements tendus simples should be done in each direction: the first battement with a turn, the second in place.

Battement Tendu Simple Backward en Tournant, with an Eighth of a Turn en Dedans. Stand in 5th position en face, right foot back, the arms opened to 2nd position.

2/4 time. On the upbeat, the working leg is drawn back to

point 4; and, at the same time, the body turns to face point 8, shifting the heel of the supporting foot well forward, without lifting it from the floor. On the first quarter, the leg returns to 5th position. On the second eighth of the first quarter, it is drawn back to point 3, and the body turns to face point 7. On the second quarter, the leg returns to 5th position. The movement then continues in the same way, facing respectively points 6, 5, 4, 3, 2, and 1. The exercise is finished with the completion of one turn.

Battement Tendu Simple to the Side en Tournant

with an Eighth of a Turn. *En dehors.* Stand in 5th position en face, right foot front, arms in 2nd position.

2/4 time. On the upbeat, the working leg is drawn out to 2nd position toward point 4; and, at the same time, the body turns to face point 2. On the first quarter, the leg closes in 5th position back. On the second eighth of the first quarter, the leg is drawn out to 2nd position to point 4, the body remaining as it is. On the second quarter, the leg closes in 5th position front. On the upbeat of the following measure, the leg is drawn out to 2nd position to point 5, the body turning to face point 3, and the leg closes in 5th position back; then the leg is drawn out to 2nd position without a turn and closes in 5th position front. Then follow the turns to face points 4, 5, 6, 7, 8, and 1. The exercise is finished with the completion of one turn.

En dedans. Stand in 5th position, right foot back, arms in 2nd position.

2/4 time. On the upbeat, the leg is drawn out to the side to 2nd position toward point 2; and, at the same time, the body turns to face point 8, shifting the heel of the supporting foot well forward. On the first quarter, the leg closes in 5th position front. On the second eighth of the first quarter, the leg is drawn out to 2nd position to point 2 without a turn of the body. On the second quarter, the leg closes in 5th position back. Then follow the turns to face points 7, 6, 5, 4, 3, 2, and 1. The exercise is finished with the completion of one turn.

Battement tendu simple en tournant to the side, en dehors and en dedans, can also be done with one battement in each direction; the leg is drawn out with a turn of the body and brought in without a turn. Turning en dehors, the first battement closes in 5th position back, the second closes front, etc. Turning en dedans, the first battement closes front, the second back, etc.

Battement tendu simple en tournant en dehors and en dedans, forward, to the side, and backward, is done in exactly the same way with quarter turns. And these, as well as other movements executed en tournant, can also be done with half turns.

Battement Tendu Jeté

In a battement tendu jeté, the leg is sharply thrown forward, to the side, or backward from 1st or 5th position to a height of 45°. With the acceleration of the tempo or the execution of battements tendus jetés in eighth or sixteenth notes, the height to which the leg is thrown is lowered from 45° to 22.5° or even less.

At first, the throw and return of the stretched leg are performed evenly, without an accent; but in its final form, the accent falls at the end of the movement when, after a sharp and energetic throw, the working leg returns to the supporting leg.

Study begins at a slow tempo with pauses, each direction taken separately. Later on, the directions are joined into one combination, and the movement is done in the usual sequence: front, side, back, side.

The working leg is thrown out, from 1st or 5th position, in the required direction to a height of 45° with the toe sliding along the floor (as in battement tendu simple). On the return to

1st or 5th position, the toe again slides along the floor. It is necessary to watch carefully for the correctness of this movement, and not allow a careless throw of the leg straight up from 1st or 5th position, or a careless return of the leg to 1st or 5th position, from a height of 45° (eliminating the part of the movement that is identical with battement tendu simple).

When one throws out the leg, if the instep and toes are not stretched simultaneously, and, on the return, if they flex prematurely, the foot will lose its assembly and the calf muscles will not be sufficiently worked.

In doing battement tendu jeté to the side, the toe of the working leg should attain a uniform height each time, directly opposite the supporting leg. If the leg is thrown out somewhat forward of this point (before returning it to 5th position front) or somewhat behind (before returning it to 5th position back), a deviation in the movement of the leg results, which will disturb the thigh and prevent the development of its capacity to move in a turned-out condition. Later on, this defect will affect jumps in which the leg is thrown out to the side (e.g., assemblés, jetés, ballonnés, et al.).

Battement tendu jeté in its final form is done twice as fast as battement tendu simple. The rules for the execution of both are the same. The musical time is 4/4 or 2/4.

Study Sequence

1. In four quarters. 2/4 time. On the first quarter of the first measure, the leg, from 1st or 5th position, is thrown out in the necessary direction. On the second quarter, the position is held. On the first quarter of the second measure, the leg returns to 1st or 5th position. On the second quarter, the position is held.
2. In one quarter. 2/4 time. On the upbeat, the leg is thrown out. On the first eighth, it returns. On the second eighth, the leg again is thrown out. On the third eighth, it returns, etc.

3. Final form, in one eighth. 2/4 time. On the upbeat, the leg
    is thrown out. On the first eighth of the first measure, it
    returns to 1st or 5th position and. again is thrown out. On
    the second eighth, the leg returns to the initial position and
    once more is thrown out. On the third and fourth eighths,
    it does the same thing, etc.

    Thus, in one measure of 2/4, four battements tendus
    jetés are done.

    Battement tendu jeté can be done in the poses at the
    barre and in the centre of the room, and, like battement
    tendu simple, can finish in demi-plié in 1st or 5th position.

    Battement tendu jeté en tournant is done according to
    the rules for battement tendu simple en tournant.

Battement Tendu Jeté Pointé

This is a battement tendu jeté; but, after the throw
to 45°, the leg does not immediately return to 1st or 5th position
(as in battement tendu jeté) but is lowered to the floor with a
stretched instep and toe, then sharply raised one or several
times before completing the movement in 1st or 5th position. It
is done, like all battements, forward, to the side, and backward,
from 1st or 5th position.

The movement begins on the upbeat, with a throwing out of
the leg to 45° and, at first, is broken down into four parts: on
one eighth, there is the throw of the leg; on the next eighth, the
toe returns to the floor. Then, from the toe, another throw to
45° is done, after which the leg returns to the initial 1st or 5th
position. In the final form, battement tendu jeté pointé is done
in one eighth and is repeated in succession from three to five
times before finishing in 1st or 5th position.

It is also possible to change the direction of the leg at the
height of 45° and, after that, continue the jetés pointés in
another direction. In all directions and at all tempos, however,
the touching of the toe to the floor must be short and abrupt.

Battement Tendu pour Batterie

Battement tendu pour batterie prepares for and accompanies the study of beats.

It is done only at the barre in the form of an independent combination, and consists of transfers of the working leg in front and in back of the supporting leg, the number of which is determined by one or another kind of beat. It does not have an invariable place in the daily exercise; but, when included, it is most often done at its conclusion. The study of this battement is begun somewhat earlier than the actual study of beats and is continued systematically until the beats are learned. It is done in the following manner: stand in 5th position with the right foot front. For the préparation, open the arm to 2nd position and raise the stretched leg, with stretched instep and toes, to a height of 45° to the side in 2nd position.

The working leg, from the initial position at 45°, is sharply lowered, allowing the foot to flex, and the thigh strikes the thigh of the supporting leg in front. The working leg must be brought in to a 5th position more crossed over than is usual, keeping the legs taut and turned-out to the utmost, with the heel of the working leg emphatically held forward.

After striking the supporting leg, the working leg, with the knee stretched, rebounds slightly to the side, and then comes in to strike the supporting leg in back, also thigh to thigh (in a deep 5th position), before being thrown out to the side, with a stretched instep and toes, in 2nd position to a height of 45°. From here, the movement is repeated in the opposite direction, striking first in back.

In throwing out the leg and returning it for the beat, the working foot must be stretched, but on the floor itself, the instep flexes; and, during the transfer of the leg for the next beat, the foot remains flexed. The accent of the movement comes on the throw of the leg out to the side at 45°.

Battement tendu pour batterie is done in 2/4 time. The first beat in front, the rebound to the side, the beat in back, and the throw of the leg out to the side at 45° all are done in one quarter.

Two or more transfers are also done in one quarter, but the number of transfers should not exceed three, the number necessary for the most complicated beat, an entrechat-huit.

According to the increase in the number of transfers, the movement is done more quickly.

Grand Battement Jeté (Basic Form)

This is a big battement, done from 1st or 5th position, forward, to the side, and back, in which the leg is thrown out to 90° or higher.

Elementary study is done at a slow tempo, taking each direction separately. The throwing out of the leg and its return are done evenly at first. In the final form, the accent falls on the return of the working leg to the initial position.

Study of the movement begins with a throwing of the leg forward from 1st position, then to the side. Grand battement to the back should at first be studied facing the barre (for not less than one week of daily lessons).

Later on, the battements are studied in two directions, forward and to the side, no less than four in each direction, which is repeated with the other leg; then they are practised backward and to the side in the same manner.

After this, it is possible to go on to the execution of grands battements forward, to the side, backward, and to the side, four in each direction.

In the centre of the room, the same sequence is maintained.

RULES FOR THE EXECUTION OF GRAND BATTE-MENT JETÉ. The movement is done from 1st or 5th position. The working leg is energetically thrown out to a height of at least 90°, with the toe sliding along the floor, as in battement tendu and tendu jeté.

The throw is done lightly, freely, and with a leg that is strongly stretched, turned out, and pulled up tightly in the hip joint, without which the battement loses its support.

In the return to the initial position, the leg must not be dropped, but should be lowered with control, accentuating the return to the closed position. It is necessary to observe this moment strictly, since, during the return of the leg, the foot must actively take part in the movement, sliding the toe along the floor.

The direction in which the leg is thrown forward or backward is determined by the initial position (4th position opposite either 1st or 5th); to the side, it is determined by the line of 2nd position.

In doing battements forward or to the side, the body remains erect, pulled up in the middle. But, in doing battements backward, while the body remains pulled up, the torso is allowed to incline slightly forward (this increases the height of the throw and precludes the possibility of injury to the kidneys and the lower back). The torso is allowed to incline simultaneously with the throw of the leg, and comes erect together with the return of the leg to the initial position. During this, the head must also incline forward in alignment with the torso.

Care should be taken that, during the battements, the shoulder of the arm that is on the barre is not raised (this is most often observed in battements to the side). In battements backward, the hand that is on the barre must not move forward; the hips and shoulders are held level; and the arm that is in 2nd position moves slightly forward with the torso.

During grand battement jeté in all directions, the knee of the supporting leg must always be strongly stretched.

The incorrect execution of grands battements most often

results from a premature attempt to throw the leg higher than 90°. While the movement is being learned, a height of more than 90° should not be allowed, even where the natural gifts of the student permit it. The mastery of the correct method of execution of grands battements is very important, since these battements are used in all kinds of pas allegro, where the proper execution of the jump depends on the correct manner of throwing out the leg.

Study Sequence

1. In two measures. 2/4 time. On the first quarter of the first measure, the working leg, from 1st or 5th position, is taken out in the necessary direction as if doing a battement tendu. On the second quarter, the stretched leg is thrown from the tendu position (the toe to the floor) to a height of 90°. On the first quarter of the second measure, it is lowered with a stretched toe to the floor. And on the second quarter, it returns to the initial position.

2. In one measure. 2/4 time. On the first quarter of the measure, the leg is thrown out to 90° from 1st or 5th position. On the second quarter, it returns to the initial position.

3. Final form. 2/4 time. At first the tempo is slow, but as the movement is mastered, it is gradually speeded up. On the upbeat, the leg is thrown out to 90° from 1st or 5th position. On the first quarter, it returns to the initial position.

   In intermediate and advanced classes, grand battement can be done with a pause (holding the leg at a height of 90°), with a rise to demi-pointe at the moment the leg is thrown, completely on demi-pointe (with a preliminary préparation in 5th position on demi-pointe), or with a demi-plié on the supporting leg during the throw of the leg (straightening the knee of the supporting leg as the working leg returns to 5th position).

Grand Battement Jeté Pointé

This is done according to the rules for grand battement jeté from lst or 5th position; but, after the throw, the leg is lowered with a stretched toe to the floor, the next battement being done from the stretched position and returning to the same position. After a given number of repetitions, the last battement returns to the initial lst or 5th position.

The accent of the movement is on the lowering of the leg with a stretched toe to the floor, and, for the last battement, the accent falls on the return of the leg to lst or 5th position.

The distribution of the movements on the musical counts is the same as for the final form of grand battement jeté.

Grand battement jeté and grand battement jeté pointé, like many other movements, are done not only in quarters, but also in eighths. The acceleration of the tempo develops speed and agility in the throw of the leg to a great height.

It should be noted that, in the execution of grand battement backward in eighths, the body only barely inclines forward, all the time being held erect, with a strongly pulled up middle and tight lower back. If the body were to be allowed to really incline, the co-ordination of the movement would be destroyed, since the body would have to come erect each time on the return of the leg to the initial position.

"Soft" Grand Battement Jeté

"Soft" grand battement is done from 5th position to 5th position, forward, to the side, and backward at 90°.

The working leg is thrown out and upward by means of a développé. In spite of the energetic throw of the leg, the développé gives the movement softness, which determines the character of its execution.

The accent of the movement falls on the return of the stretched leg to its initial position.

This battement can also be done with a rise to demi-pointe at the moment of the développé, in which case the supporting leg is lowered onto the whole foot as the working leg returns to 5th position.

In combination with other kinds of grands battements, the "soft" battement may also be finished with a stretched toe on the floor in any direction; but it always begins from 5th position. Having done a "soft" battement to the toe, do the next battement from the toe with a stretched leg, and then finish in 5th position.

Grands battements jetés, grands battements jetés pointés, and "soft" battements can be done in the centre of the room with a turn of the body en dehors or en dedans, according to the rules given in the section on battement tendu en tournant.

Grand Battement Jeté Balancé

Battements balancés ("rocked") are done forward and backward to 90°, passing through lst position. To the side, they are done only in the centre of the room in either lst or 5th position, alternating the legs.

The accent of the movement falls on the throw of the working leg upward.

Standing in lst position at the barre, do the préparation as follows: on the first chord, raise the right arm to lst position; on the second, open the arm to 2nd position and simultaneously draw the right leg back to 4th position with the toe to the floor (according to the rules for battement tendu simple) and turn the head to the right.

Then the working leg is thrown forward, through lst position, to 90°, with the body simultaneously inclining backward. The leg is then lowered through lst position and thrown backward, with the body simultaneously inclining forward. Then the leg is again thrown forward, backward, etc.

During the entire exercise, the head is turned toward the arm that is opened to 2nd position.

The body inclines backward as far as possible, but must maintain a straight, pulled-up lower back and level shoulders. During the inclination forward, the shoulders must also be level, with the small of the back tightly pulled up.

It is particularly important in grand battement jeté balancé to achieve the correct inclination of the body (especially in back) simultaneously with the throw of the leg.

In the beginning, grands battements balancés are practised with each battement done separately, stopping in 1st position or in 4th position (in which case, the toe will be to the floor). In the final form, the battements are done in succession, passing through 1st position.

In battements balancés executed in the centre of the room, from 5th position towards 2nd position, the body inclines to the side, away from the working leg. For a description of the position of the body, see the section on développé ballotté.

Study Sequence

1. 2/4 time. On the first quarter of the first measure, the working leg, from 4th position back, is thrown forward through 1st position. On the second quarter, it is lowered to 1st position. On the first quarter of the second measure, the leg is thrown backward. On the second, it returns to 1st position, etc.

2. Final form. 2/4 time. On the first quarter of the first measure, the leg is thrown forward, through 1st position, from 4th position back. On the second quarter, it is lowered and, through 1st position, is thrown backward. On the first quarter of the second measure, the leg is again thrown forward. On the second quarter, it is thrown backward, etc.

Grand Battement Jeté Passé

This is done according to the rules for grand battement jeté, but with a transfer of the leg from one direction to another by means of a passé at the height of 90° (passé, "passed through"). It is done in two directions only: forward and backward. The accent of the movement falls on the throw of the leg into the air.

The working leg, from 1st or 5th position (although the movement may also be done from 4th position with the toe to the floor), is thrown forward to 90°, the body slightly inclining backward. Then the leg, bending in the knee, passes beside the supporting leg at the same height (the toe at the level of the knee); the body, at this moment, comes erect. Continuing the movement, the working leg is extended backward at 90°, and the body inclines forward. Then the leg is lowered and the body comes erect before the leg is again thrown forward through 1st position, etc.

The movement is done in the reverse direction in the same manner.

Care should be taken that, after having thrown the leg forward, as the knee bends, the thigh must be drawn back as much to the side as possible, with the heel directed forward. On extending the leg to the back, one must maintain this turn-out of the thigh without lowering the knee.

In doing the movement in the reverse direction, after having thrown the leg backward, as soon as the knee begins to bend, one must hold the thigh back for as long as possible, leading forward the lower leg first, with the heel held well forward.

Later on, it is recommended that, after the throw of the leg, the height during the passé be raised somewhat, and that the stretching backward or forward be higher than 90°.

Example. 2/4 time. On the first quarter of the first measure, the working leg is thrown forward to 90°. On the second quarter, passé is done at the same height, and the leg is stretched backward. On the first quarter of the second measure, the leg is lowered and is thrown forward to 90° through lst position. On the second quarter, it again is transferred back by means of a passé, etc.

Usually this battement is included in a combination with other kinds of grands battements jetés; but it can also be combined with rond de jambe par terre, alternating with grand rond de jambe jeté.

Grand Battement Jeté, Taking the Leg Around a Quarter or a Half of a Circle

This is done according to the rules of grand battement jeté, but with the leg taken around in the air to a new direction, which furthers the development of flexibility in the hip joint.

Grand battement jeté with a quarter or a half of a circle is done from lst or 5th position (or from 2nd or 4th, when the leg is lowered to a position with the toe to the floor) in two directions: en dehors and en dedans. The accent of the movement comes on the return of the leg to the initial position. The study is begun at the barre, from lst position.

En dehors. The working leg, from lst position, is thrown forward somewhat lower than 90°; then, without interrupting the movement, it is taken to the side, gradually coming up to a height of 90°. Having passed thus through a quarter of a circle, it is lowered to lst position. Then the leg is thrown out to the side, is taken back, gradually gaining height, and, having completed the second quarter of the circle, is lowered to lst position. As the leg is taken around to the back (moving en dehors), after the throw to the side, the body slightly inclines forward. However, during the throw, the body must never be allowed to lean toward the barre in order to facilitate the movement of the leg.

En dedans. The working leg, from 1st position, is thrown backward somewhat lower than 90°, then, without interrupting the movement and gradually coming up to a height of 90°, it is taken around to the side a quarter of a circle before being lowered to 1st position, etc.

During the throw of the leg backward and the taking of it around to the side (moving en dedans), the body is lifted and must never incline toward the barre.

The successful execution of these complicated movements is determined by a turned-out and tensed thigh of the working leg, during the circular movement en dehors or en dedans, and a pulled-up and correct position of the body.

This battement is also done taking the working leg around a half of a circle en dehors or en dedans, from 1st or 5th position. The rules remain the same: the height of the working leg is increased gradually, the highest point in the direction en dehors being in back and, in the direction en dedans, in front. It is necessary to frequently practise grand battement jeté taking the leg around a quarter of a circle and, especially, a half of a circle, before the study of grand rond de jambe jeté, since it prepares the legs well for this movement.

After this battement has been learned from 1st position, it is done from 5th position. Then one should go on to the study of the same movement, from either 1st or 5th position, with a lowering of the leg to the floor with a stretched foot; in this case, each succeeding battement is done from the toe, en dehors or en dedans.

Battement Frappé

Battement frappé (a "struck" battement) is done forward, to the side and backward from 2nd position, at first with the toe to the floor, then at a height of 22.5°. One should begin its study first to the side, and then forward and backward. During the learning stage, the movement is done at a slow tempo, with pauses, and the bending and stretching of the working leg must be given equal musical value. In its final form, the accent of the movement falls on the stretching of the working leg in the required direction, which must be sharp and energetic.

Begin in 5th position with the right foot in front. For the préparation at the barre, open the right arm through 1st position to 2nd, and at the same time, draw the right leg out to 2nd position, finishing with a stretched foot, toe to the floor. The working foot then energetically strikes the supporting leg sur le cou-de-pied devant before being sharply extended to 2nd position, barely grazing the floor at the last moment, with a stretched instep and toe to the floor. The instep stays stretched when, from 2nd position, the foot strikes (but more softly) sur le cou-de-pied derrière and, without delay, is again sharply extended to 2nd position.

In the position sur le cou-de-pied devant, the foot of the working leg clasps the ankle of the supporting leg; the heel is in front, above the ankle joint; the toe is in back, behind the Achilles tendon; the instep and toes are tautly stretched. In the position sur le cou-de-pied derrière, the inside face of the heel of the working foot fits closely by the ankle of the supporting leg in back, the instep and toes stretched and taken back.

In the final form of battement frappé, the foot, after striking sur le cou-de-pied devant or derrière, without delay literally rebounds from the supporting leg and is extended in the given direction to a height of 22.5°.

During the bending and stretching of the working leg, the thigh must be completely turned out and immobile.

In battement frappé forward, one must be especially careful, when extending the leg, to hold the thigh in a completely turned-out position, and not permit it to move forward, whereas the lower leg and the heel must actively be moved forward. And in bending the leg to bring the foot sur le cou-de-pied devant, the thigh should be actively taken back to the side.

In battement frappé backward, the turn out of the thigh must be maintained and the knee must not be lowered. When bending the leg to place the foot sur le cou-de-pied, hold the thigh well turned out.

The character of the movement and the rules for the execution of battement frappé forward and backward are the same as for those done to the side.

In battement frappé executed to a height of 22.5°, the working leg, extending from the position sur le cou-de-pied, each time must get to the same point in the air at a height of 22.5°.

Study Sequence

1. Two measures of 2/4 time. On the first quarter of the first measure, the working leg, bending, is brought in from 2nd position to the supporting leg, the foot striking it sur le cou-de-pied. On the second quarter, the foot is held in this position. On the first quarter of the second measure, the leg is extended in the given direction. On the second quarter, the position is held, etc. The movement is timed equally and has no accent.

2. One measure of 2/4 time. On the first quarter of the first measure, the working leg bends and the foot strikes the supporting leg sur le cou-de-pied. On the second quarter, the leg is extended, etc. The movement is still timed equally and has no accent.

3. One measure of 2/4 time (with an accent). On the upbeat, the working leg bends and the foot strikes the supporting leg sur le cou-de-pied. On the first quarter of the first measure, the leg is extended with an accent. On the second quarter, it remains in this position, etc.

4. Final form (in one quarter). 2/4 time. On the upbeat, the working leg bends and the foot energetically strikes the supporting leg sur le cou-de-pied. On the first eighth, the

leg is sharply extended with an accent. After the second eighth, the working foot strikes the supporting leg sur le cou-de-pied. On the third eighth, it is stretched, etc.

Beginning with the second year, frappés are done on demi-pointe.

Battement Double Frappé

This movement is similar to battement frappé but has a double transfer of the working foot sur le cou-de-pied (devant and derrière, or in the reverse order) before the leg is extended.

The rules, the character of execution, the initial position, and the accent of the movement, are the same as for battement frappé.

During the learning stage, the movement is done at a slow tempo, each part executed separately with pauses, at first with the toe to the floor, then at a height of 22.5°, and, finally, on demi-pointe at the same height and in all directions.

Study Sequence

1. 2/4 time. On the first eighth of the first measure, the working leg, from 2nd position, bends, and the foot strikes the supporting leg sur le cou-de-pied devant. On the second eighth, the leg slightly unbends (halfway to 2nd position), during which the thigh is held well turned-out and immobile. On the third eighth, the leg bends, and the foot strikes the supporting leg sur le cou-de-pied derrière. On the fourth eighth, the foot is held in this position. On the first eighth of the second measure, the leg is extended in the given direction, and, during the remaining three eighths, the stretched position is held. From here, the movement is repeated.

2. Final form. 2/4 time. On the upbeat, the working foot, from 2nd position, strikes the supporting leg sur le cou-de-pied

devant and is transferred to the position sur le cou-de-pied derrière. On the first eighth of the first measure, the leg is extended in the given direction. On the second eighth, the foot does a double transfer sur le cou-de-pied, beating back and front. On the third eighth, the leg is extended. On the fourth eighth, the foot again does a double transfer, etc.

Thus a double transfer of the working foot and the extension of the leg are done during one quarter.

Battement double frappé can also be done more rapidly. In this case, the working foot does a double transfer sur le cou-de-pied and the leg is extended, all during one eighth.

Having learned battement double frappé on the whole foot, and then on demi-pointe, it is possible to introduce a more complicated form, which includes the supporting leg more actively in the work. For this, the double transfer of the working foot sur le cou-de-pied is accompanied by a rise to demi-pointe; as the leg is extended with the toe to the floor or at a height of 22.5°, the heel of the stretched supporting leg is lowered to the floor.

Another variant is also useful. The double transfer of the working foot sur le cou-de-pied is done on demi-pointe, and, on extending the leg with the toe to the floor or to a height of 22.5°, the supporting leg comes down in demi-plié.

General Remarks. Doing battement frappé and double frappé, it is necessary, each time, to accent the movement of the working foot at its greatest distance from the supporting leg (forward, to the side, or backward), otherwise the frappé will lack sharpness and clarity.

Battement frappé and double frappé in the centre of the room can also be done en tournant with eighth or quarter turns, in a direction en dehors or en dedans. The working foot strikes the supporting leg sur le cou-de-pied at the moment of the turn of the body, and the leg is extended without a turn. The striking is done alternately in front and in back.

In battement double frappé, the double transfer of the working foot is also done simultaneously with the turn of the body and the extension without a turn.

In the beginning of the study of this movement, at least two battements should be done in each direction, the second being done without a turn.

In general, it is very difficult to do battements frappés, doubles frappés, petits battements sur le cou-de-pied, and ronds de jambe en l'air, en tournant. Doing each of these movements, one must pay special attention to the turn-out and the immobility of the thigh of the working leg.

One must not destroy the character of the movement, the sharpness of the stretching of the leg, the clarity of the transfers sur le cou-de-pied, the fixing of the point to which turns are done; nor may the movement be done limply and slug-gishly.

In doing all movements en tournant, good stability on demi-pointe, in combination with a correct execution of the movement itself, is essential.

Petit Battement sur le Cou-de-Pied

This movement consists of a transfer of the working foot from the initial position sur le cou-de-pied devant to the position sur le cou-de-pied derrière by means of an unbending of the working leg half the distance to 2nd position. From here the movement is repeated. The number of transfers of the foot depends upon the given instructions.

The lower part of the working leg moves freely in the knee, but the thigh maintains the utmost possible turn-out, and absolute immobility. During the unbending of the leg, the toe must be directed precisely to the side.

The movement is first studied with each part done separate-ly, with pauses, and at a slow tempo, without an accent. Each transfer of the working foot to the position sur le cou-de-pied is timed equally. As it is mastered, the tempo is accelerated, until it becomes very fast.

Later on it is studied with an accent which falls on the bending of the leg to bring the foot sur le cou-de-pied devant, the foot being brought sur le cou-de-pied derrière on the upbeat. Thus, the position sur le cou-de-pied devant will come on the first eighth of each quarter, and is accentuated by the striking of the working foot against the supporting leg sur le cou-de-pied. This position is then fixed for a moment with a pause. In the reverse direction, the accent falls on the position sur le cou-de-pied derrière, the foot being brought sur le cou-de-pied devant on the upbeat.

When petits battements are done in succession, without an emphasised accent, the leg, free in the knee, unbends and bends to the position sur le cou-de-pied evenly and clearly.

A préparation on two introductory chords precedes the movement. On the first chord (at the barre), the right arm, from preparatory position, is raised to 1st position, and the right leg, from 5th position, is taken to 2nd position with a stretched foot, toe to the floor. On the second chord, the arm is brought to 2nd position, and, bending the leg in the knee, the foot is brought sur le cou-de-pied devant.

In doing this préparation on demi-pointe, one rises to demi-pointe at the moment when the leg bends sur le cou-de-pied devant.

Later on, the préparation is done more simply, in the following manner: the right arm is raised to 1st position; then the right leg, from 5th position, together with the arm, is taken to 2nd position; and from here the movement begins.

Study Sequence

1. 2/4 time. On the first quarter of the first measure, the working leg, from the initial position with the foot sur le cou-de-pied devant, unbends halfway to 2nd position. On

the second quarter, the position is held. On the first quarter of the second measure, the working leg bends, placing the foot sur le cou-de-pied derrière. On the second quarter, the position is held. Continuing the movement, the leg unbends to the side and returns the foot to the position sur le cou-de-pied devant, etc.

2. 2/4 time. On the first quarter of the first measure, the working leg unbends to the side. On the second, it bends, and the foot is placed sur le cou-de-pied derrière, etc.

3. Final form. 2/4 time. On the upbeat, the working leg, from the initial position with the foot sur le cou-de-pied devant, unbending to the side, transfers the foot to the position sur le cou-de-pied derrière. On the first eighth of the first measure, it again unbends and the foot is transferred sur le cou-de-pied devant. On the second eighth, the working foot is transferred sur le cou-de-pied derrière. On the third eighth, it is transferred sur le cou-de-pied devant, and, on the fourth eighth, sur le cou-de-pied derrière, etc. Thus, in one measure, two complete movements are done. They are executed without an accent, evenly.

Doing these movements with an accent and with a pause sur le cou-de-pied devant, on the upbeat, transfer the working foot to the position sur le cou-de-pied derrière. On the first eighth of the first measure, return it to the supporting leg, striking sur le cou-de-pied devant. On the second and third eighths, hold the position. On the fourth eighth, transfer the working foot again to the position sur le cou-de-pied derrière; and on the first eighth of the second measure return it, with an accent, sur le cou-de-pied devant, etc.

Petits battements, like battements frappés and frappés doubles, are combined with themselves in various rhythmic patterns, as well as with other movements of the barre and centre exercise.

In the centre of the room, petits battements sur le cou-de-pied are also done on demi-pointe and en tournant.

Battement Battu sur le Cou-de-Pied

Battement battu is executed on demi-pointe in a forward or backward direction with épaulement effacé or croisé. The movement consists of a striking of the working foot on the supporting leg.

Battements battus forward are done in the conditional position sur le cou-de-pied devant. The toe of the working foot strikes the upper part of the inside face of the heel of the supporting foot and, staying bent in the knee, slightly opens somewhat forward. Backward, the strike is done in the basic position sur le cou-de-pied derrière with the heel of the working foot on the ankle (the cou) of the supporting leg and then slightly opens somewhat backward. The working leg, with maximum turn-out, moves freely forward or backward from the knee. The accent of the movement must be away from the supporting leg. In petits battements, each movement finishes in the position sur le cou-de-pied, whereas, in battements battus, it finishes a short distance from the supporting leg.

Battements battus produce quick, free mastery of the lower leg (from the knee to the toe), with the turn-out and immobility of the position of the upper part (the thigh).

The slight openings of the lower leg forward and backward after the strike (the battu) are considerably harder than the openings of the leg to the side in petits battements sur le cou-de-pied. Therefore, battements battus are studied only in advanced classes.

A préparation for the movement is executed on two introductory chords. On the first chord, the right arm is raised from preparatory position to 1st position and opens a little toward 2nd; the right leg opens from 5th position to the side at 45°, while, simultaneously, the supporting leg rises to demi-pointe. On the second chord, the leg bends in the knee and the foot is brought sur le cou-de-pied devant or derrière; the arm is lowered to preparatory position, and the body turns to épaulement effacé or croisé.

Study Sequence

1. 2/4 time. Before the measure, the working foot slightly opens somewhat forward from the initial conditional position sur le cou-de-pied devant. On the first quarter of the measure, the working foot does two short beats (battus) on the heel of the supporting foot, rebounding a short distance forward. On the second quarter, there follow two more beats, etc.

2. Final form. 2/4 time. Before the measure, the working foot slightly opens somewhat forward from the initial conditional position sur le cou-de-pied devant. On the first quarter of the first measure, four beats are done on the heel of the supporting foot. On the second quarter, four more short beats follow, etc.

Battements battus are executed at a quick tempo. At the beginning of their study, they are done in one eighth each; later, they are done in one sixteenth, and, still later, in one thirty-second each.

Battements battus can finish in a small pose effacée or croisée, devant or derrière, toe to the floor, in plié, or at 90° on demi-pointe in the big poses effacée or croisée devant or attitude effacée or croisée.

In the centre, battements battus are also executed with épaulement effacé or croisé and can be executed en tournant (with forward beats, turning en dehors; with backward beats, turning en dedans) and combined with pas courus.

Battement Fondu

Battement fondu ("melted" or "flowing") is a complicated movement consisting of a bending of the working leg to the position sur le cou-de-pied, with a simultaneous demi-plié on the supporting leg, followed by an opening of the working leg in any direction, with a simultaneous straightening of the supporting leg from demi-plié. The conditional position sur le cou-de-pied devant is used. In this, the toe of the stretched working foot touches the front of the supporting leg just above the ankle joint; the heel is strongly moved forward and must not touch the leg. In fondu back, the basic position sur le cou-de-pied derrière is used.

The study of this battement at first is done at a slow tempo to the side, then forward and backward, finishing each battement with the toe to the floor. Then battement fondu is learned, raising the working leg to a height of 45°, while the supporting leg remains with the heel on the floor. And, finally, the working leg is raised to 45° or 90° in all directions, as the supporting leg simultaneously rises to demi-pointe. The bending and stretching of the leg always takes place smoothly, evenly, and in a co-ordinated fashion.

The study sequence for battement fondu in the centre of the room is the same as at the barre.

General Remarks. In stretching the working leg from the position sur le cou-de-pied to the floor, it must not be raised; the thigh must be held well turned-out and the heel actively moved forward.

In stretching the working leg to a height of 45°, one should watch that the toe each time goes to the same point and is fixed there. The thigh must be held well turned out, and its tendency to move forward resisted.

When bending the leg to the position sur le cou-de-pied devant from the forward direction from a height of either 45° or 90°, the thigh must not be lowered immediately; it should be taken to the side at that height, while the leg bends halfway in the knee; then, from there, the foot is gradually lowered to the position sur le cou-de-pied devant.

Bending the leg from a height of 45° in 2nd position to the position sur le cou-de-pied, the thigh must not be lowered immediately. First, the leg bends halfway in the knee, holding the thigh immobile at a height of 45°; then, continuing the movement, the thigh is gradually lowered until the foot is sur le cou-de-pied.

Extending the leg backward, with the toe to the floor or at a height of 45°, it is necessary to watch carefully that the turned-out position of the thigh is maintained and the knee is not lowered.

During the bending of the leg to the position sur le cou-de-pied derrière from a height of 45° or 90° in back, the thigh also is held back in a well turned-out position, while the lower part of the working leg is actively brought into the supporting leg. The thigh is held at a height of 45° or 90° as the leg bends halfway in the knee; then, continuing the movement, the thigh is lowered until the foot is sur le cou-de-pied derrière.

The bending and stretching of the legs is done smoothly and in a co-ordinated fashion, the supporting leg stretching simultaneously with the working leg.

It is necessary to maintain the turn-out of the thigh of the supporting leg as well, especially during the transfer from demi-pointe to demi-plié, keeping the heel well forward throughout. The body is erect and pulled up; and, particularly in the demi-plié, an inclination forward must not be allowed.

Battement fondu is done in 2/4 and 4/4 time. In the beginning (at the barre), the following préparation precedes the movement: the right arm opens through 1st position to 2nd, and, simultaneously with the movement of the arm to the side, the right leg, from 5th position front, is taken to 2nd position with a stretched foot, toe to the floor. Later on, battements fondus are done directly from 5th position, without a préparation.

Study Sequence

1. 2/4 time. On the first quarter of the first measure, the working foot, from the initial position (2nd position, with

the toe to the floor), is brought to the conditional position sur le cou-de-pied devant; the supporting leg remains stretched. On the second quarter, the position is held. On the second measure, demi-plié on the supporting leg. On the third measure, straighten the supporting leg from demi-plié, holding the working foot sur le cou-de-pied. On the first quarter of the fourth measure, the leg is extended in the given direction with a stretched foot, toe to the floor. On the second quarter, the position is held. From here, the movement is repeated. In doing fondu to the side, the position sur le cou-de-pied devant should be alternated with the position sur le cou-de-pied derrière.

2.   2/4 time. On the first measure, the working foot is brought sur le cou-de-pied, and, at the same time, the supporting leg does a demi-plié. On the second measure, the working leg is extended in one direction or another, and, at the same time, the supporting leg straightens from demi-plié.

3.   Final form. 2/4 time. Stand in 5th position with the right foot in front, the arm in preparatory position and the head turned to the right.

On the upbeat, the arm, unbending slightly, is taken a little to the side. Then, on the first quarter, the working foot, from the initial 5th position, is raised sur le cou-de-pied devant with a simultaneous demi-plié on the supporting leg; the arm returns to preparatory position, and the head turns straight forward. On the second quarter, the working leg is stretched in the given direction as the supporting leg simultaneously straightens from demi-plié; the arm opens through 1st position to 2nd; the head remains straight. From here, the movement is repeated.

During the exercise, the arm remains in 2nd position and the head stays straight forward.

Later on, for the development of co-ordination, a lowering and raising of the arm, with a turn of the head, may be introduced with the movement of the legs, in the following

manner: bending the legs, lower the arm to preparatory
position and turn the head straight; on stretching the legs,
bring the arm through 1st position to 2nd and turn the head in
the direction of the arm. To do this on each battement is not
obligatory; it is possible to combine the arms and head in any
number of ways.

Battement fondu can also be done in one quarter: on the first
eighth, the working foot is brought to the position sur le
cou-de-pied, with a simultaneous demi-plié on the supporting
leg; on the second eighth, the working leg is extended,
with a simultaneous straightening of the supporting leg.

Regardless of the acceleration of the tempo, the bending and
stretching of the legs always remains smooth, elastic, and
co-ordinated.

In battement fondu to 90°, the leg is raised by means of a
développé. The raising of the thigh and the stretching of the
working leg are done smoothly and simultaneously with the
stretching of the supporting leg from demi-plié.

The rules for the execution of these battements at 90° are the
same as for their execution at 45°. In the beginning of the study
of battement fondu at 90°, one movement is done in two
measures of 2/4; later, it is done in one measure.

Double Battement Fondu

Double battement fondu (two fondus) is done
according to the rules for battement fondu in all directions to a
height of 45° or 90° in 2/4 time.

On the first eighth, the working foot is brought to the
position sur le cou-de-pied simultaneously with a demi-plié on
the supporting leg. On the second eighth, the supporting leg is
straightened, but the working foot remains sur le cou-de-pied.
On the third and fourth eighths, the working leg is stretched in
the given direction, while the supporting leg again bends in a
demi-plié and straightens with a rise to demi-pointe. On this

second demi-plié, the working leg unbends halfway; then, during the straightening of the supporting leg and rise to demi-pointe, the working leg continues the movement, softly unbending the rest of the way.

In the execution of double battement fondu to 90°, the toe of the working leg is raised from the position sur le cou-de-pied to the knee of the supporting leg, and the leg is extended at 90° by means of a développé.

Battement fondu and double battement fondu at the barre and in the centre of the room can also be done at 45° or 90° in the various poses.

For the changing of the poses and the directions, in addition to the usual alternation of the positions sur le cou-de-pied devant and derrière, one may include a passé through 1st position while in demi-plié; one may bring the stretched leg around a quarter or a half of a circle, in plié or without a plié; and one may also employ a double transfer of the leg sur le cou-de-pied. In the centre of the room, half turns en dehors and en dedans are also done, as are transfers from one leg to the other, without interrupting the exercise, by means of a step (either tombé or coupé) or a substitution of one leg for the other in 5th position.

Battement Fondu en Tournant

Battement fondu and battement double fondu can be done also with eighth or quarter turns (i.e., en tournant), extending the leg forward (for a turn en dehors), backward (for a turn en dedans), or the side (for a turn either en dehors or en dedans).

En dehors. Simultaneously with an eighth or a quarter turn of the body in the direction of the front foot, the foot that is in front is raised from 5th position to the position sur le cou-de-pied devant as the supporting leg does a demi-plié; then, the leg is extended forward as the supporting leg straightens from demi-plié. Again, the same foot is brought sur le cou-de-pied devant simultaneously with a demi-plié on the supporting leg and a turn of the body (in the same direction) another eighth or quarter turn, etc.

En dedans. Simultaneously with an eighth or quarter turn of the body in the direction of the front foot, the foot that is in back is raised from 5th position to the position sur le cou-de-pied derrière as the supporting leg does a demi-plié; then, the leg is extended backward as the supporting leg straightens from demi-plié, etc.

Battement fondu en tournant with an extension of the leg to the side is done in the same way as battement fondu en tournant extending the leg forward or backward. In the beginning, at least two battements should be done in each direction. Turning en dehors, an alternation of the positions sur le cou-de-pied devant and derrière takes place; turning en dedans, the alternation is derrière and devant.

Battement Soutenu

Battement soutenu ("continuous" or "uninterrupted") is done from 5th position forward, to the side, and backward, with the toe to the floor and also at 45° and 90°.

Having passed the foot through the position sur le cou-de-pied (in front, the conditional position sur le cou-de-pied is used; in back, the basic position), the working leg is stretched in the required direction; at the same time, the supporting leg is lowered in demi-plié. Then, the working leg, sliding the foot along the floor with stretched toe, is brought up to the supporting leg in 5th position, simultaneously with a rise to demi-pointe.

In doing battement soutenu with the toe to the floor, the working leg must not be raised higher than the level of the position sur le cou-de-pied. The working leg is extended to a height of 45° from the position sur le cou-de-pied, gradually stretching, and is raised to a height of 90° by means of a développé.

In extending the working leg forward, one must hold the thigh turned-out as long as possible and actively move forward the turned-out lower part of the leg and the inner face of the heel.

In extending the leg backward, the turn-out of the thigh must also be maintained, and the knee must not be allowed to lower.

To the side, the movement is done with the thigh turned out to its utmost.

When first studied, the movement is done without an accent; in the final form, the accent falls on the return of the leg to 5th position on demi-pointe. Battement soutenu can be combined with battement fondu and with battement frappé and is executed in 2/4 time.

Study Sequence

1. In four measures of 2/4 time. On the first quarter of the first measure, the working foot, from the initial 5th position, is brought to the conditional position sur le cou-de-pied devant with a simultaneous demi-plié on the supporting leg. On the second quarter, the working leg, extending in the given direction, is lowered with a stretched toe to the floor in the following manner: at half the distance to the final point, the toe begins to slide along the floor; the leg is then completely stretched with the toe to the floor, while the supporting leg remains in demi-plié. On the second measure, the position is held. On the third measure, the stretched working leg is brought to 5th position, meeting the supporting leg, which simultaneously stretches from demi-plié. On the fourth measure, the position is held.

The exercise is done on the whole foot (i.e., without a rise to demi-pointe).

2. In two measures of 2/4 time. On the upbeat, the working foot is brought sur le cou-de-pied with a simultaneous demi-plié on the supporting leg. On the first quarter of the first measure, the working leg is stretched in the given direction, the supporting leg remaining in demi-plié. On the second quarter, the position is held. On the first quarter of the second measure, the working leg is brought up to the supporting leg, which is simultaneously stretched from demi-plié; and the legs join in 5th position on demi-pointe. On the second quarter, the position is held.

    In the beginning, the movement is done with the toe to the floor; then, after this has been mastered, the movement is done at a height of 45° and 90°.

3. Final form. In one measure of 2/4 time. On the upbeat, the working foot is brought sur le cou-de-pied. On the first quarter, simultaneously with a demi-plié on the supporting leg, the working leg is extended in the required direction, the supporting leg remaining in demi-plié. On the second quarter, the stretched working leg is brought up to the supporting leg in 5th position on demi-pointe. From here, the movement is repeated.

    In one measure of 2/4 time, the movement is also done to a height of 45° and 90°.

    Battement soutenu can also be done more rapidly, as follows:

4. In one quarter. 2/4 time. On the upbeat, the working foot is brought sur le cou-de-pied and the leg extended simultaneously with a demi-plié on the supporting leg, after which it is brought up to the supporting leg in 5th position on demi-pointe. On the second quarter, the movement is repeated.

Battement Développé

Battement développé is done forward, to the side, and backward at a height of 90° or higher (depending on the individual capabilities of the student).

From the initial 5th position, the working leg, bending, and sliding with a stretched toe along the supporting leg, is raised to the knee, after which it is extended in one or another direction to at least 90° before being lowered to 5th position.

Like the preceding movements of the barre exercise, battement développé is learned with each leg separately, at first to the side, then forward and backward. The movement backward should at first be studied facing the barre.

General Remarks. In raising the working leg from 5th position front for a développé forward or to the side, slide it along the front of the supporting leg with a stretched foot; the heel is moved well forward and does not touch the supporting leg; the thigh must be turned out to its maximum.

In extending the leg forward or to the side at a height of 90°, maintain the turn-out of the thigh, and do not allow it to move forward; actively move forward the lower part of the leg.

In raising the working leg from 5th position back for a développé backward or to the side, slide the heel along the back of the supporting leg to a point higher than the knee; and draw back the stretched toe, for it must not be allowed to touch the supporting leg.

In stretching the leg backward at a height of 90°, maintain the turn-out of the thigh and do not lower the knee. The pulled-up body must incline forward somewhat, the shoulders remaining level; however, the hand must not move forward along the barre (because movement of the hand forward before such an inclination of the body will inevitably lead to a slackening of the middle).

During the extension of the leg forward and to the side, the body remains erect and pulled up.

While extending the leg to the side, from beginning to end of the movement, maintain the turn-out of the working leg.

The leg is extended smoothly, and is lowered with control, strongly tightening the muscles to keep it stretched.

Développé is studied at a slow tempo, in 2/4 and 4/4 time.

Study Sequence

1. Four measures of 2/4 time. On the first measure, the toe of the working foot, the knee bending, is brought from 5th position to the knee of the supporting leg. On the second measure, the leg is extended at a height of 90° in one direction or another. On the third measure, the position is held. On the first quarter of the fourth measure, the stretched leg is lowered with the stretched toe to the floor. On the second quarter, it closes to 5th position. From here, the movement is repeated.

2. One measure of 4/4 time. On the first quarter, the toe of the working foot is raised from 5th position to the knee of the supporting leg. On the second quarter, the leg is extended at a height of 90° in the given direction. On the third quarter, the stretched leg begins to be lowered. And, on the fourth quarter, it closes in 5th position.

3. Final form. One measure of 4/4 time. On the upbeat, the toe of the working foot is raised from 5th position to the knee of the supporting leg. On the first quarter, the leg is extended in the given direction at a height of 90°. On the second and third quarters, it is held in this position. On the fourth, it is lowered to the initial 5th position.

In this final form of battement développé, the extension of the leg takes place in one quarter, distributed in the following way: one eighth for the raising of the working foot to the knee of the supporting leg; the second eighth for the extension of the leg at a height of 90°.

The extension of the leg at 90° must coincide with the first strong beat of the measure. This will be the basic feature of the movement of the leg in its final form, regardless of how much time it will be held in the air.

In the construction of an adagio, the extension of the leg can take place in either one or two quarters, the latter being used in the slow parts of the adagio.

Battements développés are very numerous in type.

The examples of the various kinds of développés cited below are stipulated by the study programme given in the appendix and are learned in an obligatory order.

Développé Passé

The working leg is extended at 90°, and then bends, the toe being brought to the knee of the turned-out supporting leg (near the back of the knee, but not touching it) after which the leg is again extended in one or another direction at 90°.

Bending the leg into the knee from the front, it is necessary to bring the thigh well back to the side, maintaining the turn-out of the foot.

Bending the leg into the knee from the back, the thigh is held back as much as possible, and the turned-out foot is actively brought to the supporting leg with the toe to the knee.

Bending the leg into the knee from the side, it is necessary to actively maintain the turn-out of the whole leg.

At first, passé (the bringing of the foot in to the knee from an extended position) must be done at a slow tempo, in two quarters; later on, it can be done in one quarter or in one eighth.

Développé, Taking the Leg Around to the Side a Quarter of a Circle (Demi-Grand Rond de Jambe en Dehors and en Dedans)

From 5th position, the working leg is extended forward at 90° (the développé) and, keeping it stretched, is taken around to the side at this same height.

The same is done in the opposite direction: the leg is extended backward and, keeping it stretched, is taken around to the side at the same height. Then it is extended to the side at 90° and taken either forward or backward at the same height.

In the beginning of the study of this développé, the taking around of the stretched leg from one direction to another is done in two quarters; later on it is done in one quarter.

As the leg is taken around to the side from the front, the body remains level and must not incline toward the barre.

As the leg is taken around to the side from the back, the body, inclined forward, comes erect, but must at no time incline toward the barre. Such an inclination of the body toward the barre usually occurs as the leg is taken around to the back from the side.

The decisive element in the correct execution of this kind of développé is the maintenance of the maximum turn-out of the working leg, keeping that leg tautly stretched and pulled up in the hip joint.

Développé, Taking the Leg Around a Half of a Circle (Grand Rond de Jambe en Dehors and en Dedans)

From 5th position, the working leg is extended forward at 90° and, keeping it stretched, is taken around to the back through 2nd position at this same height. For the execution in the opposite direction, the leg is extended backward at 90° and taken around to the front through 2nd position.

The finished movement is smooth and without a stop; but, during the learning stage, it can be done with pauses—that is, the leg is brought around to the side; there is a pause; then the leg is taken backward.

The rules for the position of the body are the same as for développé with a demi-grand rond de jambe. The leg must maintain a turned-out position and be well pulled up in the hip joint.

Développé Ballotté

In développé ballotté ("rocked"), the body inclines backward as the leg is extended to the front, and forward as the leg is extended to the back. During the movement of the leg to the side, the body inclines in the opposite direction, to the side of the supporting leg.

If one is standing with the left hand on the barre, the right leg in 5th position front, this développé is done forward with the right leg, and backward with the left, to a height of 90°. With the right leg in 5th position back, it is done backward with the right leg and forward with the left. Développé ballotté forward and backward can also be done with the same leg by means of a passé at 90°.

Développé ballotté to the side is done only in the centre of the room, alternating one leg with the other.

During the inclination of the body backward, the shoulders must remain level, with the small of the back tightly pulled up. The back is held straight and not allowed to collapse. During the inclination of the body forward, the shoulders are also level, and the small of the back is tightly pulled up; but the upper back is curved backward. In the movement in 2nd position to the side, the body inclines to the side of the supporting leg. The thigh of the working leg is well pulled up, and the head turns in the direction opposite the raised leg. As the leg returns to 5th position, the head turns en face.

In the beginning of the study of développé ballotté, the arm remains in 2nd position for the whole exercise, with the head turned away from the barre.

Later on, for the development of co-ordination, the arm, from preparatory position, is raised through 1st position to 2nd simultaneously with the extension of the leg at 90°, and is lowered to preparatory position together with the closing of the leg to 5th position. The head is turned toward the arm that is opening to 2nd position; then, during the lowering of the arm to preparatory position, the head turns en face.

Study Sequence

1. In two measures of 4/4 time. From the initial 5th position, on the upbeat, rise to demi-pointe. On the first quarter, the right foot, which is in front, is raised, bringing the toe to the knee of the supporting leg. On the second quarter, the working leg is extended forward at 90° with a simultaneous demi-plié on the supporting leg, the body inclining backward. On the third quarter, the position is held. On the fourth quarter, the stretched leg is brought, with the toe along the floor, up to the supporting leg in 5th position together with a rise to demi-pointe; and the body comes erect. On the first quarter of the second measure, from 5th position on demi-pointe, the left foot, which is in back, is raised to the level of the knee of the supporting leg in back. Then, on the second quarter, the working leg is extended backward at 90°, with a simultaneous demi-plié on the supporting leg, and an inclination of the body forward. On the third quarter, the position is held. On the fourth quarter, the stretched leg is brought, with the toe along the floor, up to the supporting leg in 5th position back, together with a rise to demi-pointe; and the body comes erect. The movements of the legs are analogous to those of battement soutenu at 90°.

2. Final form. In two measures of 2/4 time. On the upbeat, from the initial 5th position with the right foot front, rise to demi-pointe; then the right foot is raised, bringing the toe in front of the knee of the supporting leg. On the first quarter of the first measure, the working leg is extended forward at 90° with a simultaneous demi-plié on the supporting leg, the body inclining backward. On the second

quarter, the stretched leg is brought to 5th position front on demi-pointe, simultaneously with a rise of the supporting leg from demi-plié; and the body comes erect. On the last eighth of the measure, from 5th position, the left foot is raised to the level of the knee of the supporting leg in back. On the first quarter of the second measure, the working leg is extended to the back at 90° with a simultaneous demi-plié on the supporting leg, and the body inclines forward. On the second quarter, the stretched leg is brought to 5th position back on demi-pointe, simultaneously with a rise of the supporting leg from demi-plié, and the body comes erect.

Study Sequence for Développé Ballotté with Passé at 90°

1. In two measures of 4/4 time. On the upbeat, rise to 5th position on demi-pointe, and raise the right foot with the toe to the knee of the supporting leg. On the first quarter of the first measure, the leg is extended forward at 90°, with a demi-plié on the supporting leg; the body inclines backward. On the second quarter, the position is held. On the third quarter, the leg bends in passé at 90° (the toe near the knee); the supporting leg rises to demi-pointe, and the body comes erect. On the fourth quarter, the position is held. On the first quarter of the second measure, the right leg is extended backward at 90°, with a simultaneous demi-plié on the supporting leg; the body inclines forward. On the second quarter, the position is held. On the third quarter, the leg is bent to passé (the toe near the knee); simultaneously, the supporting leg rises to demi-pointe and the body comes erect. On the fourth quarter, the position is held. From here, the movement is repeated forward and backward, etc.

2. Final form. In one measure of 4/4 time. On the upbeat, from 5th position, rise to demi-pointe and raise the toe of

the working foot to the knee of the supporting leg. On the first eighth, the working leg is extended forward at 90°, with a demi-plié on the supporting leg and an inclination of the body backward. On the second eighth, the position is held. On the third eighth, the leg bends to passé at 90°; the supporting leg rises to demi-pointe, and the body comes erect. On the fourth eighth, the position is held. On the fifth eighth, the working leg is extended backward at 90°, with a demi-plié on the supporting leg and an inclination of the body forward. On the sixth eighth, the position is held. On the seventh eighth, the leg again is bent to passé at 90°; the supporting leg rises to demi-pointe, and the body comes erect. On the last eighth, the position is held. From here, the movement is repeated forward and backward, etc.

Développé with a Half Turn en Dehors and en Dedans

Extend the working right leg forward at 90° by means of a développé; then turn on the left leg a half turn en dedans (toward the barre), simultaneously turning the body.

As the body turns, the right leg, without lowering, rotates in the hip joint and finishes in back at 90°; the left arm, which was on the barre, opens to 2nd position and the right arm, from 2nd position, is brought forward and takes hold of the barre after the turn. The supporting leg turns in place, the heel being moved forward.

On the same supporting leg, with the working leg extended backward, it is possible to turn a half turn en dehors (away from the barre); the working leg, without changing its position in the air, will finish in front at 90°. The arms change in the following manner: one takes the barre, and the other opens to 2nd position.

To execute the movement in the reverse direction, développé

backward and turn the body on the supporting leg en dehors (away from the barre). The working leg will finish in front.

Then, on that same leg, together with the body, turn back en dedans. The working leg will finish in back.

In the turns en dedans and en dehors, one must pay attention to the tautness and the turn-out of the thigh of the working leg; and the toe should be held at one point in the air.

In the beginning of the study of this movement, each turn is done in two quarters; but, later on, it can be done in one quarter.

The movement is learned first on the whole foot, then on demi-pointe, and also with plié-relevé.

Développé Plié-Relevé with a Half Turn en Dehors and en Dedans

Développé forward and plié-relevé; but, on rising to demi-pointe, turn en dedans on the supporting leg; the working leg will finish in back. To reverse the movement, demi-plié on the supporting leg (with the working leg extended in back); rise to demi-pointe, turning en dehors; the working leg finishes in front.

Développé Balancé (Quick)

Développé balancé has a quick swing of the leg either vertically or horizontally. The character of the swing is precise and sharp.

Développé at 90° forward, to the side, or backward. Then, with a short, quick movement, slightly lower the leg and immediately return it sharply to its former height.

For the execution of the movement, the utmost tautness of the whole working leg is necessary.

Balancé is done in one quarter; one eighth is used for the lowering of the leg, the other for the raising of it.

Développé Balancé Taking the Leg Around a Quarter or a Half of a Circle and Quickly Returning It (d'ici-delà)

The working leg, from 5th position, is extended forward at 90° by means of a développé; then, at the same height, it is brought quickly to the side (a quarter of a circle) and, without a pause, is returned to the front. The movement is also done in the opposite direction: the leg, extended backward, is taken around (a quarter of a circle) to the side, and then quickly returned to the back. Or, from a développé to the side, the leg may be brought forward (a quarter of a circle) and returned to the side, or, taken backward (a quarter of a circle) and returned to the side.

Balancé is also done taking the leg around a half of a circle. For this, the leg is extended forward by means of a développé, taken quickly around to the back through 2nd position and, without pausing, returned to the front through 2nd position.

Taking of the leg around a quarter or a half of a circle may also be combined. For example: extend the leg forward by means of a développé, then take it to the back through 2nd position, then return it quickly to the side. Or, after having done a développé to the side, the leg may be brought forward before taking it quickly around to the back through 2nd position. The height of the leg must be kept at 90° throughout the movement.

The balancé movement is done in one quarter; one eighth is used for taking the leg around, the other for bringing it back; and the accent must fall on the return of the leg to its initial position.

Balancé is done with a strongly stretched leg, turned out to the utmost, and well pulled up in the hip joint.

The position of the body is the same as in développé taking the leg slowly around a quarter or a half of a circle.

Développé Tombé

Développé tombé ("fallen") is done at the barre forward, to the side, and backward, and in the poses effacées and écartées devant and derrière. In the centre of the room it is done forward, to the side, and backward, and in the poses croisées, effacées, and écartées devant and derrière.

At the barre and in the centre of the room, développé tombé can be done as an independent adagio, and also in combination with other kinds of développé.

Développé Tombé at the Barre.

One measure of 4/4 time. On the first quarter, the right (the working) leg is extended forward at 90° by means of a développé; and, simultaneously, the right arm opens through 1st position to 2nd. On the second quarter, the supporting leg is raised to demi-pointe; and the right leg is "thrown", so to speak, upward in an arc. On the third quarter, moving the body forward, "fall" forward onto the right leg in demi-plié in a wide 4th position (the tombé), transferring the centre of the body's weight over the right leg and keeping the left leg stretched back with the toe to the floor; the middle must be strongly pulled in; the right arm remains in 2nd position, and the left hand moves forward along the barre; the shoulders are level. On the fourth quarter, the left foot is lowered from the toe to the heel, and the body comes erect, transferring the weight back onto the left (supporting) leg. The right leg, stretching and sliding the toe along the floor, is brought up to the supporting leg and, through 5th position, is extended forward again at 90° by means of a développé; the supporting left leg rises to demi-pointe, etc.

As the body's weight is centered again over the left leg, the right arm is lowered; then, simultaneously with the développé of the right leg, it opens through 1st position to 2nd; and the left hand slides back to its original position.

In elementary study, it is also possible to finish développé tombé in the following manner: on the fourth quarter, returning to the supporting leg, remain on the whole foot (with the heel on the floor), bring the right foot in to the supporting leg to the conditional position sur le cou-de-pied devant, and begin the next movement from there.

The principles governing the execution of développé tombé backward and to the side are the same as those for the movement forward. It should be noted that during the fall (the tombé) to the side, the hand that is resting on the barre must leave the barre, with the arm taking either 2nd or 3rd position; during the return of the centre of the body's weight to the supporting leg, the hand is lowered to the barre.

In executing développé tombé in the poses, one also releases the. barre on the tombé. Taking, for example, développé tombé to the pose effacée devant, after the développé at 90°, one falls in the direction effacée and, having let go of the barre, assumes the small pose effacée derrière (that is, a small 2nd arabesque with the toe to the floor); on returning to the supporting leg, again place the hand on the barre.

In the execution of développé tombé in all directions, the tombé should be done as widely as possible; one should come down from the toe to the heel with control, going to a resilient demi-plié. It should be noted that développé tombé done with a strong raising of the leg in an upward arc before the tombé, and also the active participation of the body in the movement (its striving at first upward, and then beyond the toe forward or backward, depending on the direction of the développé), unquestionably help in the correct execution of grands jetés in allegro work. And in class, during the study of grands jetés, it is useful to remind the student of the rules for the execution of développé tombé.

Besides the even distribution of développé tombé on the counts of the measure, when each separate movement is done in one quarter, in combination, the movement can be distributed in individual cases in various ways: that is, each développé tombé can be done unevenly, even within one measure. For example: the first développé can be sustained, doing it slowly in two quarters, and the subsequent développés in the same combination can follow without pauses and take one quarter each.

Battements Divisés en Quarts

Battements divisés en quarts ("divided in quarters") is a combination of several movements repeated with one leg four times, with a quarter turn of the body each time. It is executed en dehors and en dedans.

This combination of battements is also done with half turns and whole turns of the body en dehors and en dedans.

It exists in two forms, en avant and en arrière, and is done only in the centre of the room.

First form. Battements divisés en quarts en avant, en dehors.

Four measures of 4/4 time. On the upbeat, the working foot, from 5th position front, is brought up along the front of the supporting leg until the toe is under the knee. On the first quarter of the first measure, the working leg is extended forward at 90°; and, together with the movement of the leg, the arms, from preparatory position, are raised to 1st position. On the second quarter, demi-plié on the supporting leg, the arms remaining in 1st position. On the third quarter, simultaneously taking the working leg around to the side at the height of 90° and opening the arms to 2nd position, rise to demi-pointe and turn a quarter turn en dehors. On the fourth quarter, bend the working leg, bringing the toe under the knee of the supporting leg; come down from demi-pointe with a stretched knee and lower the arms to preparatory position. From here, the combination is repeated.

After the fourth time, the working leg is lowered to 5th position behind the supporting leg, and the exercise is executed with the other leg.

For the execution of battements divisés en quarts en avant, en dedans, the working leg is extended forward and, simultaneously with the rise to demi-pointe on the supporting leg and a turn en dedans, is taken to the side the same way as before.

Second form. Battement divisé en quarts en arrière, en dehors.

Four measures of 4/4 time. On the upbeat, the working foot, from 5th position back, is brought up along the supporting leg until the toe is behind the knee. On the first quarter of the first measure, the working leg is extended backward at 90°, and the arms are raised to 1st position. On the second quarter, demi-plié on the supporting leg, the arms remaining in 1st position. On the third quarter, turn a quarter of a turn en dehors on demi-pointe, and, simultaneously, take the working leg to the side and open the arms to 2nd position. On the fourth quarter, the working leg bends, bringing the toe behind the knee of the supporting leg; come down from demi-pointe, with a stretched knee and lower the arms to preparatory position. From here, the combination is repeated.

For the execution of battements divisés en quarts en arrière en dedans, the leg is extended backward at 90° and is taken around to the side simultaneously with a rise of the supporting leg to demi-pointe and a quarter turn en dedans.

For the successful execution of these battements, it is necessary to maintain a pulled up body and to exert the strength of the legs throughout. There can be no slackening in any position and a good turn-out must be maintained. The decisive moment will be the turn of the body on demi-pointe as the working leg is taken to the side.

The turn on demi-pointe must be stable to such an extent that there can be a pause on demi-pointe after the working leg has reached 2nd position. In order to do this, a single timing is very helpful. Simultaneously with the turn of the body, it is necessary to rise energetically to demi-pointe, stretching the knee strongly, and at that instant, bring the working leg, turned out and pulled up in the hip joint, to the side, as the arms open to 2nd position (at the moment they open, the arms must be resilient, helping the body).

III. Rond de Jambe

Rond de Jambe par Terre

Rond de jambe par terre is a circular movement of the foot along the floor in the direction en dehors or en dedans.

En dehors. From 1st position, the working leg is taken forward and moves in an arc through 2nd position to a position in back opposite 1st position. The foot is completely stretched, and the toe does not leave the floor. Continuing the movement, the leg, lowering the heel to the floor, is brought forward through 1st position. From here, the movement is repeated in the same direction (en dehors).

In stretching the leg forward, it is necessary to lead with the heel, strongly moving it forward, and, while drawing the leg in an arc through 2nd position to the back, one should maintain the turn-out and continue to hold the heel forward.

En dedans. From 1st position, the working leg is drawn back to a position opposite 1st position and moved in an arc through 2nd position to the front. Then, through 1st position, it is taken to the back. From here, the movement is repeated in the same direction (en dedans).

In stretching the leg backward, it is necessary to begin the movement from the toe and continue it in an arc through 2nd position to the front with a turned-out leg, holding the heel well forward.

General Remarks. In rond de jambe par terre (en dehors and en dedans), the maximum turn-out and tautness of the whole leg are maintained throughout.

It is necessary to observe the correct direction of the leg forward and backward in a straight line, placing the toe exactly opposite its initial point in lst position. For, if the toe goes beyond the limits of these points, the evenness of the rotary movement is destroyed.

In bringing the foot to lst position, it is necessary to hold up the instep, and to draw it in without rolling over onto the big toe. The muscles of the working leg must not be relaxed.

In the beginning rond de jambe par terre is broken down into parts; in its final form, it is executed in a connected manner.

Study Sequence

1. Demi-rond de jambe par terre en dehors. 4/4 time. On the first quarter of the first measure, the working leg, from lst position, is drawn forward. On the second quarter, the position is held. On the third and fourth quarters, the leg is drawn in an arc to the side. On the first and second quarters of the second measure, the position is held. On the third and fourth quarters, the leg closes to lst position. Then follows the second half of the movement.

   On the first quarter of the third measure, the leg, from lst position, is drawn out to the side. On the second quarter, the position is held. On the third and fourth quarters, the leg is drawn in an arc to the back. On the first and second quarters of the fourth measure, the position is held. On the third and fourth, the leg closes to lst position.

   This movement is done en dedans in the same manner, but moving in the opposite direction.

2. Demi-rond de jambe en dehors. 4/4 time. On the first quarter of the first measure, the leg, from lst position, is

drawn forward. On the second quarter, it is drawn in an arc to the side. On the third quarter, it closes to 1st position. On the fourth quarter, the position is held. On the first quarter of the second measure, the leg is drawn to the side. On the second quarter it is drawn in an arc to the back. On the third quarter it closes to 1st position. On the fourth, the position is held.

3. Rond de jambe en dehors. 2/4 time. A préparation is executed on the two introductory measures in the following manner. Opening the arm a little to the side, on the first quarter of the first introductory measure, demi-plié in 1st position; and lower the arm to preparatory position. On the second quarter, draw the working leg forward, strectching the foot so that only the toe touches the floor; the supporting leg remains in demi-plié; the arm is raised to 1st position, and, looking at the hand, the head inclines toward the barre. On the first quarter of the second introductory measure, draw the working leg in an arc to the side, without taking the stretched foot from the floor; and, at the same time, stretch the supporting leg, open the arm to 2nd position, and turn the head out. On the second quarter, the leg, from 2nd position, sliding the toe along the floor, is drawn in an arc to the back, and the head turns straight forward. The drawing of the leg from 2nd position to the back, on the second quarter of the second introductory measure, is the upbeat for the beginning of the movement en dehors (for the movement en dedans, the préparation is done in exactly the same manner, but the leg is moved in the opposite direction).

On the first quarter of the first measure, the working leg is drawn through 1st position forward. On the second quarter, it is drawn in an arc through 2nd position to the back. On the first quarter of the second measure, the leg again is drawn through 1st position forward. On the second quarter, it is drawn through 2nd position in an arc to the back, etc.

4. Final form. 2/4 time. The préparation from 1st or 5th position, done in one introductory measure, precedes the movement: on the first eighth, demi-plié. On the second eighth, the working leg is drawn forward, the foot stretched, the toe to the floor; the supporting leg remains in demi-plié; the arm is raised to 1st position and the head, looking at the hand, inclines toward the barre. On the third eighth, the leg, sliding the toe along the floor, is drawn in an arc to the side; simultaneously, the supporting leg is straightened from demi-plié, the arm opens to 2nd position, and the head turns out. On the fourth eighth (the upbeat), the leg, with the toe in contact with the floor, is drawn in an arc to the back and the head turns straight forward.

On the first eighth of the first measure of the musical phrase, the leg is drawn forward through 1st position. On the second eighth, it is drawn in an arc through 2nd position to the back. On the third eighth, it again is drawn forward through 1st position. Thus, an uninterrupted movement of the leg takes place. Each rond de jambe is done in one quarter.

In learning the connected form of rond de jambe par terre, the transfer from en dehors to en dedans is made from 4th position. The leg finishes the circle en dehors forward with a stretched foot and, from there, the movement is reversed: the leg is drawn through 1st position to the back for the execution of the circle en dedans.

In executing rond de jambe par terre in the centre, the préparation is exactly the same, but both arms are raised to 1st position before being opened to 2nd. It is important to remember that the head should always incline toward the supporting leg. Thus, in the préparation for rond de jambe en dedans with the left leg, the head will incline to the right, because the right leg is the supporting leg.

Rond de jambe par terre can also be done more quickly, in eighths, and also in combinations of quarters and eighths.

Rond de Jambe par Terre en Tournant

Rond de jambe par terre en tournant (i. e., turning) with turns an eighth or a quarter of a circle en dehors or en dedans is done in the centre of the room.

In the initial stage, the first rond de jambe is done with a turn and the second in place. During the turn, attention must be paid to the correct motion of the working leg, bringing it to a position in front or in back opposite 1st position.

The drawing of the working leg in an arc through 2nd position backward or forward (en dehors or en dedans) takes place simultaneously with the turn of the body on the supporting leg, the heel of which, without doing a relevé, merely shifts its position on the floor.

Rond de Jambe en l'Air

Rond de jambe en l'air is a circular movement of the lower limb in the air at the height of 45° or 90°.

Rond de jambe en l'air en dehors. Begin with the working leg in 2nd position at 45°. With an immobile thigh, bending the knee, the lower part of the leg is moved in a bow-shaped line, describing a backward arc toward the supporting leg, until the toe just touches the calf; the leg then continues the circular movement in a forward arc and is stretched in 2nd position at 45° (the initial position).

Rond de jambe en l'air en dedans. From the initial position, the working leg, bending, is moved in a forward arc toward the supporting leg; it then continues the movement in a backward arc and is stretched in 2nd position at 45°.

The movement is learned at a slow tempo.

RULES FOR THE EXECUTION OF ROND DE JAMBE EN L'AIR. In moving the leg in an arc, one must not bring it too far either in front or in back of the plane of the supporting leg; that is, one must not try to make a true circle. The circle must be lengthened out and is actually an elongated oval.

The stretching of the leg to 2nd position must be energetic, but not sharp, and without yanking the knee. Each rond is done clearly, and its completion in 2nd position is fixed for a moment with a pause each time.

From 2nd position at 45°, the toe of the working leg is brought to the middle of the calf of the supporting leg. In rond de jambe en l'air at a height of 90°, the toe of the working leg is brought behind the knee and must not cross in front or in back of the supporting leg.

During the rond de jambe, the thigh must be completely turned-out and immobile. At no time may the turn-out of the heel be disturbed, allowing the foot to sickle.

Before beginning the study of rond de jambe en l'air, it is recommended that, for a short period only, the bending and stretching of the lower leg be done without the circular movement.

Rond de jambe is preceded by a préparation, which is done on two introductory measures of 2/4. On the first quarter of the first measure, the arm is raised from preparatory position to lst position, the head inclines to the barre, and the eyes look at the hand. On the second quarter, the position is held. On the first quarter of the second measure, the arm opens to 2nd position and the head turns out; at the same time, the working leg, from 5th position, is drawn out to 2nd position, stretching the foot, toe to the floor. On the second quarter, the leg is raised to 45°

and the head turns straight forward. Later on, the préparation is done in one introductory measure, in the following manner: on the first quarter, the arm is raised to 1st position; on the second quarter, it is taken out to 2nd position and, at the same time, the leg, from 5th position, is raised to 2nd position to a height of 45°. The préparation for rond de jambe en l'air can also be a temps relevé.

Study Sequence

1. Without a rotation of the leg, in eight quarters. 2/4 time. On the first measure, the working leg, which is stretched to 2nd position at 45°, bends, and the toe is brought to the calf of the supporting leg. On the second measure, the position is held. On the third measure, the leg is stretched to 2nd position at a height of 45°. On the fourth, the position is held. Then the movement is repeated.

2. En dehors, in four quarters. 2/4 time. On the first measure, the working leg, from 2nd position at 45°, describes a backward arc, bringing the toe to the calf of the supporting leg. On the second measure, the leg continues the movement in a forward arc, closing the circle, and is stretched to 2nd position at 45°. From here, the rond de jambe is repeated. The circular movement of the leg must be smooth, completely legato; it has no accent.

   Rond de jambe en dedans is done in the reverse order.

3. En dehors, in four quarters, with a pause. 2/4 time. On the first measure, the working leg, from 2nd position at 45°, bending, describes a backward arc before bringing the toe to the calf of the supporting leg. On the first quarter of the second measure, the leg continues the movement in a forward arc and is stretched to 2nd position at 45°. On the second quarter, the position is held. From here, the movement is repeated in the same direction.

4. En dehors, in two quarters. 2/4 time. A préparation is done on two introductory measures. Then, one rond de jambe en l'air is done in one measure of 2/4, in the following manner: on the upbeat, the backward arc is described; on the first quarter, the leg is opened to 2nd position with a forward arc and stretched; on the second quarter, the backward arc of the next rond de jambe is described, etc. Thus, each rond de jambe is finished on the strong beat of the measure.

Then, in its final form, one rond de jambe is done in one quarter.

Rond de jambe en l'air, in the beginning, is done on the whole foot; but, from the second year, a rise onto demi-pointe is introduced.

It can also be executed more quickly, in eighths and sixteenths. For example, two movements can be done in quarters and three in eighths. In advanced classes, rond de jambe en l'air is combined with other movements and is done in combinations of quarters, eighths, and sixteenths.

Rond de jambe en l'air, in the centre of the room as well as at the barre, can also be done with plié-relevé, with an accent up or with an accent down.

With an accent up. The working leg, on the upbeat, bending, is moved in a backward or forward arc (en dehors or en dedans) to the supporting leg; at the same time, the supporting leg does a plié. The working leg continues the movement in an arc forward or backward and is stretched, on the strong beat, to 2nd position at 45°; at the same time, the supporting leg is also stretched and rises to demi-pointe. Both legs bend simultaneously and are stretched simultaneously.

With an accent down. On the upbeat, the working leg, bending, moves in a backward or forward arc (en dehors or en dedans) to the supporting leg and, continuing the movement, is stretched to 2nd position at 45°. As the working leg is stretched, the supporting leg does a plié. Then the working leg bends again, describing an arc toward the supporting leg; at the same time, the supporting leg is stretched and rises to demi-pointe, etc.

In the centre of the room, rond de jambe en l'air can be done en tournant with turns an eighth or a quarter of a circle en dehors or en dedans. The turns will take place on demi-pointe. In the movement en tournant, one must preserve the turn-out, immobility, and pulled-up condition of the thigh of the working leg, which is necessary not only for the correct execution of rond de jambe but also for stability on demi-pointe.

Grand Rond de Jambe Jeté

This movement consists of a big circular throw of the leg at 90° en dehors and en dedans.

Grand rond de jambe jeté en dehors. The working leg, from lst position, is drawn back along the floor to 4th position, stretching the foot, toe to the floor. Then, through lst position, the leg is thrown out forward to a half-bent position at 45°, is stretched in the direction effacée, and continues the movement in a circle at a height of 90° through 2nd position to the back. Completing the circle, the leg is lowered and, through lst position, again is thrown out forward at 45° for the succeeding rond de jambe en dehors.

Grand rond de jambe jeté en dedans. The working leg is first drawn forward to 4th position. Then, through lst position, the leg is thrown out backward to a half-bent position at 45°, is stretched in the direction effacée, and continues the movement in a circle at a height of 90° through 2nd position forward. Completing the circle, the leg is lowered and, through lst position, again is thrown out backward to 45° for the succeeding rond de jambe en dedans.

General Remarks. In the beginning, while learning this movement by itself, the drawing out of the leg to 4th position, toe to the floor, is a kind of préparation. But later on, when grand rond de jambe jeté is combined with rond de jambe par terre (the former, as a rule, following the latter), the leg is thrown out immediately from the preceding rond de-jambe par terre.

In grand rond de jambe jeté en dehors, the leg is thrown out forward to a half-bent position at 45° opposite lst position, with a turned-out and pulled-up thigh. The heel is moved well forward, the muscles of the leg are taut, and the instep and toes are completely stretched.

Under no circumstances should the leg pause after being thrown out at a height of 45°; it continues an unbroken movement in a circle, just as in rond de jambe par terre.

From the half-bent position at a height of 45°, the leg, stretching in the knee, is thrown in the conditional direction effacée devant (the point between the direction forward and to the side). Then the leg, gradually climbing to a height of 90°, goes through 2nd position to the conditional position écartée derrière (the point between the direction to the side and backward). This is the highest point of the throw of the leg in the direction en dehors. Then the leg is lowered and is drawn back to the 4th position opposite lst position. These positions effacée and écartée are called conditional because the body itself does not take on the positions effacée or écartée but remains en face.

When one is first learning rond de jambe jeté, the throwing movement of the leg is replaced by a slow, nonstop movement, taking the leg around in a circle at 90°. Later on, the rond de jambe is done with an energetic throw of the leg.

Study Sequence

1. En dehors. 4/4 time. On the first quarter, from 4th position back, toe to the floor, the working leg is thrown through lst position forward to a bent position at a height of 45°, stretching the instep and toes. On the second quarter, the leg stretches and, rising to 90°, moves in an arc to 2nd

position. On the third quarter, continuing the movement, it goes to the conditional position écartée derrière. On the fourth quarter, it is lowered to 4th position back with a stretched foot, toe to the floor, opposite 1st position.

2. 2/4 time. In two quarters, the working leg, from the initial position (4th position back with a stretched foot, toe to the floor), is thrown through 1st position forward to a half-bent position at 45°; then, stretching and rising to 90°, it goes in an arc through 2nd position to the conditional position écartée derrière and is lowered in back to 4th position with a stretched foot, toe to the floor. On the second measure, the movement is repeated, etc. During the execution of grand rond de jambe jeté, the body must remain immobile and erect, the shoulders freely open and the lower back tightly pulled up.

The movement en dedans is done in the reverse direction.

At the next stage of study, the movement is also done in one measure, but with the difference that the leg, on lowering, does not pause in 4th position back (for the movement en dehors) or in front (for the movement en dedans), fixing the position, but only passes through this position.

3. Final form. 2/4 time. On the first quarter of the first measure, from 4th position back with a stretched foot, toe to the floor, the working leg is thrown through 1st position forward to a half-bent position at 45°, then, stretching, continues the throw, rises to 90°, goes in an arc through 2nd position to the conditional position écartée derrière, and is lowered in back opposite 1st position. On the second quarter, without interrupting the movement, and passing through 4th position with a stretched foot, toe to the floor, the heel is lowered, and the leg is thrown through 1st position forward at 45° to a half-bent position, etc.

Thus, the rond de jambe is done in one quarter.

IV. Port de Bras

Port de bras is the correct passage of the arms through the basic positions with turns and inclinations of the head and movements of the body.

In classical dance, port de bras has enormous importance. The linear beauty of the arms, their softness and flexibility, the mobility of the torso, the various turns and inclinations of the head—all are produced by port de bras. In port de bras, the plastic expressiveness of dance is gradually developed.

The study of the simplest port de bras at the barre and in the centre of the room is begun in the first year of training, as soon as the positions of the arms are mastered. For example, the movement of the arms through the positions in combination with rond de jambe par terre or some other movement of the barre exercise is a preparation for port de bras. Later on, an inclination of the body forward, a bend backward, and turns of the head are included. Still later, a port de bras in a wide 4th position with a deep demi-plié on the supporting leg and an inclination of the body forward, stretching it out from the head to the toe, and a bend backward are done (for example, conclude ronds de jambe par terre).

Ports de bras are added to the study of the positions of the feet; they are executed while standing on demi-pointe on both legs or on one; and they accompany grands pliés. The musical rhythms and tempos are diverse, but the smoothness and continuity of the movements, a characteristic of port de bras, must always be maintained.

The various ports de bras are extensively used in adagio, of which they are one of the basic elements.

In advanced classes, ports de bras are combined with jumps (for example, sissonne renversée, jeté renversé, etc.)

The Basic Forms of the Academic Ports de Bras

The study of port de bras is begun standing en face and in the centre of the room with a movement of the arms through the three arm positions at a slow tempo, with a prolonged pause in each position. After this has been mastered, the basic forms of port de bras are introduced one by one.

The 1st port de bras. Stand in 5th position croisée, right leg front, the arms in preparatory position, the head turned to the right, and the body well pulled up. The initial stance for all of the following numbered ports de bras will be the same.

Two measures of 4/4 time. On the first quarter of the first measure, the arms, from the preparatory position, are raised to 1st position, the head inclines slightly toward the left shoulder, and the eyes are directed at the hands. On the second quarter the position is held. On the third quarter, the arms are raised to 3rd position and the head straightens, the eyes accompanying the hands. On the fourth quarter, the position is held. On the first quarter of the second measure, the arms open to 2nd position and the head turns to the right, with the eyes accompanying the right hand. On the second quarter, the position is held. On the third quarter, the arms are lowered to preparatory position, during which they curve somewhat, the hands gradually turning palms down; the fingers lag slightly behind and, while in motion, complete the curved line of the arms; the head remains turned to the right. On the fourth quarter, the position is held.

Later on, this port de bras is done in one measure of 4/4, at a slow tempo and in a connected fashion. Then, in accordance with mastery of the port de bras, the tempo is somewhat accelerated.

In the execution of the port de bras in 3/4 time, each position will correspond to one measure.

The 2nd port de bras (a complex use of the three positions).

A préparation is done on two introductory chords as follows: stand in 5th position croisée, right leg front. On the first chord, the arms, from preparatory position, are raised to lst position; the head inclines slightly toward the left shoulder, and the eyes are directed at the hands. On the second chord, the left arm is raised to 3rd position and the right one is taken to 2nd position; the head turns to the right, the eyes accompanying the right hand.

From here, the port de bras itself begins. The left arm opens to 2nd position and, simultaneously, the right arm is raised to 3rd position; the head turns toward the left arm and the eyes follow the hand. Then the left arm is lowered through preparatory position and raised to lst position; at this moment, the head turns to the right and the eyes are transferred to the elbow of the right arm which, during the movement of the left, has remained in 3rd position. Then the right arm is lowered to meet the left in lst position; the head straightens somewhat, and the eyes are transferred to the hands. In conclusion, the left arm is raised to 3rd position and the right arm is taken to 2nd position; the head turns to the right, the eyes accompanying the right hand.

This can also be done, later on, with grand plié in 5th or 4th position, simply or with tours sur le cou-de-pied or in the big poses.

A port de bras with inclinations of the body to the side.

This port de bras is not one of the numbered academic ports de bras, but its study is useful and is placed here because it is given before the study of the 3rd port de bras.

Stand facing the mirror, the feet in an unturned-out lst position, the heels together, the arms in preparatory position.

On two introductory chords, do a préparation in the following manner: on the first chord, raise the arms to 1st position and incline the head slightly toward the left shoulder, the eyes being directed at the hand; on the second chord, open the arms to 2nd position and bring the head straight front.

Then the body inclines as much as possible to the right, exactly to the side, without any backward inclination; and, simultaneously with the movement of the body, the left arm is raised to 3rd position (the right arm remains in 2nd position, but, in accordance with the inclination of the body to the side, it will be seen to move down); the shoulders maintain their even relationship to the torso; the head is turned to the right and the eyes are directed at the right hand. Then the body comes erect (the right arm, remaining in 2nd position, is raised as the body straightens); the left arm is lowered to 2nd position; the head turns en face. Then the body inclines to the left in the same manner.

After mastering the inclinations of the body to the side and the bends forward and backward of the 3rd port de bras (to be discussed next), it is customary to arrange them in one combination standing en face: for example, first do a bend forward and backward and repeat this; then do an inclination to the right and to the left and repeat this (a port de bras with various movements of the body).

This combined port de bras is done either in an unturned-out 1st position or in 5th position and may be used to conclude the lesson.

The 3rd port de bras (a bend of the body forward and backward).

Stand in 5th position croisée with the right leg in front. On the préparation, the arms, through 1st position, open to 2nd; and the head turns to the right.

Then the body inclines forward, maintaining a straight line from the base of the spine to the top of the head and tightly pulling up the middle; simultaneously with the bend of the body, the arms are lowered to preparatory position; the head turns straight forward and the eyes are directed at the hands. It is imperative that, during the bend, the head and the body form one straight line. That is, as the body inclines, one must not arch the back, cave in the small of the back, draw together the shoulder blades, or loosen the buttocks muscles. The whole point of the movement consists precisely in the preservation of the straight and pulled-up position of the body as it goes forward. At the end, the torso gives forward a bit more.

After this, the body resumes its initial position; the arms are raised to 1st position and then continue on to 3rd position. As the body straightens, the eyes follow the hands to 1st position; then the head turns to the right, the eyes being directed slightly higher than the elbow of the right arm.

This is followed by a bend of the body backward (first the shoulders incline, then the back bends in the waist). The back must be well held and the middle tightly pulled up; the stomach should not be allowed to protrude when the shoulders are back; the head must not be thrown back, but should form one line with the body, and stays turned to the right; the arms remain in front of the head for the duration of the bend. The legs must be stretched, their muscles taut (especially at the moment of extreme bend). One must not increase the bend of the body by bending the knees. Then the body comes erect in reverse order (first the lower back and then the shoulders), and the arms gradually open to 2nd position.

At the conclusion of the port de bras, lower the arms to preparatory position.

The 4th port de bras (a complicated twist of the torso).

Stand in 5th position croisée with the right foot in front. For the préparation, the left arm opens to 3rd position and the right to 2nd position (as for the 2nd port de bras). The body turns to the left until the back is to the mirror and the right shoulder forward. The thorax is open and the back tightly pulled up. At the very end, the body bends backward, the shoulders remaining level and the hips immobile. Simultaneously with the turn of the body, the left arm is lowered to 2nd position and goes back in the direction of point 4 of the classroom plan; the right arm goes from point 2 to point 8 at the height of 2nd position, during which time the arms gradually lengthen out; the fingers are stretched and the palms turn down, the arms, therefore, taking on the position of 4th arabesque. At the final movement, when the body bends backward, the arms flex slightly in the elbows.

Especially important in this port de bras is a free, soft movement of the arms, which serves to emphasise the complicated twist of the torso.

In the beginning, when the left arm is lowered to 2nd position, the head turns to the left; the eyes are directed at the left hand and follow its movement to 2nd position. With the twist of the torso, the head turns toward the right shoulder; the right arm is brought forward and the eyes are directed at the right hand.

In conclusion, the left arm, through preparatory position, joins the right in 1st position; the body returns to its initial position; the head inclines slightly toward the left shoulder, and the eyes are directed at the hands. Then, the left arm is raised to 3rd position and the right is taken to 2nd; the head turns to the right, and the eyes follow the right hand.

The 5th port de bras (a complicated inclination of the body backward, with a preliminary turn and bend to the side).

Stand in 5th position croisée, right leg front. The préparation is as for the 2nd and 4th ports de bras; i.e., the left arm is in 3rd position, the right in 2nd. Before beginning the port de bras, on the upbeat, the head turns straight forward and the eyes are directed upward to the left hand. Then the body inclines forward, maintaining a straight and tightly pulled-up posture.

As the body inclines, the left arm is lowered to 1st position, the eyes following its movement; and, simultaneously, the right arm is lowered to preparatory position and is raised to join the left in 1st position, the eyes being transferred to the hands. Then the body comes erect and slightly turns to the left (during this, it is necessary to watch that the shoulders are not raised); the left arm goes to 2nd position and the head turns to the left, the eyes following the left hand; and, at the same time, the right arm is raised to 3rd position. After this, the body bends back and then comes erect; the arms are transferred simultaneously, the left going to 3rd position and the right to 2nd position; the head turns to the right, the eyes accompanying the right hand.

The 6th port de bras (a complicated form of grand port de bras having a deep inclination of the body forward stretching it out in one line).

As a préparation, on the first chord, demi-plié in 5th position; then take the right leg forward in the direction croisée, sliding the toe along the floor, while the left leg remains in demi-plié (plié-soutenu); the arms are raised to 1st position and the head inclines slightly to the left, the eyes being directed at the hands. On the second chord, transfer the centre of the body's weight onto the right leg, passing (without a pause) through demi-plié in 4th position to the pose croisée derrière (the left leg is back with a stretched foot, toe to the floor). During this, the left arm is raised to 3rd position and the right to 2nd position; the head turns to the right, the eyes accompanying the right hand.

Before beginning the port de bras, on the upbeat, the head turns straight forward and the eyes are directed at the left hand. Demi-plié on the right leg and, simultaneously, draw the left toe (with a stretched foot) along the floor further back, remaining in the position croisée (but lengthening it out). With the movement of the legs, the straight and pulled-up body is lowered to the thigh of the supporting leg;

the left arm remains in 3rd position and the right in 2nd position; the eyes follow the left hand.

At the moment of maximum inclination of the body forward in a deep demi-plié, the left arm is lowered from 3rd position to 1st, and the right arm is brought up through preparatory position to meet with the left in 1st position. It is necessary to watch that the head, body, and left leg form a straight, inclined line, going from the top of the head to the toe of the left foot. The middle remains strongly pulled up, the body maintaining a relatively even line with the centre of its weight over the supporting right leg. Then the straight and pulled-up body, with the help of a push from the supporting right leg, sharply comes erect; and the weight is transferred onto the whole foot of the stretched left leg (the toe remaining in place); the right leg straightens (but without the toe coming up off the floor) and is drawn in toward the supporting left leg to a distance of an easy step, remaining with a stretched toe (in the pose croisée devant); the arms remain in 1st position; the head inclines toward the left shoulder and the eyes are directed at the hands.

Then the body bends backward, slightly turning back with the left shoulder, during which the hips must remain level and immobile; simultaneously, the left arm is taken to 2nd position and the right arm is raised to 3rd position; the head turns to the left, the eyes being directed at the left hand and accompanying its movement. The body continues to bend back; the left arm is transferred to 3rd position, and the right arm opens to 2nd position; the head turns to the right, with the eyes now following the movement of the right hand.

In conclusion, the torso straightens and, simultaneously, the body's weight is transferred from the left leg onto the right, passing through a demi-plié in 4th position to the pose croisée derrière, the initial position.

In the enumerated ports de bras, basic inclinations, bends, and turns of the body are done in combination with the movements of the arms and head. Later on, a great number of diverse forms of port de bras are built on this foundation.

In adagio, port de bras can finish in a préparation for tours in the big poses en dehors and en dedans, or in a préparation for small pirouettes (tours) with the foot sur le cou-de-pied.

Port de bras to a préparation for tours

For big tours en dehors, do the sixth port the bras up to the transfer of the body to the concluding position, that is, remain in the pose croisée devant. Then, transfer the weight of the body onto the right leg to a wide 4th position in demi-plié, the left leg remaining back with the knee stretched, heel on the floor. The centre of the body's weight is on the right leg, such a wide position being necessary for the execution of tours in the big poses.

Simultaneously with the transfer to 4th position, the left arm, from 3rd position, is lowered in front to the level of the left shoulder (the hand opposite the shoulder), the right one remaining in 2nd position; then the arms are elongated and the palms turn down as in 3rd arabesque.

The transfer at the conclusion of this port de bras to a préparation for small pirouettes en dehors is the same, only the 4th position is narrower.

In the execution of this port de bras to a préparation for tours en dedans, the movement of the arms is somewhat different. From the position croisée devant (the supporting leg is the left leg; the left arm is in 2nd position and the right in 3rd), transfer the weight forward onto the right leg to a wide 4th position and lower the right arm from 3rd position, through 2nd, to preparatory position before raising it to 1st position; the left arm remains in 2nd position and the line of the arms is curved.

This same port de bras to a préparation for tours en dehors

or en dedans can also be done in another manner: after the deep stretching out in demi-plié on the right leg, without transferring the body's weight onto the left leg, bring the left leg toward the right, which remains in demi-plié, and, from a stretched toe, put down the whole foot in a wide 4th position. At this moment, the body comes erect and the arms are joined in 1st position. Then follow the bend of the body and the movement of the arms analogous to the previous port de bras, which finishes in a préparation for tours either en dehors or en dedans.

V. Temps Lié

Temps lié is a term for a whole series of conventionally connected movements executed in the centre of the room. In dance training, temps lié, as an independent form, has a great importance in the development of the co-ordination of the movements of the arms, legs, head, and body. It is always done smoothly. Elements of temps lié are often introduced in the construction of an adagio.

Temps lié is studied from the simplest forms to the most complicated. It is complicated by bends of the body, execution at 90°, the introduction of a rise to demi-pointe, and tours from demi-plié and grand plié. The student begins with the basic form, at a slow tempo. The musical time may be 2/4, 4/4, or 3/4.

Basic form. (This form of temps lié is described in detail; the examples following it will be given in an abbreviated form, with the exception of the additions.) 4/4 time. Stand in 5th position croisée, right leg front, the arms in the preparatory position and the head turned to the right. (This preparatory position before the exercise will be the same for all versions of temps lié.) On the first quarter of the first measure, demi-plié in 5th position; the head is turned to the right, the arms are in preparatory position. On the second quarter, draw the right leg, with a sliding movement and without taking the toe from the floor, croisé devant. The left leg, which is the supporting leg, remains in demi-plié, with the centre of the body's weight over it; simultaneously, the arms are raised to 1st position and the head slightly inclines toward the left shoulder. On the third quarter, pass through demi-plié to the pose croisée derrière on the right leg, transferring onto it the centre of the body's weight After this, both legs are stretched, the left leg in back with a stretched toe to the floor. The transfer from the left leg onto the right is done smoothly, passing through the demi-plié in 4th position. At the moment of transfer, the left arm is raised to 3rd position and the right to 2nd; the head turns to the right, the eyes following the right hand. On the fourth quarter, the left leg closes in 5th position back with épaulement croisé; the arms remain where they are.

On the first quarter of the second measure, demi-plié in 5th position. Simultaneously, the body turns en face; and the eyes are directed to the left hand, which is lowered to 1st position, the right arm remaining in 2nd. On the second quarter, draw the right leg, stretching it, with a sliding movement along the floor, to 2nd position, with a stretched toe; the left arm opens to 2nd position; and the head maintains its position en face. On the third quarter, transfer the centre of the body's weight onto the stretched right leg, the left leg stretching with the toe to the floor; the arms remain in 2nd position, and the head turns to the left. On the fourth quarter, the left leg closes in 5th position front with épaulement croisé; the arms are lowered to preparatory position, and the head is turned to the left. Then this combination is repeated, starting with the left leg front, and then all is done backward in the reverse direction.

In 3/4 time (waltz form), each position is allotted one measure.

Temps Lié with a Bend of the Body

4/4 time. Stand in 5th position croisée, right leg in front. On the first quarter of the first measure, demi-plié in 5th position. On the second, draw the right leg, stretching it, croisé devant without taking the toe from the floor; the arms are simultaneously raised to 1st position. On the third quarter, passing through demi-plié, transfer the centre of the body's weight onto the right leg to the pose croisée derrière; the left leg is back with a stretched toe; at the moment of the transfer of the weight, the left arm goes to 3rd position and the right to 2nd; the head turns to the right. On the fourth quarter, the pose croisée derrière is held. On the first and second quarters of the second measure, the body bends back, the arms and head remaining in the same position. During the bend of the body, one must not put weight on the toe of the leg that is in back; the centre of the body's weight must remain on the supporting leg. On the third quarter, the body straightens, the arms remaining in the same position. On the fourth quarter, the left leg closes in 5th position back with épaulement croisé. On the first quarter of the third measure, demi-plié in 5th position, turning the body en face; the left arm is lowered to 1st position, with the eyes accompanying its movement; the right remains in 2nd position. On the second quarter, draw the right leg, stretching it along the floor to 2nd position, the head maintaining its position en face, and open the left arm to 2nd position. On the third quarter, the centre of the body's weight is transferred from the left leg onto the stretched right leg, the left stretching to 2nd position with the toe to the floor; the arms hold 2nd position, and the head turns to the left. On the fourth quarter, this position is held. On the first and second quarters of the fourth measure, the body inclines to the left; the left arm, remaining in 2nd position and maintaining its level relationship to the shoulder, is lowered together with the body, the eyes following the hand; the right arm is raised to 3rd position. In the inclination of the body to the side, as in the bends back, one must not lean onto the toe of the leg that is stretched to the side. On the third quarter, the body straightens; the right arm opens to 2nd position, the head turning first en face and then to the right, the eyes directed at the right hand. On the fourth quarter, the left leg closes in 5th position front with épaulement croisé; the arms are lowered to preparatory position; and the head turns to the left.

This combination is repeated with the left leg, and then all is done in the reverse direction.

In temps lié backward, the bend of the body will be done backward as before, but in the pose croisée devant. The inclination of the body to the side will be done toward the supporting leg.

Temps Lié par Terre with a Tour

4/4 time. Begin in 5th position, the right leg in front with épaulement croisé. For the préparation, demi-plié in 5th position on the upbeat; the right arm is raised to 1st position, the left to 2nd; and the head is straight forward to point 8. On the first quarter, do a tour en dehors on the left leg on demi-pointe; the right leg is bent sur le cou-de-pied devant, and the arms come together in 1st position finishing to point 8. (For a detailed description of the technique of the execution of tours from 5th position en dehors and en dedans, see Chapter X, "Tours on the Floor and in the Air".) On the second quarter, demi-plié on the left leg as the right leg, stretching from the position sur le cou-de-pied devant, is lowered to the floor and slides with the toe along the floor, croisé devant; the arms are in 1st position; the eyes are directed at the hands, and the head inclines slightly toward the left shoulder. On the third quarter, transfer the body's weight onto the right leg, passing through demi-plié in 4th position, to the pose croisée derrière; the left arm is raised to 3rd position and the right to 2nd; the head turns to the right. On the fourth quarter, the left leg closes in 5th position back with épaulement croisé, the arms maintaining the same position. On the last eighth of the fourth quarter, demi-plié, the right arm bending to 1st position; the left is in 2nd and the head is straight forward to point 1 (the préparation). On the first quarter of the second measure, tour en dehors on the left leg (finishing en face to point 1), the right foot sur le cou-de-pied devant. On the second quarter, demi-plié on the left leg as the right leg, stretching from the position sur le cou-de-pied devant, is lowered to the floor and slides, with the toe along the floor, to 2nd position; the arms open to 2nd position; and the head is en face. On the third quarter, transfer onto the stretched right leg, the left stretching, with the toe to the floor, to 2nd position; and turn the head to the left. On the fourth quarter, the left leg closes in 5th position front; the arms are lowered to preparatory position; and the head remains to the left. This combination is then done in the reverse direction with tours en dedans, raising the working leg sur le cou-de-pied derrière.

Temps Lié at 90°

4/4 time. Begin in 5th position croisée, with the right leg in front. On the first quarter of the first measure, demi-plié on the left leg, simultaneously bringing the toe of the right foot in front of the knee of the supporting leg; the arms are in 1st position; and the head is to the left. On the second quarter, the left leg remaining in demi-plié, the right is stretched croisé devant at 90°; the arms hold 1st position; and the eyes are directed at the hands. On the third quarter, transfer onto the stretched right leg to the big pose attitude croisée; the left arm is raised to 3rd position, the right to 2nd; the head turns to the right. On the fourth quarter, the pose attitude croisée is held. On the first quarter of the second measure, bring the left leg to 5th position, demi-plié on it, turning the body en face; simultaneously, the right leg bends and the toe is brought in front of the knee of the supporting leg; the left arm is lowered to 1st position and the right remains in 2nd. On the second quarter, the right leg is stretched to the side at 90°; the left arm is taken to 2nd position; the head is en face. On the third quarter, transfer the centre of the body's weight onto the stretched right leg, through an extended 2nd position, raising the left leg to the side at 90°; the arms remain in 2nd position; the head turns to the left. On the fourth quarter, the left leg is lowered to 5th position front; the body turns, with the left shoulder forward; the arms close to preparatory position; the head is turned to the left (épaulement croisé).

In temps lié, the drawing out of the working leg to 90° croisé devant and to the side at 90° takes place from 5th position simultaneously with demi-plié on the supporting leg. To the pose attitude, the bent leg is raised according to the rules of relevé. In the execution backward, the movements follow in the reverse order. The drawing out of the leg to 90° croisé derrière and to the side at 90° is done in the same way as in front, with the exception of the movement to the big pose croisée devant, where the leg must be taken out through 5th position (trasferring onto the supporting leg, it is necessary to bring the working leg up to the supporting leg before taking it out at 90° by means of a développé).

In the transfers to the pose attitude croisée, to the side at 90°, and to the pose croisée devant, the working leg is placed on the floor from the stretched toe onto the whole foot.

Temps lié at 90° is also done on demi-pointe. In the transfers to the pose attitude croisée, to the side at 90°, and to the pose croisée devant, the working leg is placed immediately on demi-pointe. After fixing the pose, the working leg closes in 5th position also on demi-pointe; then, from demi-pointe the leg is lowered to demi-plié in 5th position and, from here, the movement continues.

In advanced classes, temps lié at 90° can be done in one measure in the following manner:

4/4 time. On the upbeat, demi-plié on the left leg; the right leg bends and the toe is brought in front of the knee of the supporting leg. On the first quarter, the right leg is stretched croisé devant at 90°, the left remaining in demi-plié; the arms are raised to 1st position; the eyes are directed at the hands. On the second quarter, transfer to the pose attitude croisée, raising the left arm to 3rd position and the right to 2nd, and turning the head to the right. On the last eighth of the second quarter, the left leg is lowered, brought up to the right in 5th position croisée, and bends in demi-plié; the right leg, at the same time, quickly bends, lifting the toe in front of the knee of the supporting leg (the transfer from the right leg to the left is done passing through 5th position and ends with a quick substitution of one leg for the other); the left arm is lowered to 1st position, the right remaining in 2nd; the body and head come en face. On the third quarter, the right leg is stretched to the side at 90°, the left remaining in demi-plié; the left arm is brought to 2nd position, the right remaining in 2nd; the head is en face. On the fourth quarter, transfer onto the stretched right leg, through an extended 2nd position; the left leg, stretching, is raised to the side at 90°; the arms are in 2nd position; the head turns to the left. For the continuation of the combination with the other leg forward, on the last eighth of the fourth quarter, bend the left leg, bringing the toe in front of the knee of the supporting leg; simultaneously, demi-plié on the supporting right leg; the body turns with the left shoulder forward (épaulement); the arms are lowered to preparatory position; the head turns to the left.

Temps Lié at 90° with a Tour

4/4 time. Begin in 5th position croisée, with right leg front. For the préparation, demi-plié on the upbeat in 5th position, and raise the right arm to 1st position, the left to 2nd, turning the head straight forward to point 8. On the first quarter of the first measure, do a tour en dehors on the left leg, the right foot sur le cou-de-pied devant. On finishing the tour (to face point 8), bring the toe up in front of the knee of the supporting leg. On the second quarter, demi-plié on the left leg and stretch the right leg croisé devant at 90°; the arms are in 1st position; the eyes are directed at the hands; the head inclines toward the left shoulder. On the third quarter, transfer to the pose attitude croisée, bringing the left arm to 3rd position and the right to 2nd; the head turns to the right. On the fourth, the left leg is lowered to 5th position back in demi-plié, the right arm going to 1st position, and the left to 2nd (the préparation). On the first quarter of the second measure, tour en dehors on the left leg, the right foot sur le cou-de-pied devant (the tour finishes en face, raising the thigh to bring the toe in front of the knee of the supporting leg). On the second quarter, demi-plié on the left leg, the right leg stretching to the side at 90°, the arms open to 2nd position; the head is en face. On the third quarter, transfer the centre of the body's weight onto the stretched right leg, through an extended 2nd position, raising the left leg to the side at 90°; the arms remain in 2nd position; the head turns to the left. On the fourth quarter, the left leg closes in 5th position front with épaulement croisé; the arms are lowered to preparatory position; the head is turned to the left.

Then the combination is repeated with the left leg forward and then all is executed in reverse. In the execution of temps lié in reverse, the tour is done en dedans with the foot sur le cou-de-pied derrière or with a transfer of the foot from the position sur le cou-de-pied devant to the position sur le cou-de-pied derrière. In either case, on finishing the tour, it will be necessary to raise the thigh in order to bring the heel behind the knee of the supporting leg before the extension.

Temps Lié at 90° with a Tour from Grand Plié

4/4 time. Begin in 5th position croisée with the right leg in front. On the introductory chords, open the arms through 1st position to 2nd.

On the first and second quarters of the first measure, grand plié in 5th position; the left arm is in 2nd position, and the right is raised through the preparatory position to 1st position (the préparation), the head turning straight forward to point 8. On the last eighth of the second quarter, coming up from the grand plié, do a tour en dehors on the left leg (for a description of tours from grand plié, see Chapter X, "Tours on the Floor and in the Air"), the right foot sur le cou-de-pied devant (on finishing the tour, raise the thigh to bring the toe in front of the knee of the supporting leg). On the third quarter, demi-plié on the left leg and stretch the right leg croisé devant at 90°; the arms are in 1st position; the eyes are directed at the hands; the head inclines slightly toward the left shoulder. On the fourth quarter, transfer to the pose attitude croisée, bringing the left arm to 3rd position and the right to 2nd; the head turns to the right. On the last eighth of the fourth quarter, the left leg is lowered to 5th position back, knees straight, with épaulement croisé; the left arm goes to 2nd position. On the first and second quarters of the second measure, grand plié in 5th position; the left arm remains in 2nd position and the right, through the preparatory position, is raised to 1st (the préparation); the head turns straight. On the last eighth of the second quarter, coming up from grand plié, do a tour en dehors on the left leg, bringing the right foot sur le cou-de-pied devant. On the third quarter, demi-plié on the left leg, stretching the right to the side at 90°; the arms open to 2nd position; the head is en face. On the fourth quarter, transfer the weight of the body to the right leg, through an extended 2nd position, as the left leg, stretching, is raised to the side to 90°; the arms remain in 2nd position; the head turns to the left. On the last eighth of the second measure, the left leg closes in 5th position front croisé; the arms are held in 2nd position; and the head turns to the left. From here, the combination continues with the left leg forward. In reverse, a tour en dedans is done, which finishes by bringing the heel up behind the knee of the supporting leg before the extension.

Temps lié at 90° with a tour and with a tour from grand plié are both done on demi-pointe.

Having mastered the combination with one tour, one can begin practising it with two tours.

VI. The Poses of Classical Ballet

The students are acquainted with the poses of classical dance in the first year. In the beginning, they learn each pose separately, toe to the floor, without raising the leg. Later on, the study continues with the raising of the leg to 90°. The poses can also be done at 45° (for example, battements fondus in a pose). In this case, one arm usually opens to 2nd position and the other to a half-1st position (i.e., between 1st and preparatory position).

It is generally accepted that the study should begin with the poses croisée devant and derrière, then effacée and écartée devant and derrière. After that, one goes on to the four arabesques.

Initial study is done at a slow tempo. The musical time is 2/4, 4/4, or 3/4.

The Initial Study of the Poses Croisées

The Pose Croisée Devant. As in the concept croisé, so in the poses croisées, a position of the figure with crossed lines is emphasised. It is as if the turn of the head crosses the direction of the turn of the body, the legs also being crossed.

Stand in 5th position with épaulement croisé, the right foot in front and the right shoulder forward; the head is turned to the right and the arms are in preparatory position.

Two measures of 4/4 time. On the first quarter of the first

measure, raise the arms to 1st position and, inclining the head toward the left shoulder, direct the eyes at the hands. On the second quarter, the position is held. On the third quarter, take the right leg forward, stretching the foot but not taking the toe from the floor (the toe of the working leg should be opposite the heel of the supporting leg); raise the left arm to 3rd position and take the right arm to 2nd; turn the head to the right, the eyes following the right hand, and incline the torso slightly back. This will be the pose croisée devant. On the fourth quarter, the position is held.

On the first quarter of the second measure the left arm is lowered to 2nd position, the right one remaining in 2nd; the body is inclined back as before, and the right leg has a stretched toe to the floor. On the second quarter, the position is held. On the third quarter, the arms are lowered to preparatory position; the right leg closes in 5th position front; and the torso comes erect. On the fourth quarter, the final position is held.

The Pose Croisée Derrière. The initial position is the same as for the pose croisée devant. From 5th position croisée, the left leg is taken back with a stretched toe; the left arm is raised through 1st position to 3rd, the right arm to 2nd; the head is turned to the right; the centre of the weight of the erect and pulled-up body is transferred to the supporting leg.

The movements of the head and arms are as for the pose croisée devant; but, unlike the pose croisée devant, the torso remains erect throughout.

The Initial Study of the Poses Effacées

The Pose Effacée Devant. In the poses effacées, as in the concept effacé, an open position of the figure is emphasised.

Stand in 5th position with épaulement effacé, the right foot in front and the left shoulder forward; the arms are in preparatory position; the head is turned to the left. Not taking the toe from the floor, extend the right leg forward with a stretched foot and, through 1st position, raise the left arm to 3rd, and the right arm to 2nd. At the moment when the arms are in 1st position, turn the head straight forward, directing the eyes at the hands. As the arms open (the left arm to 3rd position and the right to 2nd), incline the torso slightly back and turn the head to the left, directing the eyes at a point slightly higher than the elbow of the left arm.

The Pose Effacée Derrière. The initial position is the same as for the pose effacée devant. From 5th position, take the left foot back, sliding the toe along the floor and stretching the foot; and, through 1st position, raise the left arm to 3rd and the right arm to 2nd position. At the moment when the arms are in 1st position, turn the head straight forward; and, as the arms open to 3rd and 2nd positions, turn the head to the left, directing the eyes to a point slightly higher than the elbow of the left arm, and transfer the centre of the body's weight slightly forward onto the supporting leg.

Later, the poses are practised in a single measure of 4/4, each position corresponding to one quarter. In 2/4 time, the pose is distributed over two measures. In 3/4 (waltz form), each position corresponds to one measure.

The study of the other poses (the poses écartées and the 4 arabesques) also takes place at first with the toe to the floor and then with the leg at a height of 90°. The distribution of the poses on the musical counts is the same as in the poses croisées and effacées.

The Basic Big Poses Croisées

In the beginning of the study of the big poses, the raising of the leg to 90° is done with a relevé, later on, with a développé.

The Pose Croisée Devant. Stand in 5th position with épaulement croisé, the right foot in front and the right shoulder forward; the head is turned to the right; the arms are in preparatory position.

4/4 time. On the first and second quarters of the first measure, from 5th position croisée, the right leg bends, bringing the toe to the knee of the supporting leg; the arms are raised to 1st position; the head is inclined slightly to the left, the eyes being directed at the hands. On the third and fourth quarters, the leg is stretched out to the pose croisée devant at 90°; the left arm is raised to 3rd position, and the right arm is brought to 2nd; the head is turned to the right, the eyes following the right hand; the torso is inclined slightly back. On the first and second quarters of the second measure, the pose croisée devant is held. On the third quarter, the left arm is lowered to 2nd position, but the leg remains raised at the height of 90°. On the fourth quarter, the arms are lowered to preparatory position, and the working leg simultaneously is lowered to 5th position; the head remains to the right; and the torso comes erect. From here, the pose is repeated.

The Pose Croisée Derrière. The initial position is as for the previous pose. From 5th position croisée, draw the left foot back and up to 90°, raising the left arm, through 1st position to 3rd and the right arm to 2nd. At the moment the arms reach 1st position, the head is slightly inclined to the left, the eyes directed at the hands; then as the left arm is raised to 3rd position and the right is taken to 2nd position, the head turns to the right, the eyes following the right hand; the torso is slightly inclined forward.

To finish the pose in the initial position, lower the left arm to 2nd position, leaving the torso and the right arm in their previous positions. Then, simultaneously, lower the arms to preparatory position; place the foot in 5th position, and straighten the torso; the head, as before, is turned to the right.

At the next stage of study, the poses are done in a single measure of 4/4, each position corresponding to one quarter.

The Pose Attitude Croisée. Begin in 5th position croisée with the right foot in front. From 5th position, the left leg bends, bringing the heel behind the knee of the supporting leg; then, in a bent position, but unbending slightly, it is raised to 90° croisé derrière, forming, at the final point, an obtuse angle (i.e., greater than 90°). It is necessary to take back the turned-out thigh of the working leg as far as possible, not lowering the knee. The position is considered correct when the toe is horizontally in alignment with the knee. Simultaneously with the raising of the leg, the left arm is raised through 1st position to 3rd, and the right to 2nd; the head turns to the right, the eyes following the right hand; and the torso, with level shoulders, is slightly inclined forward; the middle of the body is tightly pulled in.

The Basic Big Poses Effacées

The Pose Effacée Devant. Stand in 5th position with épaulement effacé, the right foot in front and the left shoulder forward; the arms are in preparatory position; the head is turned to the left.

The right leg is drawn forward and raised to 90°; the left arm, at the same time, opens through 1st position to 3rd and the right arm opens through 1st position to 2nd; at the moment the arms reach 1st position, the head turns straight forward and the eyes are directed at the hands; then, as the arms open, the head turns to the left, the eyes being directed toward a point slightly higher than the elbow of the left arm; the torso inclines slightly back.

To finish the pose in the initial position, open the left arm to 2nd position, the eyes accompanying the left hand as it lowers; the torso and the right arm remain in their previous positions.

Then, simultaneously, the arms are lowered to preparatory position; the leg is lowered to 5th position; the head remains turned to the left; the body comes erect.

The Pose Effacée Derrière. The initial position is as for the previous pose. From 5th position effacée, draw the left leg back and raise it to 90°; raise the left arm through 1st position to 3rd and the right arm through 1st position to 2nd; at the moment the arms reach 1st position, turn the head straight forward and direct the eyes at the hands; then, as the arms open, turn the head to the left, directing the eyes toward a point slightly higher than the elbow of the left arm, and incline the torso, preserving the back well pulled in the middle, slightly forward.

To finish the pose in the initial position, open the left arm to 2nd position, the eyes accompanying the hand; the body and the right arm remain in their previous positions. Then, simultaneously, lower the arms to preparatory position; lower the leg to 5th position; and, leaving the head turned to the left, bring the torso erect.

The Pose Attitude Effacée. Starting as before from 5th position effacée, the left leg bends, bringing the heel behind the knee of the supporting leg and, in the bent position, but unbending slightly, is raised to 90° effacé derrière, forming, at the conclusion, an angle more obtuse than that of attitude croisée (about 135°), the thigh of the working leg being taken well back, with the toe and knee horizontally in alignment; simultaneously, the left arm is raised through 1st position to 3rd, and the right through 1st position to 2nd; when the arms reach 1st position, the head turns straight forward, the eyes directed at the hands. During the opening, as the arms open to 3rd and 2nd positions, the head turns to the left, the eyes directed to a point slightly higher than the elbow of the left arm; the torso, with level shoulders, inclines forward slightly; the middle is well pulled in.

To finish the pose, lower the left arm to 2nd position; the head is to the left, the eyes following the left hand as it moves; the working leg straightens in back at 90° in the direction effacée. Then, simultaneously, the arms are lowered to preparatory position; the leg is lowered to 5th position; the head is turned to the left; and the torso comes erect.

The Basic Big Poses Écartées

The Pose Écartée Devant. Stand in 5th position with épaulement croisé; the right leg is in front and the right shoulder forward, with the head turned to the right and the arms in preparatory position. The body is positioned as if along a diagonal in relationship to the audience.

Draw the right leg to the side and raise it to 90° toward point 2 of the classroom plan; at the same time, raise the right arm through 1st position to 3rd, and the left through 1st position to 2nd; at the moment the arms reach 1st position, incline the head slightly to the left and direct the eyes at the hands; during the opening of the arms, turn the head to the right, directing the eyes at a point somewhat higher than the elbow of the right arm, and incline the body to the side away from the raised leg, preserving the turned-out position of the body along the diagonal (the initial position, épaulement croisé, is intensified).

As a result of the inclination of the body, the shoulders take on a tilted position, the right shoulder higher than the left; but, in spite of this inclination, maintain a level relationship to each other. The left arm, in correspondence with the inclination of the body, is lowered, maintaining 2nd position; the right arm is in 3rd position (in front of the plane of the head).

In the poses écartées, it is especially necessary to maintain the turn-out; the thigh of the working leg is turned out to the utmost, taken well to the side. To finish the pose in the initial position, the right arm is lowered to 2nd position and, simultaneously with the left arm, which remains in 2nd, the hands are turned palms down. The arms form one straight line and the body remains inclined. As the right arm is lowered, the eyes are directed at the right hand and follow its movement to 2nd position. Then, simultaneously, the arms are lowered to preparatory position; the leg is lowered to 5th position front; the body comes erect; the head is turned to the right.

The Pose Ecartée Derrière. The initial position is en face, the feet in 5th position with the right foot in front. The right leg is drawn to the side and raised to 90° to point 4 of the classroom plan; the right arm goes to 3rd position, and the left arm to 2nd. At the moment the leg is taken out and the arms are opened, the entire body turns, pivoting on the supporting leg, so that it is on the diagonal from point 8 to point 4.

In the pose écartée derrière, as in the pose écartée devant, there is the same inclination of the body and the same position of the arms and shoulders; the difference is in a small bend of the body backward; the head is turned to the side of the arm that is in 2nd position, and the eyes are directed at the hand.

During the return to the initial position, at the moment when the right arm lowers from 3rd position to 2nd, the head is turned to the left. Then, simultaneously, the arms are lowered to preparatory position; the leg is lowered to 5th position back; and the body straightens.

Arabesques

1st Arabesque. Stand with the body turned in profile, the left shoulder to the audience, placing the feet in a half-turned-out 5th position (in 1st and 2nd arabesque, a half-turned-out position is sufficient for the supporting leg), right foot front, the head turned to the left, and the arms in preparatory position. The left leg is then drawn back and raised to 90°; the arms are simultaneously raised to 1st position; the head turns straight forward; and the eyes are directed at the hands. Then the right arm is stretched out forward so that the hand is opposite the right shoulder and on a level with it; the left arm, at the same time, is brought to the side and also stretched out (the hand opposite the left shoulder and on a level with it); the palms gradually turn down, and the fingers are stretched out. The body is slightly forward, and the back and the thigh of the working leg are tightly pulled up.

During the study of 1st arabesque, it is necessary to pay attention to the position of the torso and shoulders, which must be level. In no case may a turn of the torso toward the audience be allowed; nor may the left shoulder be allowed to go back: the pose would then be elongated, and the back would lose its curve, and its assembly; the beauty of line would be destroyed. One must also be careful not to tilt the body forward or to the side.

2nd Arabesque. The initial position is as for 1st arabesque. From 5th position, the left leg is drawn back and raised to 90°, the arms are simultaneously raised to 1st position, the head turns straight forward. Then the left arm is stretched out forward, according to the rules for arabesque; and the right arm is brought back through 2nd position and continues the line of the shoulders; the palms of both hands are turned down; the head is to the left, the body slightly forward. The middle of the back is securely held and the thigh of the working leg is well pulled up.

3rd Arabesque. Stand in 5th position with épaulement croisé, the right foot and the right shoulder forward; the head is turned to the right; the arms are in preparatory position.

The left leg is drawn out croisé derrière and raised to 90°, the arms simultaneously are raised to 1st position, and the head turns straight forward. Then the left arm is stretched out

11*

forward (the hand opposite the shoulder and on a level with it), the eyes directed at the tips of the fingers; and the right arm is stretched out and taken to the side; the palms are turned down and the fingers stretched out; the body is slightly forward (but not inclined to the side), the back securely held in the middle, and the thigh of the working leg tightly pulled up.

4th Arabesque. The initial position is as in the previous pose. From 5th position, the left leg is drawn out croisé derrière and raised to 90°; the arms simultaneously are raised to 1st position, the head turned straight forward. Then the right arm is stretched out forward, as the left arm, moving through 2nd position, is taken back, together with the left shoulder, so that the body is strongly turned with its back to the audience (more so than in 2nd arabesque). At the conclusion of the twist of the body, the left thigh and the left side are strongly pulled up. The arms are in a straight line with the shoulders, the palms of both hands turned down, and the fingers stretched out. The head is turned to the right and slightly inclines back, in accordance with the turn of the shoulders and body, the eyes are directed toward the audience.

In 4th arabesque, the body is not forward; it is held high, and the shoulders must remain level. The line of the arms is softened, the elbows being slightly lowered.

The turned-out thigh of the working leg is strongly pulled up to the side.

The Small Poses

The small poses are extremely varied. However, in all of them, except the small arabesque poses, the arm that is in 2nd position is held at full height; the arm that is in 1st position is held a little lower, between 1st and preparatory positions. In the small arabesque poses, both arms are at a half-height. The arms open through 1st position as for the big poses; but they are lowered directly to preparatory position at the end, after having turned the palms down.

The Small Pose Croisée Devant. The right leg is stretched forward croisé, toe to the floor or at 45°. 1. The left arm may be in 2nd position, the right in 1st position, the head turned to the right. 2. The right arm may be in 2nd position, the left in 1st, the head turned to the right (as a variant, the head may be turned to the left).

The Small Pose Croisée Derrière. The left leg is stretched backward, toe to the floor or at 45°. 1. The left arm may be in 2nd position, the right in 1st, the head to the right. 2. The right arm may be in 2nd position, the left in 1st, the head to the right (as a variant, the head may be turned to the left).

As a variant of the poses croisées, devant and derrière, the arm corresponding with the supporting leg may be stretched forward, the other opened to the side; both hands are turned palms up; the eyes are directed at the hand that is outstretched forward; the torso and the head lean a little backward.

In the small pose croisée devant, one can bend the body strongly forward toward the toe of the working leg, if the pose is in plié. In the pose croisée derrière, the torso may also be bent strongly forward, if it is in plié; or it may also be bent backward, the head turned to the side of the supporting leg (as a variant, the head may look back toward the toe of the working leg).

The Small Pose Effacée Devant. The right leg is stretched forward effacé, toe to the floor or at 45°. The right arm is in 2nd position, the left in 1st, the head to the left.

The Small Pose Effacée Derrière. The left leg is stretched in back, toe to the floor or at 45°. The right arm is in 2nd position, the left in 1st, the head to the left; the torso is slightly forward and raised as if it were in "flight". As a variant, the arms may be in a small 2nd arabesque.

The Small Pose Écartée Devant. The left leg is stretched forward, toe to the floor or at 45°. 1. The left arm may be in 2nd position, the right in 1st, the head to the left. 2. The arms may be opened from preparatory position directly to the side at a half-height (45°), the head and torso as in the big pose.

General Remarks. All the poses are finished with a return to the initial position, the arms being lowered to the preparatory position. In returning to preparatory position from the arabesque poses, the arms maintain the line taken for the arabesque and are curved only on arriving in preparatory position.

The correct organisation of the arms, body, and head is basic to all the poses. Especially serious attention must be paid to the middle of the body and to the thigh of the working leg, both of which must be well pulled up. One most often observes an incorrect form in 1st and 4th arabesques, therefore, it is necessary to study these poses most carefully.

The maintenance of the correct form in the poses is important not only for the poses themselves, but also for the successful execution of tours and jumps in the big poses.

The positions described for the arms, body, and head in the poses are basic. In elementary study, they must be adhered to strictly. Later on, it is possible to combine the positions of the arms and head in different ways, preserving, however, the characteristic position of the body, which is fixed, since on it depend the positions of the arms and head.

VII. Connecting and Auxiliary Movements

Pas de Bourrée

Pas de bourrées are a diverse kind of step used in the centre exercise, in adagio, and in jumps, as connecting and auxiliary movements in order to travel in any direction.

They may be done with or without a turn, with an opening of the leg to a height of 45°, without an opening, etc.

The study of pas de bourrée begins facing the barre and then continues in the centre of the room.

At first, it is done at a slow tempo; later, the tempo is accelerated; and, still later, pas de bourrées included in a combination are done in the tempo of the combination.

In the elementary years, pas de bourrées are done with precision, sharply raising the feet sur le cou-de-pied. In the intermediate and advanced years, such pas de bourrées remain only in the centre exercise and in adagio, for in jumps, they are done in a different way: the feet are not raised precisely sur le cou-de-pied; rather, the stepping over from leg to leg is soft and easy, raising the feet only slightly from the floor and rising onto a low demi-pointe, which gives a flowing, light transition from one jump to another. Pas de bourrées with an energetic raising of the feet sur le cou-de-pied would disturb the fluidity of the transitions (especially at a quick tempo).

When such precise pas de bourrées are used in adagio and in the centre exercise at a slow tempo, they do not disturb the fluidity of the transitions from pose to pose or from movement to movement.

The conditional position sur le cou-de-pied devant is used for pas de bourrée (see Chapter II, "Battement Fondu"). The working foot should not be pressed against the supporting leg sur le cou-de-pied, for this would make the pas de bourrée stodgy, destroying its light character. Instead, it should be held a short distance away from the supporting leg.

The musical time is 4/4, 2/4, or 3/4.

Pas de Bourrée Changing the Feet (Changé) Facing the Barre. 4/4 time. Stand in 5th position with the right leg in front and place the hands on the barre (opposite the shoulders); lower the elbows to a free, relaxed position; the head and body are erect.

En dehors. On the upbeat, demi-plié on the right leg, simultaneously raising the left foot sur le cou-de-pied derrière; turn the head to the right. On the first quarter of the first measure, step onto the left leg on demi-pointe and raise the right foot sur le cou-de-pied devant (the conditional position sur le cou-de-pied devant is used) holding it a small distance from the supporting leg; bring the head straight forward. On the second quarter, step over onto the right leg on demi-pointe, taking it slightly to the side at a distance of a small step (an almost negligible movement, stepping almost in place, a kind of step that is maintained in all kinds of pas de bourrée, with or without changing the legs, with the exception of pas de bourrée en tournant), simultaneously raising the left foot sur le cou-de-pied devant, the centre of the body's weight going over onto the right leg. In the transfer from leg to leg, the arms move along the barre lightly, and the hands again are placed opposite the shoulders. On the third quarter, come down on the left leg in demi-plié, simultaneously raising the right foot sur le cou-de-pied derrière; and turn the head to the left. On the fourth quarter, the position is held.

On the first quarter of the second measure, step onto the

right leg on demi-pointe, simultaneously raising the left foot sur le cou-de-pied devant; bring the head straight forward. On the second quarter, step over onto the left leg on demi-pointe, taking it slightly to the side, and simultaneously raising the right foot sur le cou-de-pied devant. On the third quarter, come down on the right leg in demi-plié, raising the left foot sur le cou-de-pied derrière; and turn the head to the right. On the fourth, the position is held, etc.

After the given number of repetitions, the last pas de bourrée finishes in 5th position in demi-plié.

This pas de bourrée is also done in the reverse direction.

En dedans. Stand in 5th position with the right leg in front. On the upbeat, demi-plié on the left leg, raising the right foot sur le cou-de-pied devant; and turn the head to the right. On the first quarter, step onto the right leg on demi-pointe, raising the left foot sur le cou-de-pied derrière; and bring the head straight forward. On the second quarter, step over onto the left leg on demi-pointe, slightly taking it to the side, and raise the right foot sur le cou-de-pied derrière. On the third quarter, come down on the right leg in demi-plié, behind the left, raising the left foot sur le cou-de-pied devant; and turn the head left. On the fourth quarter, the position is held.

Pas de Bourrée Changing the Feet in the Centre of the Room. Stand in 5th position croisée with the right leg in front; the arms are in preparatory position; the head is turned to the right.

En dehors. 3/4 time. On the upbeat, demi-plié on the right leg, simultaneously raising the left foot sur le cou-de-pied derrière, opening the arms to a half-second position; the body is erect and pulled up. On the first quarter of the first measure, step onto the left leg on demi-pointe, raising the right foot sur le cou-de-pied devant; and turn the body en face (the head straight forward), lowering the arms to preparatory position.

On the second quarter, step over onto the right leg on demi-pointe, taking the leg slightly to the side, and raising the left foot sur le cou-de-pied devant. On the third quarter, come down on the left leg in demi-plié with épaulement croisé (left shoulder forward), raising the right foot sur le cou-de-pied derrière; turn the head to the left; and open the arms to a half-2nd position. From here, pas de bourrée continues to the other side. After the given number of repetitions, finish the last one in 5th position in demi-plié with épaulement croisé. Other kinds of pas de bourrées (with and without changing the feet), which have an opening of the leg forward, backward or to the side at 45° (as well as to the small poses croisées, effacées, and écartées at 45°), all finish simply with an opening of the leg forward, backward, or to the side or in the given pose. Then, separately, on concluding chords, the working leg closes in 5th position. This pas de bourrée is done in the same way in the reverse direction (en dedans), the head turning in the direction of the working leg.

Pas de bourrée changé en dehors can also begin from the pose croisée derrière. Stand on the right leg with épaulement croisé, the left leg extended backward in 4th position with a stretched foot, toe to the floor; the arms are in preparatory position; and the head is turned to the right. On the upbeat, demi-plié on the right leg, simultaneously raising the left foot sur le cou-de-pied derrière and opening the arms to a half-2nd position. Then step up onto the left leg on demi-pointe, turning the body en face, etc. In the reverse direction (en dedans), pas de bourrée is done from the pose croisée devant.

It is also possible to begin with the arms in another position. For example, one arm may be in 1st position (opposite the raised leg) and the other in 2nd position; then, on the first step, they close to preparatory position and, at the end of the pas de bourrée, open again, one to 1st position (opposite the raised leg) and the other to 2nd position.

Pas de Bourrée Without Changing the Feet (sans Changé) in the Directions Croisée Devant and Croisée Derrière. Stand in 5th position with épaulement croisé, right leg front, arms in preparatory position, the head turned to the right. On the upbeat, demi-plié on the right leg, simultaneously raising the left foot sur le cou-de-pied derrière, and open the arms to a half-second position. Then step onto the left leg on demi-pointe, raising the right foot sur le cou-de-pied devant; turn the head straight forward; and lower the arms to preparatory position. Step over onto the right leg on demi-pointe, taking the leg forward in the direction croisée the distance of a small step and simultaneously raising the left foot sur le cou-de-pied derrière. Then come down on the left leg in demi-plié, as the right leg, the foot passing through the position sur le cou-de-pied devant, is taken softly to the pose croisée devant at 45°; the left arm is raised to 1st position, and the right to 2nd; the head turns to the right; and the body inclines slightly backward.

From here, the pas de bourrée is done in the reverse direction. Step onto the right leg on demi-pointe, bringing it, without bending the knee, in front of the left; the left foot is raised sur le cou-de-pied derrière; the arms are lowered to preparatory position; the head turns straight forward; and the body comes erect. Step over onto the left leg, taking it backward in the direction croisée derrière the distance of a small step, simultaneously raising the right foot sur le cou-de-pied devant. Then come down on the right leg in demi-plié, as the left leg, the foot passing through the position sur le cou-de-pied derrière, is taken to the pose croisée derrière at 45°; the right arm is raised to 1st position and the left arm to 2nd; the head turns to the right; and the body, pulled up in the waist, inclines forward. Then the first pas de bourrée may be repeated.

Pas de bourrée sans changé is done to the poses effacées and écartées devant and derrière in exactly the same way.

When this step is combined with inclinations of the torso forward and backward, it is called pas de bourrée ballotté.

Pas de Bourrée Without Changing the Feet (sans Changé), to the Side, with an Opening of the Leg at 45°. Stand in 5th position with épaulement croisé, the right leg in front and the arms in preparatory position; the head is turned to the right. On the upbeat, demi-plié on the right leg, simultaneously raising the left foot sur le cou-de-pied derrière and opening the arms to a half-2nd position. Then step onto the left leg on demi-pointe, turning the body en face; the right foot simultaneously is raised sur le cou-de-pied devant; the head is straight forward, and the arms are lowered to preparatory position. Step over onto the right leg on demi-pointe, taking it to the side the distance of a small step, simultaneously raising the left foot sur le cou-de-pied derrière. Come down on the left leg in demi-plié while the right, the foot passing through the position sur le cou-de-pied devant, is softly taken to the side to a height of 45°; the arms open to a half-2nd position; the body inclines to the left (the side opposite the raised leg); and the head is turned to the left.

From here, the pas de bourrée continues to the other side. Step onto the right leg on demi-pointe, bringing it in front of the left, simultaneously raising the left foot sur le cou-de-pied derrière; the arms are lowered to preparatory position; the body comes erect; and the head turns straight forward. Step over onto the left leg on demi-pointe, taking it to the side the distance of a small step, simultaneously raising the right foot sur le cou-de-pied devant. Come down on the right leg in demi-plié, as the left leg, the foot passing through the position sur le cou-de-pied derrière, is taken to the side at 45°, the arms open to a half-2nd position; the body inclines to the side away from the raised leg; and the head turns to the right.

Pas de Bourrée Dessus-Dessous, Changing the Legs. In translation, dessus means "over", dessous means "under". In pas de bourrée, the term dessus-dessous indicates in what way the working leg is brought for the substitution of one leg for the other; i.e., if the working leg is brought in front of the supporting leg, the movement is dessus; if in back, the movement is dessous.

Dessus. Stand in 5th position with épaulement croisé, right leg front, and the arms in preparatory position. On the upbeat, turning en face, demi-plié on the right leg and, simultaneously, take the left leg, the foot passing through the position sur le cou-de-pied derrière, softly to the side at 45°; open the arms to a half-2nd position; and turn the head to the left. Then step onto the left leg on demi-pointe (in doing this, bring it, without bending the knee, in front of the right leg), and simultaneously raise the right foot sur le cou-de-pied derriére; turn the head straight forward; and lower the arms to preparatory position. Step over onto the right leg on demi-pointe, taking it to the side the distance of a small step, simultaneously raising the left foot sur le cou-de-pied derrière. Come down on the left leg in demi-plié, as the right leg, the foot passing through the position sur le cou-de-pied devant, is taken out to the side at 45°; open the arms to a half-2nd position; and turn the head to the left.

Dessous. Stand in 5th position with épaulement croisé, the right leg in front and the arms in preparatory position. On the upbeat, turning en face, demi-plie on the left leg, simultaneously taking the right leg, the foot passing through the position sur le cou-de-pied devant, to the side at 45°; open the arms to a half-2nd position; and turn the head to the left. Then step onto the right leg on demi-pointe (in doing this, bring it, without bending the knee, in back of the left) and simultaneously raise the left foot sur le cou-de-pied devant; lower the arms to preparatory position; turn the head straight forward. Step over onto the left leg, taking it to the side the distance of a small step, simultaneously raising the right foot sur le cou-de-pied devant.

Come down on the right leg in demi-plié, as the left leg, the foot passing through the position sur le cou-de-pied derriére, is taken to the side at 45°; open the arms to a half-2nd position; and turn the head to the left.

Pas de bourrées dessus and dessous usually are done one after the other.

Beginning with the fourth year, all the pas de bourrées described above are done not only en face, but also en tournant. In the execution of pas de bourrée en tournant, the following are the general rules: the substitution of the legs occurs in place, one leg being placed near the other in front or in back; the turn is executed around one's own vertical axis. However, in doing this, one must not actually turn on the supporting leg, but must step onto demi-pointe simultaneously with a turn of the body.

Pas de Bourrée en Tournant en Dehors, Changing the Legs. Stand in 5th position with épaulement croisé, the right leg in front and the arms in preparatory position, the head turned to the right. On the upbeat, demi-plié on the right leg, simultaneously raising the left foot sur le cou-de-pied derrière; the arms are opened to a half-2nd position. Step onto the left leg on demi-pointe, simultaneously making a quarter turn to the left (the body is placed, with the back to the audience, on a diagonal, with the right shoulder to point 8 of the classroom plan), raising the right foot sur le cou-de-pied devant; the body is pulled up, but the upper torso bends slightly backward; the arms are quickly raised through preparatory position to a low 1st position, which gives stability during the bend of the body; the head, during this first half of the pas de bourrée, is turned to the right, toward the mirror, and afterward, in the second half, turns to the left. Then, stepping onto the right leg on demi-pointe, in back of the left foot, make a quarter turn in the same direction toward the mirror, simultaneously raising the left foot sur le cou-de-pied devant; the body comes erect; and the head turns toward the mirror. Come down on the left leg in demi-plié with épaulement croisé, simultaneously raising the right foot sur le cou-de-pied derrière; the arms open to a half-2nd position; and the head turns to the left.

In all pas de bourrées en tournant, the head is turned to the mirror during the first part of the movement and then returns to the same spot at the end of the turn. The head must not lean back or incline toward the shoulder. The position of the head during the turn is vertical.

Pas de Bourrée en Tournant en Dedans, Changing the Legs. Stand in 5th position with épaulement croisé, the left leg in front, the arms in preparatory position, and the head turned to the left.

On the upbeat, demi-plié on the right leg, simultaneously raising the left foot sur le cou-de-pied devant; and open the arms to a half-2nd position. Step onto the left leg on demi-pointe, simultaneously making a half-turn to the right (the body is placed with the back to the audience), raising the right foot sur le cou-de-pied derrière; raise the arms through the preparatory position to a low 1st position; and bend the upper torso, from the shoulders, slightly backward. Then, stepping over in front of the left foot onto the right leg on demi-pointe and straightening the body, make a half turn in the same direction, simultaneously raising the left foot sur le cou-de-pied derrière. Come down on the left leg in demi-plié épaulement croisé, simultaneously raising the right foot sur le cou-de-pied devant; the arms open to a half-2nd position. The movements of the head are analogous to those in pas de bourrée en tournant en dehors.

Pas de Bourrée en Tournant, Without Changing the Legs, with an Opening of the Legs Forward and Backward.

En dehors. Stand in 5th position with épaulement croisé, the right leg in front and the arms in preparatory position. On the upbeat, demi-plié on the right leg, simultaneously raising the left foot sur le cou-de-pied derrière; and open the arms to a half-2nd position. Step onto the left leg on demi-pointe, and simultaneously make a three-quarter turn to the right (the right leg raised sur le cou-de-pied devant), lowering the arms to preparatory position. Stepping over onto the right leg on demi-pointe in front of the left, make a half-turn in the same direction, simultaneously raising the left foot sur le cou-de-pied derrière. Come down on the left leg in demi-plié en face, taking the right leg, the foot passing through the position sur le cou-de-pied devant, forward at 45°; and open the arms to a half-2nd position; the pulled up body inclines slightly back, with the head straight forward.

En dedans. This is done as a continuation of pas de bourrée en tournant en dehors. Step onto the right leg on demi-pointe (bringing the right leg, without bending the knee, in front of the left), and make a half turn to the right, simultaneously raising the left foot sur le cou-de-pied derrière; lower the arms to preparatory position; and straighten the body. Then, stepping over onto the left leg on demi-pointe behind the right, again make a half-turn in the same direction, simultaneously raising the right foot sur le cou-de-pied devant. Come down on the right leg in demi-plié, taking the left leg, the foot passing through the position sur le cou-de-pied derrière, backward at 45°; and open the arms to a half-2nd position; the pulled-up body simultaneously inclines slightly forward.

This pas de bourrée can also finish in the small poses croisées. In the ending for the pas de bourrée en dehors, open the right leg to the pose croisée devant; in the ending for the pas de bourrée en dedans, open the left leg to the pose croisée derrière.

Pas de bourrée en tournant to the small poses effacées and écartées finishes in exactly the same way: effacé en dehors finishes in the small pose effacée devant; en dedans, in the pose effacée derrière; écarté en dehors, in the pose écartée derrière; en dedans, in the pose écartée devant.

The position of the body, arms, and head, in each case, corresponds to that used in the small poses croisées, effacées, and écartées.

Pas de Bourrée Dessus-Dessous en Tournant, Changing the Legs.

Dessus, en dehors. Stand in 5th position with épaulement croisé, the right leg in front and the arms in preparatory position. On the upbeat, demi-plié on the right leg, simultaneously taking the left leg, the foot passing through the position sur le cou-de-pied derrière, to the side at 45°; open the arms to a half-2nd position (the palms turned down, the hands extended); and turn the head to the left. Step onto the left leg on demi-pointe (bringing it, without bending the knee, in front of the right); simultaneously making a half-turn to the right, raising the right foot sur le cou-de-pied derrière; lower the arms to preparatory position; and turn the head to the left toward the mirror. Then step over onto the right leg on demi-pointe in front of the left, with a half turn in the same direction toward the mirror, simultaneously raising the left foot sur le cou-de-pied derrière; and at the end of the turn, turn the head to the initial point toward the mirror. Come down on the left leg in demi-plié, taking the right leg, the foot passing through the position sur le cou-de-pied devant, to the side at 45°; open the arms to a half-2nd position; and incline the body slightly away from the raised leg, turning the head to the left.

Dessous, en dedans. This can be done as a continuation of pas de bourrée dessus en dehors. Step onto the right leg on demi-pointe (bringing it, without bending the knee, in back of the left), simultaneously making a half turn to the right, raising the left foot sur le cou-de-pied devant; lower the arms to preparatory position and turn the head to the left toward the mirror. Then step over onto the left leg on demi-pointe in back of the right, with another half turn in the same direction, toward the mirror, simultaneously raising the right foot sur le cou-de-pied devant; and turn the head to the initial point. Come down on the right leg in demi-plié, taking the left leg, the foot passing through the position sur le cou-de-pied derrière, to the side at 45°; and open the arms to a half-2nd position (palms down, the hands extended), turning the head to the left.

Pas Couru

Pas couru is a run in any direction. In classical dance, it is used as an auxiliary movement preceding jumps, as a connecting movement in order to change the direction of the pattern of the dance, and for joining different parts of a dance phrase. The term pas couru also designates a run on pointe in an unturned-out 1st position (a kind of pas de bourrée suivi).

Pas couru is not studied independently. It is done at first (in the third year) in combination with the stage form of sissonnes in the arabesque poses at 45°, which are varied by traveling in different directions. Later, it is used much more widely.

Pas couru, as a running start before a jump, consists of no fewer than three steps. It is done from 5th position croisée or from the pose croisée devant or derrière, toe to the floor, or with the leg at a height of 45° or 90°. From the position sur le cou-de-pied, pas couru more often is done after a jump which finishes in that position. Pas couru with the legs alternating between 5th and 2nd positions is done only in a movement of the body sideways, during which the legs preserve their full turn-out.

In all cases, pas couru is preceded by demi-plié. In executing it from the pose croisée derrière, it is necessary first to do a demi-plié on the leg that is forward. In executing it from the pose croisée devant, demi-plié is also done on the leg that is forward, transferring onto it the centre of the body's weight.

Coupé

The name of the movement itself (from the French couper, "to cut") indicates its quick, sharp character. Coupé is a quick substitution of one leg for the other, serving as an impetus for a jump or some other movement. Coupé has no independent importance. It is always done on the upbeat, in the space between two quarters or in the space between two measures.

Coupé can be either in place or moving out in any direction.

Coupé in Place. The foot of the working leg is raised sur le cou-de-pied, or to a height of 45° or 90° in any position, pose, or direction. Then it is brought up to the supporting leg (which simultaneously rises to demi-pointe) with a short movement, and as if strikes the supporting leg, before being placed down in demi-plié, lowering from the toe through the whole foot. In this manner it replaces the supporting leg from the front (coupé dessus) or the back (coupé dessous).

The transition from leg to leg in jumps by means of coupé takes place without a rise to demi-pointe, simply passing through 5th position in demi-plié. For example, having done a jeté derrière with the right leg, the left foot is sur le cou-de-pied derrière, the following jump can be preceded by a coupé dessous by putting the left foot down in 5th position demi-plié in such a manner (with a kind of stamp) as to provide the impetus for an assemblé, ballonné or another jeté, the right foot being sharply cut out from under oneself.

In non-jumping movements in the barre and centre exercise, it takes place in demi-plié with a transfer onto the whole foot or demi-pointe with a stretched leg. For example, standing, with the left hand on the barre, on the left leg on demi-pointe and with the right leg extended to the side at 45°, first do a tombé dessus in place: the right leg comes down in front of the left in 5th position in demi-plié. A coupé dessous onto demi-pointe is effected by sharply stepping onto the left leg on demi-pointe behind the right leg and immediately stretching the right leg out to the side at 45°. A coupé dessus is executed analogously. During the tombé in place, the head will turn to the side of whatever leg is in front and then turns straight forward on the coupé.

Coupé Traveling (Step-Coupé). This is done passing through 4th position in any direction. It can begin from the poses croisées, effacées, or écartées, devant or derrière, with the leg open at 45° or 90°, or from the position sur le cou-de-pied, or from 5th position. The working leg does a step forward, is placed in 4th position demi-plié through the foot (from the stretched toe to the heel) and immediately, strongly, with a short movement, pushes off from the floor. The other leg immediately is thrown out with a grand battement forward. In the jump, the required pose is taken. Simultaneously with the movement of the working leg, which goes to 4th position front, the centre of the body's weight is transferred onto that leg and the body inclines forward, the small of the back being well held (see page 218, Example of grand jeté with a step-coupé). If, in the initial pose, both feet are on the floor, the working leg is raised slightly and brought up to the supporting leg before the step-coupé.

Step

In classical dance, a step is also used as an auxiliary or connecting movement in a change of poses with a transfer of the body's weight from one leg to the other.

The step can begin with a stretched or bent leg, raising it to the position sur le cou-de-pied or to a height of 45° or 90°.

Most often, the step is preceded by demi-plié on the supporting leg. In the step, the foot is placed on the floor, going through the foot from a stretched toe to the heel. A step also can be done immediately onto demi-pointe (posé). There is a step-tombé ("fallen") as well, which finishes in plié. Transferring onto the working leg with the help of step-tombé to the demi-plié, it is necessary to keep the body erect and pulled-up. Jumps, pirouettes with the foot sur le cou-de-pied, and tours in the big poses en dehors and en dedans, are often preceded by a step-tombé from a height of 45° or 90°.

Flic-flac

Flic-flac is a connecting movement that consists of an energetic brush of the working leg through 5th position front and back (or back and front) close to the supporting leg and then its return to the initial position.

The study of flic-flac begins, at the barre and in the centre of the room, from 2nd position at 45°, broken down into two counts, en dehors and en dedans. Then it is done in one count. Later on, flic-flac is done en tournant en dehors and en dedans at the barre and in the centre of the room.

The final version is done quickly and fluently, in one count, from and to various poses and positions. The accent of the movement takes place on the opening of the working leg in one or another direction, whatever height is required.

Study Sequence

1. *En dehors.* 2/4 time. On the préparation, the right arm, through 1st position, is brought to 2nd; and, simultaneously, the working leg, from 5th position, is raised to 2nd position at 45°. On the upbeat, the working leg is quickly lowered to the floor in 2nd position with a stretched toe. Then it bends in the knee and, sliding the ball of the foot along the floor, passes through 5th position back, goes up to the toe of the supporting leg and comes off the floor a

little, the toes then being stretched. On the first eighth of the first measure, the same leg at the level of the position sur le cou-de-pied derrière, is stretched and thrown out to 2nd position at 45°. On the second and third eighths, the position is held. On the fourth eighth, the leg again is quickly lowered to the supporting leg, passing this time through 5th position front (the rules for the movement of the leg are the same as in the first case). On the first eighth of the second measure, the leg at the level of the position sur le cou-de-pied devant is stretched and thrown out to 2nd position. On the second, third and fourth eighths, the position is held. In flic-flac en tournant en dehors, the throwing of the leg back and front is done in the same manner.

The exercise is repeated en dedans with the opposite alternation, throwing the leg in front of the supporting leg and in back. Flic-flac en tournant en dedans will have the same alternation.

For several lessons, flic-flac is studied without a rise to demi-pointe. Then, on the first movement, while the working leg is brought in past the supporting leg and taken out to 2nd position at 45°, the supporting leg remains on the whole foot. On the second movement, after the throw of the leg in past the supporting leg, a rise to demi-pointe is added as the leg is taken out to 2nd position at 45°.

2. 2/4 time. On the upbeat, the working leg, from 2nd position at 45°, is lowered sharply past the supporting leg in back and then is taken out to 2nd position, during which it only partially straightens (to about half the distance of a stretched 2nd position). Then, sliding the ball of the foot along the floor, it quickly passes in front of the supporting leg. On the first eighth of the first measure, the working leg is thrown out to 2nd position at 45° and, simultaneously, the supporting leg rises to demi-pointe. On the second and third eighths, the position is held. On the fourth eighth, the

leg is sharply lowered past the supporting leg in back; and the heel of the supporting leg is lowered to the floor. Then the working leg is placed halfway to 2nd position and is brought sharply past the supporting leg in front. On the first eighth of the second measure, the leg is thrown out to 2nd position at 45°, and the supporting leg rises to demi-pointe, etc.

Thus, throwing the working leg past the supporting leg in back, bringing it halfway to 2nd position, throwing it past the supporting leg in front, and out again to 2nd position at 45°, all takes place during one quarter, in one count.

As mastery of flic-flac increases, the exercise is supplemented with arm movements (in execution at the barre with one arm; in the centre, with both), as a preparation for flic-flac ,en tournant, in which the arms provide force for the turn of the body.

Together with the throw of the working leg in past the supporting leg, the right arm, from 2nd position, is lowered to preparatory position and, at the moment the leg is thrown to 2nd position at 45°, is brought through 1st position to 2nd, the left arm remaining on the barre.

Flic-flac en Tournant (with a Half Turn). The study of flic-flac en tournant begins at the barre with a half turn en dedans,with the working leg stretched forward at 45°; or with a turn en dehors,with the working leg stretched back at 45°; or with a turn either en dehors or en dedans, with the working leg opened to 2nd position at 45°.

En dedans. With the left hand on the barre, the right leg (which is the working leg), from the initial position forward at 45°, is sharply lowered to the toe of the supporting leg, the ball of the foot sliding on along the floor and coming off the floor a little (with the toes stretched). Then the body makes a half turn en dedans (to the left) on demi-pointe on the supporting leg, while, simultaneously, the working leg, remaining bent, sliding the ball of the foot along the floor away from the toe of the supporting leg, goes through the position sur le cou-de-pied derrière and is thrown backward at 45°. During the turn, the arms are lowered and brought together. At the end the right arm goes to the barre, and the left to 2nd position.

En dehors. With the left hand on the barre, the working right leg, from the position in back at 45°, is sharply lowered to the toe of the supporting leg, the ball of the foot sliding along the floor and coming off the floor a little (with the toes stretched). Then the body makes a half turn en dehors (to the right) on demi-pointe on the supporting leg, while simultaneously, the working leg, remaining bent, sliding the ball of the foot along the floor away from the toe of the supporting leg and through the conditional position sur le cou-de-pied devant, is thrown forward at 45°. The arms, as in flic-flac en tournant en dedans, are lowered and brought together during the turn. Then the right arm goes to the barre and the left arm opens to 2nd position.

From 2nd position at 45°, flic-flac with a half turn en dehors is done in the following manner: the right leg is sharply lowered to the supporting leg through 5th position back (with the toe sliding past the toe of the supporting leg), the ball of the foot sliding along the floor and coming off the floor. Then the body makes a half turn en dehors on demi-pointe on the supporting leg, while, simultaneously, the working leg, remaining bent, sliding the ball of the foot along the floor away from the toe of the supporting leg and through the conditional position sur le cou-de-pied devant, is thrown forward at 45°. The position of the arms corresponds to that in the preceding examples.

For the execution of flic-flac en tournant en dedans from 2nd position at 45°, with a half turn, the working leg is sharply lowered to the toe of the supporting leg in front. Then the body makes a half turn en dedans on demi-pointe on the supporting leg, while, simultaneously, the working leg, sliding the ball of the foot along the floor away from the toe of the supporting leg and through the position sur le cou-de-pied derrière, is thrown backward at 45°.

From 2nd position at 45°, the movements can be combined in the following manner: with the right leg do flic-flac with a half turn en dedans, throwing the leg backward at 45° at the end; and, with the same leg, do flic-flac en dehors, throwing it to 2nd position at 45° at the end; then do flic-flac with a half turn en dehors, throwing the leg forward at 45° at the end; and, with the same leg, do flic-flac with a half turn en dedans, throwing the leg to 2nd position at 45° at the end, etc.

In order to increase the combination possibilities, including half turns en dehors and en dedans, it is possible to interpolate several other movements. For example, coupé and battement fondu may be used for the transitions from one leg onto the other through 5th position, or the stretched working leg may be brought around a quarter or a half circle at a height of 45°, etc.

Flic-flac en Tournant (with a Whole Turn).

En dehors. The working leg, from the initial position (2nd position at 45°), is sharply lowered behind the supporting leg through 5th position (the toe sliding past the toe of the supporting leg), the ball of the foot sliding along the floor, and comes off a short distance. Then the body makes a full turn en dehors on demi-pointe on the supporting leg. Simultaneously with the turn of the body, the working leg, remaining bent, slides the ball of the foot along the floor away from the toe of the supporting leg and through the conditional position sur le cou-de-pied devant, and is thrown out to 2nd position at 45°. During the turn of the body, the arms provide the force, passing through preparatory position and 1st position before opening to 2nd.

During the turn en dehors, the arm that is opposite the working leg must work most actively. The supporting leg, before rising to demi-pointe, pushes off from the floor with the heel and gives direction to the turn. The head, at the moment of the turn, remains directed towards the initial point as long as possible and returns to that same point at the end of the turn.

En dedans is done analogously but in the opposite direction.

Flic-flac with a complete turn is done connectedly and in one count, on one-quarter beat, starting on the upbeat.

Doing flic-flac en tournant, it is necessary to watch carefully the turn-out of the thigh of the working leg, especially at the moment of the second throw of the leg, which is done with the turn of the body. It is inadmissible, after the first throw of the leg, to hold the toe on the floor and push off with it to help the turn. It is also inadmissible to rise to demi-pointe on the first throw of the leg. After the first and second throw of the leg, the leg is raised immediately. In the execution of flic-flac en tournant from one pose to another, the arms open from the pose to 2nd position, and then, through preparatory and 1st position, take their required positions. From the arabesque poses, the arms are lowered immediately to preparatory position and, through 1st position, open to the required positions.

In flic-flac en dehors and en dedans, the "flic" is always done on the whole foot, and the "flac" on demi-pointe.

Passé

Passé is a connecting movement used in transferring the leg from one position to another, and from one pose to another.

Passé can be done through 1st position on the floor, as well as at a height of 45° and 90° in any direction. It also is done with a jump (passé sauté).

Let us cite several examples:

1. With the right leg, do a battement fondu forward at 45°. Then, going to demi-plié, take the right leg through 1st

position backward and raise it to 45° (after passing through 1st position in demi-plié, the leg is stretched).

2. Stand in 1st arabesque on the right leg (on the diagonal) and, bending the left leg in the knee at a height of 90°, bring the left toe beside the knee of the supporting leg, and stretch it croisé devant at 90°. The same thing can be done by lowering the left leg from 1st arabesque and, after it is brought through 1st position, raising it forward at 90° to the pose croisée devant.

3. Raise the right leg to the side at 90° en face, then lower it and bring it along the floor, through 1st position, to attitude croisée or 3rd arabesque. The same thing can be done bending the right leg in the knee at 90°, taking the toe beside the knee of the supporting leg, before opening it to attitude or arabesque.

4. Do a grande sissonne ouverte to 3rd arabesque on the right leg; then, pushing off from the floor with the supporting leg, at the moment of the jump, bend the left leg in the knee (taking the left toe past the right knee), and stretch it forward to the pose effacée devant at 90°. Or do the sissonne to 2nd arabesque and change the épaulement during the passé sauté, finishing effacé.

As is evident from the examples, passé is any transfer of the working leg past the supporting leg from one position to another, along the floor or through the air, in a stretched or bent position, on a stretched supporting leg or in demi-plié.

Temps Relevé

Temps relevé is an auxiliary movement that involves a rise of the supporting leg from demi-plié and a straightening of the working leg from a bent position. It serves as a préparation for certain movements (for example, rond de jambe en l'air). It also can be a complicated means of executing small pirouettes with the foot sur le cou-de-pied and tours in the big poses.

In the beginning, however, temps relevé is studied independently, at the barre and in the centre of the room, with the leg at 45° or at 90°, en dehors and en dedans. Then it is combined with other movements of the exercise and adagio with and without tours.

Temps relevé requires careful study, since its correct execution also determines the quality of tours temps relevés.

Petit Temps Relevé

Study Sequence

1. At the barre. 4/4 time. Stand in 5th position, with the right leg in front. The left hand is on the barre, the right arm is held in preparatory position; the head is turned to the right.

    En dehors. On the first quarter, demi-plié on the supporting leg, while, simultaneously, the foot of the working leg goes to the conditional position sur le cou-de-pied devant; the right arm is raised to 1st position; and the head inclines slightly toward the left shoulder, the eyes being directed at the hand. Before the second quarter, the working leg, with a thigh that is well turned out and secured in the hip joint, is taken forward, at the height of the conditional position sur le cou-de-pied, a few inches in front of the supporting leg, remaining in a half-bent position. Then, without pausing, the working leg stretches and continues the movement in an arc to the side at a height of 45°, finishing on the second quarter; simultaneously, the supporting leg stretches from demi-plié and rises to demi-pointe, the right arm opens to 2nd position; and the head turns to the right. In the earliest study, however, temps relevé is done without a rise to demi-pointe. On the third quarter, the 2nd position at 45° is held. On the fourth quarter, the leg returns to 5th position.

En dedans. Stand in 5th position, right leg back. Demi-plié on the left leg, bringing the right foot sur le cou-de-pied derrière; and raise the right arm to 1st position. Then the lower part of the right leg (with an immobile and turned-out thigh) is taken backward a few inches, stretches and continues the movement in an arc to the side at 45°. During the movement of the leg in an arc, the left leg rises to demi-pointe; and the right arm goes to 2nd position. The details of execution are the same as in the version en dehors.

2. 2/4 time. Stand in 5th position, right leg front.

En dehors. On the first eighth of the first measure, demi-plié on the left leg, bringing the right foot sur le cou-de-pied devant and raising the right arm to 1st position. On the second eighth, the position is held. On the third eighth, the right leg is brought forward and in an arc to the side at 45°, while, simultaneously, the supporting leg rises from demi-plié to demi-pointe, the right arm opening to 2nd position. On the fourth eighth, the position is held. On the first eighth of the second measure, for the repetition of the movement en dehors, the right leg is brought sur le cou-de-pied devant simultaneously with a demi-plié on the supporting leg, etc.

Temps relevé en dedans is done in exactly the same way in the reverse direction.

Temps relevé as a préparation for tours is done somewhat differently: while the working leg is taken forward and in an arc to the side at 45°, the supporting leg stays in demi-plié; then the tour en dehors follows, with the foot of the working leg simultaneously brought sur le cou-de-pied devant and the supporting leg stretching and rising to demi-pointe. The bringing of the working leg sur le cou-de-pied and the rise to demi-pointe are done at the same time and energetically.

The version en dedans is done in the same manner.

Grand Temps Relevé.

Grand temps relevé is done according to the principle of petit temps relevé, the only difference being that the toe of the working leg is raised in front of the knee of the supporting leg for the execution en dehors, and behind the knee of the supporting leg for the execution en dedans. Then the working leg is brought forward or backward at that same height, stretches, and continues the movement in an arc to 2nd position at 90°.

The arms are held in the same position as that used in petit temps relevé. Tours in the big poses are done with a grand temps relevé.

VIII. Jumps

Jumps comprise one of the basic categories of the movements of classical dance. They are extremely diverse in kind and are done at various tempos. They may be generally divided into small and big jumps, those that go upward only, those that travel lengthwise, and those that travel along a trajectory (where height and length are equally important).

Small jumps are divided, in turn, into those of minimal elevation, such as petit changement de pieds, petit échappé, glissade, and those of a maximum elevation having a throw of the working leg out to a height of 22.5° or 45° (such as petit assemblé, jeté, ballonné, etc.).

Big jumps are done with a throw of the leg to 90° or higher (depending on the individual capability of the dancer).

Jumps may also be subdivided into five categories, according to the character of their execution: those that go from two feet onto two, from two feet onto one, from one foot onto two, from one foot onto the same foot, and from one foot onto the other. Jumps from two feet onto two include changement, échappé, sissonne fermée, etc.; those from two feet onto one include all other kinds of sissonnes, jeté from 5th position, etc.; those from one foot onto two include cabriole fermée, etc.; those from one foot onto the same foot include temps levé in a pose, ballonné, cabriole, etc.; those from one foot onto the other are jetés. All jumps begin and end with a demi-plié.

In the study of jumps, it is necessary to pay special attention to the development of ballon, that is, the ability to pause in the air in a definite pose. To be able to do this, the maximum point of the jump must be attained as quickly as possible; for this will help the dancer to suspend poised in the air. Ballon is especially effective in dancers having a big jump.

General rules for the execution of jumps. The bound from the floor is always done from a demi-plié on the whole foot and especially from the heel; therefore, in no case should the heel come off the floor in the demi-plié.

At the high point of the jump, the knees, insteps, and toes must be taut and stretched to the utmost, if the jump is done from both legs. In a jump on one leg, the other (the working) leg must take on the position required by the pose with a well turned-out thigh.

After the jump, the return to the floor must always be soft. At first, the toes touch the floor, then the weight is taken through the whole foot onto the sole, coming down into a good demi-plié before straightening the legs.

Temps Levé

Temps levé is the very simplest jump from two feet onto two in 1st, 2nd, 4th, and 5th positions.

At first, temps levé is studied facing the barre, holding the barre with two hands; then it is practised in the centre of the room.

Study Sequence

1. In two measures of 2/4 time. Stand in 1st position en face, the arms in preparatory position. On the first quarter and on the first eighth of the second quarter, demi-plié. On the second eighth, jump up equally off of both feet. On the first quarter of the second measure, come down in demi-plié. On the first eighth of the second quarter, come

up from demi-plié, straightening the knees. On the second eighth, the position is held. Then repeat the sequence. The movement should be practised no fewer than four to eight times.

2. In one measure of 2/4 time. On the upbeat, demi-plié and jump. On the first quarter and the first eighth of the second quarter, come down in demi-plié and deepen it. On the second eighth, jump again. On the first quarter of the second measure and the first eighth of the second quarter, demi-plié and deepen it. On the second eighth, jump again, etc.

3. Final form. In one quarter 2/4 time. On the upbeat, demi-plié and jump. On the first eighth, come down in demi-plié. On the second eighth, jump again, etc.

General Remarks. A change of the position of the legs after the jumps from 1st position takes place, in the first form, by means of a battement tendu from 1st position to 2nd, and from 2nd to 4th or to 5th position. Later on, when the jumps are done in succession, the change of position takes place during the jump.

Temps levé can also be done on one leg. Thus, for example, after a jump that finishes on one leg (the other in the position sur le cou-de-pied or open at a height of 45° or 90°), the jump is repeated in that same pose. Repetition more than once is also possible, but the pose and the height of the raised leg must not be altered.

Temps levé can also be done en tournant with quarter and half turns.

Changement de Pieds

Changement de pieds is a jump from two feet onto two, from a demi-plié in 5th position to a demi-plié in 5th, changing the position of the legs at the end of the jump, at the moment of the return to the floor in demi-plié. The leg that was in front goes back, and the one that was in back goes front. During the change of the legs, they must not be separated widely to the side but moved apart only so far as to make it possible to change them in 5th position. The rules for execution and the study sequence are the same as those for temps levé.

Petit changement de pieds is done at a low height and does not require great muscular effort for the jump, but the legs must be stronglv stretched in the knees, the insteps, and toes; and the jump must be well organised.

In their final form, petits changements de pieds are done at a quick tempo in one eighth each, but the tempo must not be accelerated too much.

It is possible to do petits changements de pieds en tournant with an eighth or a quarter turn each. The turn must be done at the moment of the jump. The head and eyes remain directed toward the audience; then, quickly turning the head, direct the eyes to the point toward which one has turned. The turn is always begun in the direction of the leg, that is in 5th position front. Thus, if the right leg is front, the turn is to the right; if the left leg is front, the turn is to the left.

Grand changement de pieds is done at a maximum height and demands great tautness of the leg muscles and a deep demi-plié, which makes possible the necessary strong push from the floor.

In their final form, grands changements de pieds are done in one quarter each and at a moderate tempo. However, one should remember that an extremely slow execution can weaken the leg muscles, causing one to "sit on the legs". This is true not only of changement de pieds, but all jumps in general.

Grand changement de pieds en tournant is done at first with quarter and half turns. The most difficult grand changement de pieds, that with a full turn, can serve as a good preparation for tours en l'air. The turn is done according to the rules for petit changement de pieds.

It is useful to combine changements de pieds en tournant in small combinations with other pas.

Example. 2/4 time. Stand in 5th position with épaulement croisé, left foot front. With the right leg, double assemblé; then, changement de pieds with a full turn to the right, one entrechat-quatre with the left foot in front, two brisés forward and three petits changements de pieds en tournant, turning to the right, 1/8 each. Then repeat the combination starting with the other leg.

In reversing this combination, the tour must also be done in the direction of the leg that is in 5th position front.

Pas Échappé

Échappé ("escaped"), a jump with an opening of the legs, actually consists of two jumps, one done from two feet onto two from 5th position to 2nd, and then another from 2nd to 5th. The technique of execution is the same as for temps levé. Échappé can be done with or without changing the legs. In the first case (échappé changé), the leg that is in 5th position front finishes the second jump (from 2nd position to 5th) in back; in the second case (échappé sans changé), the leg returns from 2nd position to 5th position front.

Petit échappé is done at a low height, with the legs opening directly to 2nd position in the air. Grand échappé is done at a great height and from a deeper demi-plié; and the legs, during the jump upward, hold the 5th position in the air, one ankle in front of the other, with the feet tightly stretched. Only at the moment of the return to the floor do they open to 2nd position. Both petit and grand échappé can also be done to 4th position croisée and effacée. In the second jump, the feet are brought together in 5th position immediately.

The second jump, from either 2nd or 4th position to 5th, can also finish on one leg, the other being raised sur le cou-de-pied

13*

devant or derrière, or to various poses at 45° and 90° croisée and effacée devant and derrière. The small poses will be preceded by a petit échappé and the large poses by a grand échappé. The leg will be raised to the pose by means of a relevé, that is without a développé. A jump from 2nd or 4th position, with a transition to a pose, can be done in place or traveling in any direction

In the closing jump (from 2nd or 4th position to 5th), it is inadmissible, as often happens, to open the legs wider than the established norms for these positions permit. After pushing off from the floor from 2nd or 4th position, the legs, without a pause, come together in 5th position in the air. A pause would hinder, later on, the execution of a beat from 2nd or 4th position to 5th.

Petit and grand échappés are done en tournant with both quarter and half turns. Grand échappé is also done with a full turn, but it is studied only after the student has mastered grand échappé without a turn. It is necessary to learn échappé en tournant gradually, in the following manner: at first, it is mastered with a quarter turn, then with a half turn, and, finally, with a complete turn. In doing this, the first jump (from 5th position to 2nd) is done with the turn, the second jump is done in place, etc. Later on, complicating the movement, it is possible to do each jump (from 5th position to 2nd and from 2nd position to 5th) with a turn. If the échappé en tournant is repeated in one direction, then it is usually done without changing the legs. At the next stage of study, échappé is done with a beat (for the explanation of échappé battu see Chapter IX, "Batterie").

Study Sequence

1.   In four measures of 2/4 time. Stand in 5th position en face, right foot front; the arms are in preparatory position; the head is straight forward.

On the first quarter and the first eighth of the second quarter, demi-plié. On the second eighth, jump, opening the legs to 2nd position. On the first quarter of the second measure and the first eighth of the second quarter, land in 2nd position with a controlled lowering through the feet into demi-plié. Simultaneously with the jump, the arms, through the half-1st position, open to the half-2nd position; the head is turned to the right. On the second eighth, jump, bringing the legs together in 5th position in the air; close the arms to preparatory position; and turn the head straight forward. On the third measure, finish in 5th position with a controlled lowering through the feet into demi-plié. On the first quarter of the fourth measure, straighten the legs from demi-plié. On the second quarter, the position is held. From here the exercise continues.

2. In two measures of 2/4 time. On the upbeat, demi-plié in 5th position and jump, opening the legs to 2nd position. On the first quarter and the first eighth of the second quarter of the first measure, land in 2nd position with a controlled lowering through the feet into demi-plié. On the second eighth, jump, bringing the legs together in 5th position in the air. On the first quarter and the first eighth of the second quarter of the second measure, finish in 5th position with a controlled lowering through the feet into demi-plié. On the second eighth, jump, opening the legs to 2nd position, etc.

3. Final form. In one measure of 2/4 time. On the upbeat, demi-plié in 5th position with épaulement croisé and jump with an opening of the legs to 2nd position. On the first eighth of the first measure, come down in demi-plié in 2nd position en face. On the second eighth, jump, bringing the legs together in 5th position in the air. On the third eighth, come down in demi-plié in 5th position, with épaulement croisé. On the fourth eighth, jump, opening the legs to 2nd position, etc.

Grand échappé is learned in the same sequence as the petit échappé; however, in grand échappé, on the first jump, the arms open through a full 1st position to 2nd, and the feet hold the 5th position in the air for as long as possible before coming down in 2nd position.

Pas Assemblé

Pas assemblé (meaning "assembled", from the French *assembler*, "to gather together") is a jump from two feet onto two feet from 5th position to 5th, with the working leg thrown out at a height of 45° (for petit assemblé) or 90° (for grand assemblé) forward, to the side, or backward. The basic characteristic of pas assemblé is the joining (or assembling) of the legs in 5th position in the air. Assemblé may be done en face, or in a pose croisée, effacée, or écartée. The elementary preparation for learning assemblé takes place first at the barre and then in the centre of the room, broken down, and at a slow tempo. In its completed form, assemblé is done in a connected and fluent manner.

Petit Assemblé. From a demi-plié in 5th position, the working leg is thrown out at 45° in a given direction while at the same time the supporting leg pushes off from the floor; the working leg instantly is brought up to the supporting leg, the legs in this way uniting in the air in 5th position; care should be taken not to let the supporting leg move toward the side of the working leg.

Assemblé may be done with a progression forward downstage (assemblé dessus). For this, the leg that was in 5th position back will be thrown out to the side and brought up to the supporting leg in front so that, by throwing out the right and left legs alternately, a natural progression forward is obtained. In moving backward upstage (assemblé dessous), the leg that was in 5th position front must be thrown out to the side and brought up to the supporting leg in back.

It is also possible to move forward in a different manner, which may be called assemblé porté: the working leg, from 5th position, is thrown out in a forward direction; and, at the same time, the supporting leg, after the push from the floor, is brought up to the working one, the legs being united in the air in 5th position; and the body moves forward according to the rules of grand assemblé (see below). Just the opposite procedure is used to travel backward: the working leg is thrown out backward and the supporting leg, after the jump comes up to join it in the air, as the body travels in a backward direction.

Assemblé porté may also be done traveling to the side, usually in combination with other jumps. Note that in all assemblés portés the supporting leg comes up to join the working leg in 5th position in the air, while in the previously described assemblé just the opposite is the case.

Example. 2/4 time. With the right leg, assemblé in the small pose croisée devant traveling forward; the right arm is raised to a half-1st position and the left to 2nd position; the head is turned to the right; the body bends slightly backward but comes erect on landing from the jump in demi-plié. Then, do an entrechat-quatre, during which the arms are lowered to preparatory position, the head remaining in the previous position.

Assemblé in the small pose croisée derrière, traveling backward toward the left leg; the right arm is raised to 2nd position and the left to a half-1st position; the head is turned to the left, and the body inclines slightly forward but straightens on landing from the jump in demi-plié. Follow this with an entrechat-quatre, the arms being lowered to preparatory position, and the head turned to the right. Then, en face, with the left leg, assemblé to the side, turning the head to the left, and with the right leg, assemblé to the side, turning the head to the right, each time closing in front to effect a progression forward (two assemblés dessus); for this the arms open to a half-2nd position. Finish the last jump in demi-plié, with the right shoulder forward and the head turned to the right (épaulement croisé). Then, end the combination with three petits changements de pieds with a transition from épaulement through the position en face to épaulement again, finishing the last changement with the left shoulder forward. On these three petits changements, lower the arms gradually to preparatory position. Then, repeat the same combination starting with the other foot.

Petits assemblés portés or in place may also be combined with other movements. Petit assemblé porté, traveling in one direction or another, is an excellent preparation for the study of grand assemblé at 90°.

In learning assemblé, a definite sequence must be observed: first the student studies assemblés to the side at 45°, then assemblés forward (en avant) and backward (en arrière) en face, then in the poses croisées, effacées, and écartées (also porté, traveling forward and backward), the double assemblé, and, finally, assemblé battu (see Chapter IX, "Batterie").

Study Sequence

1. In one measure of 4/4 time (progressing forward down-stage). Stand in 5th position en face, left foot front, the arms in preparatory position. On the first quarter of the first measure, demi-plié in 5th position. On the second quarter, the right foot, sliding along the floor, is taken to 2nd position; the knee, instep, and toes are completely stretched. On the third quarter, throw the working leg up to 45° and, at the same time, push off from the floor with the supporting leg, which has been held in demi-plié; in the jump, unite the legs in 5th position, right leg front, and then land in demi-plié in 5th position; the head is turned in profile to the right. On the fourth quarter, straighten the

legs from demi-plié; and turn the head straight forward. After this, the jump is repeated with the other foot.

　　In executing assemblé in the reverse direction (progressing backward upstage), bring the leg, that was in front, to 5th position in back; and turn the head to the side opposite the working leg.

2.　In one measure of 2/4 time. Begin in 5th position en face with the left foot in front. On the first quarter and the first eighth of the second quarter of the first measure, demi-plié in 5th position. On the second eighth, the right foot, from 5th position, slides out along the floor; the leg is stretched and thrown out to the side at 45°, simultaneously with a push off from the floor with the supporting leg. On the first quarter and the first eighth of the second quarter of the second measure, after having united the legs in 5th position in the air, bringing the right leg front, land in demi-plié in 5th position, with the head turned to the right. On the second eighth, the left foot, from 5th position, slides out along the floor; the leg is stretched and thrown out to the side, simultaneously with a push off from the floor with the supporting leg, and the head turns straight forward. On the first quarter and the first eighth of the second quarter of the third measure, after having united the legs in the air in 5th position, the left leg in front, land in demi-plié in 5th position, with the head to the left. On the second eighth, the right leg, from 5th position, is thrown out to the side at 45°, simultaneously with a push off from the floor with the supporting leg; and the head turns straight forward. On the first quarter and the first eighth of the second quarter of the fourth measure, after having united the legs in 5th position in the air, the right leg in front, land in demi-plié, with the head to the right, etc.

3.　Final form. 2/4 time. Start in 5th position en face, left foot front. Before the measure, on the upbeat, demi-plié in 5th position and, throwing the right (the working) leg out to the side at 45°, simultaneously push off from the floor with the supporting leg and jump. On the first eighth of the first measure, having brought the right leg to 5th position front in the air, land in demi-plié, with the head to the right. On the second eighth, the left leg, from 5th position, is thrown out to the side at 45°; simultaneously push off from the floor with the supporting leg, and jump; turn the head straight forward. On the third eighth, having brought the left leg to 5th position front in the air, land in demi-plié, with the head to the left. On the fourth eighth, the right leg is thrown out to the side at 45°; simultaneously push off from the floor with the supporting leg; turn the head straight forward, etc. Thus, in its completed form, assemblé is done in one quarter.

In combinations of movements, assemblé very often serves as a linking jump between other jumps. It also is used as a concluding jump; but, for this, it is necessary that one foot already be in the air. For example, after a jump that finishes in a pose where the leg is raised at 45° or 90° in one direction or another, push off from the floor with the supporting leg and bring the raised leg to the supporting leg in the air, finishing the jump in a demi-plié in 5th position.

Double Assemblé. Double assemblé consists of two assemblés done from 5th position, throwing out the leg to the side at 45°; the first is done without changing the legs, and the second with a change. The rules for execution are the same as those for simple assemblé to the side.

RULES FOR THE EXECUTION OF PETIT ASSEMBLÉ. For the correct execution of assemblé, a single timing is very important, that is, the throw of the working leg out to 45° and the strong push off from the floor by the supporting leg must be simultaneous. When these two movements do not coincide, a kind of "sitting" in demi-plié is produced, and a "throwing away" of the leg to the side results, which impedes the union of the legs in the air in 5th position and their tight assemblage.

Usually, in petit assemblé, the working leg is thrown out to the side at 45°; but, with the acceleration of the tempo, the height of the working leg, as well as the height of the jump, automatically is lowered. In any case, the supporting leg must succeed in stretching to the maximum. Therefore, in the execution of all the various petits assemblés, it is necessary to remember that the height of 45° is conditional (i.e., relative); but the height of the working leg must not exceed the height at which the leg is thrown out in the exercise of battements tendus jetés.

The working leg is energetically thrown out from 5th position in the given direction, with a sliding movement, the heel actively participating in the bound from the floor; at the beginning of the throw, there must be a moment during which the whole foot slides out along the floor.

The positions of the legs, body, head, and arms are as follows: in assemblé to the side, the working leg must be thrown out exactly to 2nd position, without deviation from that line either forward or backward. The body is held erect, and rocking or inclining it to the side is inadmissible. In assemblé croisé and effacé forward and backward, the working leg is thrown out, preserving the relationship of the legs in 5th position (i.e., the toe of the working leg will be opposite the heel of the supporting leg). In assemblé écarté, the working leg is thrown out to 2nd position on a diagonal and does not deviate from the line of 2nd position either forward or backward. In assemblé to the side, if the foot that was in 5th position back comes front, the head is turned to the side of the working leg; if the foot that was in 5th position front goes back, the head turns to the side opposite the working leg. In each case, the head is turned to a profile position. In the execution of assemblé with épaulement, the working leg is thrown out to the side in 2nd

position en face. At the moment the legs are united in 5th
position in the air, a turn of the body is made, with either the
right or the left shoulder advancing (épaulement). However,
under no circumstances should the shoulder be especially
pushed or thrust forward; during the jump, the shoulder is
delayed and moves only in correspondence with the turn of the
body. In assemblé with a progression forward downstage
(assemblé dessus), the head is turned to the side of the working
leg at the moment of assembling the feet in 5th position in the
air. In assemblé with progression backward upstage (assemblé
dessous), the head is turned to the side opposite the working
leg, simultaneously with the throw of the working leg to 45°.
The positions of the body, arms, and head for assemblé in the
poses croisées, effacées, and écartées devant and derrière,
correspond to the positions described for these poses. The
positions of the arms may vary as to 1st and 2nd positions, or
half-1st and half-2nd positions. (See also the general rules for
the execution of jumps in the opening part of this chapter.)

In the 5th class, petit assemblé may also be executed with
quarter turns. For example, beginning in 5th position with
right leg front: with the right leg, assemblé to the side, at the
same time turning to face point 3; at the end of the assemblé,
the right leg is in back. Then, also with the right leg, do another
assemblé to the side, at the same time turning to face point 5; at
the end, the right leg is in front. The third and fourth
assemblés are done in the same manner with the right leg,
turning to points 7 and 1.

It is also possible to begin with the back leg, turning also to
the right. Each assemblé effects a quarter turn, finishing first in
front and then in back. Both of these assemblés must be
practised with the other leg as well, changing the legs on each
one and each time effecting a quarter turn to the left.

Grand Assemblé. Grand assemblé is done with a
throw of the working leg out to 90° forward or to the side.

Grands assemblés with a throw of the working leg backward are not used as an independent step on the stage or in the classroom; they are encountered only as a link between other jumps (as, for example, after a grande sissonne ouverte; see the above section, "Petit Assemblé"). Grand assemblé may be done en face, in the poses croisées, effacées, or écartées, with various auxiliary movements and jumps (for example, from a step-coupé, an ordinary step, pas de bourrée, glissade, failli, sissonne-tombée, etc.). Grand assemblé is always done traveling in the direction of the working leg. The learning of grand assemblé is begun with the simplest preliminary movements; for example, with a step, with glissade, etc. The combinations must be uncomplicated, the grand assemblé being linked with simple jumps that will not take attention and strength away from the main task—learning the grand assemblé. Once it is mastered in various ways, it is used widely in more complicated combinations. Grand assemblé with a compound beat, entrechat-six de volé ("flown"), is learned after having mastered grand assemblé without a beat; and, in the beginning, it also is learned in only the simplest combinations. (For the explanation of the compound beat entrechat-six de volé see Chapter IX, "Batterie".)

Example of the study of grand assemblé from a step. 2/4 time. Stand in 5th position croisée, left foot front, arms in preparatory position, head turned to the left. On the upbeat, raise the stretched left leg forward croisé to a low height (however, not lower than 22.5°); and, simultaneously, together with the movement of the leg, raise the arms from preparatory position directly to 2nd position. Then, on the first quarter of the first measure, transfer the centre of the body's weight to the left leg and lower it from the extended toe through the foot to the heel (a step to demi-plié) before strongly pushing off from the floor, and at the same time, energetically throwing out the right leg, through 1st position, with a grand battement at 90°, to point 2 of the classroom plan. The throw of the leg is directed exactly to the side in 2nd position, so in order to do this, on moving the body to follow the throw of the leg, it is necessary to place it on a diagonal with the right shoulder forward (épaulement). The supporting leg, after the push, instantly is brought in back of the thrown-out leg, joining it in 5th position in the air. The right arm passes through preparatory position and 1st position, and is raised to 3rd, as the left goes through 1st to 2nd position; at the climax of the jump, the hands are turned palms down; the head is turned to the right; the eyes are directed beyond the fingers of the right hand. On the second quarter, the jump is concluded in demi-plié, in 5th position croisée, right foot front. On landing, the pose that was achieved at the top of the jump is held. On the first quarter of the second measure, straighten from demi-plié and lower the arms to preparatory position. The head remains turned to the right. On the second quarter, the stretched right leg is raised forward croisé at 22.5°, and the arms are raised directly to 2nd position. From here, the jump is repeated with the other leg.

Grand Assemblé en Tournant (a Jump with a Whole Turn of the Body). In grand assemblé en tournant, the leg is thrown out at 90° always to the side, regardless of the direction in which the step is being done (directly forward or backward, directly to the right or to the left, on a diagonal downstage or upstage, in a circle, etc.). The basic rules are the same as those governing grand assemblé without a turn. The study of grand assemblé en tournant is begun with the simplest preliminary movement: a step-tombé at 45°. Later on, the most often-used preliminary movements are pas chassé and pas couru (for a running start), which are the strongest ways of getting into the jump and enable one to execute it at a very great height.

Example of the study of grand assemblé en tournant with step-tombé at 45°. Start in 5th position en face, right foot front, arms in preparatory position. On the upbeat, demi-plié on the left leg, and at the same time, take the right leg out through the

conditional position sur le cou-de-pied to the side at 45°; the
arms open through 1st position to 2nd. Then, fall onto the right
leg (tombé). The left leg slides along the floor, passing through
1st position, stretches, and is energetically thrown out to the
side at 90°, simultaneously with a push-off from the floor with
the supporting leg and a half turn of the body to the side of the
thrown-out leg, so that the back is to the audience; the arms,
moving from 2nd position through preparatory and 1st
positions, are raised to 3rd. After the push-off from the floor,
the supporting leg is instantly brought up to join the working
leg in 5th position back. If the dancer doing the step stands en
face to the audience and, after the step-tombé onto the right
leg, throws out the left leg, then the turn of the body will be to
the right with the left shoulder brought forward. The first
movement of the turn of the body brings the dancer's back to
the audience and the final movement brings the body en face
once again. With the other leg, all will be done to the opposite
side. Later on, according to what is required, one can vary the
position of the arms; for example, the right arm may be raised
to 1st position and the left to 3rd, etc. The body is transferred
to the side of the thrown-out leg, and completes the turn with
the participation of the arms, which provide force to help the
turn of the body in the air. During this, the legs hold 5th
position in the air, and the arms maintain the position taken at
the first moment of the jump. The jump is finished in 5th
position, right foot front, in demi-plié, en face (changing the
feet at the last instant). The head, during the jump, is turned
across the left shoulder, looking toward the audience for as
long as possible, then quickly turns, following the turn of the
body, and again returns to the initial position. One must take
care that the thrown-out leg passes along the floor near the
supporting leg by way of 1st position, and does not move
forward away from the supporting leg, making an arc-like
movement "scooping the floor", as if thereby to provide force
for the turn (particularly at the first moment of the jump, when

the turn of the body itself and the force of the arms are
sufficient); moreover, with an incorrect movement of the
thrown-out leg, it is impossible to achieve a strong and free
throw to 2nd position at 90°. The thrown-out leg must be pulled
up in the hip joint; the buttocks muscles must be pulled up and
tense; the body must be held in a vertical position, the shoulder
directed toward the toe of the thrown-out leg. It is necessary to
see that the body does not bend to the side away from the
thrown-out leg (which, however, is often observed in those
doing this step). In grand assemblé en tournant, the turn of the
body does not present a particular difficulty; the real difficulty
consists in attaining the maximum height and flying quality of
the jump with the throw of the leg to 90°, holding the body at
this height. This can be assisted by pulling up the thighs, the
buttocks muscles, and the whole torso. The full turn of the body
is executed as a single movement but, even so, it is necessary to
become clearly aware of the two parts of the jump: the first part
is the throw of the working leg to the side at 90°, simultaneously
with the jump and the first half turn of the body; the second
part is the quick pulling up of the supporting leg to the
thrown-out leg, uniting them in 5th position, together with the
further turn of the body to face the front.

Following the mastery of grand assemblé en tournant, the
student learns, in order of difficulty, grand assemblé en
tournant with a compound beat (entrechat-six de volé) and
grand assemblé en tournant with a double turn of the body. All
of the rules, conditions, and positions set forth above fully
relate also to these complicated kinds of assemblé; but, for the
double turn, a greater force must be provided by the arms,
body, and legs to give impetus in the direction of the turn.

One can do grand assemblé en tournant without changing
the feet or with a change; in the latter case, the change of the
feet occurs at the last, the final, moment of the turn.

The musical pattern for the initial study of grand assemblé en
tournant is the same as that for grand assemblé en face.

RULES FOR THE EXECUTION OF GRAND ASSEM-
BLÉ. The working leg is thrown out at 90° with a grand
battement simultaneously with a strong push-off from the floor
by the supporting leg and a movement of the arms, which
render significant aid to the jump. Before the jump, it is
imperative that the arms open to 2nd position, and only at the
moment of the bound from the floor and the throwing out of
the working leg will they pass through preparatory position and
1st position, opening in the air, to one or another pose,
according to what is required. The movement of the arms is
free, not tense; and from the shoulder to the elbow there must
be felt a slight resiliency of the muscles, which keeps them from
sagging. The simultaneous movements of the working and
supporting legs, together with the movement of the arms,
give the necessary single timing, thanks to which the possibility of the jump, and of its being held in the air, is
increased.

Regardless of the approach from which the assemblé is done,
it is necessary, before the bound from the floor, while pressing
down in demi-plié, to transfer the centre of the body's weight to
the supporting leg, thus freeing the other leg for the throw, and
then to carry the body after the thrown-out leg during the
jump. After the push, the supporting leg instantly is brought
up to the thrown-out leg, joining it in 5th position back in the
air. In pushing off with the supporting leg, it is necessary to
direct the strength of the push not only to the jump lengthwise,
but also to the jump in height; that is, the jump must be
extended with as much flight as possible. It is necessary to hold
the thrown-out leg as high as possible, and up to this highest
point quickly bring the supporting leg. A great help is given by
pulled-up buttocks muscles, a pulled-up body, and thighs that
are prepared (somewhat tensed) before the jump, in demi-plié.
An undisciplined, loose body or a body that is settled onto the
legs, prevents the execution of a jump of full value. On the
return to the floor after the jump, the body, legs, head, and

arms remain well pulled up, held, as in the jump, to preserve the form and expressiveness of the given pose.

Pas Jeté

A jeté is a jump from one foot to the other, with the exception of jeté fermé (in which, immediately after the jump, the second leg closes in 5th position, and the jump takes place as if from two feet to two). During the jump, one leg is sharply thrown forward, to the side, or backward, and the other is stretched in the air. In this manner, the centre of the body's weight is transferred from one leg to the other.

Jetés are extremely diverse in form.

Petit Jeté. The rules for the execution of petit jeté correspond, basically, to the rules for the execution of petit assemblé, but the throw of the leg to the conditional height of 45° must be slightly higher than for petit assemblé.

Standing in 5th position, demi-plié. The working leg stretches as it is thrown forward, to the side, or backward at 45°; simultaneously, the supporting leg springs from the floor. Then, the working leg is brought up to the supporting leg in front or in back in the air; and, on landing in demi-plié, the supporting leg bends in the knee and takes the position sur le cou-de-pied devant or derrière (the conditional position sur le cou-de-pied devant is used).

In all petits jetés that finish sur le cou-de-pied, the throw of the working leg from the position sur le cou-de-pied for the succeeding petit jeté takes place by passing the foot through 5th position. This method co-ordinates the throw of the working leg with the spring of the supporting leg from the floor and makes possible the pull-up of the thighs. It is necessary to observe it especially in the elementary classes (the first, second, and third), when the thighs and other muscles have not yet been sufficiently strengthened. Later on, the working leg is thrown out from the position sur le cou-de-pied with only the front part of the foot brushing against the floor.

Petit jeté can be done en face or in a pose croisée, effacée, or écartée.

Jeté is learned first at the barre, then in the centre of the room, broken down, and at a slow tempo. The final form is done in a connected manner.

Beginning the study of petit jeté in the centre of the room, the arms are held in preparatory position. Later on, simultaneously with the throw of the working leg, the arms, from preparatory position, are freely thrown up to 2nd position and extended with the palms down; then, during the return to the floor, after the jump, the arm that is opposite the working leg is brought to 1st position, and the other remains in 2nd; that is, the right arm is in 1st position if the left foot is sur le cou-de-pied derrière, and the left arm is in 1st position if the right foot is sur le cou-de-pied derrière. At the end of the movement the arms are curved, and the head turns in the direction of the leg in demi-plié.

In the execution of petit jeté in the reverse direction, the positions of the arms in relation to the legs are the same. The head turns in the direction of the front leg on landing in demi-plié. However, these basic positions of the arms and head for petit jeté can be changed according to the requirements of the teacher.

Petit jeté can be done either in place or traveling (springing out in one direction or another), in which case it is termed porté.

Petit jeté to the side. Do several petits jetés in succession, throwing first one leg out to the side, and then the other. Begin with the right leg in 5th position back. The right leg, or working leg, comes in front of the supporting leg at the end of the jump, taking its place. On landing on the right leg in demi-plié, the supporting leg bends to the position sur le cou-de-pied derrière. Then the left leg, which is now the working leg, from the position sur le cou-de-pied, is thrown out to the side at 45° and comes in front of the supporting leg, at the end of the jump, taking its place; on landing in demi-plié, the right leg goes to the position sur le cou-de-pied derrière, etc. A natural progression forward thus results.

Petit jeté moving backward is done according to the same principle, but the working leg, at the end of each jump, must be substituted for the supporting leg in back.

Progressing forward, the head turns towards the working leg after the jump from the floor. Moving backward, the head turns away from the working leg simultaneously with the jump.

Petit jeté porté. This jeté is done traveling in one direction or another. It begins with a special jump; during the jump, the supporting (or jumping) leg is brought up to the working leg (which has been thrown out at 45°) and takes the position sur le cou-de-pied, the body following in the direction of the leg that has been thrown out in the air. In the execution of the ordinary petit jeté, the working leg is brought back to the supporting leg in front or in back and bends sur le cou-de-pied.

Petit jeté porté to the side, as a rule, is not done consecutively with alternate legs but is combined with other jumps.

This jeté is not only an independent pas but, at the same time, serves as an excellent preparatory exercise for grand jeté at 90°, jeté fondu at 90°, jeté fondu-passé, as well as some other jumps; for during all of these, one must hold oneself in the air for as long as possible after the leg has been thrown out to 45° (in petit jeté) or to 90° (in grand jeté) and fly beyond the tip of the toe forward, to the side, or backward in the jump. The given pose (i.e., the position of the arms and the turn of the head) must be expressed during the flight through the air as well as in the landing in demi-plié. Petits jetés portés can be done in the poses croisées, effacées, and écartées, devant and derrière.

Study Sequence

Petit jeté porté forward in the pose croisée.

1. Two measures of 2/4 time. Begin in 5th position with épaulement croisé, right leg front. On the first quarter,

demi-plié. Between the first and second quarters, jump upward, throwing the right leg forward, with a sliding movement along the floor, to a height of 45° in the direction croisée; the arms, from preparatory position, are raised to 1st position, and the hands open slightly; the head is turned to the right. On the second quarter, having flown beyond the tip of the toe, come down in demi-plié, the left foot in the position sur le cou-de-pied derrière.

On the first quarter of the second measure, assemblé back, closing the legs in 5th position in demi-plié and lowering the arms to preparatory position through 2nd. On the second quarter, straighten from demi-plié. From here, the movement is repeated the required number of times en diagonale.

2. One measure of 2/4 time. On the upbeat, demi-plié and do the jeté forward in the direction croisée. On the first quarter, come down in demi-plié. On the second quarter, assemblé, bringing the legs together in 5th position in demi-plié. From here, the movement is repeated.

Jeté porté backward in the pose croisée is learned in exactly the same way, the head being turned toward the shoulder analogous to the leg that is sur le cou-de-pied at the conclusion of the jump.

In intermediate and advanced classes, petit jeté porté forward can be finished in a small pose attitude; in this case, the arms, in the small attitude, open to 1st position, or one arm can take 1st position and the other 2nd. In the same way, petit jeté porté backward, which, in the elementary years, finishes in the position sur le cou-de-pied devant, can be finished, later on, in a pose with the leg stretched forward at 45° or with the leg taken out through the conditional position sur le cou-de-pied devant to a height of 45°.

Example of a combination of petits jetés portés. 4/4 time (executed in two measures). Begin in 5th position with épaulement croisé, left leg front. On the upbeat, demi-plié. On the first quarter, with the right leg, petits jeté portés to the side, the left foot taken to the position sur le cou-de-pied devant. On the second quarter, petit jeté porté forward in the direction croisée. On the third quarter, assemblé backward. On the fourth quarter, entrechat-quatre.

On the next measure, petit échappé in 4th position croisée and petit échappé in 2nd position (changing the feet). Repeat the combination with the other leg. Then do the same thing in the reverse direction.

Petit Jeté Fermé. Jeté fermé (from the French fermer, "to close") is a jump from two feet onto two. It is done to the side and in all the small poses. Petit jeté fermé to the side may be done with or without changing the legs; in the second case, several jetés can be done in succession in one direction. It is studied after the mastery of petit jeté porté.

Example of the study of jeté fermé to the side (without changing the legs).

1. 4/4 time. Begin in 5th position with right leg front. On the first quarter, demi-plié. Between the first and second quarters, slide the left foot out along the floor, throw it to the side at a height of 45° and jump, the body inclining to the right; simultaneously, the arms, from preparatory position, open to 2nd position, and the head turns to the right. Travel sideways to the left, beyond the tip of the toe, opening the right leg sideways also to a height of 45° (not any lower than the left). On the second quarter, come down in demi-plié on the left leg; then bring the right, sliding the toe along the floor, to 5th position front in demi-plié. On landing, the centre of the body's weight is transferred onto the left leg; the body inclines to the left; the arms close to preparatory position; and the head, following the movement of the body, turns to the left. On the third and fourth quarters, come up from demi-plié and, straightening the body, turn the head to the right. From here repeat the movement.

2. 2/4 time. On the upbeat, demi-plié and jump. On the first quarter, come down on the left leg in demi-plié; on the second quarter, the right leg closes in 5th position front in demi-plié. The next jeté fermé is done from here.

In the execution of petits jetés fermés to the side in 2/4, the body does not straighten between the first and second jetés, but is smoothly transferred from one leg to the other (inclining to the side), as indicated in the first example.

In its final form, this jeté can be done in one quarter.

Example of a combination of jetés fermés. Eight measures of 2/4. Begin in 5th position with épaulement croisé, right foot front. On the upbeat, demi-plié.

First measure: jeté fermé to the side (to the left), without changing the legs.

Second measure: repeat the jeté fermé once again.

Third measure: two jetés fermés to the side (to the left), without changing the legs, 1/4 each.

Fourth measure: entrechat-cinq derrière and pas de bourrée en tournant en dehors. Finish in 5th position, left foot front.

Fifth measure: with the left leg, jeté fermé forward in the small pose croisée.

Sixth measure: with the right leg, jeté fermé backward in the small pose croisée.

Seventh measure: entrechat-cinq devant and pas de bourrée en tournant en dedans. Finish in 5th position, right foot front.

Eighth measure: with the right leg, jeté fermé forward in the small pose 3rd arabesque and royale.

Petit Jeté Traveling to the Side with Half Turns (Petit Jeté en Tournant). This jeté is done either to the side (from point 7 to point 3 and vice versa) or on a diagonal (from point 6 to point 2 and from point 4 to point 8). During each jeté, a half turn of the body is done (two jetés make a full turn).

Example of petit jeté en tournant traveling to the side from point 7 to point 3. 2/4 time. Begin in 5th position, right leg front. On the upbeat, demi-plié; the right arm is in 1st position, the left in 2nd. Then throw the right leg out to the side, jump, and open the arms to 2nd position. Fly to the right with as much force as possible, while doing a half turn en dedans (to the right) in the air. During the jump, the head turns to the left, toward the audience, and at the end takes on a profile position, with the eyes directed across the left shoulder. On the first quarter, come down in demi-plié with the back toward the audience, and pause with the left foot sur le cou-de-pied derrière, the left arm is in 1st position, and the right in 2nd. In the second jeté, throw the left leg out to the side; and in the jump, simultaneously open the left arm to 2nd position. Fly in the direction of the toe and the left hand, with a half turn in the air en dehors (to the right). On the second quarter, come down in demi-plié with the right foot sur le cou-de-pied devant; the right arm is in 1st, and the left in 2nd position; the head is en face.

GENERAL RULES FOR THE EXECUTION OF PETIT JETÉ EN TOURNANT. It is necessary to fix the jump in the air in the position en face; only at the last moment is the body turned halfway around.

The second petit jeté (with a turn of the body en dehors), beginning from the position with the back to the audience, must not be weaker than the first, which usually happens with the inexperienced. In fact, to create an impression of uniformity in the series of jetés en tournant, the height of the second jump and the span of the flight to the side in the air must actively be somewhat stronger than in the first jeté.

Beginning the first jump with the right leg, turning en dedans, one must turn the body clearly, moving the left shoulder forward; in the second jump, turning en dehors, the body turns by taking the right shoulder back. During the pause after the jump onto the right leg, the thigh and the buttocks muscles of the left leg, which is sur le cou-de-pied derrière, must be well pulled up. Pausing on the left leg, it is necessary to pull up the thighs and buttocks muscles of the right leg, which is bent sur le cou-de-pied devant.

At the moment of the jump, when the arms open to 2nd position to help the flight, the hands, extending, are turned palms down. On finishing the jump the arm that is to be bent in 1st position must be "caught up" by the hand to 1st position from down below. The arm must not go through preparatory position, but this active and fleeting movement of the hand helps assemblé the body during the turn.

Petit jeté en tournant can be done with opposite turns. If the movement travels to the right, then the right leg begins in 5th position back. After throwing the right leg out to 2nd position for the jump, one turns en dehors by taking the left shoulder back; for the second jeté, the left leg is thrown out, followed by a turn en dedans, moving the right shoulder forward. After the first jeté, the left foot is in the position sur le cou-de-pied devant; and after the second jeté, the right foot is sur le cou-de-pied derrière.

Petit jeté with half turns of the body, on a diagonal moving downstage from an upstage corner, is done according to the rules for petit jeté in a straight line, except that the position of the head is slightly different. As an example, let us take the diagonal from point 6 to point 2. Beginning in 5th position, with the right leg in front, the right shoulder, the head and eyes are directed to point 2. Finishing the first jeté on the right leg, after turning en dedans, pause with the left shoulder to point 2, the head turned across the left shoulder. After the second jeté, with the left leg and a turn en dehors, the head turns in a profile position across the right shoulder to point 2.

Thus, moving with half turns in a straight line from point 7 to point 3 or vice versa the head turns alternately in profile and en face; but, in moving on a diagonal, the turns of the head alternate between one profile position and the other. This same rule also applies in the execution of emboîté en tournant at 45°, to the side and on the diagonal.

Grand Jeté. On the stage, grand jeté is assigned an important place. It is done with a jump forward to the poses attitude croisée and effacée, and to 1st, 2nd, 3rd, and 4th arabesques. More rarely, it is done with a jump backward to the big poses croisée and effacée devant.

Preliminary movements to the jump are numerous and include a passing step-coupé, pas couru, glissade, chassé, sissonne-tombée-coupée, etc. All approaches must be so co-ordinated as to energetically give impetus to the grand jeté, before which there is a strong springboard-like push from the floor. All preliminary movements are done on the upbeat.

In intermediate classes, at the beginning of the study of grand jeté, it is useful for several lessons to do jeté simply from 5th position. Later it is preceded by a step-coupé, then by pas couru, by glissade, and by chassé.

The rules for the execution of grand jeté are in many ways analogous to the rules for the execution of petit jeté porté (see "Petit jeté porté forward in the pose croisée"), but with the difference that the leg is thrown out to a height of 90°. This throw of the leg up to 90° goes out in an upward arc, the body pulled up and aspiring upward. The position of the body at the moment of the jump, and the transfer of the body's weight onto the supporting leg in demi-plié, have much in common with développé-tombé. It is necessary to call the attention of the students to this. During the jump (in the execution of grand jeté en avant), the leg that is in back takes the position of attitude croisée, effacée, or arabesque. The pose must be clearly expressed in the jump itself and then be held, after the jump, in demi-plié. The jump is as high as possible and ends elastically and softly in demi-plié with a pulled-up back and leg muscles. The jeté can then be finished with an assemblé.

Example of grand jeté with a step-coupé to attitude croisée (elementary study).

1. 4/4 time. Préparation: the right leg is in the position croisée derrière with a stretched leg, toe to the floor (for men, the

knee is relaxed and the ball of the foot is on the floor), the instep stretched; the arms are in preparatory position; and the head is turned to the left. On the upbeat, after opening the arms directly to 2nd position, take a wide step forward with the right leg in the direction effacée, and demi-plié; at the moment the centre of weight is transferred onto the right leg, strongly incline the body forward and slightly to the right; simultaneously, the arms are lowered to pre-paratory position, and the head inclines to the right. Using the heel, push off from the floor strongly with the right leg (the coupé); throw out the left leg forward in the direction croisée to a height of 90°; and, providing force with the arms from below, open the right arm to 3rd and the left to 2nd position; turn the head to the left; straighten the body, and jump. Flying beyond the toe, hold the left leg at the height of 90° for as long as possible, while the right bends to attitude croisée. The demi-plié on the right leg and the jump both take place on the first quarter. On the second quarter, come down from the jump in demi-plié on the left leg with the right in attitude. On the third and fourth quarters, lower the arms and place the right leg in the initial position, the préparation derrière. From here, the movement is repeated, traveling on a diagonal from point 6 to point 2.

It is essential to remember that in grand jeté the body and the arms actively help the jump. A body that is pulled up and raised upward during the jump (going up, forward, and over beyond the toe) increases not only the height but also the length of the jump.

In the jump, it is necessary to be conscious of tautness in the legs, and, particularly, the pull-up of the thigh muscles; in no case, should the buttocks muscles be relaxed. Looseness of the muscles leads to a slack jump and makes it impossible to establish the pose in the air.

2. 4/4 time. Grand jeté in this form is done without pauses;

that is, after the first jeté, done on the first and second quarters, the leg from the position attitude croisée immediately does a step-coupé and executes a second jeté, etc.

One should note that this method of studying grand jeté with a step-coupé was formerly considered suitable only for women; and the opinion was that, in the men's class, to learn jeté with a running start was much easier. However, experience has shown that, in perfecting the form and height of the jump, it is difficult to get rid of the lack of precision and orderliness inherent in this easier approach, whereas a step-coupé well co-ordinates the position of the body, the arms, and head before the jump, and, in this very way, helps the jump.

Let us look closely at the execution of the step preceding the coupé. From 4th position croisée derrière, the leg, with stretched toes, and bending a little in the knee, passes forward close by the supporting leg, just barely coming off the floor, but not brushing against the floor with the toe. At the distance of a wide step forward from the supporting leg, the toe of the working leg is placed on the floor with a forward sliding movement; and, immediately, the whole foot is lowered onto the floor in demi-plié in a well turned-out manner, the heel accenting the pressure in plié, and the body inclining toward this leg. A careless step, in which the leg is placed down in demi-plié directly from above, without the forward sliding movement, does not give the necessary result.

Example of grand jeté with pas couru. A pas couru is a running start before the jump; it can consist of three or five quick steps, of which the last will be a step-coupé. Like the preliminary movement step-coupé, the pas couru also begins with a préparation croisée derrière, the first step forward being done with the leg that is in the position croisée derrière.

During the run, the arms open to 2nd position, and the body is slightly inclined backward; the centre of the body's weight is transferred forward onto the jumping leg only on the step-coupé. The dynamics and tempo of the running start (done on the upbeat) do not allow one to incline the body forward at the moment of the coupé as strongly as is done in grand jeté with a step-coupé. The inclination of the body and the step-coupé will be only "in passing", just helping to provide force with the arms from below and to raise the whole body upward during the jump to attitude croisée or to the pose 3rd arabesque. The movement travels forward along a diagonal.

Example of grand jeté with pas chassé. Grand jeté with a preliminary pas chassé (a jump in which one foot catches up with the other in the air, from the French chasser, "to chase"; see "Pas chassé") is a variation of the approach with pas couru and is used in advanced classes.

Préparation: the right leg is croisé derrière. Having taken the right leg forward in the direction effacée, do an easy sliding jump (chassé) forward bringing the left leg up to 5th position back in the air; the arms are in 2nd position allongée. Land on the left leg, freeing the right for a sliding step-coupé, and throw the left leg forward at 90° for the grand jeté. The movement travels on a diagonal. Pas chassé, like pas couru, is done on the upbeat.

Example of grand jeté with glissade in a straight line to the side in 1st arabesque. 4/4 time. Begin in 5th position with épaulement croisé, left leg front, and the arms in preparatory position. The movement is to the side in a straight line from point 7 to point 3. Demi-plié and, on the upbeat, glissade, with the right leg, to 2nd position (directly to point 3), finishing in 5th position croisée with the left leg in front in demi-plié. During the glissade, the arms open to 2nd position and come down together before the jeté; the head is turned to the left.

On the first quarter, both finish the glissade and push off from the floor, turning the body to the right to point 3 while throwing out the right leg forward at 90° and leaping toward point 3; the arms, passing through 1st position, open to the pose 1st arabesque; and the eyes are directed over the right hand, which is brought upward. On the second quarter, having transferred the body forward, come down on the right leg in demi-plié and hold the pose 1st arabesque. On the third quarter, assemblé, bringing the legs together in the air in 5th position croisée, with the left leg in front, and come down in demi-plié. On the fourth quarter, straighten the legs from demi-plié. Or, on the fourth quarter, it is also possible to do an entrechat-quatre or any pas that finishes on both legs without changing the feet. From here, repeat the movement in the same direction.

RULES FOR THE EXECUTION OF GRAND JETÉ WITH GLISSADE. The glissade is done with a jump, but without breaking contact with the floor; it must be finished, in the classroom, in a precise 5th position (4th position, although permitted on the stage, is not recommended for academic work).

Finishing the glissade, do not pause in the demi-plié, for this will turn the glissade from an auxiliary movement into an independent pas and will hinder the spring from the floor and weaken the force of the jump.

At the finish of the glissade, the push from the floor for the jeté is done with both legs; but the main task must fall to the leg that finishes the glissade (i. e., if the right leg begins the glissade, then the left leg will provide a greater push for the jump). After opening the arms during the glissade, and then bringing them down together, they should be energetically opened to the pose during the jeté without a trace of sluggishness; that is, one must vigorously provide force for the jump with the arms.

Doing the glissade in 2nd position directly to point 3 with épaulement croisé, the left shoulder is forward and the head turned to the left throughout; but, at the last moment, before the jeté, the right shoulder should be taken further back, preparing the position of the body for the subsequent pose—1st arabesque, directed to point 3.

As in all grands jetés, the body is pulled up simultaneously with the jump and directed forward.

Example of grand jeté in 1st arabesque with glissade on a diagonal. Begin in 5th position with épaulement croisé, left leg front. The movement is done from point 6 to point 2. The glissade, as in the previous example, is done without changing the legs and begins with the right leg moving forward in the direction of point 2, the grand jeté to 1st arabesque also being done to point 2. The right foot, sliding in the glissade forward in the direction effacée, determines the direction of the throw of the right leg forward at 90°, at the moment of the jeté. The left shoulder remains forward the whole time (for the rules of execution, see "Rules for the Execution of Grand Jeté with Glissade"). However, if the grand jeté is done to attitude effacée, from point 6 to point 2, then, at the beginning, the right leg can as well be in 5th position front. In this case, the glissade is done forward in the direction écartée, with the right shoulder to point 2; and only at the moment of the jeté does the body turn effacé.

Example of grand jeté in 2nd arabesque with glissade on a diagonal. Begin in 5th position with épaulement croisé, left leg front. The movement is on a diagonal, from point 6 to point 2. The glissade, done without changing the legs, is begun with the right leg moving forward in the direction effacée toward point 2; and the grand jeté in 2nd arabesque also is done with the right leg to point 2. Then the left leg, which is in back in the pose 2nd arabesque at 90°, lowers and quickly passes along the floor near the right supporting leg before sliding forward, to do the second glissade in the direction between point 1 and point 2. This glissade finishes in 5th position with the right leg in front. Immediately, the left leg is thrown out at 90°, for the jeté, in the direction of the second glissade. From here, the movement is repeated with the right and with the left leg. The arms, as in the previous examples, open to 2nd position in the glissade and are lowered to preparatory position before the jeté. The first glissade is done with the left shoulder forward, the head to the left. On finishing the glissade, slightly lower the head; then, in the jeté, the head is again directed over the left shoulder, the left arm stretched forward and the right to the side. Doing the second glissade, it is necessary to turn the head to the right and to lower the arms directly from the pose 2nd arabesque before raising them again, in the second jeté.

The rules for the execution of the glissade and the grand jeté are the same as in the previous examples.

In advanced classes, these jetés can be done in a circle around the room. The circle can begin, traveling to the right, from point 8, go past points 1, 2, and 3, and finish by moving on a diagonal, from point 4 to point 8; or, continuing around past points 4 and 5, it can finish moving diagonally forward from point 6 to point 2. To the left, the movement begins from point 2 and continues past points 1, 8, 7, etc. Or, after doing the jetés moving on a diagonal forward, one can continue them in a circle. In this case, after moving on a diagonal from point 6 to point 2, begin the circle turning to the right (after a diagonal from point 4 to point 8, begin the circle turning to the left).

Jeté Fondu at 90°. Jeté fondu ("melted") is a big jump from two legs finishing on two, executed to the side and in all the big poses devant and derrière. This jeté can be compared to grand jeté done from 5th position; however, at the end of the jump, the leg does not remain in the air, but softly closes to 5th position.

Example of the study of jeté fondu to the pose 3rd arabesque.
1. 4/4 time. Begin in 5th position with épaulement croisé, right leg front, arms in preparatory position. Opening the arms a little before the beat, on the first quarter, demi-

plié. Between the first and second quarters, jump, throwing the right leg out forward to a height of 90° in the direction croisée, and fly forward beyond the toe of the right foot; at the same time, raise the left leg croisé derrière at 90° and open the arms through 1st position, the left forward and the right to 2nd position. On the second quarter, come down on the right leg in demi-plié. Between the second and third quarters, the left leg, with the toe to the floor, is brought in to 5th position back in demi-plié; simultaneously, the arms are softly lowered to preparatory position. On the third quarter, the left leg, in 5th position, somewhat deepens the demi-plié, which creates the character of fondu. On the fourth quarter, straighten from the demi-plié.

2. Final form. 2/4 time. On the upbeat, demi-plié and do the jeté forward. On the first quarter, come down on the right leg in demi-plié. On the second quarter, bring the left leg to 5th position back in demi-plié, and lower the arms to preparatory position. From here, the movement is repeated the required number of times.

The characteristic feature of jeté fondu at 90° is a smooth, soft execution; and inherent in it is a moderate waltz tempo. In executing it in 3/4 time, each measure will be equal to one quarter of a two-count measure. These jetés are done in all the poses and in all directions.

Jeté Passé. There are three basic types of jeté passé: petit, executed at 45°; grand, executed at 90° (both of which are executed en avant and en arrière); and grand, executed in 2nd position with a bending of the leg for the passé at the height of 90°, or with a passé with straight legs through 1st position. They may be preceded by a passing step or a pas couru.

Petit jeté passé en arrière preceded by a step. 2/4 time. Préparation: the right leg is croisé derrière. On the upbeat, step forward with the right leg in the direction effacée, with the toe to the floor. On the first quarter, demi-plié on the right leg, transferring the centre of the body's weight forward onto it; the right arm is in 1st, and the left in 2nd position; the head and eyes are directed at the right hand. Between the first and second quarters, jump and, pushing away from the floor, throw the left leg out backward in the direction effacée at 45°; at the moment of the jump, the body, coming erect, slightly bends backward; the arms, with open hands, go to 2nd position; and the head turns to the left. On the second quarter, the left leg is lowered in demi-plié to the place on the floor from which the right leg jumped, and the right leg is thrown out backward in the direction croisée to a half-bent position at 45°; the right arm remains in 2nd position, and the left bends to 1st position; the head remains turned to the left. Repeating the movement, again take a step forward in the direction effacée with the right leg and, lowering the right arm, with a passing movement bring it together with the left in 1st position, after which, having bent the body forward a little before the jump, bring the left arm to 2nd position, etc. The movement goes on a diagonal from point 6 to point 2.

RULES FOR THE EXECUTION OF PETIT JETÉ PASSÉ EN ARRIÈRE PRECEDED BY A STEP. In the jump, there must be a moment when both legs are in the air, one in the position effacée, and the other, croisée derrière. The legs, changing in the air, pass near one another, but do not actually come into contact.

When inclining the body forward before the jump, the shoulders must be kept completely level. To achieve this, it is necessary, at the moment of the plié on the right leg, to move the left shoulder slightly forward. A common mistake is to allow this shoulder to lag behind, which gives a crookedness to the body at the moment of the jump and disturbs the line of the backbend.

The smooth transfer of the body from the inclined position forward to the small bend backward takes place during the jump itself (which is very important) and is maintained in the final pose in demi-plié.

These rules also apply to jeté passé en arrière at 90°.

Petit jeté passé en arrière with a pas couru. Pas couru (a running start) can consist of three or five steps. The last step is done with an emphasis on the plié.

The initial position is the pose croisée derrière with the toe to the floor.

In the pas couru, which is done on the upbeat, the arms are in preparatory position; in the jeté passé, they take on the small poses described in the first example. When the movement is done several times in succession, the arms should be lowered to preparatory position during the pas couru.

The rules for the execution of jeté passé en arrière with a preliminary pas couru are the same as for jeté passé en arrière preceded by a step.

Jeté passé en arrière at 90°. 2/4 time. Préparation: the right leg is croisé derrière. As in petit jeté passé, the step forward in the direction effacée is done with the right leg, but the position in demi-plié is slightly wider, and the inclination of the body forward is greater.

At the moment of the jump, the left leg is thrown out backward in the direction effacée to 90°, the right, to croisé derrière. Finishing the jump in demi-plié on the left leg, hold the right in attitude croisée.

Before the beginning of the jump, the right arm is in 1st position, the left in 2nd. In the jump, the right arm is raised through 2nd to 3rd position and the hand opens outward; the left remains in 2nd position. In the final pose, the hands can be allongé or may take on the usual 3rd or 2nd position. The bend of the body backward in the jump is considerably greater than in petit jeté passé.

Musically the movement is divided into quarters, as in the first example. This jeté can also be done with pas couru.

Jeté passé en avant at 90°. 2/4 time. Préparation: the left leg is croisé devant with the toe to the floor; the arms are in preparatory position; the head is turned to the left.

On the upbeat, the left leg takes a step backward in the direction effacée; the arms, passing through 1st position, are brought to 2nd position with open hands. On the first quarter, demi-plié on the left leg and incline the body, with level shoulders, slightly backward; then, before the second quarter, throwing the right leg forward to 90°, jump; during the jump, the left leg does a développé forward at 90°. On the second quarter, come down in demi-plié on the right leg, finishing the movement in the big pose croisée devant. The arms, from 2nd position, rotate inward so that the hands turn out at the end; the left arm remains in 2nd position, and the right is brought from 2nd to 3rd; or the left arm may be raised with the right remaining in 2nd position. The head turns to the right or to the left, according to what is required.

These jetés can also be done with pas couru. Pas couru backward is done on low demi-pointe in contrast to pas couru forward, in which the feet are placed down through the foot, from the toe to the heel.

Jeté passé at 90° to 2nd position, finishing in 3rd arabesque. This jeté is done from 5th position onto one leg, and can finish with an assemblé or a pas de bourrée changé. Another pas usually precedes it; for example, grande sissonne ouverte to attitude croisée, assemblé to 5th position, and then jeté passé to the side, finishing in 3rd arabesque. Or it is possible, at the end of an allegro combination, to do a glissade, jeté passé to 3rd arabesque and pause in the pose in plié at the end.

Let us analyse the given example. Begin in 5th position with épaulement croisé, the left leg in front, arms in preparatory position, head to the left. On the upbeat, demi-plié, then glissade with the right leg to 2nd position without changing the legs, opening the arms slightly to the side. On the first quarter, finish the glissade and lower the arms. Between the first and second quarters, pushing off from the floor, jump, throwing the right leg out to the side to 90°; the arms, from below, open directly to 2nd position; and the position of the head and body is en face. Having flown as far as possible in the direction of the right leg, on the second quarter, come down on the right leg in demi-plié, quickly bringing the left leg, which, in the jump, has formed a right angle with the floor, through 1st position to demi-plié, croisé derrière at 90° (that is, to 3rd arabesque); the right arm remains in 2nd position, the left, at the moment of the passé through 1st position, is lowered before being raised forward; the eyes, having followed the movement of the left arm, are directed forward over the left hand.

Jeté passé at 90° to 2nd position, finishing in the pose effacée devant. In this example, jeté passé is combined with a pas de bourrée changé.

2/4 time. Begin in 5th position with épaulement croisé, the left leg in front. On the upbeat, demi-plié and jump with a throw of the right leg to 2nd position at 90°; the arms, from preparatory position, open directly to 2nd position, with the hands turned palms down; the body and the head are en face. Having flown in the direction of the right leg, come down, on the first quarter, on the right leg in demi-plié; at the moment of landing, the body, with level shoulders, turns to point 8 (i. e., effacé); the left leg does a développé to the pose effacée devant; the right arm is raised to 3rd position, the left remains in 2nd; and the head turns to the right. Between the first and second quarters, without lingering in the pose, fall (tombé) onto the left leg in demi-plié (a little bit wider than usual) in the direction of point 8; and, bringing the right leg up to the left in back on demi-pointe, do a pas de bourrée changé forward (en dehors en face); simultaneously, the right arm opens to 2nd position and is lowered together with the left. After finishing the movement, on the second quarter, in 5th position (the right leg in front), immediately throw out the left leg to 2nd position at 90°, with a jump, and continue by repeating all the pas with the other leg.

RULES FOR THE EXECUTION OF JETÉ PASSÉ AT 90° TO 2ND POSITION. This jeté must convey a free, dancelike character. It is done traveling widely from side to side.

In pushing off for the jump from demi-plié, the leg must be thrown out at 90° with a strong sliding movement along the floor, in no case freeing it in the demi-plié.

In combination with this kind of jeté passé, pas de bourrée is done as a passing movement and does not require a distinct fixing of the rise to demi-pointe with the foot sur le cou-de-pied.

Jeté Renversé. Jeté renversé ("overturned", from the French "renverser") is done en dehors and en dedans with a big jump, throwing the leg to 2nd position. Before beginning its study, it is necessary to master well renversé in the centre exercise and adagio.

It is customary to begin jeté renversé en dehors with the leg that is in 5th position back, and jeté renversé en dedans with the leg that is in front.

Jeté renversé en dehors. 2/4 time. Begin in 5th position with épaulement croisé, left leg front, arms in preparatory position. On the upbeat, demi-plié and jump, throwing the right leg to 2nd position at 90°; the arms open to 2nd position, palms down; the position of the body and head is en face. On the first quarter, having flown to the side in the direction of the right leg, come down in demi-plié on the right leg, taking the left to attitude croisée (the left leg is thrown out to 90° directly from the floor and bends to attitude croisée on landing); the left arm is in 3rd position, and the right in 2nd; the head is turned to the right. Between the first and second quarters, bring the left leg up to the supporting leg and step onto it on demi-pointe, raising the right foot to the conditional position sur le cou-de-pied devant; the body inclines backward; simultaneously make a half turn to the left away from the audience; at this time, the right arm is lowered and then raised to 1st position; the left arm remains in 3rd position; the head is turned across the right shoulder, with the eyes directed at point 1. Hold this inclination for an instant in the turn, and then step onto the right leg on demi-pointe (in place of the left), raising the left foot sur le cou-de-pied devant, and finish the turn of the body en dehors toward the mirror; simultaneously, lower the left arm, from above, to 1st position, and bring it together with the right; leave the head turned to the right as long as possible. On the second quarter, finish the movement in 5th position with épaulement croisé, the left leg in front; turn the head to the left; and open the arms slightly to 1st position at half height (the half-1st position).

RULES FOR THE EXECUTION OF JETÉ REN-VERSÉ EN DEHORS. On finishing the jump jeté to attitude croisée the exact position of épaulement croisé must be observed; in no case should the back be turned to the audience prematurely.

When going onto demi-pointe, the body should be held in the bend as long as possible, with the head turned toward the audience; only at the last moment should the renversé be completed with the turn of the body.

Despite the necessity for establishing both the first position of the body (the attitude croisée) and the second (the transfer onto demi-pointe, with the bend of the body backward), renversé must have a legato character.

At the end of the renversé, the body straightens without a jerk, smoothly, controlling the demi-plié in 5th position.

While observing the similarity of renversé in jumps and in adagio, it is necessary to clearly distinguish the difference, which comes in the initial moment of the renversé, that is, in adagio, the rise to demi-pointe in attitude croisée takes place on the supporting leg, but in jumps, this comes during the transfer onto the leg that is in back in attitude, that is, at the moment of the pas de bourrée with which the renversé ends. This rule applies also to jeté renversé en dedans.

Jeté renversé en dedans is done like jeté renversé en dehors, but the turn of the body and the concluding pas de bourrée will be done en dedans. Usually, after the jump in 2nd position, this renversé begins from the pose croisée devant; but there is also a more complicated variant, in which the jump finishes in the pose écartée devant. (For both variants, see Chapter XI, "Turning Movements Used in Adagio".)

Once mastered from 5th position, jeté renversé can be done with a preliminary glissade.

Jeté Entrelacé. Jeté entrelacé, "interlaced", is one of the basic, as well as one of the most difficult, pas of classical dance. The student who has really mastered such movements as jeté entrelacé, saut de basque, and grande cabriole, can be considered to have mastered the technique of classical ballet. These pas are perfected and become more complicated over a period of years, not only in school, but also during the dancer's career on the stage.

Jeté entrelacé is done in all directions: on a diagonal traveling upstage from one of the downstage corners, moving downstage from one of the upstage corners, in a straight line across the stage, in a straight line upstage from downstage, and also in a circle around the stage to the right or to the left. At first, it is learned with a wide step, and then with chassé (by women, it is also done with pas couru).

In the jump, the arms are usually in 3rd position; at the end, any one of a number of positions can be used: for example, 1st, 2nd, and 3rd arabesques, 3rd position, 1st and 3rd positions, 2nd and 3rd positions, etc.

Study Sequence

1. Jeté entrelacé with a step. 4/4 time. The movement travels on the diagonal from point 2 to point 6 of the classroom

plan. Stand on the right leg, facing point 2; the left leg is stretched effacé derrière, with the toe to the floor; the left arm is forward and the right is in 2nd position; the head is turned to the left; thus, the pose is 2nd arabesque. On the upbeat, demi-plié, and raise the left leg to 45°, the body inclining a little forward. On the first quarter, with a wide step, go, from the toe through the foot, onto the left leg in demi-plié, opening the arms to 2nd position; throw the right leg forward, through 1st position, to a height of 90° toward point 6; and push off from the floor with the left leg for the jump; at this moment, the arms provide force, going down from 2nd position, then quickly up through 1st to 3rd position; in the jump, the left leg also is thrown out, directed toward the right leg (the legs almost come together, as if they were interlaced); the body is strongly pulled upward and turns in the air. On the second quarter, finish the jump on the right leg in demi-plié; the left leg is in back at a height of 90°; and the head and arms are in the position 1st arabesque, facing point 2. On the third and fourth quarters, the pose is held. From here, the movement is repeated the necessary number of times.

RULES FOR THE EXECUTION OF JETÉ EN-TRELACÉ WITH A STEP. The throw of the leg forward to 90° must be quick, strong, and exactly in the forward direction; the buttocks muscles are taut and the thigh of the thrown-out leg is completely stretched.

Also, the leg is thrown out along the floor precisely through 1st position. Non-observance of these two rules leads to disconnectedness of the legs in the jump.

In finishing the jump, it is necessary to come down on the same spot from which the jump began, and not to allow a deviation of the body from the diagonal set in the beginning.

Strictly watch that, in the air, the legs pass near one another. If it is the right leg that is thrown forward, then, coming down, the left leg should be brought exactly backward and not be allowed to veer to the side (a fault encountered quite often). In order to do this, the thigh of the left leg and the left side must be held as if "pulled in", and the shoulders must be kept level.

Before the beginning of the jump, the body, which is inclined forward in demi-plié, remains on the supporting leg as long as possible, and only at the moment of the throw of the leg forward and the jump does it straighten, and then turns in the air. If the body turns beforehand, then, instead of an entrelacé, you get at first a turn, and then a jump over from one leg to the other. Finishing the jump, it is necessary to hold the torso well pulled up, and only at the last moment transfer its weight forward onto the supporting leg in demi-plié. In fact, in the beginning of the study of this jump, it is useful to finish jeté entrelacé on the second quarter with the arms in 3rd position, and only on the third and fourth quarters transfer the torso forward, lowering the arms to 1st arabesque.

The head, during the step backward (if the movement goes from point 2 to point 6), turns to point 2, and during the throw of the leg forward, is turned across the right shoulder; then, simultaneously with the turn of the body, it again turns to point 2.

The arms, coming down from 2nd position and going up to 3rd position in the jump, must be elastic, strong, and actively help the jump.

2. Jeté entrelacé with a step, moving in a straight line upstage. 2/4 time. Stand on the left leg, near point 1, the right leg stretched croisé derrière with the toe to the floor; the hands are in the arabesque position; the head and eyes are directed beyond the right arm; thus the pose is 3rd arabesque. On the upbeat, demi-plié on the left leg and raise the right to 45°; the body inclines a little forward toward the supporting leg; the arms, curving the hands, open to 2nd position; and the head turns toward the left shoulder. On the first quarter, with a wide step, go, from

the toe through the foot, onto the right leg in demi-plié and, pushing off for the jump, throw the left leg forward, through 1st position, to a height of 90° toward point 5; simultaneously with the passé through 1st position, the arms are lowered and then raised through 1st to 3rd position (providing force for the jump); and the body is pulled upward; in the jump, the right leg is thrown out toward the left leg and as if interlaces with it in the air; the body turns; the head remains turned toward the audience, and only at the last moment follows the turn of the body. On the second quarter, the jump finishes on the left leg in demi-plié, facing point 1, the right leg stretched backward at 90°; the arms remain in 3rd position; and the head is turned to the left, the body slightly turned with épaulement croisé.

For the repetition of the movement, the body inclines slightly forward on the supporting leg; the arms, from 3rd position, open to 2nd and then are lowered and provide force for the next jump.

3.   Jeté entrelacé with chassé. Final form. Pas chassé (see below) belongs to the category of jumping movements that have a strong push from the floor. However, in this instance, pas chassé is a passing movement, an approach to the big jump, and is done with a minimum push from the floor, just permitting the toes to stretch in the jump. Several teachers call this approach glissade, soutenu, etc., but we feel that the term chassé most fully expresses the essence of this short pas.

2/4 time. The movement proceeds on the diagonal from point 2 to point 6. Stand on the right leg, facing point 2; the left is stretched effacé derrière with the toe to the floor; the arms are in the position 2nd or 1st arabesque. On the upbeat, demi-plié and raise the left leg to 45°, the body inclining forward toward the supporting leg; then, with a wide step, go onto the left leg; and moving on the diagonal upstage, bring the right leg in the jump (the chassé) to 5th position front (on bringing the legs together in 5th position, one must be sure not to bring the right leg up to the left as if stepping over after it, which is sometimes encountered in a careless execution of this chassé); the body straightens and follows the movement of the legs, turning on the diagonal, with the right shoulder to point 2 and the left to point 6; the arms, from arabesque, are brought to 2nd position; the head and eyes are directed across the right shoulder, to point 2. Sliding out as far as possible (for this "running start" gives a good impetus for the jeté), and opening the hands, with the palms turned down, take a step onto the left leg; and, on the first quarter, throw the right leg forward to 90° toward point 6, and jump, throwing the left leg toward the right; the arms are lowered before the jump, then, quickly going up to 3rd position, provide force for the jump. Having turned the body in the air, on the second quarter, come down on the right leg in demi-plié in 1st arabesque, facing point 2. From here, the movement is repeated. (For a detailed description of the execution of jeté entrelacé, see the first example, "Jeté entrelacé with a step".)

Jeté entrelacé in a circle. This is done in the same way as jeté entrelacé with chassé, but in a circle around the room. If the movement goes to the right, it begins from point 8 and goes past points 1, 2, 3, 4, 5, etc., back to point 8; or, going around in a circle only to point 6, one can then turn, with the back to point 2, and continue the movement downstage on the diagonal toward point 2.

RULES FOR THE EXECUTION OF JETÉ EN-TRELACÉ IN A CIRCLE. During the running start, the chassé and step, the body, with level shoulders, is turned to face the outside part of the circle, that is, toward the walls of the room past which the movement goes; the arms are opened to 2nd position; the head and eyes are directed toward the left shoulder (if the movement goes to the right).

After each jeté entrelacé, the position of the whole body is in arabesque in a profile relative to the walls of the room.

After the jump, one must not slur over the pose arabesque; it is fixed with a pause.

Observing the squareness of the musical phrase, in a three-count waltz tempo, eight jetés entrelacés will be done in sixteen measures.

The turn for the execution of the jetés on the diagonal from point 6 to point 2 takes place after the fifth jeté entrelacé, during the running start and the sixth jeté. The diagonal finishes with the seventh and eighth jetés. Thus, during the execution of the last three jetés, the body is turned with the back to point 2.

Double jeté entrelacé. This most difficult virtuoso step can be executed only by especially gifted male dancers who have a strong technique.

It is done with a preliminary running start (chassé) and with a double turn in the air during the jump. It begins from point 2 and moves along the diagonal upstage to point 6. After the chassé, when pushing off from the floor for the jump, the right leg is thrown forward at 90° toward point 6; the left leg quickly comes together in the air with the right leg; the body leans back so much that the whole figure, from the head to the stretched feet, assumes a horizontal position in the air; the arms are raised to 3rd position, the right arm providing the force and control for the turn; the body, while preserving the horizontal position, does a double turn in the air, during which the shoulders must be forcibly turned, sharply taking the left shoulder back and move the right one forward; the back and thighs are pulled up to the utmost. The pause, after the jump, is taken on the right leg in demi-plié, facing point 2, in the pose 1st arabesque.

The rules for the execution of the chassé and the beginning of the jeté remain the same as for the simple jeté entrelacé.

Complicated double jeté entrelacé (a compound step). Stand facing point 8 on the right leg, the left stretched croisé derrière with the toe to the floor; the left arm is extended forward, the right arm to the side; thus the pose is 3rd arabesque. Demi-plié on the right leg, raising the left to 45°; and chassé on the diagonal upstage toward point 4, pulling up in the chassé to 5th position with the right leg in front; the right shoulder is turned toward point 8, the left toward point 4; the head is also turned toward point 8. Step onto the left leg, and throw the right leg forward to 90° toward point 4, as in a simple jeté entrelacé; the arms, gathering force from 2nd position, are quickly raised to 1st position; at the same time, the left leg is instantly thrown out toward the right leg, coming together with it in back in 5th position in the air; the body does a double turn in the air, during which, the left shoulder is forcibly taken back. Land on the right leg in demi-plié, facing point 2, and throw the stretched left leg out croisé devant to a height of 90°; at the same time, open the right arm from 1st position to 3rd, and the left arm from 1st to 2nd.

RULES FOR THE EXECUTION OF THE COMPLI-CATED DOUBLE JETÉ ENTRELACÉ. In learning this pas, it is necessary to carefully analyse the double turn in the air, although we see that pausing in the pose croisée devant facing point 2 breaks off, as it were, the second part of the double turn; in fact, only one and a half turns actually take place. To provide just the right force for one and a half turns is extremely difficult. If we take force for one turn, we risk not getting around again. Therefore, it is necessary to take force for a double turn and be able to "put on the brakes", as it were, at the last moment.

The body, from a horizontal position during the turn-and-a-half in the air, straightens in demi-plié in the pose croisée devant.

The arms, resilient and strong in 1st position, should not lose their resilience on opening to the pose croisée; they must, however, give stability to the finish of the step.

In the given example, the right arm provides the force for the turn. The head, which is turned to point 8, toward the audience, before the jump, is held straight during the turn-and-a-half in the air, and, in the final pose croisée, distinctly turns toward the left shoulder.

Jeté entrelacé battu (with a beat). This is done according to the rules for simple jeté entrelacé with a preliminary running start (chassé). If the movement goes on a diagonal from point 2 to point 6, and, in the big jump, the right leg is thrown forward (to point 6), then the left leg, coming to the right at a height of 90°, strikes the right leg in back, is transferred front and then back, and, after the turn of the body, is thrown backward to the pose arabesque.

To make the beat more complex, one may do a double transfer: front, back, front, back. As in all beats, these transfers are done with both legs completely stretched.

Grand Jeté-Pas de Chat. This big compound pas appeared on the stage comparatively recently (in the late forties) and only in the last few years has been included in the school programme for the study of classical dance. But jeté-pas de chat is used in many Soviet ballets: *Romeo and Juliet, Laurencia, The Fountain of Bakhchisarai,* and others.

In some variations, because it is considered more effective, jeté-pas de chat has now replaced grand pas de chat en arrière, although it has not completely ousted it, for both these movements are studied and used in dance.

Jeté-pas de chat can be done as a series of uninterrupted big jumps on a diagonal, or it may be combined with other jumps moving on a diagonal, in a straight line, or in a circle.

Jeté-pas de chat is not studied directly from 5th position; pas glissade or coupé always precedes it.

Grand jeté-pas de chat on a diagonal. Stand in 5th position with épaulement croisé, left leg front. The movement travels from point 6 to point 2 of the classroom plan. Do a short glissade without changing the legs, beginning with the right leg and moving forward on the diagonal; at the same time, slightly open and then lower the arms. For the jump, push off from demi-plié with both legs; at the moment of the jump, the right leg, with strongly stretched toes, is brought up, in an unturned-out position, with the toe to the knee of the left leg, and, without a pause, is thrown forward, completely stretched, to 90°; precisely at that instant, the left leg must be already stretched backward in the air at 90°; for it is the simultaneous opening of the legs in the air and their maximum arrest at a height of 90°, together with a strong movement forward beyond the toe of the right leg, that culminates this jump. The right arm opens through 1st to 3rd, and the left to 2nd position, in the form characteristic of arabesque, that is, allongé. The jump finishes in a demi-plié in which first the right leg is lowered to the floor, and then the left, with a barely noticeable delay, comes to 5th position front. This describes only the exact position of the legs on the floor; but there is no pause in 5th position: hardly does the left leg touch the floor when it immediately pushes off again, as if from a trampoline (a kind of coupé), for the next jeté-pas de chat.

RULES FOR THE EXECUTION OF JETÉ-PAS DE CHAT. The first glissade is done as if it were a running start for the first grand jeté-pas de chat; the following jetés are done with a short push from the floor (a coupé). This coupé must be so quick and assembled that the moment of contact with the floor is almost imperceptible to the eye. The dancer must seem to fly above the floor, rushing forward through the air, an effect which is achieved by the utmost opening of the legs, with taut muscles, and a maximum arrest of the legs in the air in a form resembling a split.

The momentum of these jetés is so great that their execution is successively intensified: that is, the second jeté is stronger than the first, the third is stronger than the second, etc.

The student's ability to hold the torso and the back is so developed by the time he begins to learn these jetés (in the 8th year), that, in teaching the jumps, it is necessary only to indicate the strong shift of the torso forward. An erect body, or one that is inclined backward, will cut short the distance traveled forward during the jump.

In the execution of several jetés-pas de chat in succession, the arms are not lowered but remain in the position they took in the first jump, and do only a barely noticeable wavelike movement in the air.

Grand Jeté en Tournant. These jetés are done in the poses attitude croisée, attitude effacée, and 3rd and 1st arabesques. As with all big jetés, they may be done in a direction croisée devant or effacée devant, on a diagonal, or in a circle.

The auxiliary approaches to the jump are sissonne tombée-coupée, sissonne-coupée, or coupé.

Grand jeté en tournant in attitude croisée with sissonne tombée-coupée. 2/4 time. Begin in 5th position with épaulement croisé, right leg front, arms in preparatory position.

On the upbeat, demi-plié and sissonne tombée forward to 4th position croisée, finishing on the first quarter (for a detailed description of sissonne tombée see the section "Sissonne"); the centre of the body's weight is transferred forward onto the right leg in demi-plié; the left leg, stretched back, has the whole foot on the floor; the right arm is in 1st position, and the left is in 2nd; the head turns to the right. Between the first and second quarters, coupé dessous and grand jeté en tournant, finishing on the second quarter.

Doing the coupé, the left leg is brought quickly in back of the right, to the position sur le cou-de-pied derrière, and it is then placed down in demi-plié as if "pushing away", displacing the right leg, which, half-bent, comes off the floor forward to a height of 45°; simultaneously, the body turns effacé to point 2, the arms elastically come together in 1st position, and the head turns to the left. In the jump (the jeté), the right leg, stretching, is thrown forward to a height of 90° and, after describing a big arc to the right in the air, comes down in demi-plié; the left arm opens to 3rd, and the right to 2nd position, the head is turned to the right. At the end, the pose attitude croisée is held for a moment.

Then, on the first quarter of the second measure, assemblé, bringing the legs together in 5th position in the air and landing in demi-plié, and lower the arms to preparatory position. On the second quarter, stretch the knees. The movement is repeated several times.

Later on, royale, entrechat-quatre, entrechat-six, or a series of other jumps can be done after the assemblé, followed by a repetition of jeté en tournant with the right or the left leg.

RULES FOR THE EXECUTION OF GRAND JETÉ EN TOURNANT TO ATTITUDE CROISÉE WITH SISSONNE TOM-BÉE-COUPÉE. At the end of the sissonne tombée, the body must be inclined forward over the supporting right leg. In the coupé, when transferring the body's weight onto the left leg, the body is inclined slightly back in the position effacée. This complicated transfer of the body's weight from one leg to the other, the quick inclination of the body forward and then to the left, with a strong pulling in of the back and buttocks muscles, gives the prerequisite necessary for raising the body upward in the jump and turning it in the air. The push from the floor (the coupé) is the fundamental moment for the jump.

The jeté en tournant includes: a) motion upward, b) a turn in the air, and c) flight forward. These three elements must be present in the jump to an equal degree (a mistake frequently made in its elementary execution is jumping with a turn in the air, but without any movement forward).

The movements of the arms and head, inseparably linked with the movement of the body, give substantial aid in the correct execution of the step. The arms, which are elastically brought together in 1st position in the coupé, strongly open to 3rd and 2nd positions in the jeté; and, precisely at the moment the body turns with the left shoulder forward, it is necessary to move the left arm forward from 3rd position, for this helps not only the turn of the body, but also its movement forward. The head, which is turned to the left in the coupé, in the jeté quickly turns to the right, which also assists the turn to the right.

Finishing the jeté in attitude croisée, the body should be held in demi-plié in the correct position. The force generated by the arms and turn of the head and the body to the right can lead to an undesirable inclination of the body to the right at the end of the jump, and even to the loss of equilibrium. To avoid this and hold the body, it is necessary, on coming down in demi-plié, to pull up strongly on the left side and the left thigh.

Grand jeté en tournant to attitude effacée, with sissonne tombée-coupée. Begin in 5th position with épaulement croisé, the right leg in front, the arms in preparatory position. Demi-plié and sissonne tombée forward to 4th position effacée, in the direction of point 2; the weight is transferred onto the right leg in demi-plié, and the body inclines forward; the shoulders are level; the right arm is in 1st position, and the left is in 2nd; and the head and eyes are directed over the right arm. The left leg does a short coupé dessous, coming down in plié behind the right foot, and the right leg comes off the floor in a half-bent position forward at 45°; the body, remaining in the position effacée, leans back and to the left; the arms come together in 1st position; and the head turns to the left. In the jump (the jeté en tournant), the right leg is thrown forward at 90°; the left arm opens to 3rd, and the right to 2nd position; the head turns to the right. Turn to the right, describing a complete circle in the air; and, having flown forward in the direction of point 2, finish on the right leg in attitude effacée in demi-plié.

The rules for its execution, and the distribution of the musical counts, are the same as in grand jeté en tournant to attitude croisée. But, in this case, the turn in the air is somewhat greater than in the jump to attitude croisée.

Grand jeté en tournant to attitude croisée with sissonne-coupée. 4/4 time. Stand on the right leg, near point 1; the left leg is stretched croisé derrière with the toe to the floor; the left arm is extended forward, and the right to the side; the hands are in arabesque position (3rd arabesque), and the eyes are directed over the left arm.

On the upbeat, demi-plié and a small jump (the stretched left leg comes slightly off the floor); the body inclines forward; the left arm is curved in 1st and the right in 2nd position; the head turns to the right. (In form, this jump should be regarded as belonging to the sissonne category of jumps.) On the first quarter, the demi-plié deepens; with a wide step go through the foot onto the left leg in demi-plié; the head remains turned to the right; the arms, with a free movement, open to 2nd position; the left shoulder is slightly brought back, the body remaining in a foreshortened position croisée. Between the first and second quarters, coupé dessous: the right leg is placed behind the left in plié and gives a push from the floor for the jump; the arms, lowering, are quickly brought to 1st position. Then, having thrown the left leg out forward to a height of 90°, do the jump (jeté en tournant); the right arm opens to 3rd and the left to 2nd position; the body turns to the left with the right shoulder forward; and the head is to the left. On the second quarter, come down on the left leg in demi-plié in attitude croisée. On the third quarter, assemblé, bringing the legs together in 5th position in the air, the left leg in front, and landing in demi-plié. On the fourth quarter, one can take a step forward with the right leg to the initial position, the left leg croisé derrière, and repeat the movement, or one can step onto the left leg and do the jeté with the other leg. Jeté en tournant is also done in the same manner to 3rd arabesque. (For the rules of execution, see the example of grand jeté en tournant to attitude croisée with sissonne tombée-coupée.)

Grand jeté en tournant in a circle (autour de la salle). These jetés, done to attitude effacée, are often used at the end of variations, and even more frequently in codas.

Before studying the execution of grands jetés en tournant in a circle, it is recommended that they be practised on a diagonal going downstage from an upstage corner, using the same auxiliary step to be used in their execution around the room.

Studying the jetés with a turn to the right, stand on the diagonal from point 6 to point 2. Do the first jeté with a sissonne tombée-coupée effacée as described in the section on grand jeté en tournant to attitude effacée. After finishing on the right leg in attitude effacée, do a short coupé with the left leg, placing it behind the right, and, without delay, repeat the jeté en tournant. In this coupé, the centre of the body's weight is quickly transferred onto the left leg, as in the execution of the coupé that follows the sissonne tombée. The arms, opening from attitude through 2nd position, are quickly brought down to 1st position in the coupé and, with an elastic movement, help the jump; they then open in the air to the pose. The second jeté is finished with an assemblé.

To make the movement more complicated, do the first jeté with sissonne tombée-coupée and then two more with coupé only. Gradually increase the number of jetés until it is possible to execute a series of eight in a row. Only after having done this can one go on to their execution in a circle.

RULES FOR THE EXECUTION OF GRAND JETÉ EN TOURNANT. Each coupé must be as short as possible; and, after a strong push from the floor, one must emphasise the jeté by holding it (with ballon) in the air. Assembled leg and back muscles, mastery of the arms and the turns of the head are extremely important for these jetés.

It is necessary to consider the body at the moment of the turn in the air, and its landing in attitude effacée. In the execution of a large number of jetés with coupé in succession, the body involuntarily begins to incline to the right (if the jetés are done turning to the right). It often happens that one observes a dancer, doing jetés en tournant in a circle, soaring in the air with an inclination of the whole figure toward the centre of the room at an angle of 80° or 90°, thus bringing his execution close to being an intricate, but not at all artistic, acrobatic feat. Even though in some cases such an execution on stage is an individual feature of the dancer, it cannot be a general rule or model for the study of this pas. In order to avoid such an undesirable inclination of the body, it is necessary first of all to hold correctly the leg that is bent in attitude. The slightest taking of the upper part of the leg to the side (a lack of discipline of the thigh) immediately affects the position of the body. Traveling to the right, the left arm also must not be taken to the side and back. A pulled-in hip and side of the left leg, and a slight pulling upward of the whole right side of the body, will give these jetés their proper form.

The execution of these jetés in a circle traveling to the right begins from point 8; to the left, they start from point 2.

Their character is expressive and dynamic. They are encountered, for example, in the ballets *Nutcracker* (coda), *Laurencia* (variation, 3rd act), and *Don Quixote* (last act, coda).

Example of a combination of grands jetés en tournant. Four measures of 4/4. Begin in 5th position, right leg front.

First measure. Sissonne-tombée forward to 4th position croisée, coupé dessous, and grand jeté en tournant to attitude croisée. Finish with assemblé derrière and entrechat-six.

Second measure. Repeat the same thing with the left leg.

Third measure. With the right leg, toward point 2, sissonne-tombée to 4th position effacée, coupé dessous, and grand jeté en tournant to attitude effacée, coupé dessous, and a second jeté en tournant to attitude effacée. Finish with an essemblé to 5th position, left leg front.

Fourth measure. With the left leg and moving in a straight line to the left, sissonne-tombée, pas de bourrée, finishing in 5th position, right leg front. Relevé to demi-pointe in 5th position croisé, demi-plié, and two tours en l'air to the right. At the end, the left leg will be in front.

Jeté en Tournant par Terre. The very name jeté par terre indicates that this movement does not belong to the category of big aerial jumps. A jump rushing out horizontally, with the legs split above the floor, a dynamic striving forward with the aim of covering great distances—these are the characteristic features of jeté par terre.

This jeté consists of two parts: a jump that slides along the floor without taking off from it, and a low jump in the air en tournant.

Done in a straight line, on a diagonal, or in a circle to the right or to the left, jeté par terre is often encountered at the end of variations and in codas.

Study Sequence

1. 2/4 time. The movement proceeds on a diagonal from point 6 to point 2. Begin in 5th position, with épaulement effacé, right leg front, arms in preparatory position. On the upbeat, demi-plié and, pushing off from the floor with the left leg, throw the right leg forward with a wide sliding movement, without taking off from the floor, toward point 2. On the first quarter, come down on the right leg in plié; the left leg is raised in back not higher than 10° or 15°; the body is sharply inclined forward, as if spread out low above the floor; the right arm, passing through 1st position, is extended forward, and the left arm is to the side (thus, the

pose is 1st arabesque); the eyes follow the right hand. Between the first and second quarters, a jump in the air is done from the position arabesque, tearing away from the floor and finishing on the second quarter; for this, bring the left leg up to the right in back, so that the legs come together in 5th position in the jump. This jump is done with a complete turn in the air and finishes on the left leg in demi-plié, the right foot, with stretched toes, sur le cou-de-pied devant. In the jump, the body takes on a vertical position and, at the end of the turn, is facing point 2 in the position effacée; the arms, helping the turn of the body, are quickly taken down to a low 1st position; the head, during the first part of the turn in the air, is turned across the left shoulder to point 2; at the end of the turn it faces point 2; and, at the final moment in demi-plié, it is turned to the left. The movement is done several times in succession, the sliding jump along the floor being done with the right leg from the position sur le cou-de-pied devant.

2.   Final form. 2/4 time. This is done in the same way as the preceding example, but each jeté par terre is executed in one quarter; and the sliding jump begins without preliminary épaulement effacé, directly from épaulement croisé. The sliding jump begins on the upbeat and finishes on the first quarter; the jump in the air with a turn is done between the first and second quarters, and the next jeté is begun immediately. Thus, the accent of the movement falls on the first half of the jeté par terre en tournant on the *one*. It is essential to emphasise this. If the movement is done to a phrase of four measures of 2/4, then eight jetés are executed. In this case, it is permitted to finish in the pose arabesque allongée on the eighth jeté, eliminating the turn in the air. One can also finish such a musical phrase, or one twice the length, after the seventh or fifteenth jeté, transferring the centre of the body's weight to any pose on

the right leg (if one is traveling to the right) after the jump with the turn in the air.

Jetés par terre are often finished with swift tours chaînés, and they are also frequently combined with grands jetés en tournant.

RULES FOR THE EXECUTION OF JETÉ PAR TERRE EN TOURNANT. In this jeté, it is especially necessary to hold the muscles of the back at the moment when the weight is transferred onto the supporting leg in the sliding jump and the whole body (in the pose arabesque allongée) takes on a horizontal position. Particularly at that time, the small of the back and the abdominal muscles must be tightly pulled up.

The shoulders must be completely level. The left shoulder, if the sliding jeté is done onto the right leg, or the right shoulder, if the jeté is done onto the left leg, should not be permitted to lag behind.

During the second jump in the air, the body actively comes erect and turns with pulled-up thighs in a perfectly vertical position, the feet held tightly together.

The arms and head energetically help the turn in the air. If the turn is done to the right, and the left arm provides force, then, at the end of the turn, it is necessary to take the right shoulder back; if the turn is done to the left (the right arm providing the force), the left shoulder is taken back.

Jeté par Terre Elancé. This jeté is a variation of the jeté par terre just described. It is much easier to study after the rules for the execution of jeté par terre have been mastered. It also consists of two elements: a jeté élancé and a coupé dessous en tournant. It is done in all directions, as well as in a circle.

The musical time and the accent of the movement are analogous to those of jeté par terre. Beginning from 5th position, with the right leg in front, and moving on the diagonal from point 6 to point 2, do a low, light jeté in 1st arabesque, at first sliding the toe along the floor and, having flown forward through the air, pause for a moment in plié; the body is spread out above the floor, the left leg is raised not higher than 45°. Then, closing the arms to preparatory position and straightening and turning the body to the right, place the left leg in plié behind the right (a coupé dessous en tournant); the right foot takes the position sur le cou-de-pied devant. The body turns at the moment of the coupé and finishes in épaulement effacé toward point 2. From here, the next jeté is done immediately. These jetés also can be done to a small attitude effacée.

RULES FOR THE EXECUTION OF JETÉ PAR TERRE ÉLANCÉ. The jump in the air begins on the upbeat, and the accent, on the musical quarter, always falls on the plié. The coupé en tournant and the beginning of the next jeté take place on the eighth between two quarters.

The coupé, which gives the push off the floor and which is done during the turn, must have a quick and natural character, emphasising the execution of the jeté élancé.

The arms actively help the turn and then elastically come down together and, passing through 1st position, open to the pose arabesque or attitude in the jeté.

During the coupé the head and eyes are directed across the left shoulder (if the movement is done with the right leg toward point 2, or in a circle to the right), or across the right shoulder in the execution to the left.

In the execution of jeté élancé, it is necessary each time to throw the leg in a precise direction on a diagonal, in a straight line, or in a circle.

Sissonne

Sissonnes are jumps from two legs to one (with the exception of sissonne fermée, sissonne tombée, and sissonne fondue, in which the step finishes on two legs), and can be divided into two categories, petite and grande. To the category of petites sissonnes belong sissonne simple, sissonne ouverte at 45°, sissonne fermée, and sissonne tombée at 45°; to the category of grandes sissonnes belong sissonne ouverte at 90°, sissonne fondue, sissonne tombée at 90°, sissonne renversée, and sissonne soubresaut. All of these sissonnes can be done en tournant and battue (with a beat).

The study of sissonne begins in the first year with sissonne simple, at first at the barre (for several lessons), then in the centre of the room.

Sissonne Simple

Study Sequence

1. 4/4 time. Begin in 5th position en face with the right leg in front and the arms in preparatory position. On the first quarter, demi-plié. Between the first and second quarters, push off from the floor with the heels and jump, bringing the legs together, one ankle in front of the other, with the knees and toes strongly stretched. On the second quarter, come down in demi-plié on the left leg, bending the right leg to the conditional position sur le cou-de-pied devant. On the third quarter, the right leg is lowered to join the left in 5th position in demi-plié. On the fourth quarter, the knees straighten. The movement is repeated at least four times, then it is done with the other leg, after which it is practised in the reverse direction. To do the movement in reverse, bend the leg that was in 5th position back to the position sur le cou-de-pied derrière on coming down in demi-plié after the jump.

2. 4/4 time. Begin in 5th position with épaulement croisé, right leg front. On the first quarter, demi-plié. Between the first and second quarters, jump. On the second quarter, come down in demi-plié on the left leg, bending the right sur le cou-de-pied devant. At the end of the jump, the right

arm is in 1st position, the left in 2nd (or, at the discretion of the teacher, the left arm can be in 1st position and the right arm in 2nd); the head is turned to the right. On the third quarter, after sliding the toe of the right leg forward along the floor, assemblé in place, bringing the legs to 5th position in the air before landing in demi-plié; on landing, the arms are lowered to preparatory position. On the fourth quarter, straighten the knees. The same thing is done with the other leg, then with the right and with the left leg back.

3. Final form. 2/4 time. On the upbeat, demi-plié and jump, finishing on the first quarter in demi-plié. Between the first and second quarters, assemblé, finishing in demi-plié on the second quarter. From here, the movement is repeated the necessary number of times.

RULES FOR THE EXECUTION OF SISSONNE SIMPLE. The demi-plié before the jump of the sissonne must be done with taut leg muscles. The knees are turned out and directly in alignment with the toes. The heels press on the floor and provide the push for the jump. The body is erect, with pulled-up back and buttocks muscles.

The demi-plié after the jump is elastic, resembling the demi-plié in fondu. One must come down into the plié from the jump through the foot, from the stretched toe onto the heel, maintaining an erect and pulled-up body.

Pausing in demi-plié on one leg (the other leg bent sur le cou-de-pied), both legs must be kept equally turned-out, with the knees held back.

The arms are raised in the jump to a low 1st position and, at the end of the jump, take on the given pose.

In the concluding assemblé from the position sur le cou-de-pied, both legs must be brought together in 5h position in the air before coming down in demi-plié.

Sissonne Ouverte. Sissonne ouverte (an open sissonne) is a jump equally off of both feet, at the end of which one of the legs opens at 45° or 90° to a small or big pose.

Petites sissonnes ouvertes are done with a jump in place and en tournant; grandes sissonnes ouvertes are done with a jump in place or traveling in any direction, with half tours, with a complete tour (en tournant), and with beats (battu). Its study begins with the simplest form: sissonne ouverte to 2nd position with the toe to the floor.

Study Sequence

1. 4/4 time. Begin in 5th position en face, with the right leg in front. On the first quarter, demi-plié. Between the first and second quarters, jump. On the second quarter, come down in demi-plié on the left leg; the right foot, passing through the conditional position sur le cou-de-pied devant, opens to 2nd position with the toe to the floor. Between the second and third quarters, pushing off with the heel of the left foot and slightly raising the right leg from the floor, assemblé, bringing the legs together in the air in 5th position with the right leg in back. On the third quarter, come down in 5th position in demi-plié, right leg back. On the fourth quarter, straighten the knees.

   Repeat the movement with the other leg. To do the movement in the reverse direction, open the leg that is in 5th position back by passing the foot through the position sur le cou-de-pied derrière; finishing with an assemblé, the leg from 2nd position is brought to 5th position front.

Sissonne ouverte forward (en avant) and then backward (en arrière) are studied in exactly the same way. After this, épaulement and movements of the arms are introduced. Before beginning the sissonne ouverte, stand in 5th position with épaulement croisé. On the upbeat, open the arms slightly to the side and, having brought them together in preparatory position in demi-plié, raise them halfway to a half-1st position in the jump. At the end of the jump, the arms open to a half-2nd position (demi-seconde); and in the assemblé, they are lowered to preparatory position. Doing sissonne ouverte to the side, opening the leg through the conditional position sur le cou-de-pied devant, the head turns toward the supporting leg at the end. In the reverse direction, the head turns toward the open leg. In the execution forward and backward, the head is en face.

Sissonne ouverte at 45°. 4/4 time. Begin in 5th position with épaulement croisé, right leg front. On the upbeat, open the arms slightly to the side. On the first quarter, demi-plié, bringing the arms together in preparatory position. Between the first and second quarters, jump, raising the arms to a half-1st position. On the second quarter, come down in demi-plié on the left leg; the right leg, passing through the conditional position sur le cou-de-pied devant, opens without a pause to the side at 45°; the arms, at the same time, open to a half-2nd position; and the head turns to the left. Between the second and third quarters, firmly pushing off from the floor with the left heel, assemblé, bringing the legs together to 5th position in the air with the right leg in back, and close the arms to preparatory position. On the third quarter, come down in demi-plié, right leg back, the head turned to the left. On the fourth quarter, straighten the knees.

Sissonne ouverte at 45° forward, backward, and then to the small poses croisée, effacée, and écartée devant and derrière, is studied in exactly the same way.

Sissonne ouverte at 45° to the small pose croisée devant. Final form. 2/4 time. Begin in 5th position with épaulement croisé, right leg front. On the upbeat, open the arms slightly, then demi-plié and jump. On the first quarter, finish in demi-plié on the left leg; the right leg, passing through the conditional position sur le cou-de-pied devant, opens forward croisé at 45°; the right arm is in 1st position and the left is in 2nd; the head is turned to the right (or, at the discretion of the teacher, the left arm can be in 1st position and the right in 2nd). Between the first and second quarters, assemblé, bringing the legs together in the air. On the second quarter, finish in 5th position in demi-plié, lowering the arms to preparatory position. From here, the movement is repeated.

RULES FOR THE EXECUTION OF SISSONNE OUVERTE AT 45°. In addition to the general rules set forth in the preceding sections on jumps, it is typical of all kinds of sissonne ouverte at 45° to pause after the jump in demi-plié on one leg with the other leg stretched in the air.

A basic mistake is to open the working leg after the supporting leg has already come down in demi-plié, whereas, for correct execution, the working leg should already be stretched in the given direction at the moment of the return to the floor in plié.

The opening of the leg must take place through the position sur le cou-de-pied, but without pausing for a moment in that position.

In the final assemblé, the leg that is open to 45° must be brought up to the supporting leg in the air, before coming down in demi-plié in 5th position. It would be a mistake to bring the supporting leg up to the leg that is open at 45°, for this would entail a displacement of the body; and the assemblé must finish in the place where it began.

In studying sissonne ouverte, one must not neglect the assemblé, or regard it as something of minor importance. In other words, the second jump (the assemblé) must not be weaker than the first (the sissonne ouverte), since this type of final assemblé beneficially affects the development of the student's jump.

Example of a combination of sissonnes ouvertes at 45°. Four measures of 4/4.

First measure. Begin in 5th position croisé, with the right leg in front. On the first quarter, with the right leg, do sissonne ouverte croisée forward. On the second, assemblé. On the third quarter, with the right leg, sissonne ouverte effacée forward. On the fourth, assemblé, finishing in 5th position with the right leg in back.

Second measure. On the first quarter, with the left leg, sissonne ouverte to 2nd position. On the second, temps levé. On the third quarter, pas de bourrée dessous en tournant. On the fourth, royale.

Third measure. On the first quarter, with the left leg, sissonne ouverte croisée backward. On the second, assemblé. On the third quarter, with the left leg, sissonne ouverte effacée backward. On the fourth, assemblé, finishing in 5th position, with the left leg in front.

Fourth measure. On the first quarter, with the right leg, sissonne ouverte to 2nd position. On the second, temps levé. On the third quarter, pas de bourrée dessus en tournant. On the fourth, entrechat-quatre. The combination is then repeated, beginning with the other leg.

Sissonne Ouverte at 45° en Tournant. This is done with a tour in the air en dehors to the small poses croisée devant, effacée devant, and ecartée derrière; or with a tour en dedans to the poses croisée derrière, effacée derrière, and écartée devant. It is done either en dehors or en dedans, to 2nd position.

Elementary study with a tour en dehors. 4/4 time. Begin in 5th. position with épaulement croisé, right leg front. On the first quarter, demi-plié; the right arm is raised to 1st position, the left to 2nd; the head turns en face to point 8 (the préparation). Between the first and second quarters, jump with a tour to the right (en dehors). At the moment of the push from the floor, the left arm joins with the right in 1st position to provide force for the tour; the head, at the beginning of the tour, is turned across the left shoulder to point 8 and, at the end, turns toward the mirror. On the second quarter, come down on the left leg in demi-plié, having opened the right leg through the conditional position sur le cou-de-pied devant to 2nd position at 45° en face; the arms open to a half-2nd position; and the head is turned to the left. On the third quarter, assemblé, bringing the legs together in 5th position (right leg back), before coming down in demi-plié with épaulement croisé. On the fourth quarter, straighten the knees. In doing a sissonne ouverte en tournant en dedans to the right, open the left leg to 2nd position at the end, the foot passing through the position sur le cou-de-pied derrière.

Sissonne ouverte en tournant to all the small poses is studied in exactly the same way.

Sissonne ouverte en tournant at 45° to the pose effacée devant. Final form. 2/4 time. Begin in 5th position with épaulement croisé, right leg front. On the upbeat, demi-plié, turning the head en face to point 8 of the classroom plan and raising the right arm to 1st and the left to 2nd position (the préparation); jump upward with a tour to the right (en dehors), bringing the arms together in 1st position. On the first quarter, come down on the left leg in demi-plié, having opened the right leg through the conditional position sur le cou-de-pied devant, effacé forward at 45°. The body thus is in the small pose effacée devant to point 2; the shoulders are level; the right arm is in 2nd position and the left in 1st; and the head is turned to the left and inclined somewhat back. Between the first and second quarters, assemblé, finishing on the second quarter in 5th position in demi-plié, with the right leg in back; the arms are lowered to preparatory position; the head remains turned to the left but comes erect, the épaulement is croisé.

RULES FOR THE EXECUTION OF SISSONNE OUVERTE AT 45° EN TOURNANT. This jump is done with a complete tour in the air, bringing the legs together in 5th position, one ankle in front of the other; and only at the last moment, in the lowering from the jump into demi-plié, does one leg pass through the position sur le cou-de-pied (without a pause) and open in the air in the given direction.

The jump must begin facing the point toward which the preliminary demi-plié is done, and only in the jump is the tour executed. It would be a mistake to turn the body directly from the demi-plié without first having reached the maximum height of the jump—rushing, as it were, to do the tour.

The préparation must be well assembled: before doing the tour to the right, the right shoulder must not be brought forward, since it is precisely this one that is taken back in the air, and it is the left shoulder that goes forward. Pulled-up thighs, an erect back, a turn of the head and shoulders, force provided by the left arm—all are indispensable for the completely co-ordinated tour of the body in the air.

Grande Sissonne Ouverte at 90°. It is recommended that sissonne ouverte at 90°, like the small sissonnes ouvertes, be studied first to the side. This allows the student more easily to control the turn-out of the legs and the correctness of the execution.

Study Sequence

1. 4/4 time. Begin in 5th position with épaulement croisé, right leg front. On the upbeat, open the arms slightly to the side. On the first quarter, demi-plié a little more deeply than usual (for such a demi-plié prepares the muscles of the legs and the heel for a strong push into the air) and lower the arms to preparatory position; the head is en face, the eyes being directed at the hands. Between the first and second quarters, having pushed off strongly from the floor with the heels, jump very high; the right foot, without pausing, slides up the leg, passing through the conditional position sur le cou-de-pied devant with stretched toes, to

the knee of the tautly stretched left leg; the arms are raised to 1st position. On the second quarter, the left leg comes down in demi-plié; the right leg simultaneously opens to 2nd position at 90°—in other words, by means of a développé; the arms also open to 2nd position; and the head is en face. Between the second and third quarters, assemblé, bringing the right leg to the left in the air in 5th position in back; and lower the arms. On the third quarter, demi-plié in 5th position with épaulement croisé, right leg back; the head turns to the left. On the fourth quarter, straighten the knees.

The movement continues with the other leg, and then is done in the reverse direction, with the leg that is in 5th position back opening to the side at 90°. In exactly the same way, in 4/4 sissonne ouverte at 90° is studied forward and backward and, after that, to all the big poses.

The following order for the study of grande sissonne ouverte to the poses is recommended:

1) attitude croisée and the pose croisée devant;

2) 3rd arabesque;

3) attitude effacée, 1st and 2nd arabesques, and the pose effacée devant;

4) the poses écartée derrière and écartée devant, and 4th arabesque.

Grande sissonne ouverte at 90°. Final form. In their final form, all sissonnes ouvertes at 90° are done in the following manner: on the upbeat, demi-plié and jump; on the first quarter, finish the jump in the pose with demi-plié; on the second quarter, conclude with an assemblé to a full demi-plié.

Example of the study of grande sissonne ouverte to 1st arabesque. 2/4 time. Begin in 5th position with épaulement croisé, right leg front.

On the upbeat, open the arms slightly to the side and then, returning them to preparatory position, demi-plié; the body, with a pulled-up back, inclines to the left; the head turns to the left, and the eyes are directed at the hands. Then, pushing off from the floor with the heels, do a big jump directly upward; turn the body in the air to point 3, with the left shoulder well forward; open the arms through 1st position to 1st arabesque; and throw the left leg out backward at 90° by means of a battement. On the first quarter, come down in demi-plié on the right leg in 1st arabesque, facing point 3; the shoulders are level; the back and the thigh of the left leg must be well pulled up. Between the first and second quarters, assemblé, bringing the left leg in back of the right in 5th position in the air and lowering the arms. On the second quarter, demi-plié in 5th position with épaulement croisé, right leg front. The movement is then repeated with the same leg. For the repetition of the movement with the other leg, the assemblé finishes in 5th position with the left leg in front.

Sissonne ouverte to 1st arabesque can also be finished on the diagonal: with the right leg, the body will be directed to point 2; and, with the left, it will be directed to point 8.

RULES FOR THE EXECUTION OF GRANDE SISSONNE OUVERTE AT 90°. In petite sissonne ouverte, the arms only co-ordinate the movement, but in sissonne ouverte at 90°, they actively aid the jump. On the upbeat, the arms open slightly, then are lowered with the demi-plié, and, with an elastic movement, they are raised to 1st position, in order to provide force at the moment of the jump, when they immediately open to the given pose.

All grandes sissonnes ouvertes to the big poses can be done either with a développé or by opening the stretched leg to 90° with a grand battement. However, when the jump is done to the big poses derrière, the second method is used most of the time; but to the poses devant, either may be used.

The concluding assemblé must correspond to the sissonne, insofar as the strength of the jump is concerned.

Grande sissonne ouverte at 90° traveling (with a flying start). The study sequence is the same as for grande sissonne ouverte with a jump directly upward; that is, in the beginning the movement should be studied broken down in 4/4; only afterward are the demi-plié and the jump executed on the upbeat, as in the preceding example.

All sissonnes to the poses derrière are done traveling forward; and all sissonnes to the poses devant are done traveling backward. Grandes sissonnes traveling to the side are rarely done. In fact, it is possible to cite only one instance where they occur: the male variation of the old pas de trois from the ballet *Paquita* includes grande sissonne to 2nd position, flying off to the side and traveling in a circle.

As in all big jumps done with a flying start, the initial take-off for the jump will be upward. After reaching the highest point of the jump (in attitude or arabesque), one must throw the leg out forward with a strong movement of the thigh and, transferring the body forward, move in the air in the direction croisée or on a diagonal before coming down through the foot, from the toe to the heel, in demi-plié; then, having done an assemblé, the movement finishes in 5th position in demi-plié.

Doing grande sissonne ouverte traveling backward (to the poses croisée or effacée devant), it is necessary, after having pushed off with the heels from demi-plié for the jump, to immediately transfer the body back. Otherwise it is not possible to move backward.

Example of a combination with grande sissonne ouverte traveling. Four measures. 4/4 time. Begin in 5th position with the right leg in front.

First measure. On the first quarter, with the right leg, grande sissonne ouverte to attitude croisée; on the second, assemblé; on the third and fourth quarters, grand échappé en tournant with a half turn to the right, ending with the left leg in front.

Second measure. On the first quarter, with the left leg,

grande sissonne ouverte to attitude croisée (flying forward in a direction between points 5 and 6); on the second, assemblé; on the third and fourth quarters, grand échappé en tournant with a half turn to the left (toward the mirror), ending with the right leg in front.

Third measure. On the first quarter, with the right leg, do a grande sissonne ouverte to attitude effacée, traveling in the direction of point 2; on the second quarter, assemblé, finishing in 5th position, with the left leg in front; on the third quarter, with the left leg, do a grande sissonne ouverte to attitude effacée, flying forward in the direction of point 8; on the fourth, assemblé, finishing in 5th position with the right leg in front.

Fourth measure. On the first quarter, with the right leg, do a grande sissonne ouverte écartée derrière, flying forward on the diagonal from point 4 to point 8; on the second, assemblé, finishing in 5th position with the right leg in back; on the third quarter, with the left leg, do a grande sissonne ouverte effacée devant, flying backward on a diagonal in the direction of point 4; on the fourth, finish with an assemblé to 5th position with the left leg in back.

The combination is repeated with the other leg, then is done in the reverse direction. For the reversal, begin in 5th position with the right leg in front. Grande sissonne ouverte croisée devant, flying backward, and assemblé; grand échappé en tournant with a half tour to the right; grande sissonne ouverte croisée devant, flying backward, and assemblé; grand échappé en tournant with a half tour to the left, toward the mirror; grande sissonne ouverte, with the right leg, effacée devant, flying backward on a diagonal to point 6, and assemblé, right leg back; grande sissonne ouverte, with the left leg, effacée devant, flying backward on a diagonal to point 4, and assemblé, left leg back; grande sissonne ouverte, with the left leg, écartée devant, flying backward on a diagonal to point 4, and assemblé, left leg front; grande sissonne ouverte, with the left leg, to attitude effacée, flying toward point 8, and assemblé, right leg front.

Repeat this with the other leg.

Grande Sissonne Ouverte with a Half Tour. This is done with tours en dedans to the poses attitude croisée and effacée, to 1st, 3rd, and 4th arabesques, and to the pose écartée devant. With tours en dehors, it is done to the poses croisée and effacée devant and écartée derrière.

Grande sissonne ouverte with a half tour en dedans to attitude croisée. 4/4 time. Begin in 5th position, right leg front. On the upbeat, open the arms slightly to the side and, closing them to preparatory position, demi-plié; the head inclines slightly to the left; and the eyes are directed at the hands. Then do a jump to attitude croisée, first going upward and then, making a half tour to the right, move forward between points 4 and 5 of the classroom plan. On the first quarter, finish the jump in demi-plié on the right leg. On the second quarter, assemblé. On the third and fourth quarters, repeat the grande sissonne ouverte to attitude croisée with a half tour to the right toward the mirror, and finish with assemblé.

RULES FOR THE EXECUTION OF GRANDE SIS-SONNE OUVERTE WITH A HALF TOUR. Jumping upward, as in all sissonnes, it is necessary to travel forward at the moment of the turn in the air. In the instance cited, open the right leg forward and travel in a direction between points 4 and 5 of the classroom plan. In other words, it would be an error to execute the jump with a half tour in place, around one's own axis.

The arms and head help the jump by aiding the turn of the body and the movement of flying off forward. At the moment of the jump, as one opens the left arm to 3rd and the right to 2nd position, it is necessary to help the movement of the body, especially with the left arm, which must be forward somewhat more than the form of 3rd position requires; simultaneously, the body turns to the right with the active participation of the left shoulder, and the head turns toward the right shoulder, helping the turn and accentuating the pose.

In sissonne with a half tour, it is especially necessary to keep the hip pulled-in on the side of the leg that is bent in attitude, and also to correctly come down from the jump in plié through the foot, from the toe to the heel, moving the heel well forward in order to preserve the turn-out.

Grande sissonne ouverte with a half tour en dehors to the pose croisée devant. Begin in 5th position, right leg front. Demi-plié and jump upward with a half tour to the right, flying backward in a direction between points 1 and 8 of the classroom plan. The right shoulder, actively taken back, and the turn of the head to the right, both help the turn of the body. Finish with an assemblé, and repeat the sissonne with a turn toward the mirror, flying off backward in a direction between points 4 and 5.

Example of a combination of grandes sissonnes ouvertes with a half tour. Four measures of 4/4 time. Begin in 5th position, right leg front.

First measure. On the first quarter, with the right leg, do a grande sissonne ouverte to the pose écartée derrière, flying on a diagonal toward point 8; on the second, assemblé, finishing with the right leg in back; on the third quarter, grande sissonne ouverte with a half tour to the right to 4th arabesque, facing point 6 (jump onto the right leg, the left leg stretched backward); on the fourth, assemblé, finishing with the left leg in back, facing point 6.

Second measure. On the first quarter, grande sissonne ouverte, with a half turn, onto the right leg to 1st arabesque on the diagonal to point 2; on the second, assemblé, finishing with the left leg in back; on the third quarter, grande sissonne ouverte, with a half tour, to attitude effacée facing point 6; on the fourth, assemblé, finishing with the left leg in back.

Third measure. On the first quarter, grande sissonne ouverte, with a half tour, to the pose effacée devant (flying backward toward point 6 and finishing facing point 2); on the second, assemblé, finishing with the right leg in back; on the third and fourth quarters, brisé dessus with the right leg and brisé dessous with the left.

Fourth measure. On the first and second quarters, with the right leg, toward point 2, do pas couru, step-coupé, and grand assemblé croisé devant, finishing with the left leg in front; on the third and fourth quarters, do a turn to the right in 5th position on demi-pointe and stop in 5th position on demi-pointe, right leg front; the right arm is in 3rd position, the left in 2nd; the head is turned to point 8.

Grande Sissonne Ouverte en Tournant. This is done with tours en dehors and en dedans in the same way as small sissonnes en tournant (see "Sissonne en Tournant"), the only difference being that the demi-plié is deeper, the jump is higher, and, at the end, the working leg opens to one of the poses at 90°.

Study Sequence (example executed to the pose croisée devant)

1. . 4/4 time. Begin in 5th position with épaulement croisé, right leg front. On the first quarter, demi-plié; the right arm bends to 1st position and the left goes to 2nd position; the head turns en face to point 8 of the classroom plan. Between the first and second quarters, pushing off from the floor with the heels, jump upward. Having reached the highest point of the jump, turn en dehors 360° (a complete tour in the air). At the moment of the push from the floor, the left arm, with a resilient movement, comes together with the right in 1st position, in order to provide force; the right shoulder is taken back and the left moved

forward; the head, also helping the turn, at first looks across the left shoulder, to point 8, then quickly straightens and, in the final pose, is turned to the right. At the moment of the jump, the legs are brought together in the air in 5th position, right leg front. At the end of the jump, the right leg, without delay, opens (with a développé at 90°) croisé devant; and, simultaneously, the left arm opens to 3rd and the right to 2nd position. The pause in the pose in demi-plié comes on the second quarter. On the third quarter, assemblé to 5th position, landing in a full demi-plié. On the fourth, stretch the knees.

2. Final form. 2/4 time. The demi-plié and the jump are done on the upbeat. On the first quarter, pause in the pose in demi-plié. Between the first and second quarters, assemblé, finishing on the second quarter in 5th position in demi-plié.

In the study of grandes sissonnes ouvertes en tournant en dehors and en dedans it is recommended that they be done at least four times to each pose, after which combinations of the various poses may be permitted.

The most complicated form of these sissonnes are the grandes sissonnes ouvertes en tournant with a double turn of the body in the air. Their execution demands, in addition to pulled-up thighs and good control of the back, strong force provided by the arms, a turn of the shoulders, and the precise turns of the head necessary for any tour ("spotting"). If sissonne en tournant is begun facing point 2, before a tour to the left (en dehors or en dedans), then the head, in the jump, looks across the right shoulder to point 2; between the first and second tours, the head turns en face, the eyes again fixing on point 2, then, as the body continues the tour, the head looks across the right shoulder to point 2 as long as possible, before returning to that point at the end of the double tour en dehors or en dedans. Thus, the head, in the initial position, is turned to the left in épaulement croisé; in the demi-plié, it turns straight to point 2; in the double tour in the air, it has four positions: to the right; straight to point 2; to the right; and straight to point 2. The shoulders, freely lowered, also aid the turning of the body: the left is brought backward and, simultaneously, the right goes forward.

All sissonnes en tournant can begin en face from point 1; in this case, the turns of the head will be across the shoulder to point 1.

Sissonne Tombée. Sissonne tombée is a "fallen" jump from two legs onto two; but the "fall" after the jump (the tombé) does not take place simultaneously onto two legs, but first onto one and then, after a brief delay, onto the other. It is done passing through a form of sissonne ouverte croisée, effacée, or to the side, and finishes with either pas de bourrée or a sliding par terre jump, a kind of assemblé in which the legs are brought together in 5th position just above the floor before ending in demi-plié.

Sissonnes tombées at 45° and 90° are done en face and en tournant both as independent pas and also as linking movements before big jumps (for example, sissonne tombée-coupée and grand jeté or grand assemblé, etc.).

Sissonne tombée can also be done to a préparation in 4th position croisée or effacée for tours in the big poses.

Small sissonne tombée to the pose croisée devant. 2/4 time. Begin in 5th position, with épaulement croisé, right leg front. On the upbeat, open the arms slightly to the side; then, lowering them to preparatory position, demi-plié and jump; the right leg, passing through the position sur le cou-de-pied devant, quickly opens in the direction croisée devant and, on the first quarter, comes down in demi-plié in 4th position croisée. The left leg comes down in demi-plié slightly earlier than the right (practically on the upbeat) and, at the moment of the fall (the tombé) onto the right leg in plié, is stretched croisé derrière with the toe to the floor. The centre of weight is transferred forward onto the right leg; and the arms, which are raised slightly in the jump to a half-1st position, assume their final position—the right in 1st and the left in 2nd—on the plié in 4th position (or the left arm can be in 1st position and the right in 2nd); the head is turned to the right. Between the first and second quarters, do a sliding par terre jump (that is, a jump without breaking away from the floor), traveling forward, during which the left leg is brought up to the right and joins it in 5th position; the arms are lowered to preparatory position. On the second quarter, demi-plié in 5th position. Repeat the movement several times, then practise it in the opposite direction.

Small sissonne tombée to the side, finishing with a pas de bourrée. 2/4 time. Begin in 5th position with épaulement croisé, right leg front. On the upbeat, open the arms slightly to the side; then, lowering them to preparatory position (the head turned to the left and the eyes directed at the hands), demi-plié and jump upward, raising the arms slightly to a half-1st position; the right foot, passing through the position sur le cou-de-pied devant, opens to the side at 22.5°; and the arms open to the side with the leg, the head and eyes following the right hand. On the first quarter, fall onto the right leg in demi-plié at the distance of 2nd position; the left leg is stretched with the toe to the floor, the centre of weight having been transferred onto the right leg; the head is turned to the right. Between the first and second quarters, without pausing in this position, pas de bourrée en dehors en face, changing the legs, finishing on the second quarter in 5th position in demi-plié with the left leg in front. During the pas de bourrée, the arms are smoothly lowered, and the body is straightened; the head is turned to the left. In this instance, pas de bourrée is done as a passing, linking movement, without sharply fixing the feet sur le cou-de-pied. This form of sissonne tombée with a pas de bourrée is useful as a preparatory movement for the execution of tours en l'air from 5th position. After finishing pas de bourrée, do relevé in 5th position on demi-pointe, then demi-plié and do a tour en dehors to the left. Having finished the tour in 5th position with the left leg in back, repeat the movement several times in succession across the room.

Sissonne tombée at 90°. This is done in the same way as small sissonne tombée, but the leg is opened with a développé at 90°. The tombé is wide, with a clearly marked transfer of the centre of weight onto the leg.

Sissonnes tombées at 90° can finish with a sliding jump, bringing the legs together in 5th position, but usually they finish with a pas de bourrée and precede some big jump.

Small sissonne tombée en tournant, with a tour en dehors. Elementary study. 4/4 time. Begin in 5th position, épaulement croisé, right leg front.

On the first quarter, demi-plié; the right arm is raised to 1st position and the left to 2nd; the head turns en face to point 8. Between the first and second quarters, jump upward with a tour en dehors (to the right), bringing the arms together in 1st position; the head is turned in the direction of point 8. On the second quarter, after passing the right foot through the position sur le cou-de-pied devant and opening the right leg croisé, fall onto the right leg in demi-plié in 4th position croisée, transferring the centre of weight forward onto the right leg; the right arm is in 1st position and the left is in 2nd; the head spots point 8 and, at the end of the tour, is turned to the right. Between the second and third quarters, bring the legs together in a par terre jump, sliding forward along the floor. On the third quarter, finish the jump in 5th position in demi-plié, lowering the arms to preparatory position. On the fourth quarter, stretch the knees.

The final form of sissonne tombée en tournant is analogous to small sissonne tombée en face: the demi-plié and jump are done on the upbeat, etc. The rules for execution are the same as those for sissonne ouverte en tournant.

For the execution of sissonne tombée en tournant at 90°, the jump is higher and the leg opens at 90° with a développé.

Two sissonnes tombées, one done croisé and the other to 2nd position, make up the conventional temps lié sauté at 45° or 90°, en face and en tournant.

For a description of the quick tours sissonne-tombées done in a series (tours "blinchiki") see Chapter X, "Tours on the Floor and in the Air".

Sissonne Fermée. Sissonnes fermées ("closed") are small jumps from two legs onto two, done with a flying start and traveling to the side, with or without a change of the legs, forward, backward, and to the poses croisée, effacée and écartée, devant and derrière, and to the 1st, 2nd, 3rd, and 4th arabesques.

Study Sequence

1. Sissonne fermée without changing the legs (elementary classes). 4/4 time. Begin in 5th position en face, right leg front, the arms in preparatory position. On the first and second quarters, demi-plié. Between the second and third quarters, pushing off from the floor with the heels, jump out, traveling to the left in a straight line to the side; the body follows the left leg; and the right leg, stretching, opens to 2nd position at approximately 22.5° (the position of the legs in the air resembles that of slightly opened scissors). On the third quarter, the legs simultaneously close in 5th position in demi-plié, right leg front; the left leg is lowered to the floor immediately, through the foot, from the toe to the heel, while the right, which is in 2nd position in the air, first touches the floor with strongly stretched toes at the point of 2nd position and is then quickly brought to 5th position, according to the principle of battement tendu. On the fourth quarter, the knees are stretched.

   The movement is repeated several times. It is then studied with the other leg, and after that, forward and backward.

The jump can also be done between the first and second quarters. In that case, come down from the jump in demi-plié on the second quarter; on the third, stretch the knees; and, on the fourth quarter, pause.

2. Sissonne fermée changing the legs. 4/4 time. Begin in 5th position, with épaulement croisé, right leg front. On the upbeat, open the arms slightly to the side. On the first quarter, demi-plié, lowering the arms to preparatory position. Between the first and second quarters, jump, flying off to the left; the right leg is raised to the side at 22.5°; the arms open to a half-2nd position, palms down; and the head turns to the left. On the second quarter, finish the jump in 5th position in demi-plié with épaulement croisé, bringing the right leg back; simultaneously, the arms are lowered to preparatory position; the head remains turned to the left. On the third quarter, stretch the knees. On the fourth, there is a pause. The movement is then repeated with the left leg.

Sissonne fermée in the reverse direction is done in exactly the same way: during the jump, the leg that was in back in 5th position opens to 2nd position, the head turned toward it; at the end of the jump, it is brought, with the toe sliding along the floor, to 5th position front; the head remains turned toward the front shoulder.

3. Sissonne fermée changing the legs. Final form. 4/4 time. Begin in 5th position, with épaulement croisé, right leg front. On the upbeat, open the arms slightly to the side, then demi-plié and lower the arms to preparatory position; jump, opening the right leg to the side at 22.5°, flying off to the left in a straight line to the side; the arms open to a half-2nd position, palms down; the head turns to the left. On the first quarter, the jump finishes in demi-plié in 5th position, right leg back; the arms remain in the half-2nd position; the head is to the left (épaulement croisé). On the second quarter, the movement is repeated with the left leg,

traveling to the right. On the third and fourth quarters, the movement is repeated with the right and then with the left leg. On the fourth sissonne fermée, the arms are lowered to preparatory position.

In executing the movement to the side in the reverse direction, the leg that is in 5th position back opens, and at the end of the jump it is brought to 5th position front. The head, at the moment of the jump, turns toward the leg that is opened at 22.5°.

Sissonne fermée in the pose croisée, traveling forward. 4/4 time. Begin in 5th position, with épaulement croisé, right leg front. On the upbeat, open the arms slightly to the side, then lower them to preparatory position with a demi-plié; jump, flying forward in the direction croisé, with the stretched left leg opening croisé derrière at no higher than 22.5°; the left arm is raised to 1st position and the right to 2nd; the head and eyes are directed forward across the left arm; and the body travels forward in the air. On the first quarter, the jump finishes in demi-plié; the left leg, sliding the toe along the floor, closes in 5th position simultaneously with the right; the arms and head remain in the same position. From here, the movement is repeated four to eight times. On the last movement, the arms are lowered to preparatory position and the head turns to the right. The position of the head can be varied; for example, the head can be turned toward the right shoulder throughout.

In executing sissonne fermée flying off in the direction croisée derrière (with the right leg in front), the arms assume a small pose croisée devant, either with the left arm in 1st position and the right in 2nd, or with the right in 1st and the left in 2nd; in both cases, the head is to the right.

In the poses effacées, one arm is also in 1st position and the other in 2nd. In the pose écartée derrière, the arms open to a half-2nd position. In the pose écartée devant, the arms also open to a half-2nd position but the hands are turned palms down.

RULES FOR THE EXECUTION OF SISSONNE FER-
MÉE. The basic rule for the execution of this jump is that there
must be, first, a flying take-off with a simultaneous opening of
the legs, and then a simultaneous closing of the legs in 5th
position, without the least delay and with an accentuated return
to demi-plié (the foot of the closing leg is brought in with the
toe sliding along the floor, as in battement tendu), for this is
what makes the step fermé ("closed").

The leg toward which the jump is done opens in the direction
of the jump, with the body following after it through the air to
the side, forward, or backward.

Doing several sissonnes fermées in a series, one must avoid
doing a double plié, for, after landing resiliently in demi-plié, it
is necessary to push off immediately for the next jump without
relaxing the muscles.

In doing a succession of jumps in the same pose, one should
not open the arms and then lower them to preparatory position
each time, since this can create an impression of discontinuity.
Light, unstrained arms hold the pose taken in the first jump,
and only on the last movement should they be lowered to
preparatory position.

Example of a combination with sissonnes fermées. 4/4 time, two
measures. Begin in 5th position, with épaulement croisé, right
leg front.

First measure. On the first and second quarters do two
sissonnes fermées, changing the legs, in 2nd position, first with
the right leg and then with the left, taking to the back each time
the leg that is in 5th position front; on the first jump, the arms
open to a half-2nd position; and on the second jump, they are
lowered to preparatory position. On the third and fourth
quarters, do three sissonnes fermées to 2nd position with the
right leg, the left, and again with the right, one eighth each; the
arms, opening on the first jump, hold the pose on the second
jump, and, on the third, are lowered to preparatory position.

Second measure. On the first quarter, do a sissonne fermée

with the left leg in the pose effacée derrière, flying off on the diagonal forward to point 8 and finishing with the right leg in 5th position front. On the second quarter, do a sissonne fermée with the right leg to the pose effacée derrière, flying off on the diagonal forward to point 2 and finishing with the left leg in 5th position front. On the third and fourth quarters, do three brisés forward, in a direction between points 2 and 3, in one eighth each.

The combination is repeated with the other leg, and then it is done in the reverse direction.

Sissonne Fondue. A sissonne fondue ("melted") is a big jump, done, as is sissonne fermée, from two legs onto two, flying off in any direction, in the poses at 90°. The leg that opens in the jump at 90° is lowered to 5th position with a slight retard, and the demi-plié on the supporting leg is simultaneously deepened. Thus these sissonnes are given a fondu ("melted"), soft character, which distinguishes them from sissonnes fermées.

Study Sequence

1. *Example of execution to the side, changing the legs. Elementary study.* 2/4 time. Begin in 5th position with épaulement croisé, right leg front. On the upbeat, open the arms slightly to the side and then lower them to preparatory position; the body, with a pulled-up back, slightly bends forward, the head inclining to the right; demi-plié a bit deeper; then do a big jump, flying off to the left in a straight line, the right leg opening to the side at 90° by means of a grand battement; simultaneously, the arms open to 2nd through 1st position; the body straightens and is carried after the left leg, the head turning to the left. On the first quarter, the left leg comes down in demi-plié. Between the first and second quarters, the right leg softly

and smoothly is brought to 5th position back; and, on the second quarter, the demi-plié deepens; simultaneously with the leg, and just as softly and smoothly, the arms are lowered to preparatory position; the head, remaining to the left, inclines downward. From here, the movement is repeated with the left leg, flying off to the right. In executing the jump in the reverse direction, travel toward the leg that is in 5th position front; the leg that is in back is thrown out to 90° and taken to 5th position front at the end.

2.   *Example of execution to the pose 3rd arabesque.* Final form. 2/4 time. Begin in 5th position with épaulement croisé, right leg front. On the upbeat, open the arms slightly to the side and lower them to preparatory position with a demi-plié, the eyes directed at the hands; then do a big jump, flying off forward in the direction croisée; the body is carried after the right leg, which opens forward in the air as the stretched left leg opens croisé derrière at 90°; the movement of the legs is like a pair of scissors; the arms assume the position 3rd arabesque, with the eyes directed at the left hand. On the first quarter, the right leg comes down in demi-plié; the left, a little later, is softly lowered to 5th position; and the demi-plié is deepened; the arms, simultaneously with the left leg, close to preparatory position. On the second quarter, the movement is repeated.

It is also possible not to lower the arms on the first sissonne fondue but, having slightly "breathed" with them, to leave them in the position 3rd arabesque and lower them to preparatory position only at the end of the second jump.

Sissonne Renversée. Sissonne renversée ("flipped over") is a compound jump consisting of a grande sissonne ouverte and a renversé. It is done to attitude croisée with a renversé en dehors, and to the big pose croisée devant with a renversé en dedans.

En dehors. 2/4 time. Begin in 5th position with épaulement croisé, right leg front. On the upbeat, demi-plié and grande sissonne ouverte to the pose attitude croisée, finishing, on the first quarter, in demi-plié on the right leg. Without pausing in plié, between the first and second quarters, step onto the left leg on demi-pointe, at the same time bringing it up to the right, and raise the right foot to the conditional position sur le cou-de-pied devant; the body, bending back, makes a half turn toward the audience (to the left); the right arm bends to 1st position, the left maintaining 3rd position; and the head is turned to the right, toward the mirror. With a turn en dehors, step over onto the right leg on demi-pointe, raising the left foot sur le cou-de-pied devant; the body increases the bend and, at the end of the turn toward the mirror, straightens; the arms come together in 1st position. On the second quarter, come down in 5th position in demi-plié, left leg front; the hands open to a low 1st position; and the head turns to the left.

Sissonne renversée en dedans is done in exactly the same way. (The rules for the execution of renversé will be found in the section "Renversé" in Chapter XI, "Turning Movements Used in Adagio".) In beginning the study of sissonne renversée, the student may do it in place with only a vertical jump and then go on to do it flying off forward or backward, as in the ordinary grande sissonne ouverte.

Sissonne Soubresaut. This is a compound jump consisting of a soubresaut (a strong jump holding the feet together in 5th position) and a grande sissonne ouverte and is done flying off forward to the pose attitude croisée or attitude effacée or backward to the big pose croisée or effacée devant.

2/4 time. The demi-plié and the jump are done on the upbeat. The end of the jump, in demi-plié, comes on the first quarter. On the second quarter, an assemblé or a coupé-assemblé is usually done.

Sissonne soubresaut to attitude effacée. Begin in 5th position with épaulement croisé, right leg front. The movement is done on the diagonal from point 6 to point 2.

Open the arms slightly to the side; then, bending the body forward, lower the arms to preparatory position, simultaneously doing a somewhat deeper demi-plié than is usual. Pushing off from the floor with the heels, do a big jump, strongly bringing the feet together in the air in 5th position; the body, turning effacé in the direction of point 2 and forcefully bending back, is hurled forward, forcing the legs to be thrown back slightly; the arms are raised to 1st position; and the eyes are directed at the hands. The jump finishes in demi-plié on the right leg, the left leg opening effacé derrière at 90°; the right arm is opened to 2nd position and the left is raised to 3rd; the hands are turned outward, away from the body (allongé); the head is to the left, and the eyes are directed at the left hand. Then do an assemblé, bringing the legs together in 5th position in demi-plié, left leg back; the body returns to the épaulement croisé, with the arms lowered to preparatory position. Repeat the movement several times.

RULES FOR THE EXECUTION OF SISSONNE SOUBRESAUT. The good execution of soubresaut depends almost entirely on the correct position of the body: it must be curved back in the jump, with the lower abdominal muscles strongly pulled up. It is precisely the tautness of these muscles that makes it possible to hold the body in the air for a moment with the legs thrown back, giving to the whole figure, in profile, the look of a curved bow. The pulled-up body and the shoulders, also thrown back, help one to fly off forward on a diagonal.

In soubresaut, a general rule for jumps is modified: the knees, at the moment of the jump, are slightly bent, and the legs are actually brought together not along their whole length but only at the feet.

Sissonne soubresaut to the pose croisée derrière is done in exactly the same way.

Sissonne soubresaut to the poses croisée or effacée devant is nearer to simple sissonne ouverte at 90°. At the moment of the jump, the legs are held together in 5th position in the air, after which the leg that is in front opens at 90° by means of a grand battement.

Example of a combination with sissonne soubresaut and sissonne renversée. 3/4 time (waltz), sixteen measures. Four measures: from point 6 to point 2, do pas couru and grand jeté to attitude croisée two times. Four measures: assemblé back and three entrechats-six. Four measures: with the right leg, sissonne soubresaut to attitude croisée and assemblé; then sissonne renversée en dehors. Four measures: with the left leg, on a diagonal to point 8, sissonne soubresaut to attitude effacée; assemblé, finishing in 5th position with the right leg in back; and, with the left leg, to point 8, do six tours chaînés, stopping in a pose on the left leg, with the right leg effacé derrière, toe to the floor, the left arm in 2nd position and the right in 3rd.

Grande Sissonne à la Seconde de Volée en Tournant en Dedans. This compound step is done facing the mirror or on a diagonal with a preliminary step-coupé, a small sissonne tombée to 4th position croisée, or a pas chassé; and it finishes with a pas de bourrée dessus en tournant or a soutenu en tournant en dedans.

Grande sissonne à la seconde de volée en tournant en dedans, with a preliminary step-coupé. 4/4 time. Begin in 5th position with épaulement croisé, right leg front. On the upbeat, demi-plié, raising the right foot to the conditional position sur le cou-de-pied devant, but at a short distance from the supporting leg; the right arm is raised to 1st position and the left to 2nd. On the first quarter, do a step-coupé to 4th position croisée on the right leg, transferring onto it the centre of weight; then, pushing off from the floor with the heel, do a big jump upward, throwing the left leg to 2nd position at 90° (à la seconde) by means of a grand battement; simultaneously, raise the arms to 3rd position with a strong movement through 2nd position. Thus, for an instant, the jump is fixed en face; then do a complete turn in the air en dedans (to the right) with the leg at a height of 90°; the head is turned across the left shoulder to point 1. On the second quarter, finish the jump to point 1 in demi-plié on the right leg, the left leg maintaining its position at 90° à la seconde; the arms are in 3rd position, and the head is straight forward. Between the second and third quarters, open the arms to 2nd position and do a pas de bourrée dessus en tournant (also to the right), finishing, on the third quarter, in 5th position in demi-plié, right leg front. On the fourth quarter, stretch the knees.

One can do the same movement with a preliminary small sissonne tombée to 4th position croisée. The position of the arms is the same as that described above.

If this pas finishes with a soutenu en tournant en dedans, then the soutenu is done between the second and third quarters; on the third quarter, pause in 5th position on demi-pointe; and, on the fourth quarter, come down in demi-plié.

Grande sissonne à la seconde de volée en tournant en dedans with a preliminary pas chassé. 4/4 time. Begin in 5th position with épaulement croisé, right leg front. On the upbeat, demi-plié and do a small passing sissonne tombée croisée devant, finishing in 4th position on the first quarter. Between the first and second quarters, pas chassé. On the second quarter, the centre of weight is transferred onto the right leg in demi-plié to a small 4th position croisée; the right arm is in 1st and the left in 2nd position, as when doing it with a preliminary step-coupé. Between the second and third quarters, do the grande sissonne à la seconde de volée en tournant en dedans, as described in the preceding example. On the third quarter, end the jump facing point 1 in demi-plié. The pas de bourrée dessus en tournant en dedans finishes in 5th position in demi-plié on the fourth quarter. The movement should be repeated several times with one leg before being done in the other direction with the other leg.

On a diagonal, the movement is done in exactly the same way; with the right leg, from point 4 to point 8; with the left, from point 6 to point 2. The positions of the arms are as in the preceding example.

RULES FOR THE EXECUTION OF GRANDE SIS-SONNE À LA SECONDE DE VOLÉE EN TOURNANT EN DEDANS. During the jump, the body maintains a strongly vertical position. The leg that is thrown out at 90°, locked in the hip joint, must not lose the position à la seconde, and in no case must it move forward, which can happen if the buttocks muscles and thigh muscles are undisciplined.

For the tour in the air to the right, the left arm provides force; for a tour to the left, the right does. When raising the arms to 3rd position energetically, the elbow of the arm that is providing the force should slightly move forward, without, however, disturbing the correct form of 3rd position over the centre of the body.

The movement of the head also helps the tour: in a tour to the right, it remains turned toward the mirror (or to the point on the diagonal) across the left shoulder for as long as possible, and at the end of the tour, quickly returns en face; in a tour to the left, the head remains turned across the right shoulder, and then returns en face.

Soubresaut

A soubresaut is a big jump from two legs onto two, from a demi-plié in 5th position to another demi-plié in 5th, without changing the legs and with a strong movement forward, executed with a backward bend of the body.

Study Sequence

1. 4/4 time. Begin in 5th position with épaulement croisé, right leg front. The arms open halfway to the side (half-2nd position) on the upbeat. On the first quarter, demi-plié a bit more deeply than usual; lower the arms to preparatory position; and incline the body somewhat forward and down (but with a pulled-up back); the eyes are directed at the hands. On the second quarter, hold the position. Between the second and third quarters, pushing off from the floor with the heels, jump traveling forward to the left; the legs are thrown back, with stretched toes; the feet are held together in 5th position; the knees are allowed to slightly bend; the body, directly from its inclined position, is projected forward and also strongly bends backward; simultaneously, the arms, helping the movement of the body, are raised to 1st position; and the head turns to the right. The jump finishes, on the third quarter, in demi-plié. On the fourth quarter, the knees are stretched; the body comes erect; and the arms are lowered to preparatory position:

In the elementary study of soubresaut, holding of the arms in 1st position during the jump not only helps the movement forward, but also facilitates the complicated co-ordination of bending the body backward and throwing the legs backward at the same time.

2. 4/4 time. Begin in 5th position with épaulement croisé, right leg front.

On the upbeat, open the arms to the side to a half-height; incline the body forward and down; demi-plié, lowering the arms to preparatory position; and look at the hands. Then demi-plié a bit deeper and jump, traveling forward and strongly bending the body backward (the position of the legs is the same as in the first example); simultaneously with the jump, the arms are raised: the left to 3rd position and the right to 1st allongée (the position of the forward arm in arabesque); and the head turns to the right. On the first quarter, come down in 5th position in demi-plié. On the second quarter, hold the position. On the third quarter, bring the body smoothly erect, lower the arms to preparatory position; and stretch the knees. On the fourth quarter, pause.

3. Final form. 2/4 time. This is done in the same way as in the second example: the jump finishes on the first quarter. On the second quarter, remaining in demi-plié, smoothly straighten the body and slightly "breathe" with the arms, holding them in 1st and 3rd position; turn the head toward the left shoulder and incline it slightly downward. Then, from this position, do the next soubresaut.

It is recommended that, in classroom study, no fewer than four soubresauts be performed in succession, with the arms lowered to preparatory position only on the last jump. However, in stage practice, one encounters soubresauts done in succession somewhat differently. The first soubresauts are small jumps, with the body inclined forward; then the jumps get larger and the body straightens and bends back; this sequence occurs in *Giselle,* Act II.

With further mastery, soubresaut can also be done in 1/4.

RULES FOR EXECUTION. An airy, light soubresaut requires a strong push from the floor with the heels and, simultaneously, a quick, almost sharp, bend of the body backward in the air. After the jump, the body comes erect in a legato manner, smoothly; the muscles of the back must prevent the body from making a sharp transition to an erect position.

The arms are held easily, without tension, and give soubresaut a limpid, light character.

Rond de Jambe en l'Air Sauté

Rond de jambe en l'air sauté is done at 45° and 90°, en dehors and en dedans.

In elementary study, it is done with a single rond de jambe; when this is mastered, double rond de jambe is practised.

There are two methods of execution for rond de jambe en l'air sauté: 1) having done a sissonne ouverte to 2nd position at 45°, push off from the floor with the heel of the supporting leg and jump (a temps levé); during the jump, the leg that is opened to the side does a single or double rond de jambe en l'air; 2) from 5th position in demi-plié, push off for the jump with both legs; in the air, one leg is perpendicular to the floor, while the other is thrown out to the side at 45° and does a single or a double rond de jambe en l'air.

If the working leg begins in 5th position front, a rond de jambe en dehors is done; if the working leg begins in back, it will do a rond de jambe en dedans.

In a small rond de jambe en l'air sauté, the arms open to a half-2nd position; in a big one, done at 90°, the demi-plié is deeper and the jump is higher; the arms open to a full 2nd position. The body inclines slightly to the side of the supporting leg, which enables the working leg to do the rond de jambe more freely.

A basic rule for this pas is the execution of the rond de jambe simultaneously with the jump. The legs must be well prepared by the barre and centre exercise.

Example of a combination with rond de jambe en l'air sauté at 45°. 4/4 time, four measures. Begin in 5th position, right leg front.

First measure. On the first quarter, sissonne ouverte with the right leg to 2nd position at 45°; on the second quarter, rond de jambe en l'air sauté en dehors; on the third, repeat the rond de jambe; on the fourth, assemblé, finishing in 5th position with the right leg in back.

Second measure. On the first quarter, do a small jeté porté battu with the right leg, traveling to the side in 2nd position, finishing with the left foot sur le cou-de-pied devant; on the second quarter, do a small jeté porté, traveling forward croisé, with the left leg; on the third quarter, coupé with the right leg and repeat the jeté porté croisé forward with the left leg; on the fourth quarter, assemblé in back.

Third measure. On the first quarter, rond de jambe en l'air sauté en dehors with the left leg, from 5th position; on the second, assemblé, finishing in 5th position back; on the third and fourth quarters, repeat the rond de jambe and assemblé with the right leg.

Fourth measure. Do two échappés battus en tournant to the left, with one half turn each.

Repeat the combination with the other leg, and then do it in the reverse direction.

The same combination can be done with a double rond de jambe.

Pas de Basque

Pas de basque ("Basque step") is basically a jump from one leg to the other. There are two kinds of pas de basque: pas de basque par terre and pas de basque done in the air. The pas de basque par terre, which is executed without leaving the floor, is done forward (en avant) and backward (en arrière), as well as with a quarter or a half turn and, in advanced classes, with a full turn (pas de basque en tournant).

Grand pas de basque, executed in the air with a big jump, with the legs thrown out to a height of 90°, also can be done en tournant.

The study of pas de basque par terre is begun in the elementary classes.

Study Sequence

1. Pas de basque en avant (forward). Elementary study. Two measures of 3/4 time. Begin in 5th position, with épaulement croisé, right leg front.

On the upbeat, open the arms slightly to the side, then lower them to preparatory position with a demi-plié. On the first quarter, stretch out the right leg croisé devant, with the toe to the floor; raise the arms to 1st position; incline the head to the left; the eyes are directed at the hands. On the second quarter, remaining in demi-plié, take the right leg to 2nd position with a demi-rond de jambe par terre en dehors, keeping the toe to the floor; the arms open to 2nd position; the head turns to the left. On the third quarter, the position is held. On the first quarter of the second measure, spring onto the right leg, without leaving the floor; the left leg quickly stretches in 2nd position and then immediately passes (between the first and second quarters) with a sliding movement, heel to the floor, through 1st position (passé) in demi-plié, to a position croisée devant, with the toe to the floor; during the passé through 1st position, the arms are lowered and, as the leg slides croisé, they are raised to 1st position; the head inclines to the right; and the eyes accompany the hands. On the second quarter, sliding forward the toe of the left leg, with a passing movement, transfer the weight onto the left leg in demi-plié; then, bringing both legs together in a jump in 5th position, with stretched toes, move forward without leaving the floor (an assemblé par terre). On the third quarter, finish the jump in 5th position in demi-plié, opening the hands slightly and turning the head to the left. From here, repeat the movement starting with the other leg.

Pas de basque en arrière (backward) is done in the same way. Begin in 5th position, with the right leg in front.

Demi-plié; the left leg is stretched out croisé derrière with the toe to the floor; then, accompanied by the arms, it is taken around to 2nd position with a demi-rond de jambe en dedans; spring onto the left leg without leaving the floor; thé right leg does a passé through 1st position in demi-plié and is taken to the position croisée derrière with the toe to the floor; then, the left leg is brought together with the right in a sliding jump par terre (that is, without leaving the floor), traveling backward. The arms accompany the movement exactly as in pas de basque en avant. But the head does only two movements: it is turned to the right over the front shoulder on the first measure; then it turns to the left on the pas de basque.

2. Pas de basque en avant. Final form. 3/4 time. Begin in 5th position, right leg front. On the upbeat, demi-plié in 5th position and demi-rond de jambe par terre en dehors with the right leg. The rest is done as described above for elementary study.

3. 2/4 time. The demi-plié and the rond de jambe par terre are both done on the upbeat. Then, on the first quarter, spring without leaving the floor. Between the first and second quarters, passé through 1st position. Then do the sliding jump par terre, with the legs pulled together in 5th position, and, on the second quarter, finish the jump in 5th position in demi-plié with the left leg in front.

RULES FOR THE EXECUTION OF PAS DE BASQUE PAR TERRE. Pas de basque has a jump-like feeling (especially the first part), but it must not have the character of a jeté. It is inadmissible to break away from the floor; but it is equally inadmissible to creep along the floor, something which is often encountered in the execution of this pas.

Doing pas de basque en arrière, it is necessary to watch that, after the first jump, the leg, after having gone through 1st position to the position croisée derrière, is completely stretched in the knee, instep, and toes. After this, the legs are brought together in the second jump, the sliding jump par terre. A leg that is not completely stretched, and that does not reach out to the spot croisé derrière, gives pas de basque en arrière the character of a réverance.

In the final form of pas de basque, in intermediate classes, a more complicated position of the torso is introduced: in pas de basque en avant with the right leg in front, the body and the head incline to the left (toward the supporting leg) during the demi-rond de jambe. In the spring onto the right leg, the body and the head incline to the right. And finally, at the end of the pas de basque, the body and the head incline to the left.

In pas de basque en arrière (with the right leg in front), the body inclines to the right in the demi-rond de jambe, and remains in this position until the end of the jump, when it inclines to the left.

Thus, in pas de basque en avant, there are three different positions of the body and the head; in pas de basque en arrière there are only two.

Regardless of the musical time or tempo, the demi-rond de jambe par terre is done on the upbeat, and without the slightest retard. Pas de basque is learned in 3/4 time but, when combined with other steps, it is usually done in 2/4 time.

Pas de Basque en Avant en Tournant with a Quarter Turn. 2/4 time. Begin in 5th position, right leg front. On the upbeat, demi-plié, and, with the right leg, do a demi-rond de jambe par terre en dehors with a quarter turn to the right; the body inclines to the left toward the supporting leg, which remains in demi-plié; the arms, opening simultaneously with the right leg through 1st position to 2nd, help the turn, that is the right arm and shoulder give a light push, which assists the turn on the supporting leg. Having turned the body to face point 3, do the pas de basque, finishing in 5th position croisée, between points 3 and 4. A second pas de basque is done then with the left leg, turning back toward the mirror during the demi-rond de jambe par terre en dehors.

To complicate the movement, do four pas de basque en avant, or four en arrière in a circle in one direction.

After pas de basque en avant with the right leg, with a quarter of a turn, finishing to point 3, do the second pas de basque en avant with the left leg, with a turn to point 5. For this, in doing the demi-rond de jambe par terre en dehors with the left leg, turn to the right on the supporting leg (as if moving en dedans). The heel of the supporting leg, which moves forward in demi-plié, will help the turn, as will the extra force given with the right arm as the arms open to 2nd position. The third pas de basque is like the first and finishes facing point 7; the fourth is like the second and finishes facing the mirror, to point 1.

Pas de basque en arrière with four quarter turns in one direction is done analogously.

This form of pas de basque develops quickness and agility, training the student for "unexpected" turns of the whole body.

Further complicating pas de basque, it is studied with half turns.

Pas de Basque en Arrière en Tournant with a Half Turn. 2/4 time. Begin in 5th position, right leg front. On the upbeat, demi-plié in 5th position; stretch the left leg croisé derrière, with the toe to the floor; the arms are in 1st position; the body is inclined to the right, toward the supporting leg; the head is turned to the right; and the small of the back is strongly pulled up. Still on the upbeat, turn en dedans (to the right) on the supporting leg, remaining in demi-plié and moving the heel of the supporting leg forward; simultaneously, the left leg and the arms open to 2nd position; the head remains turned to the right. The turn finishes to point 5 of the classroom plan. On the first quarter, spring onto the left leg without leaving the floor. Between the first and second quarters, passé through 1st position in demi-plié, bringing the right leg croisé derrière, with the toe to the floor; then do the sliding jump traveling backward, bringing the legs together in 5th position. On the second quarter, finish the jump in 5th position in demi-plié, with épaulement croisé, between points 5 and 6, left leg front; the arms and the head are in the same positions as in the preceding example.

The second pas de basque also is done with a turn to the right: on the upbeat, demi-plié; stretch the right leg croisé derrière; the arms are in 1st position; the body is inclined to the left (toward the supporting leg); the head is turned to the left; opening the right leg and the arms to 2nd position, turn the body toward the mirror to point 1, leaving the head turned to the left toward the supporting leg. On the first quarter, spring onto the right leg without leaving the floor. Between the first and second quarters, passé through 1st position in demi-plié bringing the left leg croisé derrière, with the toe to the floor; then do the sliding jump traveling backward, finishing in 5th position in demi-plié, right leg front, with épaulement croisé, between points 8 and 1 of the classroom plan.

Pas de Basque en Avant en Tournant with a Complete Turn. 2/4 time. Begin in 5th position, with the right leg in front. On the upbeat, demi-plié and stretch the right leg croisé devant, with the toe to the floor; the arms are in 1st position; the eyes are directed at the hands. Then the body strongly inclines to the left, toward the supporting leg (which remains in demi-plié), and the head turns to the left. Without a pause, do a complete turn en dehors to the right. In beginning the turn, immediately open the arms to 2nd position, the right arm and shoulder actively assisting the turn of the body; simultaneously, the right leg opens, with the toe lightly moving along the floor, to 2nd position. Care must be taken that the foot does not rest on the floor, since an emphasised tracing of the toe along the floor inevitably will slow down the turn. The position of the body, inclined to the left toward the supporting leg, especially obliges one to keep the right hip level and the thigh of the right leg pulled up which, by its own momentum during the turn, must not be taken back beyond 2nd position.

Having finished the complete turn facing the mirror, on the first quarter, without leaving the floor, spring onto the right leg in the position en face and turn the head to the right; the left leg immediately (between the first and second quarters) stretches to 2nd position and passes through 1st position in demi-plié to the position croisée devant with the toe to the floor; the arms are lowered to preparatory position and then raised to 1st position; the eyes are directed at the hands. The sliding jump par terre travels forward and finishes, on the second quarter, in 5th position in demi-plié; the body and the head incline to the left; and the arms open slightly in 1st position.

If pas de basque is repeated with the other leg, it is recommended that, without lowering the arms, they be opened directly from the final pose of the first pas de basque to 2nd position, simultaneously with the movement of the leg.

Example of a combination with pas de basque en face. 2/4 time, four measures. Begin in 5th position, right leg front.

First measure. Small sissonne tombée croisée devant, finishing with a sliding jump in 5th position (assemblé par terre).

Second and third measures. Pas de basque en avant with the right and the left legs.

Fourth measure. With the right leg, small sissonne tombée effacée devant, finishing with a sliding jump in 5th position (assemblé par terre), left leg front.

Repeat the combination with the other leg, and then do it in the reverse direction.

Example of a combination with pas de basque en tournant. 2/4 time, four measures. Begin in 5th position, right leg front.

First measure. Pas de basque en avant with a complete turn of the body en dehors to the right.

Second measure. With the left leg, pas de basque en avant with a complete turn en dehors to the left.

Third measure. With the right leg, on the diagonal toward point 2, pas failli to the pose 2nd arabesque, finishing with a sliding jump in 5th position (assemblé par terre), left leg front.

Fourth measure. Sissonne renversée en dehors.

The combination is also done beginning with the other leg; and then is practised in the reverse direction.

Grand Pas de Basque en Avant. 3/4 time. Begin in 5th position with épaulement croisé, right leg front. On the upbeat, open the arms slightly to the side and, closing them to preparatory position, demi-plié, at the same time inclining the body a little forward. Immediately, while straightening the body and raising the arms to 3rd position, take the right half-bent leg off the floor to the position croisée devant at 45° and, stretching it, open it in an arc to 2nd position at 90° (demi-rond de jambe at 90°); the body inclines slightly toward the supporting leg; the head turns to the left. Jump onto the right leg, finishing, on the first quarter, in demi-plié; the left leg quickly bends bringing the toe near the knee of the right leg (passé at 90°) and, without a pause, stretches croisé devant at 90°; at the moment of the jump, the head turns to the right; and the arms hold 3rd position.

On the second quarter, with a wide movement, slightly inclining the body backward, fall forward onto the left leg in 4th position croisée in demi-plié, transferring onto it the centre of weight and strongly holding the back; the arms open to 2nd position; and the head turns to the left. Between the second and third quarters, do a sliding jump traveling forward, bringing the legs together in 5th position (assemblé par terre); and smoothly lower the arms. On the third quarter, demi-plié in 5th position, with the left leg in front; the head is turned to the left; the arms are in preparatory position.

Grand Pas de Basque en Arrière. Begin in 5th position with épaulement croisé, right leg front. The movements of the arms and the body are as in the preceding example. On the upbeat, demi-plié and take the half-bent left leg off the floor to the position croisée derrière at 45°, while raising the arms to 3rd position and turning the head to the right; then open the leg, in an arc, to 2nd position at 90° (demi-rond de jambe en dedans). Jump onto the left leg, leaving the head turned to the right, the right leg quickly bends bringing the toe near the knee of the left (passé at 90°) and, without a pause, stretches croisé derrière at 90°. With a wide movement, fall back onto the right leg in 4th position croisée in demi-plié, transferring onto it the centre of weight and opening the arms to 2nd position; the head turns to the left. In a sliding jump traveling backward, bring the legs together in 5th position, lowering the arms; and finish in 5th position in demi-plié, the left leg in front, the head is turned to the left.

As in pas de basque par terre, in grand pas de basque en avant there are three different positions of the head; in the movement en arrière, only two.

Grand pas de basque can also be done in 2/4. The musical counts are distributed as in the execution of petit pas de basque.

RULES FOR THE EXECUTION OF GRAND PAS DE BASQUE. Grand pas de basque can be regarded as two different jumps: the first is a big one in the air; the second, a sliding, par terre jump (a kind of assemblé).

The demi-rond de jambe at 90° must be done exactly on the upbeat. The push from the floor with the heel of the supporting leg for the jump takes place at the moment when the second leg is describing the arc to 90°. A pause in the demi-plié, or a pause when the leg is raised at 90° in 2nd position, deprives the jump of lightness.

The return to the floor after the jump must be directly beneath the point to which the toe of the working leg is extended at the end of the demi-rond de jambe to the side at 90°.

The movements of the body and arms and the turns of the head must have a legato character. As in all jumps, the small of the back must be tightly pulled up and the buttocks muscles tensed.

Saut de Basque

Saut de basque ("Basque jump"), basically a jump from one leg to the other, is one of the big jumps of classical dance. It occurs in many variations and codas, and in numerous versions: with a pause on one leg, the other leg bent at the knee; with a pause in one of the big poses; with a double turn in the air, etc. It is done in a straight line across the stage or on a diagonal, preceded by a step-coupé, pas couru, or chassé, and, in a circle, with chassé.

Study Sequence

Saut de basque with a step-coupé in a straight line to the side. Elementary study. 4/4 time. Begin in 5th position en face, right leg front. The movement is executed from point 7 to point 3 of the classroom plan. On the upbeat, one of the forms of coupé is done; the left leg does a demi-plié, strongly accentuating the movement of the heel to the floor (almost hitting it); and the right leg, with an energetic movement, bends, with the toe brought in front of the knee of the supporting leg; the right arm is in 1st position, and the left in 2nd; the head is en face. A straight, pulled-up body and well turned-out legs with taut muscles prepare the whole body in this coupé for the following strong and complicated jump. On the first quarter, opening the right arm to 2nd position, take a small step with the right leg to 2nd position in demi-plié, continuing to feel the centre of weight over the left leg. Between the first and second quarters, jump in the following manner: transferring the centre of weight onto the right leg and making a half turn to the right (so that the back will be toward the mirror), push off from the floor, throwing the left leg through 1st position to the side (toward point 3) to a height of 90°; simultaneously, the left arm, with a strong movement through preparatory position, is raised to 1st position, and the right remains in 2nd; the head remains for a moment turned toward the mirror, and then in the jump is turned in profile across the left shoulder. The jump is done upward, while also traveling beyond the toe of the left leg, thrown out at 90°. Turn in the air and finish, on the second quarter, toward the mirror, facing point 1, on the left leg in demi-plié; the right leg is bent with the toe in front of the knee. When finishing the jump, bend the right arm to 1st position and open the left to 2nd; the head and the body are en face. On the third and fourth quarters, remain in the same position, in this way consolidating the stability of the body on the supporting leg after the jump and preparing it for the next jump. Thus, the beginning of saut de basque (the coupé), which may be thought of as a préparation, is analogous to the final position of the jump. That is why it is recommended that the study of saut de basque be begun not with a step from 5th position or with a coupé sur le cou-de-pied, but precisely in this way.

The saut de basque should be repeated four times. Then practise it with the other leg, going in the other direction.

Later on, it is done without the long pause, that is, in 2/4.

Before describing saut de basque approached by means other than a step-coupé, let us consider the rules of execution, since, regardless of the preparatory steps or the tempo, these rules hold for all varieties of saut de basque.

RULES FOR THE EXECUTION OF SAUT DE BAS- QUE. The thighs and the small of the back must be completely pulled up; the least slackness during the jump deprives it of strength and the proper form.

Before the jump and at the end, the straight, pulled-up body must be securely over the supporting leg in demi-plié.

In the execution of saut de basque to the right (with the right leg), the body turns, at the moment of the jump, with the aid of the left shoulder, along with a very energetic transfer of the left arm to 1st position through preparatory position (the right arm remaining in 2nd). To finish the turn of the body the right shoulder is taken back; and, only at the last moment, in the return to the initial position in demi-plié (never earlier), does the right arm, with a resilient movement, go to 1st position.

The first half of the turn of the body takes place at the moment of the throw of the leg to 90°; the second half, when the supporting leg is quickly brought up to the knee of the leg that is thrown out to 90°. While clearly feeling these two moments, one must, all the same, do the turn of the body without a break.

The movement of the head, which, during the jump, is turned in profile across the shoulder, and quickly returns en face at the end of the jump, helps the turn.

The left leg, forcefully thrown out along the floor, through 1st position, to the side to 90°, must be turned-out and strong, and must maintain the height of 90° as long as possible, thus furthering the lightness of the jump (that is, the ballon). The body moves beyond the thrown-out leg, which heightens the quality of flight characteristic of the jump.

The right leg, after the break away from the floor, is brought up to the left and (turned-out to the utmost) bends, bringing the toe to the knee of the left leg. A leg insufficiently secured in the bent position, or a knee inclining forward or backward, will spoil the whole jump and give it a grotesque character.

The take-off from the floor in the jump must be very short, regardless of the movement that precedes the saut de basque.

For example, doing the preparatory coupé on the upbeat on the *and*, delay the step and the jump until just barely after the first quarter, and then do both very quickly.

Saut de basque with a step-coupé en diagonale, traveling downstage from an upstage corner. This is done in the same way as saut de basque with step-coupé in a straight line to the side, except that, in the jump and in the coupé-préparation, the whole body is placed on a diagonal: the head is turned across the shoulder in the direction of point 2 when the movement goes to the right, and to point 8 when it goes to the left. The throw of the leg to 90° with the jump is done toward the corner; at the end of the jump, the body and the head return to the initial position. The arms can be as follows: the right in 1st position and the left in 2nd, the right in 2nd and the left in 1st, both arms in 3rd position, or one in 3rd and the other in 1st position.

Saut de basque with chassé in a straight line to the side. Final form. 2/4 time. The movement is done from point 7 to point 3. Préparation: the right leg is croisé devant, with the toe to the floor; the right arm is in 1st position, the left in 2nd; and the head is turned to the right.

On the upbeat, demi-plié on the left leg, the right bending sur le cou-de-pied devant; the body and the head turn en face. Step with the right leg to the side, then do a pas chassé in a straight line to the right, bringing the legs together in 5th position in the sliding jump along the floor with the right leg in front; the arms open to 2nd position; then the hands are raised slightly and turned palms down. After a short delay, on the first quarter do a step-coupé by placing the right leg, with an accent, on the floor. Between the first and second quarters, do the saut de basque, finishing, on the second quarter, in demi-plié on the left leg (as described in saut de basque with step-coupé in a straight line to the side).

When pushing from the floor, and simultaneously with the throw of the leg to 90°, the arms, with a strong movement, are raised from below to 3rd position, where they remain at the end of the jump. Only on the next chassé do they open again to 2nd position. Incoherent arms, or their premature opening, interfere with the assembly of the body in the jump and a stable pause in plié after the jump. (The movements of the arms can be combined, as described in the preceding example.)

Doing saut de basque with chassé several times in a row, it is necessary to make sure that the shoulders are in alignment with the diagonal for each pas chassé and step, that is, that the body and the legs do not turn ahead of time, by their own momentum. The turn takes place only at the moment of the push from the floor. It is recommended that this be especially observed doing saut de basque with chassé traveling downstage en diagonale. In an incorrect execution, almost half of the turn of the body may be done during the chassé, in which case only a quarter of a turn will remain for the saut de basque itself. Thus, traveling in the chassé on the diagonal from point 6 to point 2, it is necessary to hold the body with the right shoulder toward point 2 and the left toward point 6 until the moment when the right leg is placed on the floor for the turn and the push for the jump (the saut de basque). On a diagonal from point 4 to point 8, the body must be held with the left shoulder to point 8 and the right to point 4.

The head, in the pas chassé, is in a profile position and is turned across the shoulder; during the jump, it turns to the same corner as the leg that is thrown out at 90°; at the end of the jump, it again takes on the profile position.

Saut de basque finishing in a big pose. This is done as described in the preceding examples, but, at the end of the jump, the leg that is bent to the knee of the supporting leg is quickly taken to the pose attitude croisée, 3rd or 4th arabesque, etc.

Saut de basque may also be finished with a pose on the knee.

Most difficult of all is saut de basque with a double tour in the air. The rules are the same as for saut de basque with one tour, but, for the double tour, stronger force is required of the arms.

Example of a combination. 2/4 time, eight measures. Préparation: standing near point 7, the right leg is croisé devant, with the toe to the floor.

First measure. Traveling in a straight line from point 7 to point 3, do chassé and saut de basque with the arms in 1st and 2nd positions.

Second measure. Repeat saut de basque with chassé.

Third measure. Sissonne tombée and grande cabriole in 1st arabesque to point 2 (on the diagonal).

Fourth measure. On the diagonal, traveling upstage from point 2 to point 6, chassé and grand assemblé en tournant with the arms in 3rd position.

Fifth and sixth measures. Opening the arms to 2nd position, do three entrechats-six and a whole turn to the right in 5th position on demi-pointe, finishing the turn with a coupé (plié on the left leg and bring the right foot sur le cou-de-pied devant).

Seventh and eighth measures. On the diagonal from point 6 to point 2, do two sauts de basque with chassé, the arms in 3rd position. Finish the second saut de basque in the big pose 3rd arabesque facing point 2 (the right leg is croisé derrière at 90°).

Pas Ciseaux

Pas ciseaux ("scissors step") is a big jump from one leg to the other, with the legs thrown forward at 90° one after the other. It is done with a preliminary step-coupé croisé devant, or may be preceded by a développé at 90° in the pose croisée devant, or by a glissade.

Study Sequence

1. Elementary form. 4/4 time. Stand on the left leg and take out the right leg croisé derrière with the toe to the floor. On the upbeat, open the arms slightly to the side and return them to preparatory position. On the first quarter, with a sharp movement, throw the right leg, through 1st position, in the direction effacée devant at 90°, simultane-

ously doing a demi-plié on the left leg and inclining the body strongly backward, with the head turned to the left and the arms in 1st position. On the second quarter, the position is held. Between the second and third quarters, pushing off from the floor with the left leg, jump upward; the left leg comes up in the air to the right leg, which maintains the height of 90°; the body is still inclined backward, and the arms are in 1st position; the left leg is immediately thrown out backward through 1st position to a height of 90°, and the right comes down in demi-plié, with the body sharply transferred forward onto the right leg to the pose 1st arabesque on a diagonal in the direction of point 2. The jump finishes, in 1st arabesque, on the third quarter. On the fourth, the position is held. On the next measure, in four quarters, take a step forward with the left leg to assume the initial position for a repetition of the movement.

2.   Final form. 4/4 time. The initial position is the same. On the first quarter, throw the right leg in the direction effacée devant at 90°. Between the first and second quarters, jump as described above. On the second quarter, finish the jump in the pose 1st arabesque. On the third and fourth quarters, step forward to the initial position.

Pas ciseaux with a step-coupé, croisé devant. 2/4 time. Begin in 5th position with épaulement croisé, left leg front. On the upbeat, demi-plié on the right leg, taking the left to the conditional position sur le cou-de-pied devant at a small distance from the supporting leg; and open the arms slightly to the side. On the first quarter, step forward onto the left leg, from the toe to the heel (the step-coupé), to 4th position croisée in demi-plié; the body inclines forward; the centre of weight is transferred onto the left leg; the head is slightly lowered; and the arms close to preparatory position. Without delay, and simultaneously with the jump, sharply throw the right leg out in the direction effacée devant to a height of 90°, strongly inclining the body backward and raising the arms to 1st position. Throw the left leg up to the right in the air, and quickly take it backward, through 1st position, to a height of 90°, as the right leg comes down in demi-plié; transfer the body sharply forward to the pose 1st arabesque. The entire pas finishes on the second quarter.

Pas ciseaux with a preliminary développé croisé devant at 90° is done in the same way. This jump is used at the end of an allegro combination, as well as in adagio. From a preparatory pose on the whole foot (the right leg croisé devant at 90°), rise to demi-pointe on the upbeat, open and lower the arms, and fall (tombé) onto the right leg in demi-plié, transferring the centre of weight onto that leg; then do the pas ciseaux as described above.

Pas ciseaux can also be done backward. From the pose effacée devant (right leg at a height of 90°), take a step backward into plié with the right leg, lowering the arms and transferring the centre of weight onto that leg; throw the left leg out, through 1st position, backward to a height of 90°, simultaneously inclining the body forward and bringing the arms together in 1st position, and jump; in the jump, throw the right leg quickly up to the left in back and then sharply forward, through 1st position, to effacé devant at 90°; the left comes down in demi-plié. The body, arms, and head again assume the initial pose effacée at 90°.

Pas ciseaux with a preliminary glissade is done in the same way. In this case, pas glissade is done on the upbeat, with a short movement forward on a diagonal.

RULES FOR THE EXECUTION OF PAS CISEAUX. The characteristic feature of pas ciseaux is the quick transfer of the body, which, in the jump, is inclined backward in a horizontal position, forward—to arabesque. The transfer of the body takes place sharply, without smooth intermediate positions. In both positions of the body, the back and thighs must be strongly pulled up.

The throw of the legs forward with a grand battement is done very quickly and with a pause in the air at the height of 90°. Coming down from the jump in 1st arabesque in demi-plié, one must not pause with the leg forward in the air, or bring it backward with a separate movement. The leg is thrown backward along the floor through 1st position to a height of 90° without the least delay, both legs taking their final position simultaneously.

Pas Ballotté

Ballotté is a rocking, swinging movement (from the French ballotter, "to toss about"). "The name is. very graphic and evokes the idea of a boat rocking on the waves," says A. Y. Vaganova in her book *Basic Principles of Classical Ballet*, concerning the character of this movement.

Study Sequence

1. Elementary study (with the toe to the floor). 4/4 time. Begin in 5th position with épaulement croisé, right leg front. On the upbeat, demi-plié and, bringing the legs together in 5th position in a jump, strongly travel forward in the direction effacée (the legs should not be excessively stretched in the knees, but the feet are tightly and strongly held together); the body is inclined backward; and the arms quickly go to a low 1st position. On the first quarter, leaving the body inclined backward, come down on the left leg in demi-plié, opening the right leg effacé devant with the toe to the floor (the opening of the leg must not be stiff, but it also must not have the character of a sissonne ouverte, in which the leg, bending in the knee, opens through the position sur le cou-de-pied; the opening of the leg is done only with the tip

of the toe, and in this way the movement is softened); the left arm opens to 1st position, and the right to 2nd; the head turns to the left. On the second quarter, coming erect and leaving the body effacé, do an assemblé, lowering the arms to preparatory position. On the third quarter, again the legs come together in 5th position in a jump that strongly travels backward to the place from which the first jump began; the body is inclined forward; and the arms are brought together in a low 1st position. The jump finishes in demi-plié on the right leg, with the left leg in the position effacée derrière, toe to the floor; the right arm is in 1st position, and the left in 2nd; the body is inclined forward; and the head and eyes are directed over the right arm. On the fourth quarter, do an assemblé, bringing the legs together in 5th position in demi-plié, left leg back.

2. Ballotté with an opening of the legs at 45°. This is done as in the preceding example, but at the end of the jump, the leg opens at 45°.

3. Final form. 2/4 time. Préparation: the left leg is croisé derrière with the toe to the floor. On the upbeat, demi-plié and jump, bringing the feet together in the air in 5th position; the arms go to a low 1st position; the body turns to the position effacée and inclines backward. Strongly travel forward in the direction of point 2, finishing the jump, on the first quarter, in demi-plié on the left leg, the right leg opening effacé devant at 45°, as in No. 1; the left arm is in 1st, and the right in 2nd position; the body is strongly inclined backward; and the head is turned to the left. Between the first and second quarters, jump strongly, bringing the feet together in the air in 5th position and traveling backward on a diagonal; the body comes erect for an instant, then immediately inclines forward; the right arm is caught up from below with the hand, and joins the left in 1st position; on the second quarter, the jump finishes in demi-plié on the right leg, with the left opening effacé

derrière at 45°; the body strongly inclines forward over the supporting leg; the right arm is in 1st position, and the left in 2nd; the eyes are directed forward over the right arm. Then the jump is repeated.

For the study of ballotté it is useful to do it from four to eight times in a series.

Ballotté can also be done with the opening of the legs, one after the other, at 90° (a famous example occurs in *Giselle*). The rules are the same as for the ballotté described above; but, at the end, the legs, in turn, open to 90° by means of a développé.

RULES FOR THE EXECUTION OF PAS BALLOTTÉ. The shifts of the torso in this jump must be smooth and co-ordinated with the movements of the legs, arms, and head. Regardless of the fact that a correct, beautifully executed ballotté demands a great tightness of the body and legs, there must not be the least noticeable effort. The pauses in demi-plié are not fixed; they should be barely apparent to the eye. The impression must be that the dancer, flying forward and backward on a diagonal, is freely and easily rocking in the air, almost not touching the floor.

In the execution of this step, a strongly pulled-up back and thighs are especially necessary.

Doing ballotté with the right leg, on a diagonal from point 6 to point 2, traveling forward and opening the right leg forward, it is necessary to watch that the shoulders remain level; to keep from raising the right shoulder, the right side must be strongly pulled up.

Traveling backward and opening the left leg, it is essential to pull up the left side, so that the left shoulder is not taken back.

The first jump begins from épaulement croisé, then the body assumes the position effacée for the remainder of the ballottés in both its elementary and its final forms.

Pas Ballonné

Pas ballonné ("bounced") is a jump on one leg, done traveling in any direction after the working leg, which is stretched during the jump, and then, at the time of landing, returns to the position sur le cou-de-pied.

The study of ballonné is begun in the elementary years (the second and third); but it must be continued in the intermediate and advanced years as well, being included as often as possible in the first or second small allegro combinations. Ballonné is encountered on the stage in ensemble dances (such as the waltz in Act I of *Sleeping Beauty* and the Dance of the Nereids in Act II), and has the character of a free dance step. However, in classwork, ballonné is a complicated and difficult pas, which develops a springboard-like jump, flying off in any direction.

Ballonné, repeated often, facilitates the execution of grands jetés and a number of other jumps which, at first glance, seem to have nothing in common with pas ballonné.

In the beginning, ballonné is studied in place, that is, with only a jump upward, and finishes with an assemblé; later, three to four consecutive jumps are done, the last one finishing with an assemblé. After this, it is possible to go on to ballonné traveling in one direction or another, beginning with a single jump and gradually increasing the number of jumps to four.

The following order of study is recommended:

1) ballonné to the side in 2nd position;
2) ballonné in the poses croisées, devant and derrière;
3) ballonné in the poses effacées, devant and derrière;
4) ballonné in the poses écartées, derrière and devant.

Study Sequence

1. Ballonné to the side in 2nd position. 4/4 time. Begin in 5th position, épaulement croisé, right leg front. On the first quarter, demi-plié. Between the first and second quarters,

pushing off from the floor with the heels, jump upward; the stretched right leg, with a sliding movement along the floor, is thrown out to 2nd position at a height of 45°; simultaneously, the left leg comes off the floor and is in the air in a vertical position; the arms, from preparatory position, open to 2nd position (the palms turned down); the body and the head are en face. On the second quarter, the left leg comes down in demi-plié; the right simultaneously bends, the foot being brought to the conditional position sur le cou-de-pied devant; the right arm goes to 1st position, the left remains in 2nd position; and the hands are curved again; the body is en face; the head is turned either straight forward or toward the right shoulder. Between the second and third quarters, sliding the toe of the right leg along the floor to 2nd position, do an assemblé, finishing it in 5th position in demi-plié, right leg back, with épaulement croisé; the head is to the left; beginning the assemblé, bring the right arm to the side, then lower both arms through a half-2nd position to preparatory position at the end. On the fourth quarter, stretch the knees.

On the next measure of 4/4, repeat the ballonné in the reverse direction; throw the right leg out to 2nd position in the jump; and come down on the left in demi-plié, while bending the right sur le cou-de-pied derrière; the right arm is in 2nd position, and the left is in 1st; the body is en face; the head is either en face or turned toward the left shoulder. Then assemblé to the side in 2nd position finishing with the right leg in front, in 5th position, with épaulement croisé.

Ballonné in the poses croisées and effacées is also learned in 4/4. In the execution of ballonné with the right leg in the poses croisées, the arms are raised from preparatory position, the left arm to 1st and the right to 2nd position; in the poses effacées, the arms are in the same position. When ballonné is repeated in the poses several times in a row, the position of the arms does not change, with the exception of ballonné to the side in 2nd position, in which the arms open to 2nd position with each jump and, on each landing, bend alternately to 1st position (if the working foot is sur le cou-de-pied devant, the same arm will be in 1st; if sur le cou-de-pied derrière, the opposite arm will be in 1st, the head always turned in the direction of the front leg).

2. 2/4 time. The demi-plié and the jump are done on the upbeat. On the first quarter, demi-plié on the supporting leg; the working leg bends with the foot sur le cou-de-pied. Between the first and second quarters, assemblé, finishing in 5th position in demi-plié on the second quarter.

3. Ballonné traveling in the pose effacée. Final form. 4/4 time. Begin in 5th position with épaulement croisé, right leg front. The movement is done on a diagonal from point 6 to point 2 of the classroom plan. On the upbeat, demi-plié (with épaulement croisé), and, pushing off from the floor, jump strongly upward, turning the body effacé to point 2; the right leg, sliding along the floor, is thrown out effacé devant to a height of 45°; the left arm is in 1st and the right in 2nd position; the head turns to the left. In the jump, travel forward toward the toe of the right leg; and, on the first quarter, come down in demi-plié on the left leg, simultaneously bringing the right foot sur le cou-de-pied devant. From this position, on the second and third quarters, do two more ballonnés, each time traveling in the direction of the thrown-out right leg; each time, the right leg, in the jump, stretches forward directly from the position sur le cou-de-pied, without touching the floor with the toe; the arms, body, and head remain in the positions taken in the first ballonné. On the fourth quarter, opening the arms slightly to the side, assemblé to the side in 2nd position and finish it in 5th position in demi-plié with épaulement croisé, right leg back, lowering the arms to preparatory position.

Repeat the movement with the other leg, then do it in the reverse direction, traveling backward on the diagonal.

Ballonné in the poses can also be done with a preliminary coupé, from épaulement croisé. A short coupé and the jump are done on the upbeat; the given pose (for example, effacée or écartée) is taken at the moment of the jump. Before a ballonné forward, at the moment of plié, the foot that is in back in 5th position is brought sur le cou-de-pied derrière; then, with a short movement, it is placed on the floor (in 5th position), accenting the plié and seeming to displace, with a push, the front leg, and immediately comes off the floor. Before a ballonné backward, the coupé is done in front. The purpose of this coupé is to give more momentum to the push from the floor.

RULES FOR THE EXECUTION OF PAS BALLONNÉ. Ballonné is a movement that develops a jump on one leg with movement through the air.

The first ballonné, from 5th position, is begun with a push from the floor with two legs; that is, it is done from two legs onto one. All of the succeeding ballonnés are done from one leg onto the same leg. The flight through the air moves toward the leg that is thrown out.

When the jump is executed several times in a row, the demi-pliés between the jumps must be resilient, so as not to lose the strength of the muscles, in order to push off effectively for the next jump.

The leg bends and the foot is brought sur le cou-de-pied simultaneously with the conclusion of the jump on the supporting leg in demi-plié. It is absolutely inadmissible to delay the bending of the working leg.

When the jump is repeated on one leg, one must not lower or raise the height of the leg that is opened at 45°, or touch the floor with the toe. In the throwing out and bending of the leg backward, it is especially necessary to take care that the buttocks muscles are tightly pulled up.

In the jump and in demi-plié, the thighs and shoulders are held level, and the back remains pulled up. For stability in plié, it is recommended that the body be restrained from inclining toward the supporting leg (such an inclination hinders the rebound from the floor and disturbs the correctness of the poses) and that the side of the body analogous with the working leg be strongly pulled up.

Example of a combination with pas ballonné for elementary classes. 4/4 time, four measures.

First measure. Begin in 5th position with épaulement croisé, right leg front. On the first quarter, ballonné with the right leg, traveling toward 2nd position. At the end of the jump, the right foot is sur le cou-de-pied devant; the right arm is in 1st, the left in 2nd position; the body is en face; the head is turned to the right. On the second quarter, do a second ballonné in the same direction; at the end of the jump, the right foot is sur le cou-de-pied derrière; the left arm is in 1st and the right in 2nd position; and the head is turned to the left. On the third quarter, do a third ballonné, the right foot finishing sur le cou-de-pied devant; the right arm is in 1st and the left in 2nd position; and the head is turned to the right. On the fourth quarter, assemblé with the right leg to 2nd position, finishing in 5th position with épaulement croisé, right leg back.

Second measure. On the first quarter, with the left leg, ballonné, traveling forward in the pose croisée devant; the right arm is in 1st and the left in 2nd position; the head is turned to the left. On the second and third quarters, do two more ballonnés, traveling in the same direction, without changing the position of the arms and head. On the fourth quarter, assemblé in 2nd position, finishing in 5th position, left leg back.

Third measure. On the first and second quarters, grand échappé to 2nd position, changing the legs; on the third and fourth quarters, grand échappé to 4th position croisée.

Fourth measure. With the right leg, do three ballonnés in a small pose croisée derrière; the right arm is in 1st and the left in 2nd position; the head is turned to the left. Then assemblé in 2nd position, finishing with the right leg in front; or assemblé back, and begin immediately to the other side.

Example of a combination for intermediate classes. 2/4 time, eight measures. Begin in 5th position with épaulement croisé, right leg front.

First and second measures. With the right leg, two ballonnés effacés devant in 1/4 each, and two in 1/8 each; in 1/4, assemblé in 2nd position, finishing in 5th position, right leg back.

Third measure. Entrechat-trois derrière (with the left leg) and assemblé croisé derrière.

Fourth measure. On the first quarter, grand changement de pieds en tournant (turning to the left); on the second, entrechat-quatre and royale (in 1/8 each).

Fifth and sixth measures. With the left leg, two ballonnés effacés derrière in 1/4 each, and two in 1/8 each; in 1/4, assemblé in 2nd position, finishing in 5th position, left leg front.

Seventh measure. Entrechat-trois devant (with the right leg) and assemblé croisé devant.

Eighth measure. Grand changement de pieds en tournant (turning to the left) and grande sissonne ouverte to attitude croisée. Stop on the left leg in demi-plié in the pose attitude croisée.

Ballonné with Half Turns. Begin in 5th position with the right leg in front. With the right leg, take a small step to the side (coupé) and jump, doing the ballonné with a half turn to the right and opening the arms to 2nd position. At the conclusion of the jump, the right arm remains in 2nd position, the left bends to 1st position, and the head is turned to the left shoulder; the left leg is bent with the foot sur le cou-de-pied derrière. Then coupé dessous with the left leg, turning a little more to the right (toward the mirror), and do a small assemblé croisé devant. Continue the sequence several times in a series traveling to the side from point 7 to point 3. Then practise in the opposite direction.

It is also possible, after the coupé dessous en tournant, to do a small cabriole in the pose écartée devant and continue this sequence several times in a series traveling to the side.

Pas Chassé

Pas chassé (from the French *chasser*, "to chase") is a jump that may travel in any direction; one leg "catches up" with the other at the high point of the jump.

Chassé exists as an independent pas allegro, it can be combined with other jumps, and it is also included in the big adagio in intermediate and advanced classes. Besides that, chassé has as well an auxiliary significance as a running start before big jumps.

In the first case (as an independent pas or in combination with other jumps), chassé is done traveling, with a strong break away from the floor, to the side, or croisé, effacé, or écarté, devant or derrière.

In the second case (as a running start), chassé is done more quickly, as a sliding jump par terre (in which the legs come together in 5th position, with stretched toes, almost without a break away from the floor), in the direction of one or another big jump, either in a straight line, on a diagonal, or in a circle.

In elementary and intermediate classes, chassé, done as a big jump, begins with a small sliding sissonne tombée or with a développé on demi-pointe at 90°; it finishes with a sliding jump par terre (i. e., without a break away from the floor) analogous to the concluding movement of a pas de basque. Between the initial sissonne tombée and the concluding jump from two to six chassés are done.

In adagio, chassé can begin from any big pose with a rise to demi-pointe, followed by a wide tombé, two chassés, and a sliding jump par terre to 5th position. However, it is more usual, in this case, to finish the chassé either in a big pose in demi-plié, or in a big préparation in 4th position for tours in the poses at 90°, en dehors or en dedans.

Chassé is also done before tours en l'air (turns in the air); in this case, it finishes in 5th position in demi-plié, in a préparation for the tours (the front arm in 1st and the other in 2nd position).

Pas chassé in 2nd position. 4/4 time, or four measures of 3/4 (waltz). Begin in 5th position with épaulement croisé, right leg front. The movement goes in a straight line to the right.

On the upbeat, open the arms slightly to the side and lower them to preparatory position, bending the body and head down and slightly to the left; simultaneously, demi-plié. Then do a slight sissonne tombée to 2nd position with the right leg, during which the body is not transferred onto the right leg, but straightens and again inclines to the left, the arms opening to 2nd position and the head inclined toward the left shoulder. On the first and second quarters, do two chassés in the following manner. Fall (tombé) onto the right leg; but immediately push off into a big jump and, in the air, bring the left leg up to the right in 5th position back. The jump must be as high as possible, with a pause in the air while traveling to the side. Having touched the floor and moved the right leg toward 2nd position, again jump, bringing the legs together in the air in 5th position and continuing the flight to the side. On the third quarter, opening the right leg slightly to the side, fall onto it in demi-plié and, in a sliding jump par terre (i. e. without breaking away from the floor), continue to move to the side. On the fourth quarter, come down in 5th position in demi-plié, at the last moment placing the left leg in front. Bending the body to the right, repeat the whole pas with the other leg, moving in a straight line to the left. Traveling to the right, the body will be inclined slightly to the left, right leg front; and, only at the very end of the pas, in 5th position, will the left leg be placed in front. Traveling to the left, the body inclines to the right, the left leg in front; at the end of the movement, in 5th position, the right leg will be placed in front.

Chassé in the directions croisée, effacée, or écartée is done in the same way. The arms can be one in 1st and the other in 2nd position, or one in 3rd and the other in 2nd position.

For example, in the pose croisée, if the movement begins with the right leg, the left arm can be raised to 3rd position, with the right in 2nd, or it can be opened to 2nd position with the head inclined under the right arm, which will be raised to 3rd, or both arms may be raised to 3rd position. In the poses effacées and écartées as well, variations of the arm positions are permitted.

RULES FOR THE EXECUTION OF PAS CHASSÉ. Chassé, as an independent jumping step, must be done broadly across the whole room in all directions in a straight line, as well as croisé and on a diagonal. The closing and holding of the legs in 5th position in the air is the same as for grand changement de pieds, with the difference that, in this case, there is no changing of the legs (changement), and one travels through the air, while jumping.

The demi-plié between the jumps must not be held; the break away from the floor is short and quick; and the pause in the air is held as long as possible.

One leg must not strike the other; neither should the leg that is in back during the movement forward (or in front during the movement backward) be allowed to lag behind, sliding along the floor. It is necessary to remember that chassé in classical dance has nothing in common with the chassé of historical and popular dance.

In the poses croisées and effacées, when doing the final jump along the floor in 5th position, the body bends slightly backward and the arms, opening to 2nd position, are gradually lowered. If chassé is done backward from a preliminary développé on demi-pointe, that is, from attitude croisée or attitude effacée, then, at the moment of the tombé, the leg stretches from attitude.

Chassé is a dynamic movement and must be done at a moderate or, more often, at a quick tempo.

Pas Glissade

Glissade (from the French glisser, "to glide") is a jump from two legs onto two. Like pas chassé, glissade can be done as an independent movement or as an auxiliary pas preceding small or big jumps.

Glissade belongs to the category of jumps par terre, i.e., jumps done without breaking away from the floor. It is done to the side, and in all directions in the small poses. Its study begins in the elementary classes.

Study Sequence

1. Glissade to the side. 4/4 time. Begin in 5th position en face with the right leg in front. On the first quarter, demi-plié and slide the right leg along the floor, reaching 2nd position with a stretched instep and toes; the left leg remains in plié. On the second quarter, this position is held. Between the second and the third quarters, pushing off from the floor with the heel of the left foot, jump onto the right leg without breaking away from the floor (in this jump, there is a moment when both legs are in 2nd position with stretched knees, touching the floor only with the stretched toes); immediately, the centre of the body's weight is transferred onto the right leg; and the left foot, sliding along the floor, is brought to the right. On the third quarter, both legs come together in 5th position in demi-plié, with the left leg in back. On the fourth quarter, the knees are stretched.

Glissade can also be done changing the legs: in the above example, the left leg would finish in front.

2. 4/4 time. Beginning as before, on the first and second quarters, demi-plié in 5th position. Between the second and third quarters, slide the right foot to second position and jump, bringing the left leg, with a stretched knee, instep, and toes, quickly to the right. On the third quarter, the legs come together in 5th position in demi-plié with the left leg in back. On the fourth quarter, the knees are stretched.

Glissade in the small poses is learned in the same way.

3. Final form. 4/4 time. Begin in 5th position, with épaulement croisé and the right leg in front. The movement goes in a straight line to the right. On the upbeat, demi-plié; quickly slide the right leg, with the toe to the floor, to 2nd position and jump, transferring the centre of weight onto the right leg; on the first quarter, the left (having stretched the knee, instep, and toes in the jump) is brought to the right in 5th position in demi-plié front. The arms, during the glissade, open halfway to the side; at the end of the glissade, they remain open, and the head turns to the left (épaulement croisé). On the next three quarters, execute three more glissades to the right with the right leg, changing the legs on each glissade. Each time, the head changes position, turning, at the end of the glissade, toward the leg that is in 5th position front. The arms remain in the original small 2nd position, and only on the last glissade are they lowered to the preparatory position.

In the execution of glissade several times consecutively in a pose (croisée, effacée, etc.), the arms assume their position on the first jump, and are lowered only with the last movement, just as in the glissade to 2nd position.

RULES FOR THE EXECUTION OF PAS GLISSADE. The object of the elementary study of glissade is the preparation of the legs for the correct execution of the jump in its final form, that is, a smooth movement from two legs onto two. In particular, the leg that finishes the movement should be carefully watched: in the par terre jump, the instep, toes, and knee of that leg must be stretched. The glissade finishes with the legs closing simultaneously in 5th position in demi-plié. In a glissade traveling forward, one must especially watch the leg that stretches in back; and similarly, in a glissade backward, one must watch the leg that stretches in front.

Glissade as an auxiliary pas for small or big jumps is done on the upbeat with a short, assembled, quick movement. It finishes on the quarter; and, on this same quarter, the main jump begins. A disconnected, wide glissade is not permitted, for it lessens, rather than increases, the impetus for the next jump (as could happen, for example, with glissade in combination with grand jeté).

In all glissades the body is transferred in the direction of the leg that begins the movement.

In its final form, glissade is done in 1/4 and in 1/8.

In advanced classes, glissade, executed before big jumps (for example, grand cabriole, grand jeté, etc.), may be begun not only from 5th position but from a préparation croisée devant. In this case, the leg, which is in 5th position front, is stretched forward croisé, toe to the floor. The arms, on the instructions of the teacher, are opened to a low 1st position or are lifted, one to 3rd and the other to 2nd allongée positions.

Example of a combination with pas glissade for elementary classes. 4/4 time, four measures. Begin in 5th position with épaulement croisé, right leg front.

First measure. On the first and second quarters, two glissades, changing the legs, in 2nd position (to the right), in 1/4 each. On the third and fourth quarters, three glissades, changing the legs, in 2nd position (to the right), in 1/8 each.

Second measure. On the first quarter, with the left leg, glissade croisée devant. On the second quarter, with the right leg, glissade croisée derrière. On the third and fourth quarters, petit échappé, changing the legs, in 2nd position.

Third measure. On the first and second quarters, with the left leg, glissade without changing the legs (preserving épaulement croisé) and a small assemblé to the side, finishing in 5th position, left leg front. On the third and fourth quarters, with the right leg, glissade to the side, without changing the legs (preserving épaulement croisé), and assemblé, changing the legs.

Fourth measure. On the first and second quarters, two glissades with the right leg, without changing the legs, in 1/4 each, in the pose écartée derrière, traveling on a diagonal toward point 2. On the third and fourth quarters, two glissades with the left leg, without changing the legs, in 1/4 each, in the pose écartée devant, traveling on a diagonal toward point 6.

Repeat the combination with the other leg and then do it in the reverse direction.

Pas Failli

Failli (from the French faillir, "to just miss") is done both as an independent allegro pas and as a connecting movement preceding such big jumps as grand assemblé or grand jeté (for example, failli, coupé, grand jeté in attitude croisée or in 3rd arabesque).

Failli is also widely used in adagio, where it can finish with a pause on one leg, with the other leg croisé derrière, the toe to the floor, or in the pose croisée, in the pose 4th arabesque, or in 4th position croisée as a préparation for tours.

Failli as an Independent Allegro Pas. (En arrière.) 2/4 time. Begin in 5th position with épaulement croisé, right leg front. On the upbeat, slightly open the arms to the side and lower them, with a demi-plié, bending the body to the left; then jump upward, strongly stretching the toes (the jump is a kind of soubresaut). In the jump, the body turns effacé to point 2 of the classroom plan; the arms are raised to 1st position, and the head is turned en face to point 2. Then come down in demi-plié on the right leg; the left, stretched, opens effacé derrière at 45°; the arms are brought to 2nd position; the head turns to the left. On the first quarter, without a pause, bring the left leg forward through 1st position in demi-plié, stretching it croisé devant, with the toe to the floor; the right leg remains in demi-plié; at the moment of the passé through 1st position, the body bends slightly back, with the small of the back strongly secured and the shoulders level; at the same time, the left arm is lowered and softly, almost involuntarily, with a free and easy elbow, brought forward to the position of 2nd or 4th arabesque (if the position is 4th arabesque, the right shoulder must be taken strongly back); the head, following the direction of the movement of the left arm, is lowered and again turns to the left. Maintaining the pose, glide forward beyond the toe of the left leg and, on the second quarter, bring the legs together in a par terre jump (that is, jump without breaking away from the floor), coming down in 5th position in demi-plié, with the left leg in front.

Failli with a pause in the big pose croisée derrière. This is done as in the preceding example, but, after the passé through 1st position in demi-plié, transfer the weight onto the stretched left leg, bringing the arms, through preparatory and 1st position, to the big pose croisée (the right arm is in 3rd position, the left in 2nd), and stretching the right leg croisé derrière with the toe to the floor.

Failli as a Springboard-like Movement Before a Big Jump. This is done on the upbeat. Both the completion of the failli and the big jump of the next pas take place on the first quarter. The beginning is the same as in the usual failli, but the body can be inclined to the left or to the right (depending upon the pose to be taken in the next jump).

The failli finishes, after the passé through 1st position, in a narrow 4th position croisée, the arms in the pose 2nd arabesque, the shoulders level; the centre of weight has been transferred forward onto the left leg in demi-plié; the stretched right leg is in back with the whole foot on the floor.

The springboard-like bound from the floor (a kind of coupé) for the following big jump is done with the left leg, although the right simultaneously slides along the floor and is thrown out to 90° (this occurs, for example, in the combination of failli with a grand assemblé, done several times on a diagonal, moving downstage).

Failli in the Opposite Direction (en Avant). 2/4 time. Start in 5th position with épaulement croisé, right leg front. On the upbeat, demi-plié; slightly open the arms to the side and then lower them, simultaneously inclining the body to the right; then leap into the air. In the jump, the body turns effacé toward point 2; the arms are raised to 1st position, and the head is turned straight forward (en face to point 2). Then, coming down on the left leg in demi-plié, the right leg, stretched in the knee, opens forward effacé at 45°; the arms open a little from 1st position (not widely); and the head turns to the left.

On the first quarter, open the arms to the side and, without a pause, take the right leg through 1st position in demi-plié croisé derrière, toe to the floor (the left leg remaining in demi-plié). At the moment of the passé through 1st position, the right shoulder, together with the right arm, is taken back; the head turns to the right. Almost at the same time, the left arm is allowed to softly fall down with a loose elbow and is taken forward; the head, following the movement of the left arm, is lowered and turns to the left.

Holding the pose (which is analogous to 4th arabesque), travel backward beyond the toe of the right leg and, before the second quarter, join the legs in 5th position in a sliding jump along the floor (assemblé par terre), landing in 5th position in demi-plié on the quarter, with the left leg in front; the arms retain their position.

Traveling forward, the legs just miss each other in back; and the step is called failli en arrière. Traveling backward, as described just above, the legs miss in front; and the step is called failli en avant.

RULES FOR THE EXECUTION OF PAS FAILLI. Failli as an independent step is one of the softest, most plastic pas of classical dance. All of the component movements must flow together in a single co-ordinated whole. This is the sole rule for its execution.

The light, unhurried flight upward, the free movement of the open arms, the one arm appearing to lower involuntarily, then its arabesque movement forward, which carries the body along after it in a gliding jump, all of this resembles a great long-winged bird accidentally happening to touch the ground with one of its wings in the course of flight.

The linking springboard-like failli is done quickly, with a short, small jump, which helps only to emphasise the following big jump. A dragged-out, slowed-down failli would be as detrimental in such a case as would an extremely wide and slowed-down glissade.

Pas Emboîté

Emboîtés are jumps with a throwing out of the legs forward or backward alternately, traveling forward or backward. They are used only in female dance, executed forward at 45° and 90° (grand emboîté) and backward only at 45°.

Pas emboîté forward at 45°. 2/4 time. Begin in 5th position with épaulement croisé, right leg front. On the upbeat, demi-plié; the right leg bends in the knee, and the foot, with a stretched instep and toes, is taken a small distance from the floor and a little forward of the supporting leg; the legs are slightly crossed, with the right toe in alignment with the toe of the supporting foot; the head turns to the right. Then jump upward, during which the right leg is stretched out forward and the left, in a half-bent position, is carried forward past the right leg and, at the conclusion of the jump, on the first quarter, bending, it finishes a short distance from the floor and a little forward of the supporting leg; the legs are slightly crossed; the head turns to the left. In the jump, the left leg is taken past the right one between the knee and the foot of the right leg (past the middle of the shin). On the second quarter, execute the following jump.

It is recommended to do not less than eight emboîtés in a series, studying the jump at first only in place. Then emboîtés are executed traveling in a straight line forward from point 5 to point 1. It is important to see that the supporting leg pushes itself from the floor in the jump without delay and immediately flies past the other leg which is stretched forward, creating a design of crossed legs in the air. At the conclusion of each jump, the head turns to the side of the leg bent in front of the supporting leg. The arms are in preparatory position.

Pas emboîté backward is done in the same way; but at the conclusion, the head is turned to the side of the supporting leg which is in demi-plié.

In the final form of pas emboîté forward it is possible to execute it en diagonale and in a circle with one arm raised to 2nd position and the other to 3rd position.

Pas emboîté forward at 90°. Executed traveling forward en diagonale and in a circle, 1/4 each. 2/4 time. Begin in 5th position épaulement croisé. Emboîté at 90° differs from emboîté at 45° in that the legs are thrown out quickly and are considerably less crossed in the air. The torso leans a little backward. The arms may be raised, one to 2nd position and the other to 3rd position, and at the discretion of the teacher may change their position during 8, 16, or more jumps. One of the basic demands for the execution of emboîté at 90° is the lightness of the jump which is achieved by a quick demi-plié and strongly pulled up buttocks muscles. The contact with the floor must be minimal and the jump, alternately throwing out the legs, must be with ballon.

In intermediate classes, a complicated form emboîté en tournant, traveling to the side in a straight line or on a diagonal, is studied directly with half turns; and, in advanced classes, it is practised traveling in a circle. In this form, each emboîté is done with a half turn; thus, a full turn consists of two emboîtés.

Emboîté en tournant on the stage is usually done only forward; in the classroom, however, in the course of training, it is recommended that it also be learned traveling backward.

Emboîté en tournant forward, traveling in a straight line to the right. 2/4 time. Begin in 5th position, right leg front. The movement is done from point 7 to point 3 of the classroom plan. On the upbeat, demi-plié; the right arm is in 1st and the left in 2nd position; then, jump upward, flying off to the right and making a half turn in the air (en dedans); in the jump, bring the left leg front, near the conditional position sur le cou-de-pied but crossed somewhat more deeply than usual. Simultaneously, the right arm opens to 2nd position. On the first quarter, pause in demi-plié on the right leg, with the back to the audience; the left arm is in 1st position and the right in 2nd; the head, during the jump, is turned toward the mirror and, at the end, is directed across the left shoulder in profile.

For the second emboîté, open the left arm to 2nd position and, bringing the stretched legs together in a jump upward, fly off to the left, making the second half of the turn (en dehors), then bring the right foot front to the conditional position sur le cou-de-pied. On the second quarter, pause on the left leg in demi-plié facing the mirror; the right arm is in 1st, the left in 2nd position; the head is en face.

From here, the movement is repeated. In the first jump, the body turns with the left shoulder forward; in the second, it turns taking the right shoulder back. At the end of each emboîté, finishing in the conditional position sur le cou-de-pied devant, the bent leg goes slightly beyond the supporting leg. It is necessary to fly off to the side equally in all the emboîtés of a series (those done consecutively as well as those done with a pause in demi-plié).

In the execution of emboîté on a diagonal, the same rules of movement are observed as when it is done in a straight line to the side; but the head, in each emboîté, is in a profile position, being turned across the shoulder.

The rules for the turns of the body and head and for the movement of the arms are the same as the rules for the execution of jetés traveling to the side with half turns (see "Jeté" above).

Emboîté is learned at a slow tempo; in its final form, it is done with only a short break away from the floor, staccato, and at a quick tempo, in 1/4 or 1/8 each.

Emboîté en tournant backward, traveling in a straight line to the right. Begin in 5th position, left leg front; the right arm is in 1st and the left in 2nd position. The movement is done from point 7 to point 3. Demi-plié, and jump upward, opening the right arm to 2nd position and turning to the left (en dehors), the left shoulder is taken back; fly off to the side (in the direction of point 3), then, bringing the left foot to the position sur le cou-de-pied derrière, pause in demi-plié on the right leg with the back to the audience; the left arm is in 1st, the right is in 2nd position; the head is turned across the left shoulder. Opening the left arm to 2nd position and bringing the legs together in the jump, fly off to the left (toward point 3) while turning (en dedans), bringing the right shoulder forward; the right leg is brought up to the left in back. Pause, facing the mirror, on the left leg in demi-plié, with the right leg bent sur le cou-de-pied derrière; the right arm is in 1st and the left in 2nd position; the head is en face.

Emboîté forward may be done on a diagonal, traveling downstage from an upstage corner; emboîté backward may be done traveling upstage from a downstage corner.

In the execution of emboîté in a circle, all the odd-numbered jumps with a half turn will finish facing the centre of the room; and all the even-numbered ones, facing the walls.

Example of a combination with pas emboîté. 2/4 time, eight measures. Begin in 5th position, right leg front.

First and second measures. Traveling on the diagonal from point 6 to point 2, four emboîtés en tournant, in 1/4 each.

Third measure. Four emboîtés en tournant in 1/8 each.

Fourth measure. Take a step with the right leg toward point 2 and do a grand assemblé en tournant, finishing in 5th position, left leg front.

Fifth and sixth measures. Seven entrechats-quatre in 1/8 each, traveling backward on a diagonal (from point 2 to point 6).

Seventh measure. In a straight line to the left, with the left leg, four emboîtés en tournant in 1/8 each.

Eighth measure. Small assemblé to the side with the left leg, finishing in 5th position back, and grande sissonne ouverte to the 4th arabesque onto the left leg, with a whole turn to the left. The combination finishes in the pose 4th arabesque at 90°.

Pas Balancé

Balancé is a small, light pas, rocking from one foot to the other, which is studied from the first class and is consistently encountered in dancing on the stage.

It is done from side to side traveling forward or backward in a straight line, on a diagonal, and en tournant, with quarter and half turns.

Balancé from side to side (de côté). 3/4 time. Begin in 5th position, right leg front. On the upbeat, demi-plié and, opening the arms slightly to the side, with the right leg do a light sliding movement (a kind of jeté par terre) toward 2nd position. On the first quarter, coming down on the right leg in demi-plié, bring the left foot behind the right leg in the position sur le cou-de-pied derrière; the body bends to the right; the left arm is brought to a low 1st position, and the right remains in 2nd; the head inclines to the right. On the second quarter, step onto the left leg on demi-pointe, raising the right foot slightly off the floor with a stretched instep and toes, to the conditional position sur le cou-de-pied devant at a slight distance from the left leg; the body and head come erect; and the arms, with an easy movement, come together in preparatory position. On the third quarter, again come down on the right leg in demi-plié, raising the left foot sur le cou-de-pied derrière; the body and head incline to the right; the right arm opens to the side and the left to a low 1st position.

From this position, the next balancé is done to the left, etc.

In all three stages of the movement, the body, head, and arms take part. It is also possible for the arms to be raised alternately to 3rd position, in which case the arm is raised through 2nd position.

When balancé is executed at a moderate or a quick tempo, the body, head, and arms cannot change their positions three times; instead, they remain, until the end, in the position taken on the first movement, and only on the next balancé do they incline to the other side.

Balancé en tournant with a quarter turn. Begin in 5th position, right leg front. On the first balancé, do a sliding jeté with the right leg, turning to face point 3; on the second balancé, done with the left leg, turn to face point 5; on the third, turn to face point 7; and on the fourth, turn to the mirror, to face point 1. The same thing is done to the left. Analogously, when balancés en tournant are done with half-turns, the turn takes place with the jeté par terre.

Pas de Chat

Pas de chat is a movement that imitates the jump of a cat (the French *chat*). It is used mainly in the female dance.

There exist two kinds of pas de chat: pas de chat en arrière, in which the legs are thrown backward, and pas de chat en avant, in which they are thrown forward.

In elementary classes, petit pas de chat (at 45°) is studied; in intermediate classes, the student progresses to grand pas de chat (at 90°).

Study Sequence

1. Pas de chat en arrière at 45°. 4/4 time. Begin in 5th position with épaulement croisé, left leg front. On the first quarter, demi-plié, and throw the half-bent right leg, along the floor, croisé derrière to 45°; the body, with a pulled-up back, inclines slightly forward; the arms are in preparatory position; the head is straight forward, the eyes are directed at the hands. On the second quarter, the position is held. Between the second and third quarters, push off from the floor with the heel of the supporting leg and jump forward on the diagonal; in the jump, the left leg, half-bent, is thrown backward effacé derrière at 45°; the legs, with turned-out thighs, meet in the air (consequently, they must not be opened too widely); the body bends backward; the hands are softly thrown upward, as the arms are raised to low positions, the left to 1st, the right to 2nd; and the head turns to the left. On the third quarter, come down in 5th position in demi-plié, left leg front (the right leg comes to demi-plié first, with the left lagging behind—but only slightly), the left leg is placed on the floor with emphasis. On the fourth quarter, the knees are stretched.

2. Final form. 2/4 time. The demi-plié and the jump are done on the upbeat. The push from the floor for the jump is done with both legs, from 5th position, without a preliminary throwing out of the right leg, as is done in elementary study. The end of the jump, in demi-plié, is on the first quarter. On the second quarter, pause in demi-plié.

Then, pas de chat is practised in 1/4 each, consecutively. Grand pas de chat en arrière is distinguished from the petit pas de chat by a higher jump and a throwing of the legs to a height of 90°. The arms and the body may take various positions. Doing several pas de chat in a row, traveling forward on a diagonal, one can begin with small pas de chat, gradually increasing the jump to a big one.

Pas de chat en avant at 45°. Begin in 5th position with épaulement croisé, left leg front. Demi-plié and jump, raising the half-bent right leg to the side at 45° and taking it forward; almost simultaneously, the left leg does the same thing and, at the end of the jump, is placed in front, in 5th or 4th position, with an accent. The positions of the arms and body, as in pas de chat en arrière, vary according to what the teacher gives. The jump is done traveling forward on a diagonal.

Grand pas de chat en avant is also done on a diagonal, throwing the legs forward to a height of 90°.

The push from the floor for the big jump is done with both legs. If the left leg is in front in 5th position, then the right leg is taken out first in the jump, the left following it.

Before the jump, the body inclines forward; in the air, it strongly inclines backward. Both arms may be raised to 3rd position, or one to 3rd and the other to 1st position, etc.

Example of a combination with pas de chat and gargouillade. 2/4 time (polka), eight measures. Begin in 5th position with the left foot in front.

First and second measures. Toward point 2, three petits pas de chat en arrière, in 1/4 each; and, in 1/4, pas de bourrée en tournant en dehors, changing the legs.

Third and fourth measures. Two gargouillades en dehors (see below), finishing each with a sliding jump in 5th position, with the right and with the left leg, in 2/4 each.

Fifth measure. Entrechat-cinq derrière, with the left leg back, and pas de bourrée en tournant en dehors, changing the legs.

Sixth measure. Gargouillade en dedans with the right leg.

Seventh and eighth measures. On the diagonal toward point 8, two petits pas de chat en avant, glissade en avant, without changing the legs, and grand pas de chat en avant.

Gargouillade (Rond de Jambe en l'Air Double)

This small allegro pas exists only in the female dance. It is done en dehors and en dedans.

Study Sequence

1. *Gargouillade en dehors.* 4/4 time. Begin in 5th position with épaulement croisé, right leg front. On the upbeat, demi-plié; the right leg slides along the floor, is brought to 2nd position at 45°, and does a rond de jambe en l'air en dehors, finishing it on the first quarter; simultaneously with the taking of the leg to the side, the arms open directly from preparatory position to a half-2nd position, and the body and head incline to the left. Between the first and second quarters, jump upward, going over onto the right leg and inclining the body and head to the right; the arms are open to the side; the left leg takes off from the floor, bends in the knee so that the toe touches the middle of the calf of the right leg, is stretched to the side at 45°, and again is brought to the calf, as if doing the second half of a rond de jambe en l'air en dehors; land from the jump onto the right leg on the second quarter, lowering the arms to preparatory position. Between the second and third quarters, the left leg is brought down, touching the toe to the floor a little in front of the supporting leg and, on the third quarter, slides croisé devant with the toe along the floor; the arms are raised to a low 1st position. Then both legs come together in a sliding jump forward without breaking away from the floor. On the fourth quarter, the movement finishes in 5th position in demi-plié, left leg front; the body is in

épaulement croisé; the arms are opened to a half-1st position; the head is turned to the left.

Gargouillade can also finish without a sliding jump forward, simply in 5th position. In this case, the left leg is put down in front in 5th position in demi-plié on the second quarter, after the second half of the rond de jambe en l'air; at the same time, the arms close to preparatory position.

In the execution of gargouillade en dedans, the movement begins with the leg that is in 5th position back; the first and second ronds de jambe en l'air en dedans are done just as in gargouillade en dehors.

2.   *Gargouillade en dehors.* 2/4 time. Begin in 5th position with épaulement croisé, right leg front. The demi-plié, the rond de jambe en l'air with the right leg, the jump onto the right leg, and the beginning of the rond de jambe with the left leg from the calf of the supporting leg, are all done on the upbeat. On the first quarter, the left leg finishes the rond de jambe en l'air and bends to the calf of the right leg. Between the first and second quarters, the left leg slides croisé devant with the toe along the floor; then the legs come together in a sliding jump forward without breaking away from the floor. On the second quarter, the movement finishes in 5th position in demi-plié, left leg front.

If gargouillade in 2/4 is done without a sliding jump, then the left leg is placed in 5th position in demi-plié on the second quarter.

3.   Final form. 2/4 time. This is distinguished from the elementary form in that the first rond de jambe en l'air begins immediately with the jump on the upbeat, from the demi-plié in 5th position, without first taking the leg to the side in plié. In the jump itself, the second rond de jambe en l'air is done. That is, both legs do rond de jambe en l'air almost simultaneously, while the body is in the air. On the first quarter, the leg slides along the floor croisé devant (or derrière, if gargouillade en dedans is being done); and the

legs come together in a sliding jump along the floor. On the second quarter, the movement finishes in 5th position in demi-plié.

Gargouillade without a sliding jump finishes in 5th position in 1/4. In all cases, the body, as in the first example, inclines away from the leg that begins the gargouillade. The positions of the arms can be varied in many ways.

Cabriole

Cabriole is one of the most difficult pas of classical dance, demanding a well-developed jump, a strong back, and ballon.

Cabrioles are divided into two categories: petite (executed at 45°), and grande (executed at 90°), and may be done in the poses effacées, croisées, and écartées, devant and derrière, as well as in 2nd position, and in the 1st, 2nd, 3rd, and 4th arabesques.

Cabrioles at 45° are done with a preliminary small sissonne ouverte, with sissonne tombée, with coupé, or with glissade.

Grandes cabrioles at 90° are done with a preliminary coupé, with glissade, with sissonne tombée, and, but very rarely, with chassé.

All cabrioles are jumps from one leg onto the same leg, with the exception of cabrioles fermées, in which the jump finishes on two legs, in 5th position. For cabriole fouettée, see "Grand fouetté sauté" (below).

Petite cabriole in the pose effacée devant (Elementary study). 4/4 time. Begin in 5th position, right leg front. On the first quarter, demi-plié, raising the stretched right leg effacé devant to a height of 45°; the body inclines backward more than in the usual pose effacée; the left arm is in 1st; the right in 2nd position; the head turns to the left. On the second quarter, the position is held. Between the second and third quarters, holding the pose, jump: the left leg, tightly stretched, and with force, strikes the right leg from below; and the right leg is slightly propelled upward from the blow. On the third quarter, the left leg returns to demi-plié, the right maintains its position in the air at 45°. On the fourth quarter, close the right leg to 5th position and stretch the knees. Then, in the same manner, without lowering the leg to 5th position, practise two, three, or more cabrioles consecutively.

Cabriole effacée derrière is studied in exactly the same way, with the arms in 1st and 2nd positions, or in a small arabesque pose.

Petite cabriole in the pose croisée devant with a sissonne ouverte. 4/4 time. On the first quarter, with the right leg, sissonne ouverte croisée devant at 45° (coming down on the left leg). Then, taking care not to linger in plié, on the second quarter, do a cabriole, throwing the stretched left leg up to the right in the jump and with it striking the right leg, which is slightly propelled upward by the blow and then remains in the air at 45° as the left returns to demi-plié. On the third quarter, repeat the cabriole. On the fourth, assemblé. Cabriole croisée derrière is studied in the same way.

The positions of the arms vary: the right may be in 1st and the left in 2nd position, or the left may be in 1st and the right in 2nd.

Petite cabriole in the pose 1st arabesque with sissonne tombée. 4/4 time. On the first quarter, with the right leg, do a small sissonne tombée effacée devant. Then, on the second quarter, throwing the left leg out to arabesque at 45°, strike it from below with the stretched right leg in a jump; from the strength of the blow, the left leg is slightly propelled upward, then remains in the air as the right leg returns to demi-plié. On the third quarter, repeat the cabriole. On the fourth quarter, assemblé; or, finish with a pas de bourrée en dehors en face, changing the legs.

Petite cabriole fermée in 2nd position with glissade. 4/4 time. Begin in 5th position, left leg front. On the upbeat, demi-plié and glissade, with the right leg, to the side, without changing the legs, finishing on the first quarter. Without a pause, between the first and second quarters, throw the right leg out to the side at 45° and jump; the left leg strikes the right from below and comes down in demi-plié on the second quarter; simultaneously, the right, propelled slightly upward by the blow, is brought, with the toe along the floor, to 5th position front in demi-plié (making the cabriole fermée). From here, the movement is repeated with the other leg.

During the glissade, the arms open slightly to the side and are lowered to preparatory position. In the cabriole, they open directly to 2nd position; the body leans to the left; and the head turns to the left. After the cabriole, the right arm, simultaneously with the right leg, which is closing to 5th position, is lowered and raised to 1st position, while the left arm remains in 2nd; the weight is transferred to the right leg; the head turns to the right.

In the next glissade with the other leg, lower the arms from the preceding pose and again open them in the cabriole.

Petite cabriole with coupé. Demi-plié on the right leg, the left foot going to the position sur le cou-de-pied derrière. With a short movement, put the left leg on the floor in place of the right (as if displacing it, pushing it away), throw the right leg out croisé or effacé devant at 45°, and, in the jump, do the cabriole.

If the cabriole is done in back, then the coupé is done with the leg that is in front in 5th position.

Grande cabriole effacée devant with coupé. 2/4 time. Préparation: the left leg is croisé devant, with the toe to the floor. Having opened the arms to a low 1st position on the upbeat, lower them on the first quarter while taking a step in demi-plié on the left leg (a kind of coupé). Then, pushing off from the floor, between the first and second quarters, jump high, throwing the right leg out, through 1st position, effacé devant to 90°; the arms in the jump take force from below and quickly, without lingering in 1st position, open—the left to 3rd and the right to

2nd position; the body, with level shoulders, a secure back, and pulled-up thighs, leans back almost to a horizontal position; the head turns to the left; in the jump, the stretched left leg is thrown out to meet the right, which is at a height of 90°, strikes it from below, and, on the second quarter, comes down in demi-plié; the right leg, propelled upward from the blow, remains at 90° or higher; the body and arms hold the pose that was taken during the jump.

For the repetition of the movement, on the next two quarters, step backward and stand in the initial position (the préparation croisée devant).

From this same préparation, it is possible to do grande cabriole écartée devant as well as cabriole fermée at 90°, in which the leg, with the toe sliding along the floor, closes to 5th position.

The préparation for grande cabriole with coupé to 1st or 2nd arabesque will be croisée derrière, with the right leg, toe to the floor; but, instead of a step backward, bring the foot sur le cou-de-pied behind the supporting leg, which is in demi-plié; then do a coupé and, throwing the left leg out backward at 90°, do the cabriole.

Grande cabriole to 3rd and 4th arabesques, as well as to 1st and 2nd, can also be done with a preliminary sissonne tombée, as described above in the section on petite cabriole.

Grande cabriole effacée devant with glissade. The movement is done on the diagonal from point 6 to point 2. From a préparation croisée devant, with the left leg, toe to the floor, open the arms slightly to a low 1st position. Then, demi-plié in 4th position and glissade, without changing the legs, forward to point 2 with the right leg; the arms open to 2nd position and, at the end of the glissade, are lowered momentarily to provide force from below for the cabriole. The glissade is done as a short assembled movement. Then push off for a big jump with the left leg, simultaneously throwing the right out to a height of

90° effacé devant. The position of the body and the arms is the same as in the preceding example.

In order to repeat cabriole with glissade several times in a row in one direction, it is necessary to combine it with some small pas: for example, assemblé to 5th position, finishing with the right leg in back, and entrechat-quatre or entrechat-cinq derrière. Or one can do two petits jetés derrière, doing the first petit jeté from the height of 90° onto the right leg and the second onto the left leg. From this position, continue the glissade-cabriole.

Grande cabriole in 1st or 2nd arabesque with glissade. The movement is on the diagonal from point 2 to point 6. Begin in 5th position with épaulement croisé, right leg front. Moving upstage on the diagonal, do glissade with the left leg to point 6, without changing the legs, in the position écartée devant. At the end of the glissade, turn the body to face point 2(épaulement effacé) and, pushing off from the floor with the right leg, simultaneously throw the left leg out backward to a height of 90° (toward point 6), then, transferring the body forward, do a cabriole in either 1st or 2nd arabesque. From here, the movement is repeated.

Beginning the glissade, open the arms slightly and, taking force from below, open them, in the jump, through 1st position (without pausing) to arabesque. In the glissade, the head is turned toward the left shoulder, then follows the turn of the body to face point 2, looking beyond the right arm in 1st arabesque or across the left shoulder in 2nd arabesque.

Variants of cabriole are so diverse that we must limit ourselves to a description of only the basic kinds and the conventional approaches to this pas. There also exists double cabriole, in which one leg strikes the other in the air two or, in a developed technique, three, or even four times. The tautly stretched legs must open slightly between each strike.

RULES FOR THE EXECUTION OF CABRIOLE. All kinds of cabrioles begin with a short springboard-like push from the floor.

Cabrioles en avant at 45° and 90° are done only with a jump upward; cabrioles en arrière, after they are learned with a jump upward, are done flying forward during the jump.

The stretching of the legs to their utmost tautness is one of the main requirements of execution; floppiness and failure to stretch the knees, insteps, and toes, are inadmissible.

The leg that has been thrown out to a height of 45° or 90° is always struck from below by the leg that pushes off for the jump (the supporting leg); a lowering of the working leg to meet the supporting leg is completely inadmissible. The striking must be well crossed over, on the inner side of the working leg; the feet and heels must not touch. It is conventional to say that the striking in cabriole is done with the calves; but, if one looks attentively at a well-executed cabriole, it is evident that the striking is done mainly with the thighs; in the process of which, however, the striking of the calves as well is not excluded.

All cabrioles en avant, especially those in the poses effacées, which are the most widely used, require level shoulders, a body that is inclined backward, and, most important of all, a strongly pulled-up thigh of the working leg. The torso must be particularly well pulled up or it will inevitably lie heavily on the supporting leg and impede the jump and the suspension of the body in the air.

A resilient, active use of the arms helps the jump and aids in maintaining the final pose in demi-plié.

Example of a combination with petites cabrioles. 4/4 time, four measures. Begin in 5th position, right leg front.

First measure. On the first quarter, with the right leg, sissonne ouverte at 45° to the pose croisée devant; on the second, petite cabriole; on the third, assemblé; on the fourth, entrechat-quatre.

Second measure. On the first quarter, with the left leg, sissonne ouverte at 45° to the pose croisée derrière; on the second, petite cabriole; on the third, assemblé; on the fourth, entrechat-quatre.

Third measure. On the first quarter, with the right leg, sissonne ouverte en tournant en dehors at 45° to the pose écartée derrière; on the second and third, two cabrioles; on the fourth, assemblé, finishing with the right leg in 5th position back.

Fourth measure. On the first and second quarters, two brisés forward with the arms in a small 3rd arabesque pose; on the third and fourth quarters, three brisés forward, 1/8 each.

Repeat the combination with the other leg; then do it in the reverse direction, with the arms for the brisés backward in a small 2nd arabesque pose.

It is possible to complicate this combination by doing all the sissonnes ouvertes en tournant.

Example of a combination with cabrioles at 90°. 4/4 time, eight measures. The movement is on the diagonal from point 6 to point 2. The préparation is with the left leg croisé devant.

First measure. On the first and second quarters, with the right leg, glissade forward to point 2 and cabriole at 90° in the pose effacée devant; on the third and fourth quarters, tombé (with a jump on the supporting leg, a kind of sissonne tombée) and pas de bourrée, changing the legs, finishing in 5th position, left foot front.

Second measure. Repeat the movements of the first measure. The pas de bourrée finishes in 5th position, left foot front.

Third measure. On the first and second quarters, with the left leg, sissonne tombée croisée devant and cabriole at 90° in the pose 3rd arabesque; on the third and fourth quarters, from 3rd arabesque do a grand jeté en tournant to attitude croisée on the right leg by means of a sissonne-tombée backward and a coupé dessous.

Fourth measure. From the pose attitude croisée, do a big

sissonne tombée effacée devant with the left leg and pas de bourrée, changing the legs, to point 8; step onto demi-pointe on the left leg to point 8 in 1st arabesque, and come down in demi-plié.

Fifth measure. The movement is now on the diagonal from point 8 to point 4. On the first and second quarters, chassé and, on the right leg, cabriole fouettée to the pose 4th arabesque; on the third and fourth quarters, chassé and, on the left leg, cabriole fouettée to the pose 1st arabesque.

Sixth measure. Step backward on the right leg; and step backward on the left leg, going to a préparation croisée devant, right leg front, toe to the floor.

Seventh measure. On the first and second quarters, demi-plié on the right leg, sissonne tombée with the left leg effacé devant and cabriole at 90° in 1st arabesque; on the third quarter, repeat the cabriole; and, on the fourth quarter, do a third cabriole (but fermée), closing the right leg to 5th position front. (All three cabrioles are done traveling forward toward point 8.)

Eighth measure. On the first and second quarters, with the right leg, chassé in a straight line forward, raising the arms to 3rd position; on the third and fourth quarters, rise to demi-pointe in 5th position and, after demi-plié, do two tours en l'air to the right, finishing in 5th position, right leg back.

This combination can also be done to a waltz (3/4), in thirty-two measures.

Grand Fouetté Sauté

The numerous kinds of grands fouettés sautés are divided into those done en face and those done en tournant. In the intermediate classes, they are studied on demi-pointe; in the advanced classes, they become complicated in adagio, and then are studied as jumps (fouetté sauté). As with the majority of the big allegro pas, fouetté sauté is preceded by a step-coupé, glissade, sissonne simple, or chassé; it is done en face to the poses effacée devant and derrière and to 1st arabesque; it is done en tournant to the pose croisée devant, attitudes croisée and effacée, and to the 1st, 2nd, 3rd, and 4th arabesques.

Grand fouetté sauté en face. 2/4 time. The préparation is with the left leg croisé devant, toe to the floor; the arms open slightly to a low 1st position. On the upbeat, lower the arms to preparatory position; and, on the first quarter, demi-plié in 4th position on the left leg (coupé). Pushing off from the floor with a jump upward, throw the right leg out along the floor to 2nd position at 90°; simultaneously raise the arms, taking force from below, with an energetic, quick movement, through 1st position to 3rd. Pause in this position as long as possible, then turn in the air to 1st arabesque facing point 7 (in profile); and, on the second quarter, maintaining the pose, come down on the left leg in demi-plié. If the movement is to be repeated immediately with the other leg, it is necessary, with a small, barely noticeable jump on the left leg, to bring the right leg to 4th position croisée devant, lowering the arms; then, pushing off from the floor, do the second grand fouetté sauté, etc. Or the first fouetté can begin with a glissade, and the remaining ones with coupé.

Another kind of fouetté en face is done by the same means. After the coupé on the supporting leg, the working leg, simultaneously with the jump, is thrown out effacé devant to 90°; it then passes through 2nd position in the air, as the body turns en face; and, on the return to demi-plié, along with the body, it assumes the pose effacée derrière. In this fouetté, the arms are in 1st position in the jump; as the body turns to effacé derrière, the arm that corresponds to the leg that is thrown out at 90° goes to 3rd position allongée, the other arm to 2nd position allongée.

This fouetté can also be done with a cabriole, following the rules for cabriole. The first fouetté can also begin with a glissade, the remaining ones with a coupé.

Fouetté sauté effacé devant en dehors. 2/4 time. Begin in 5th position with épaulement croisé, right leg front. On the upbeat, demi-plié and do a small sissonne simple devant, finishing, on the first quarter, in demi-plié on the left leg; the half-bent right leg is taken effacé devant at a small distance from the cou-de-pied; the body, during the sissonne, also turns effacé and inclines forward toward the toe of the right leg; the left arm is in 1st, the right in 2nd position; the head is inclined to the right, the eyes are directed at the toe of the right leg. Between the first and second quarters, jump on the left leg; the right leg, stretching and rising to a height of 90°, passes through 2nd position and bends effacé derrière; simultaneously, the body comes erect, passes through the position en face, and turns in the air to effacé derrière; the left arm opens, through 3rd position, to 2nd, and the right, from 2nd position, is raised to 3rd. The jump finishes in the pose effacée derrière, on the second quarter, in demi-plié on the left leg.

Fouetté effacé en dedans is done analogously. For a detailed description of the position of the body in this case see Chapter XI, "Turning Movements Used in Adagio".

Grand fouetté sauté en tournant en dedans to 3rd arabesque. 2/4 time. The préparation is taken with the right leg croisé devant, toe to the floor. On the upbeat, opening the arms slightly and lowering them to preparatory position, coupé (in plié) on the right leg to 4th position, and jump, throwing the left leg out to 2nd position en face at 90°; the arms are quickly raised to 2nd position. On the first quarter, a second jump is done with the right leg, before which the left leg does a quick passé through 1st position in plié and, together with a turn of the body to point 4, is thrown out forward, in the jump, to 90° toward point 4; the arms take force from below and elastically are raised to 3rd position. In the air, turn the body en dedans to 3rd arabesque, lowering the arms directly from 3rd position to 3rd arabesque. On the second quarter, preserving the pose (with a pulled-up back) come down in demi-plié on the right leg. During the entire pas, as well as at the end, the shoulders are level and the left thigh is strongly pulled up.

In the execution of fouetté with the same leg to attitude croisée or to 4th arabesque, the left leg, in the jump, is also thrown out forward to point 4. If the movement is done to attitude effacée, then the leg is thrown out forward to point 6. If it is executed to 1st or 2nd arabesque, the leg is also thrown out forward to point 6; but, in the jump, together with the turn of the body, it passes through 2nd position at 90° to point 1; and then the whole body turns to arabesque facing point 3. For fouetté en tournant en dehors see the section "Grand fouetté en tournant en dehors" in Chapter XI, "Turning Movements Used in Adagio".

Fouetté en tournant en dedans with a preparatory chassé. 2/4 time. This movement is on the diagonal from point 2 to point 6. The préparation is taken on the right leg, the left effacé derrière, toe to the floor; the position of the body and arms is either 1st or 2nd arabesque, facing point 2. On the upbeat, demi-plié on the right leg and, opening the arms to 2nd position, do a chassé traveling upstage (for the form of this chassé, see the section "Pas chassé" above); the right shoulder is toward point 2 and the left toward point 6; the head is turned to the right. On the first quarter, take a step on the left leg in demi-plié toward point 6 and jump, throwing the right leg, through 1st position, forward at 90° toward point 6; simultaneously, the body turns to face that same point; the arms take force from below and are raised to 1st or 3rd position; turn in the air (en dedans) to 4th arabesque and, on the second quarter, preserving the pose, come down on the left leg in demi-plié facing point 2. On the next two quarters, do a chassé, moving upstage on the same diagonal, but now with the left shoulder to point 2 and the right to point 6; step on the right leg toward point 6 and jump, turning the body and throwing the left leg forward at 90° toward point 6; then turn in the air (en dedans) to 1st arabesque facing point 2 and finish the jump in demi-plié on the right leg. This fouetté is also done with a cabriole.

Grande cabriole fouettée. From a préparation with the left leg croisé devant, toe to the floor, do a step-coupé croisé devant or a glissade to the side. Follow this with a cabriole at 90° in 2nd position en face with the arms in 3rd position; after striking the working leg with the supporting leg (in 2nd position), turn the body in the air to 1st arabesque to face point 7 (in profile); and come down on the supporting leg in demi-plié. In the arabesque, both in the air and on landing, the back must be strongly pulled up. To repeat the movement, again do a step-coupé forward to 4th position croisée (toward point 8), finishing the cabriole fouettée to point 3. This movement should be practised from four to eight times in succession. It may also be executed with a sissonne tombée-coupée.

RULES FOR THE EXECUTION OF FOUETTÉ SAUTÉ. In all fouettés sautés, the movements of the arms are co-ordinated with the turn of the body; the arms help the jump and provide force for the turn in the air; the left arm plays a more active role in the turn to the right, and the right arm—in the turn to the left.

While turning in the air and on coming down in demi-plié, one must maintain the pull-up of the thigh of the leg that is thrown out to 90°. The supporting leg comes down in plié through the foot, from the toe to the heel, which must be strongly moved forward.

As in the jump, so at the end of the fouetté, the back must be vigorously pulled up.

Example of a combination with fouetté sauté. 3/4 time (waltz), sixteen measures.

First and second measures. Beginning with the right leg, pas couru and grand jeté onto the left leg in attitude croisée toward point 2.

Third and fourth measures. From the pose, sissonne at 90° with the right leg to 2nd position and grand fouetté sauté en tournant en dedans to attitude effacée.

Fifth and sixth measures. To point 8, with the right leg, failli; with the left, coupé (under) and grand jeté onto the right leg in attitude croisée.

Seventh and eighth measures. From attitude, sissonne at 90°, with the left leg, to 2nd position, and grand fouetté en tournant en dedans to 3rd arabesque.

Ninth and tenth measures. With the left leg, glissade in 2nd position and grande cabriole fouettée to 1st arabesque on the right leg.

Eleventh and twelfth measures. Coupé and cabriole fouettée to 1st arabesque on the left leg.

Thirteenth and fourteenth measures. Coupé and cabriole fouettée to 1st arabesque on the right leg.

Fifteenth and sixteenth measures. With the left leg, failli to point 2; with the right, coupé and, throwing out the left leg forward at 90°, grand assemblé croisé devant.

IX. Batterie

In beats, or batterie (from the French battre, "to beat"), one leg strikes the other in the air. Both before and after the beat, the legs open from 5th position slightly toward 2nd position. The jump then finishes in demi-plié, either on both legs or on one. In the execution of a compound beat, that is, one in which the legs strike (or beat) each other several times, the legs open each time slightly to the side.

Beats are divided into pas battus (that is, jumping pas done with a beat) and the various kinds of entrechat and brisé.

Royale, entrechat-quatre, entrechat-six, entrechat-huit, and brisé are done from two legs onto two; entrechat-trois, entrechat-cinq, and entrechat-sept from two legs onto one; and brisé dessus-dessous is done, the first time (the brisé dessus), from two legs onto one, and then from one onto the other.

All pas battus and beats are done with the legs stretched and turned out to the utmost. The beats are done to a well-crossed (a "deep") 5th position. For women, the beat is done mainly with the calves of the legs. Men, however, beat with the upper part of the leg (the thighs as well as the calves). When the legs are properly turned-out and the beat is sufficiently deep, the heels do not touch in the air.

The smallest departure from these rules deprives the beats of clarity and makes them meaningless, since the whole point of beats is to show off the technical virtuosity and elevation of the performer (especially in entrechat-six, entrechat-huit, and entrechat-six de volé).

In the beginning (in the 3rd and 4th years), beats are studied at a moderate tempo, with a jump sufficiently high to allow a clean and turned-out execution. As the student gains strength (in intermediate and advanced classes), the height of the jump is decreased. In their final form, such beats as entrechat-trois, quatre, cinq and the small pas battus (échappé, assemblé, jeté, sissonne fermée, sissonne ouverte, etc.) are done at a quick tempo and at a low height.

It is recommended that the study of beats begin with petit échappé, followed by royale, entrechat-quatre, assemblé battu, and jeté battu, in that order.

Next in difficulty, studied in intermediate classes, are entrechat-cinq, entrechat-trois, ballonné battu, brisé, brisé dessus-dessous, sissonne ouverte and sissonne fermée battue, etc. In advanced classes, entrechat-six, grand sissonne ouverte battue, entrechat-six de volée (all in both men's and women's classes) are studied, and finally the pas specifically for men: entrechat-sept, entrechat-huit, saut de basque battu, jeté entrelacé battu, etc. The complete program for the study of beats is indicated in the 8-year syllabus in the appendix.

Petit Échappé Battu

Elementary study. 4/4 time. Begin in 5th position en face, right leg front.

On the first quarter, demi-plié. Between the first and second quarters, jump to 2nd position, finishing on the second quarter in demi-plié. Between the second and third quarters, jump, striking the legs against each other in the air, right leg front; and then open them slightly. On the third quarter, close the legs in 5th position in demi-plié, right leg back. On the fourth quarter, stretch the knees.

In its next form, échappé battu is done in 2/4; that is, it begins on the upbeat and finishes on the second quarter in demi-plié, with épaulement croisé.

Later on, échappé battu is complicated in the following manner (échappé battu with a compound beat): from 5th position, the legs, after opening in the jump, strike each other in the air (doing a beat without changing their relative positions) before coming down in 2nd position; and, from 2nd position, a second beat is done as described above.

The number of beats may be gradually increased, both in the first and the second jump. In this case, grand échappé battu is done.

Échappé battu can also finish on one leg, bending the other sur le cou-de-pied derrière or devant in one of the small poses croisée.

Preliminary Exercise for Royale and Entrechat-Quatre

4/4 time. On the first and second quarters, demi-plié in 5th position, right leg front. Between the second and third quarters, jump and quickly open the stretched legs slightly to the side. On the third quarter, just as quickly close the legs to 5th position in demi-plié, right leg back. On the fourth quarter, stretch the knees.

The quick opening of the legs is good practice for beats, both with a change of legs (preparatory to the study of royale) and without a change (preparatory to the study of entrechat-quatre).

Royale is then learned in 4/4. Begin with the right leg in front. In the jump, the legs open slightly; the right leg strikes the left in front; the legs again open slightly; and the movement finishes in 5th position in demi-plié, right leg back.

For entrechat-quatre, begin with the right leg in front. In the jump, slightly open the legs; the right leg strikes the left in back; the legs again open slightly; and the movement finishes in 5th position, right leg front.

In their final form, these jumps begin on the upbeat with épaulement and finish in one quarter, also with épaulement.

Entrechat-Trois and Entrechat-Cinq

Entrechat-trois can be compared with royale, since it is done with a change of the legs; but entrechat-trois finishes on one leg, with the other brought sur le cou-de-pied derrière or devant.

Entrechat-trois derrière. Begin in 5th position, right leg front. Jump; open the legs slightly to the side; strike the right leg in front of the left; then again open the legs slightly; landing in demi-plié, the right leg bends sur le cou-de-pied derrière.

Entrechat-trois devant. Begin in 5th position, left leg front. In the jump, the right leg strikes the left in back and at the end bends sur le cou-de-pied devant (the conditional position).

Entrechat-cinq can be compared with entrechat-quatre, for it is done without a change of legs; but, like entrechat-trois, it finishes on one leg.

Entrechat-cinq devant. Begin from 5th position, right leg front. In the jump, the legs open slightly; the right strikes the left in back; the legs again open slightly; and the movement finishes in demi-plié on the left leg, with the right bent sur le cou-de-pied devant (the conditional position).

Entrechat-cinq derrière begins in the same way but, after the beat, the left leg is bent sur le cou-de-pied derrière.

Entrechat-trois and cinq finish in the small poses croisées; that is, one arm is in low 1st position and the other in 2nd.

Entrechat-Six

Begin in 5th position, right leg front. Demi-plié and jump strongly upward; the legs open slightly; the right strikes the left in back; the legs open slightly; the right strikes the left in front; and the legs again open slightly. The jump finishes in 5th position in demi-plié with the right leg in back.

The arms in entrechat-six can remain down or, when the movement is repeated several times, they can gradually be raised to 3rd position and lowered through 2nd or be raised directly to the side and, on the last movement, close in preparatory position. The jump begins and ends with épaulement croisé; but, when accompanied by a port de bras, only the first and last entrechats have épaulement. The intervening entrechats-six are done en face.

Entrechat-Huit

Begin in 5th position, right leg front. Demi-plié and jump strongly upward; the legs open slightly; the right strikes the left in back, opens slightly, strikes the left in front, opens slightly, and strikes the left in back. After the third beat, the legs again open slightly. The jump finishes in 5th position in demi-plié, right leg front.

For a clearer and shorter explanation, we speak here of one leg striking the other, but it must not be forgotten that in all the examples of beats and pas battu described, both legs open slightly and strike each other equally.

Entrechat-Sept

Begin in 5th position, right leg front. Demi-plié and jump; the legs open slightly; the right strikes the left in back, opens slightly, strikes the left in front and again opens slightly. The jump finishes with the left leg in demi-plié, the right sur le cou-de-pied derrière.

In the men's class, entrechat-sept can finish in any small or big pose, in 2nd position, attitude, arabesque, etc. In other words, it is a sissonne ouverte with a compound beat.

Entrechat-Six de Volée

This pas is essentially a combination of grand assemblé with entrechat-six. It is done at 90° to the side in 2nd position and in the pose écartée devant by means of a step-coupé, glissade, or failli.

Entrechat-six de volée may also be done en tournant in a straight line to the side and en diagonale, with either step-coupé or chassé, in the manner described in Chapter VIII, "Jumps", under "Grand assemblé en tournant".

Entrechat-Six de Volée to the Side.

With the left leg in front, from a step-coupé or glissade, throw the right leg out to 2nd position at 90° with a big jump. In the air, bring the body and the left leg toward the right and do an entrechat-six; strike the left leg against the right in back; open it slightly and strike it in front; again open it slightly; then bring the legs together in the air and come down in 5th position in demi-plié, right leg front.

The arms, as in grand assemblé, help the flight. In the jump, they are raised to 3rd, 2nd and 3rd, or 1st and 3rd positions, and hold the pose on landing with épaulement croisé in demi-plié.

Brisé

Brisé is done moving en diagonale upstage and downstage. It can be done forward, backward, or en tournant in a circle.

Study Sequence

1. Brisé forward. 4/4 time. Begin in 5th position with épaulement croisé, left leg front. The movement is en diagonale from point 6 to point 2. On the first quarter, demi-plié; the right leg, from behind, moves forward through 1st position, with the toe to the floor, in a direction between points 2 and 3 of the classroom plan in such a way that the heel of the working right leg is in line with the heel

of the supporting leg. This same relationship of the legs to each other is maintained in the final form of brisé, when the leg is thrown to 45°, because it gives a clean beat with both legs and does not hinder the movement forward along the diagonal. On the second quarter, the position is held. Between the second and third quarters, pushing off with the heel of the left leg from the floor, jump, traveling toward the toe of the right leg; the legs strike each other in the air (left leg back), and then open slightly. The jump finishes in 5th position in demi-plié, right leg back. On the fourth quarter, the knees stretch.

In the jump, the right arm is raised to a low 1st position and the left to 2nd; the body is effacé, with level shoulders; the head is turned to the left.

2. Brisé backward. Begin in 5th position with épaulement croisé, left leg front. Demi-plié, and move the left leg backward through 1st position, with the toe to the floor, in a direction between points 6 and 7. Jump, traveling toward the toe of the left leg; the legs strike each other in the air (right leg front) and then open slightly. The jump finishes in 5th position in demi-plié, left leg front.

In the jump, the body is effacé; the left arm in a low 1st position and the right in 2nd; the head is turned to the left.

3. Brisé forward. Final form. The movement is done in 1/4, with the demi-plié and the jump on the upbeat.

Begin in 5th position with épaulement croisé, left leg front. Demi-plié and, pushing off with the heel from the floor, jump, throwing the right leg forward through 1st position at 45° in a direction between points 2 and 3. Fly beyond the toe of the right leg, striking the legs in the air (left leg back). Then, open the legs slightly and come down in 5th position in demi-plié, right leg back.

Brisé backward is done in the same way.

The basic position of the arms is as indicated in No. 1 and 2; but a number of variants can be used.

Brisé Forward en Tournant. These brisés are done traveling en dedans in a small circle, which is formed not only from the turns of the body, but also from the movement in the direction of the toe of the working leg. Eight of them are done in a circle in the beginning; then an entire circle is made with four, which is considerably more difficult.

Example with quarter turns to the right. Begin in 5th position with épaulement croisé, the right leg in front. Demi-plié and jump, throwing the left leg forward through 1st position at 45°; the body simultaneously turns a quarter turn to the right. Thus both the working leg and the jump are directed between points 1 and 2. The second brisé is done traveling forward in a direction between points 3 and 4; the third between points 5 and 6; the fourth between points 7 and 8.

The left arm can be in a low 1st position and the right in 2nd, or the left in 3rd position and the right in 2nd. The body is directed toward the left leg or may incline toward the supporting right leg.

In brisé en tournant backward (with the right leg in front), one turns to the right (en dehors), traveling beyond the toe of the right leg, which is thrown out backward: the first time, between points 4 and 5; the second, between points 6 and 7; the third, between points 8 and 1; the fourth, between points 2 and 3.

Brisé Dessus-Dessous

Brisé dessus is a brisé forward that finishes on one leg; and brisé dessous is a brisé backward that finishes on one leg. Both may be done traveling en diagonale forward or backward. The body has a more complicated part to play than in simple brisé from two legs onto two.

Study Sequence

1. Elementary form of brisé dessus. 2/4 time. Begin in 5th position with épaulement croisé, left leg front. On the upbeat, demi-plié and jump, throwing the right leg

forward through 1st position at 45° between points 2 and 3; the body leans slightly back; the arms, from preparatory position, open, with the palms down, to 2nd position; the head turns to the left. Flying forward on the diagonal, the tautly stretched legs strike in the air (left leg back); open the legs slightly and land, on the first quarter, on the right leg in demi-plié, bending the left sur le cou-de-pied devant; the body's weight, at the last moment, is transferred over the right leg and the torso inclines to the right, holding the back well pulled up; the right arm is in 1st position and the left in 2nd; the arms are curved; the head and eyes are directed toward the right hand. On the second quarter, without changing the position of the body and arms, do an assemblé croisé devant.

On the next two quarters, do a brisé dessous: from demi-plié, jump, throwing the left leg backward through 1st position at 45° between points 7 and 6; the body comes erect and, simultaneously, both arms open, with the palms down, to 2nd position, the head turning to the left; fly backward on the diagonal and beat the tautly stretched legs in the air (left leg back); open the legs slightly and come down on the left in demi-plié, bending the right sur le cou-de-pied derrière; the body's weight is transferred over the left leg with a slight inclination of the torso backward; the left arm bends to 1st position; the right is in 2nd; the arms are curved; the head turns to the left. At the end, do an assemblé croisé derrière, lowering the arms to preparatory position.

2. Final form. 2/4 time. On the first quarter, do brisé dessus (as explained above); then, directly from the position sur le cou-de-pied, throw the left leg backward at 45°, between points 7 and 6; on the second quarter, do brisé dessous, but almost in place.

In other words, in the final form, the assemblés are omitted.

Brisé dessus-dessous is also done traveling downstage en diagonale. In this case, the flight forward on the brisé dessus is increased and the brisé dessous is done almost in place.

Pas Battus

The study of the pas battus (excluding échappé, which is the first beat learned) begins after entrechat-quatre and royale have been learned in their simplest form.

Assemblé battu. From 5th position with the right leg back, demi-plié and jump, throwing the right leg out to 2nd position at 45°; with it strike the left in back; then again open it slightly and bring it to 5th position front in demi-plié. Moving in the reverse direction (i. e., progressing upstage), throw out the right leg, from 5th position front, and with it strike the left in front, finishing in 5th position, right leg back.

Jeté battu. From 5th position, with the right leg back, demi-plié and, throwing the right leg out to 2nd position at 45°, strike with it the left in back; again open it slightly and come down in demi-plié on the right leg, bending the left sur le cou-de-pied derrière.

Moving in the reverse direction (i.e., progressing upstage) from 5th position, with the right leg in front, throw the right leg out to the side, and with it strike the left in front; open it slightly and come down on the right leg in demi-plié, bending the left sur le cou-de-pied devant (conditional position).

Ballonné battu. Start in 5th position, with the right leg in front. Demi-plié and jump, throwing the right leg out to 2nd position at 45°. The right leg strikes the left in front and both open slightly; land on the left leg in demi-plié, with the right bent sur le cou-de-pied derrière.

Doing ballonné in the reverse direction, the leg that is in 5th position back is thrown out to 2nd position; it strikes the supporting leg in back and, at the end of the jump, bends sur le cou-de-pied devant (conditional position).

Sissonne ouverte battue at 45°. From 5th position, with the right leg in front, demi-plié and jump; the legs, after opening slightly, strike each other (the right in front) and again open slightly. Then the left leg comes down in demi-plié; the right, passing through the position sur le cou-de-pied, with a small développé, opens to the side or to one of the small poses croisées or effacées devant, etc. In reversing the movement, the striking is done with the leg that is in 5th position back; and the working leg opens to the side or to a small pose derrière. The number of beats can be increased, especially in the execution of grande sissonne ouverte.

Sissonne fermée battue. From 5th position, with the right leg in front, demi-plié and jump, opening the legs slightly; strike the legs, the right in front, and travel to the left side doing a sissonne fermée. The same thing may be done in the reverse direction.

Sissonne fermée battue in the poses écartées is done analogously, but it is somewhat more complicated to do it in the poses croisées and effacées.

Sissonne fermée battue croisée devant. Beginning with the right leg in front, demi-plié and jump, flying backward; open the legs slightly and strike the left in back with the right; again transfer it, opening it croisé devant at 45°; finish the sissonne fermée in 5th position demi-plié.

Sissonne fermée croisée derrière and effacée devant and derrière are done analogously.

There are many more movements and combinations with pas battus than those described—for example, saut de basque battu: begin in 5th position, with the right leg in front; step out on the right leg in demi-plié and jump, throwing out the left leg in the jump together with the first half of the turn of the body; the tautly stretched right leg, coming up to the left, strikes the raised left leg in back, opens slightly and, when the turn is completed, finishes by bending in front with the toe under the knee of the supporting leg.

Examples of combinations of batterie and pas battu.

1. 4/4 time, four measures. Begin in 5th position, right leg back.
   First measure. On the first quarter, with the right leg, assemblé battu, finishing with the right leg in front; on the second, entrechat-quatre; on the third, assemblé battu with the left leg, finishing with it in front; on the fourth, royale.
   Second measure. Repeat the combination starting with the left leg.
   Third measure. Beginning with the left leg in front, do two échappés battus, changing the legs, in two quarters each.
   Fourth measure. On the first two quarters, with the left leg, do two entrechats-quatre and royale, 1/8 each; on the third and fourth quarters, with the right leg, do two entrechats-quatre and royale, 1/8 each.
   Then reverse the combination.
2. 4/4 time, four measures. Begin in 5th position with the right leg in front.
   First measure. On the first and second quarters, entrechat-sept to the pose 3rd arabesque at 90° and assemblé croisé derrière (with the right leg); on the third and fourth quarters, entrechat-cinq derrière with the right leg back, and assemblé in back.
   Second measure. Repeat the combination with the left leg.
   Third measure. On the first and second quarters, failli and entrechat-six de volée in the pose écartée devant to point 2, raising the arms to 3rd position. On the third and fourth quarters, do two entrechats-six, with the right and with the left leg, gradually lowering the arms.
   Fourth measure. On the first and second quarters, with the right leg, step-coupé to point 2 and entrechat-six de

volée en tournant, raising the arms to 3rd position. Finish the movement in 5th position, with the left leg in front; then, on the third and fourth quarters, rise to demi-pointe on the left leg in attitude croisée, opening the arms from 3rd position, through 1st allongée position, the right to 3rd position and the left to 2nd; then, maintaining the pose, demi-plié on the left leg.

This combination can also be done to a waltz tempo in sixteen measures.

X. Tours on the Floor and in the Air

Tours for men are divided into those done par terre and those done in the air (tours en l'air); women do only tours par terre.

In the men's class, par terre tours are further subdivided into small pirouettes (which is an old term, now used only in the men's class, for, in the women's class, all kinds of turns are called tours), big pirouettes (grande pirouette), and tours in the big poses.

The small pirouettes are tours from 2nd, 5th, and 4th positions. Their préparations are studied in the elementary classes. Then, in the intermediate classes, the small pirouettes themselves are studied, followed by tours en l'air and tours in the big poses. In advanced classes, tours chaînés and grande pirouette are studied. The detailed study sequence for tours par terre and en l'air is presented in the syllabus for the study of classical dance given in the appendix.

General Remarks. For the correct execution of all kinds of tours, the following conditions are necessary: the body must be well placed, with the back held strongly in the area of the waist (particularly the small of the back); this enables one to remain in a strictly vertical position during the tour and immobile in the poses (if the tour is in arabesque, attitude, etc.). The arms must be resilient, so that they can skilfully and elastically provide force for the tour and then remain immobile during the course of it. The supporting leg must be tautly stretched on a turned-out demi-pointe (or pointe) and must be as a single piece with the body and back. The turned-out heel of the supporting leg must move forward at the moment of the spring onto demi-pointe from the préparation in demi-plié.

Clear, profile turns of the head are needed, without any inclination, at the beginning of the tour, and, at the end, there must be a quick return of the head to its position en face. At the beginning of each pirouette or tour, the head for a moment turns in profile, looking across the shoulder in the direction opposite that in which one is turning, with the eyes focused on a definite point of the room. At the moment of the tour, the head quickly comes straight en face; and, at the end of the tour, it returns to the initial point. For several tours in a row, the head and eyes each time repeat this movement. The point at which the eyes are directed must be at eye level; for, if the eyes are lowered, raised, or directed to the side, stability can be lost. On the stage, before a tour, the performer also must quickly find a point on which to fix his eyes (toward the first wing, for example).

A series of simple exercises prepares the student for stability in tours. In the beginning of the first year, at the end of the lesson, the teacher can give the pupils a tour in place using small shuffling steps to get around. The arms remain motionless in preparatory position, but the head and eyes participate in each tour, as indicated above. In the second half of the first year, this turning in place is done on demi-pointe, gently resetting the feet rhythmically during the tour (the turn-out can be disregarded).

In the second year, at the barre, half tours and then whole tours in 5th position are learned on turned-out legs on demi-pointe. They begin from a demi-plié in 5th position, followed by a spring to demi-pointe in 5th position and a simultaneous turn toward or away from the barre, moving the heels sharply forward (a kind of pivot on both legs); the arms, with a little force, are brought together in 1st position and help the tour, in which the head and eyes also participate. The tour finishes in 5th position in demi-plié. These tours in 5th position are always done in the direction of the back leg, which then finds itself in front, at the end of the tour.

In the following years, half tours from one leg onto the other are studied as well as half tours on demi-pointe on one leg. Although these have no direct relation to tours proper, they develop general mobility and adroitness.

The study of the préparations for pirouettes and the pirouettes themselves begins in the third year.

Study Sequence for Pirouettes

1. Préparation in 2nd position for pirouettes en dehors. 4/4 time, two measures. Begin in 5th position, right leg front.

First measure. On the first quarter, demi-plié en face. On the second, push off from the floor with the heels and spring onto demi-pointe in 5th position, resiliently bringing the arms together in 1st position. On the third quarter, open the tautly stretched right leg to 2nd position at a height of 45°, simultaneously opening the arms to 2nd position. On the fourth quarter, pause in this position, the well pulled-up back forming a single line with the supporting foot and thigh, perpendicular to the floor.

Second measure. On the first quarter, come down in demi-plié in 2nd position, bending the right arm to directly 1st position (the left remains in 2nd); the shoulders are level, and the right shoulder must not be allowed to move forward. On the second quarter, push off from the floor with the heels and spring onto demi-pointe on the left leg bringing the right foot sur le cou-de-pied devant (the upper part of the leg must be turned out and locked in the hip joint); simultaneously, the left arm, with a strong movement, comes to meet the right in 1st position. On the third quarter, the position is held. On the fourth quarter, finish the préparation simultaneously on both legs in 5th position in demi-plié, putting the right foot down in back; open the hands slightly forward (without dropping the elbows), freeing the arms from tension. The knees are then stretched.

For the préparation en dedans, the first half is done in the same way as for the préparation en dehors; then, after the plié in 2nd position, spring up onto demi-pointe on the right leg and bring the left foot sur le cou-de-pied devant. Finish in demi-plié in 5th position, putting the left leg down in front, and stretch the knees.

2. Final form. 4/4 time, two measures. Begin in 5th position with the right leg in front.

First measure. On the upbeat, demi-plié en face. On the first quarter, spring onto demi-pointe in 5th position, raising the arms to 1st position; on the second quarter, hold the position. On the third quarter, open the right leg to the side at a height of 45°; and open the arms to 2nd position. On the fourth quarter, hold the position.

Second measure. On the upbeat, do a short demi-plié in 2nd position, bending the right arm directly to 1st position. On the first quarter, spring onto demi-pointe on the left leg, bending the right leg, with the foot stretched, sur le cou-de-pied devant; at the same time, bring the arms elastically together in 1st position. On the second and third quarters, hold the position (in this way, stability is developed). On the fourth quarter, demi-plié in 5th position, right leg back, and open the arms easily, turning the body to épaulement croisé. Then stretch the knees.

The préparation en dedans is done analogously. In the men's class, pirouettes are also done from these préparations. They are borrowed from the women's class and effectively develop stability on demi-pointe. After they have been learned, one can go on to the specifically masculine préparations.

3. Préparation and pirouettes en dehors from 2nd position. (This form is used only by men both in the classroom and on the stage.) 4/4 time. Begin in 5th position, with the right leg in front. On the first quarter, slide the stretched right leg to the side with the toe to the floor (the first part of a battement tendu), opening the arms through 1st to 2nd position. On the second quarter, come down in 2nd position in demi-plié, bending the right arm to 1st position; the shoulders must be level. On the third quarter, without delaying, spring onto demi-pointe on the left leg, and bring the stretched right foot sur le cou-de-pied devant; simultaneously, also bring the arms, with an elastic movement, together in 1st position. On the fourth quarter, come down in 5th position in demi-plié, with the right leg in back, or one can come down on a straight left leg, placing the right foot croisé derrière on demi-pointe; the arms open slightly to a small pose; and the whole body is in épaulement croisé.

The préparation en dedans with the right leg is the same; however, one springs onto the right leg, and the left foot finishes in 5th position front in demi-plié or, one can come down on a straight right leg, placing the left foot croisé devant (derrière) on demi-pointe.

In the execution of pirouettes from these préparations the turn is to the right, with the left arm providing the force. If the préparation is with the left leg, the turn is to the left and the right arm provides the force.

In the beginning, one pirouette is done, then two, three, and more; the movement is practised at a tempo ranging from moderate to quick. It should be noted that some teachers of the Leningrad school, such as Nikolai Legat and Alexander Pushkin, taught these pirouettes with a relevé rather than a spring onto demi-pointe. Other teachers such as Enrico Cecchetti and Alexei Pisarev, taught them with a spring.

4a. Préparation and pirouettes en dehors from 4th position (example turning to the right). 4/4 time. Begin in 4th position croisée with the left leg forward in demi-plié; the right leg is stretched back with the whole foot on the floor; the centre of weight is on the supporting left leg; the shoulders are level; the right arm is forward at the level of the right shoulder and opposite it; and the left arm is open to the side, also at shoulder level; the position of the hands, with the palms down, as in 3rd arabesque; but the hands are slightly raised; the head and eyes are directed towards point 2. This is executed on two introductory chords. On the first quarter, demi-plié on both legs, leaving the centre of weight over the supporting leg. On the second quarter, push off from the floor with both heels and spring onto demi-pointe on the left leg, bringing the stretched right foot sur le cou-de-pied devant; simultaneously, bring the arms together in 1st position. On the third quarter, hold this position on demi-pointe as long as possible (a musical fermata). Then finish the préparation in 5th position in demi-plié; on the fourth quarter, with the right leg in back, or in 4th position croisée, opening the arms slightly to a small pose.

4b. Begin in 5th position croisée, right foot front. On the first quarter, demi-plié. On the second quarter, spring onto the left foot on demi-pointe and, simultaneously, turn to point 2 and bring the stretched right foot sur le cou-de-pied devant. On the third quarter, hold the position on demi-pointe. On the fourth quarter, come down in 4th position croisée, with a demi-plié on the left leg; the right leg is stretched in back with a straight knee and the whole foot on the floor. On the upbeat of the following measure, bend the knee and, pushing off the floor with the heel, spring onto demi-pointe on the left leg, bringing the right foot sur le cou-de-pied devant. On the first, second, and third quarters, hold the position on demi-pointe. On the fourth quarter, come down in demi-plié in 5th position, with the right foot in back, and stretch the knees.

By the end of the third year, the preceding form is studied with the initial demi-plié on the upbeat of the first measure. On the first, second, and third quarters, the position on demi-pointe is held. The remainder is the same.

In the préparation from 4th position, it is extremely important that, at the moment of the plié and the spring from the floor, one feels the centre of weight over the leg that is in front (that is, over the leg on which the pirouette is to be done). If the weight is distributed evenly on both legs, the body involuntarily will jerk forward during the spring onto demi-pointe and will begin to career and lose its stability during the turn. In the execution of pirouettes to the right, force is provided with the left arm. The right arm does not open to the side, but only curves to join the left in 1st position. At the beginning of the turn, the head, for a moment, remains turned over the left shoulder to point 2, with the eyes directed at that same point; then the head comes straight and, at the end, returns to point 2.

For a clean execution of pirouettes and tours, avoid beginning to turn while still in plié (something which is encountered rather often). For the turn would then actually begin with the back to the audience, after a half turn. Therefore, springing up onto demi-pointe, one must momentarily fix the position or pose in which the pirouette or tour is done, and then do the tour. However, this fixing of the pose is more an internal feeling of the performer than an actual pause, and must not be exaggerated, for it will then cut down the force and impede the tour.

5. Préparation and pirouette en dedans from 4th position (example with the turning to the left). Begin in 4th position croisée, with the left leg forward in demi-plié; the right is stretched back with the whole foot on the floor; the centre

of weight is on the left supporting leg in épaulement croisé; the right shoulder is brought slightly back and the left a little forward; the right arm, with curved hand, is in 2nd position, and the left is curved in 1st; the head and eyes are directed at point 1 of the classroom plan.

Increase the demi-plié slightly on the left leg, then spring onto demi-pointe on the left leg and turn the body en face to point 1, bringing the stretched right foot sur le cou-de-pied devant (springing onto demi-pointe in all pirouettes and tours, it is necessary to simultaneously move the heel forward); at the same time, the left arm opens to 2nd position and comes together with the right in 1st position. The préparation finishes in 5th position in demi-plié, with the right leg in front, with épaulement croisé, the arms opening to a pose.

For the execution of the pirouette en dedans on the left leg, the right arm provides the force. The head and eyes at the beginning of the tour are directed over the left shoulder to point 1, then the head comes straight. At the end, the body, head, and eyes again return to point 1 and only in demi-plié take on the épaulement croisé. When these tours are done on pointe, the working foot is always brought directly to the position sur le cou-de-pied devant; but on demi-pointe, this may be preceded by a small dégagé to the side. On the stage, the foot is sometimes held sur le cou-de-pied derrière during the tours.

From these same préparations en dehors and en dedans one may also do a tour en tire-bouchon, in which case the 4th position will be somewhat wider and, during the tour, the leg will be bent at 90°, with the toe in front of the knee instead of sur le cou-de-pied. During the tour, the arms may be in either 1st or 3rd position.

6.   Préparation and pirouette en dehors from 5th position (turning to the right). 4/4 time. Begin in 5th position en face with the right leg in front. On the first quarter,

demi-plié, raising the right arm to 1st position and the left directly to 2nd, keeping the shoulders level. On the second quarter, spring onto demi-pointe on the left leg and bring the stretched right foot sur le cou-de-pied devant; simultaneously bring the arms together in 1st position. On the third quarter, hold the position. On the fourth quarter, finish the préparation in 5th position in demi-plié, putting the right foot down in back, and stretch the knees.

For the execution of the pirouette, provide force with the left arm. The head and eyes are directed over the left shoulder to point 1. At the end of the turn, quickly bring the head and eyes to point 1, demi-plié in 5th position with épaulement croisé.

The préparation and pirouette from 5th position en dedans are done in the same way, but spring onto demi-pointe on the right leg, and bring the stretched left foot directly sur le cou-de-pied devant. At the end, put the left foot down in front.

These pirouettes are also done facing the diagonal, in which case, if the right leg is in front, the whole body and the eyes are turned to point 8 in the préparation in 5th position; when the left leg is in front, the body and eyes face point 2.

7a Préparations and tours sur le cou-de-pied en dehors and en dedans on pointe from 5th position. 4/4 time.

En dehors. Begin in 5th position with the right leg in front. On the upbeat, demi-plié. On the first quarter, spring onto the left leg on pointe, bringing the stretched right foot sur le cou-de-pied devant; the right arm is in 1st position and the left in 2nd. On the second quarter, without changing the position of the arms, come down in 5th position in demi-plié. On the third quarter, spring again onto pointe on the left leg, bringing the stretched right foot sur le cou-de-pied devant, and join the left arm to the right in 1st position. On the fourth quarter, come down in demi-plié in 5th position with the right foot in back.

En dedans. Begin as above. On the upbeat, demi-plié. On the first quarter, spring onto the right leg on pointe, bringing the stretched left foot sur le cou-de-pied derrière; the right arm is in 1st position and the left in 2nd. On the second quarter, without changing the position of the arms, demi-plié in 5th position. On the third quarter, spring onto the right leg on pointe, bringing the stretched left foot sur le cou-de-pied devant, and join the left arm to the right in 1st position. On the fourth quarter, come down in demi-plié in 5th position with the left foot in front.

7b. On the upbeat, demi-plié. On the first quarter, spring onto pointe on the supporting leg and bring the other sur le cou-de-pied; one arm is in 1st position and the other in 2nd (the préparation). On the second quarter, demi-plié in 5th position. On the third quarter, do the tour. On the fourth quarter, finish the tour in 5th position in demi-plié.

This is practised with each leg alternately, four times en dehors and four times en dedans.

Pirouettes at the Barre

At the barre, pirouettes are done en dehors and en dedans from 5th and 2nd positions. For the tour from 2nd position, the working leg is first opened to the side at a height of 45° and then, after a demi-plié on the supporting leg, bends, bringing the stretched foot sur le cou-de-pied devant as the supporting leg rises to demi-pointe from demi-plié. Along with these, tours temps relevés are also done.

In pirouettes en dehors, the arm that corresponds to the supporting leg holds onto the barre. In the demi-plié, before the pirouette, it remains on the barre, then pushes off with a light pressure of the palm to provide force for the pirouette. In the pirouettes en dedans, the arm that is open to the side provides force.

Pirouettes are studied first at the barre as a separate exercise. Only after that is their study begun in the centre of the room. Then they are introduced into combinations of fondus, ronds de jambe en l'air, petits battements, etc.

In the women's class, all of the pirouettes described are called tours. They are also done on pointe, from 5th and 4th positions, in the centre of the room.

Grande Pirouette on Demi-Pointe

The grande pirouette is the most complicated form of men's tours. It is necessary to approach its study gradually: at first, an exercise with only quarter tours is given, then one with half tours; and finally it is practised with whole tours.

A slow tempo is taken at first; as the pirouette is mastered, the tempo is gradually accelerated. In its final form, grande pirouette is done at a quick tempo in series of eight, sixteen, or thirty-two tours (depending on the student's degree of accomplishment), one quarter note for each tour.

Study Sequence

1.   Exercise with quarter tours en dehors. Begin in 5th position en face, right leg front. Do a grande préparation as follows: demi-plié and spring onto demi-pointe in 5th position, raising the arms to 1st position. Remaining on the left leg on demi-pointe, throw the stretched right leg out to the side at a height of 90° and, simultaneously, open the arms to 2nd position. After having come down in 2nd position in demi-plié and curved the right arm to 1st position, push off from the floor with the heels and spring onto demi-pointe on the left leg, again throwing the right leg to 2nd position at a height of 90° and opening the right arm to the side; simultaneously, do a quarter tour to the right. After this, do

a short plié on the supporting leg, the right leg remaining at a height of 90°, and spring again onto demi-pointe on the supporting leg, with another quarter tour to the right, etc: To finish, on two final chords, come down in 5th or 4th position, placing the right leg in back, and lower the arms to preparatory position.

From this same préparation (à la seconde) half and, finally, whole tours en dehors are practised.

2. Final form. 2/4 time. (Turning to the right.) Begin in 5th position with the right leg in front. On two introductory chords, sliding the toe along the floor, take the right leg to the side, simultaneously opening the arms through 1st to 2nd position; and demi-plié in 2nd position, curving the right arm to 1st position. On the upbeat, spring onto demi-pointe on the left leg, throwing the right leg out to 2nd position at a height of 90°; with a strong movement, take the right arm also to 2nd position, and do a quick tour (a pirouette) en dehors. On the first quarter, do a short demi-plié on the left leg, the right leg remaining in the air; and, between the first and second quarters, do a second pirouette. On the third quarter, again demi-plié; and, between the third and fourth quarters, do the next pirouette, etc. Thus, each demi-plié is done on the quarter, and each tour is done on the eighth between the quarters. It is recommended that, in the beginning, a sequence of only four pirouettes be studied; then gradually the number of tours may be increased.

Grande pirouette, in its final form, with a large number of pirouettes, is usually finished with small pirouettes sur le cou-de-pied, begun from a plié on the supporting leg. For these, the arms come together in a low 1st position.

RULES FOR THE EXECUTION OF GRANDE PIROUETTE. For the correct execution of all kinds of grande pirouette, one must pay special attention to the movements of the head. Fix the eyes on the point from which the tour begins and finish each tour with the eyes directed at that same point. For example, doing a tour to the right, the head at first looks across the left shoulder (in a turn to the left, it looks across the right shoulder); then it quickly turns en face. As the speed of the pirouette is increased, the turns of the head are also accelerated, providing force for the pirouette.

Before each tour the supporting leg does a quick, not too deep, demi-plié, then immediately pushes off from the floor, with the heel accurately rising to demi-pointe on the tour.

The working leg is tautly stretched, locked in the hip; for the duration of the series of tours, it retains the height of 90° taken on the first pirouette.

In the elementary study of grande pirouette, at a slow tempo, the leg is in exact position à la seconde (in a straight line to the side). In the final form, at a quick tempo, the leg must be slightly in front of 2nd position (without disturbing this position visually). This is because a precise position à la seconde would cause the body to involuntarily incline backward, and stability would be upset.

The arm that is curved to 1st position in the préparation provides force for the first pirouette, then the arms, resiliently rounded, remain in 2nd position. In turning to the right, the left arm each time gives a push to the right, while maintaining 2nd position; in turning to the left, the right arm each time provides force.

The back and thighs are pulled up, and the shoulders are level.

Grande Pirouette Sautillé ("Hopped")

The hopped grande pirouette is distinguished from the pirouette on demi-pointe only in that the supporting leg continuously remains in demi-plié while turning. The hops are done on the whole foot, with the heel barely leaving the floor: the heel comes up slightly to allow the supporting leg to turn. The demi-plié does not increase or decrease, since the body must all the time maintain a single level, relative to the floor. The position of the working leg, open to 2nd position at a height of 90°, the turns of the head, and the force provided by the arms are the same as those described in "Grande pirouette on demi-pointe" (above). At first four hops are done during one tour, then two, and later on, one. The movement is learned at a slow tempo; but, in its final form, it is done quickly in series of eight, sixteen, or thirty-two tours.

The grande pirouette sautillé begins with the usual prépara-tion and one grande pirouette on demi-pointe; then the supporting leg comes down in a demi-plié and the pirouette sautillé begins. The movement finishes with pirouettes sur le cou-de-pied to 5th or 4th position croisée.

Tours Sautillés in the Big Poses en Dehors and en Dedans. These tours are also used in the women's class.

Example of turning en dedans in 1st arabesque. Demi-plié in 5th position with épaulement croisé, right leg front. Bend the body to the left and do a dégagé with the right leg forward at 45° on a diagonal to point 2, or in a straight line to point 3, turning the body to face it. Opening the arms, through 1st position, to 1st arabesque, with a step, transfer the centre of weight forward onto the right leg in demi-plié, and raise the left leg backward to 90°.

Remaining in plié, slightly raise the heel from the floor (without rising to demi-pointe) and again lower it to the floor, turning to the right (en dedans) each time. In the beginning, it is necessary to do this at a slow tempo in sixteen counts: sixteen hops to one measure of 4/4 for two tours. Then the tempo is speeded up, until it is quick; and the number of tours increases.

In these tours sautillés, the heel acts as if tapping out the roll of a drum on the floor. During the tours, while taking the heel from the floor (and moving it forward each time), one must not deepen or lessen the plié. The body, directed forward, remains the whole time at the same height from the floor. The shoulders are level; and the left shoulder, in tours to the right, cannot lag behind. The leg, raised at 90°, is locked in the hip and must not change its position.

The same tours can be done in the pose 2nd arabesque and attitude effacée.

Tours sautillés en dehors can be done in the poses 3rd and 4th arabesques and attitude croisée. To begin these, one must come down in plié in the pose at 90° from a preceding tour or jump or do a step forward croisé into a plié on the supporting leg, simultaneously raising the back leg to 90°.

Tours en l'Air

Tours en l'air (in the air) are studied after the students have mastered grand changement de pieds en tournant with quarter and half tours.

Study Sequence

1. Elementary study (a single tour), 4/4 time. Begin in 5th position en face, right leg front. On the first quarter, demi-plié as deeply as possible, firmly pressing the heels onto the floor; the right arm is raised to 1st position and the left to 2nd; the shoulders are level, under no circumstances should the right shoulder be moved forward. Between the first and second quarters, do a big jump upward with a complete turn to the right. The left arm provides force for the turn and comes together with the right arm in 1st position. The head and eyes remain for a moment looking toward the mirror across the left shoulder and then, at the end of the tour, return to the initial point. The jump finishes en face on the second quarter in 5th position in demi-plié. The right leg is in back, and the arms open slightly to a small pose. On the third quarter, the knees are

stretched. On the fourth quarter, pause. Do the same thing
to the left, the force being provided by the right arm.

2. 2/4 time. On the upbeat, demi-plié and rise in 5th position
to demi-pointe; the arm that is analogous to the front leg is
raised to 1st position and the other to 2nd. On the first
quarter, demi-plié a little more deeply than usual. Between
the first and second quarters, do the tour en l'air, finishing
on the second quarter in demi-plié in 5th position.

3. 4/4 time. On the first and second quarters, chassé forward.
Between the second and third quarters, rise to demi-pointe
in 5th position. On the third quarter, demi-plié and tour en
l'air. On the fourth quarter, finish the tour in 5th position
in demi-plié.

4. With changements de pieds. 4/4 time. On the first two
quarters, do three small changements de pied in one eighth
each. Between the second and third quarters, rise in 5th
position on demi-pointe. On the third quarter, demi-plié
and tour en l'air. On the fourth quarter, demi-plié in 5th
position.

In this way, a single tour en l'air, studied from 5th
position, is gradually introduced into small combinations;
but, according to the degree of necessity, it also continues to
be studied independently.

Then a double tour en l'air is learned.

RULES FOR THE EXECUTION OF TOUR EN L'AIR.
The body must remain erect during demi-plié that precedes the
tour. Sometimes the performer, in striving to increase the
height of the jump, lets go of the back and bends the body
forward, in which case the tour en l'air gets out of hand and is
upset.

The back and the legs, with pulled-up thighs, must be in a
vertical position during the tour en l'air.

The force is always provided by the arm which is opened
beforehand to 2nd position. Although the force must be

increased for two tours, one must not take the arm back behind 2nd position in the préparation; and one must also not move forward the shoulder on the side toward which the tour is done. These devices, which supposedly provide extra force, must never be used in the classroom study of tours en l'air. Deviation from the academic form is allowed only on the stage and depends on the individual features of the dancer. Intensified movements of the arm and the turns of the head amply provide sufficient force for the execution of a double tour.

In the execution of one tour en l'air, the legs, with stretched knees and feet, are crossed in the air in 5th position for the duration of the tour and only at the last moment, on coming down in demi-plié, change (the leg that is in front going back).

For a double tour en l'air, however, it is necessary to change the legs at the very first moment of the tour, taking back the leg that is in front without an opening to the side. Thus, the change of the legs takes place immediately in the air, which appreciably assists the double tour. During the double tour itself, the legs must remain tightly pressed together.

Coming down from the tour in demi-plié, one must maintain an erect torso, with a pulled-up back, and go into demi-plié softly and resiliently.

Tours en l'air can be done facing point 1 or facing a diagonal, to the right or to the left.

Tours in the Big Poses

These tours are done from a préparation in 4th position croisée for tours en dehors, and from 4th position both croisée and effacée for tours en dedans.

The distance between the feet in 4th position must be somewhat greater than usual, since the ordinary 4th position is too narrow to allow the leg to be raised to 90° efficiently.

Tours à la seconde en dehors and en dedans and tours in the poses écartées, derrière and devant, are done from 2nd position.

The following order for the study of the préparations and tours in the big poses is recommended: 1) à la seconde, from 2nd position, en dehors and en dedans; 2) attitude croisée; 3) attitude effacée; 4) 1st arabesque; 5) à la seconde, from 4th position; 6) the poses croisée devant and effacée devant; 7) 2nd and 3rd arabesques; 8) 4th arabesque and the poses écartées, derrière and devant.

In the préparation from 4th position for tours en dehors, demi-plié is done on both legs, but for tours en dedans, only the supporting leg is bent.

In the préparation, the centre of weight, as in tours sur le cou-de-pied, must always be over the supporting leg.

Préparation and Tour à la Seconde from 2nd Position

Study Sequence

1. First form. 4/4 time, two measures. Begin in 5th position, right leg front.

    First measure. On the upbeat, demi-plié. On the first quarter, spring onto demi-pointe in 5th position, raising the arms to 1st position. On the second quarter, hold the position. On the third quarter, remaining on demi-pointe, throw the right leg out with a quick battement to 2nd position at 90°, and open the arms to 2nd position. On the fourth quarter, hold the position.

    Second measure. On the upbeat, come down in demi-plié in 2nd position, bending the right arm to 1st position. Then, on the first quarter, pushing off with the heels from the floor, spring up onto demi-pointe on the left leg, throwing the right leg out with the same quick battement to 2nd position at 90° and opening the arms to 2nd position. On the second and third quarters, the position is held. On the fourth quarter, come down in 5th position, right leg back; and lower the arms to the preparatory position.

    The préparation en dedans with the right leg is studied

in exactly the same way. The first half is the same as the préparation en dehors; then, after the demi-plié in 2nd position, spring onto demi-pointe on the right leg, throwing the left leg out to the side at 90°. In this case, finish in 5th position by placing the left leg in front.

In order to execute a tour à la seconde en dehors (with the right leg raised), after the demi-plié in 2nd position, the right arm is taken from 1st position to 2nd, providing force for the tour; the left arm, which is in 2nd position, moves slightly forward and also provides force. The head and eyes at first are directed over the left shoulder to point 1; then the head quickly comes straight and, at the end, returns to the initial point en face. The arms, during the tour, are resiliently curved in 2nd position. The heel of the supporting leg is turned out; and the leg that is raised to 90° is locked in the hip and must not lose the form of 2nd position. The back and thighs are tightly pulled up throughout.

In the execution of two tours, it is necessary to increase the force given by the right arm, but in no case should the right shoulder move forward during the plié.

2. Final form. 4/4 time, one measure. Begin in 5th position, right leg front. On the upbeat, demi-plié and rise to demi-pointe in 5th position. On the first quarter, throw the right leg out with a grand battement to the side at 90°, remaining on demi-pointe on the left leg. On the second quarter, do a short demi-plié in 2nd position. Between the second and third quarters, spring up onto demi-pointe on the left leg. Do a tour à la seconde en dehors during the third and fourth quarters. Then stop on demi-pointe, the right leg raised to 90°.

Tours en dehors in the pose écartée derrière are done with the préparation for tours à la seconde en dehors, and tours en dedans in the pose écartée devant are done with the préparation for tours à la seconde en dedans.

Tours en Dehors in the Big Poses

Préparation and tour en dehors in the pose attitude croisée. Begin in 4th position croisée, left leg front in demi-plié and the right stretched out in back with the whole foot on the floor. The centre of weight is on the left leg; and the arms are in the position used for 3rd arabesque, but with the elbows and hands slightly raised. The head and eyes are directed along the right arm to point 2. (In showing the student, for the first time, the proper width of this 4th position, one can first have him stand in 5th, then stretch the left leg, sliding the toe along the floor, croisé devant, and place it in an enlarged 4th position in demi-plié. Later on, it will not be necessary to begin in this manner.) Demi-plié on both legs, leaving the centre of weight on the supporting left leg; then, pushing off from the floor with the heels, spring onto demi-pointe on the left leg (moving the heel well forward) and throw the right leg to attitude croisée; simultaneously, the right arm is raised to 3rd position and the left curves, but remains in 2nd position; the head turns in profile toward the left shoulder. One should fix the pose on demi-pointe for as long as possible, then stretch the right leg, open the arms, and come down in 5th position in demi-plié.

In the execution of one and two tours to the right, the left arm provides the force; from the préparation position, it curves and gives a small push to the right. The right arm must not lose the form of 3rd position; the right shoulder, by being taken slightly back, also helps provide force for the tour. The head remains immobile, in the profile position, which is characteristic of the basic pose attitude croisée.

Later on, in advanced classes, many variants of the arm positions are used. In turning to the right, for example, one can raise the left arm to 3rd position, bending the right to 1st, or raise both arms to 3rd, etc.

Préparation and tour en dehors in the pose 3rd arabesque. Begin in 4th position, left leg front. The position of the legs, body, and arms is the same as in the preceding example of a tour in attitude croisée. From the demi-plié on both legs, pushing off from the floor with both heels, spring onto demi-pointe on the left leg (with the heel well forward), and throw the right leg out in the direction croisée derrière to 3rd arabesque; the arms remain in the position taken in the préparation, but the line is slightly elongated. It is very difficult to take force for the tour in the pose 3rd arabesque; but, essentially, the left arm and hand give a push to the right, while at the same time remaining in the pose arabesque. It is as if the body, in the tour, were following the right arm, which is extended forward. The right leg, pulled up in the thigh and pushed back croisé derrière, also assists the tour. The head remains immobile and is turned toward the right arm.

Préparation and tour en dehors in the pose 4th arabesque. The préparation is done in the manner described above, in 4th position croisée with the left leg forward. In springing onto demi-pointe on the left leg from demi-plié for the tour, it is necessary to lower the left arm with a passing movement and bring it forward to meet the right arm in 1st position before taking the pose 4th arabesque. This movement of the arms (the left will then be extended forward and the right, together with the shoulder, will be taken back) provides enough force for the execution of one or two tours.

Préparation and tour en dehors in the pose effacée devant. Begin in 4th position croisée, the left leg front in demi-plié and the right stretched out in back, with the whole foot on the floor. The centre of weight is on the left leg. The right arm is extended forward, and the left is to the side, the palms turned down and the hands slightly raised. With a short movement, demi-plié on the right leg, transferring onto it the centre of weight. Then, pushing off with the heel, spring onto demi-pointe on the right leg; throw the left leg out in the direction effacée devant at 90°; and turn the whole body to point 8 of the classroom plan; the hands are curved; the left arm remains in 2nd position; the right arm, at the moment of the demi-plié, is brought to the side and, from 2nd position, is raised to 3rd; the head is turned to the right, with the shoulders level; the thigh of the left leg and the back are tightly pulled up.

In the women's class, the transference to the demi-plié on the right leg is done differently: first, the instep and the toes of the right foot are quickly stretched; and then the leg is lowered in demi-plié. This can also be done in the men's class.

For the execution of one or two tours en dehors, the right arm, which is raised to 3rd position (the tour will be to the left), provides the force. The head remains immobile and is turned toward the right shoulder.

Préparation and tour en dehors à la seconde from 4th position. Begin in 4th position croisée, left leg front. The position of the body and arms is as in the previous préparations. Demi-plié on both legs and, pushing off with the heels, spring onto demi-pointe on the left leg, throwing the right leg out to 2nd position at 90°; the right arm curves and is taken to 2nd position; the left arm also curves but remains in 2nd position; the whole body is directed to point 2 of the classroom plan.

For the execution of one or two tours to the right, the right arm, which opens to 2nd position, provides the force; a light movement with the left hand to the right provides additional force. The head, at the beginning of the tour, is turned over the left shoulder to point 2 and then returns to the position en face.

It is recommended that all the préparations and tours just described be done springing slightly forward onto demi-pointe. This places the body well over the supporting leg, helps to hold the heel in a turned-out position and, since it fixes the pose for a fleeting second, facilitates the tours.

Tours en Dedans in the Big Poses

Préparation and tour en dedans in the pose attitude effacée. Begin in 4th position croisée, right leg front in

demi-plié, the left leg stretched out in back with the whole foot
on the floor. The body is in épaulement croisé, with the centre
of weight on the supporting right leg. The left shoulder is back,
and the right shoulder forward. The left arm, with a curved
hand, is in 2nd position, and the right in 1st. The head is turned
to point 1 of the classroom plan. Increasing the demi-plié on
the right leg (the left leg remaining stretched), push off with
both heels and spring onto demi-pointe on the right leg
(moving the heel well forward); and, raising the left leg to
attitude effacée, turn the whole body to point 2. While
springing up onto demi-pointe, sharply bring the right arm
from 1st to 2nd position; and raise the left arm, which is in 2nd
position, to 3rd. The centre of weight is thus brought forward
over the supporting leg, and the head turns to the left.

For the execution of one or two tours to the right, the right
arm, brought sharply to the side from 1st position, provides the
force; and the left arm, being raised to 3rd position, provides
additional force. The head is motionless once the pose is taken.

In the beginning, the arm can be raised to the pose through
1st position. Later, numerous variants of the arm positions are
used in the pose: both arms in 3rd position, one arm in 1st
position and the other in 3rd, etc.

Préparation and tour en dedans in the pose 1st arabesque. Begin in
4th position croisée, right leg front. The préparation is the
same as for attitude effacée: the right arm is in 1st position and
the left in 2nd. Increasing the plié on the right leg, push off
with both heels and spring onto demi-pointe on the right leg,
turning the body to point 3; simultaneously, the left leg, with a
pulled-up thigh, is thrown out to arabesque at 90°; the right
arm extends forward; the left arm goes to the side; the level
shoulders and head turn to point 3; and the eyes are directed
beyond the right hand.

In this préparation, it is extremely important, when springing from 4th position to the pose, to bring the left shoulder
forward immediately; if the shoulder lags, or if there is any

looseness in the left thigh, the pose will be disturbed and the tour impeded.

In the execution of one or two tours to the right, the body, with a well pulled-up back, is strongly moved forward over the supporting leg; the right arm, which extends forward with an energetic movement, provides the force (it is as if it were cutting through the air, with the whole tour following it); the left arm is opposite the shoulder in the arabesque position and balances the pose; the head is directed straight forward to point 3.

Préparation and tour en dedans in the pose 2nd arabesque. The préparation is as in the previous two examples. Springing onto demi-pointe on the supporting right leg, turn the whole body to point 3, simultaneously raising the left leg in back to a height of 90° and locking it in the hip (the torso is somewhat more erect than it is in 1st arabesque); the left arm is brought forward through 1st position, and the right arm (together with the shoulder) is taken back; the head turns to the left. The movement of the arms and the movement forward of the heel of the right foot provide sufficient force for one or two tours to the right.

Préparation and tour en dedans à la seconde. Begin in 4th position croisée, right leg front. The right arm is in 1st position and the left in 2nd. Spring onto demi-pointe on the right leg, throwing the left leg out to 2nd position at 90°; the body simultaneously turns en face to point 1 with the arms in 2nd position.

In the execution of one or two tours to the right, the pose en face is fixed (as are all poses) and the right arm provides the force. The head, for a moment, remains turned toward the mirror over the left shoulder; and then returns to point 1. These tours can also be done raising the arms through 2nd position to 3rd.

Préparation and tour en dedans in the pose croisée devant. From 4th position croisée, with the right leg in front, do the préparation for tours en dedans à la seconde, as explained in the previous example. Then, without permitting the left leg to linger in 2nd position at a height of 90°, take it croisé devant at the same height. One must pull up the thighs strongly, so that the leg does not go past the position croisée devant. The arms, at first, are opened to 2nd position, and then take on the pose croisée, the right arm in 3rd position and the left in 2nd.

The left arm and hand provide the force for one or two tours to the right. The head is turned in profile toward the left shoulder.

All the examples of tours en dedans just described can also be done from a préparation in 4th position effacée. In this case, the préparation with the right leg will be to point 2; and the préparation with the left leg will be to point 8.

"Quatre pirouettes" is a term for a combination of big tours en dedans, each preceded by a grand (6th) port de bras. Usually, the tours take the following order: à la seconde, attitude effacée, en tire-bouchon, and 2nd arabesque; but other combinations are possible.

Tours by Various Other Means

In the centre exercise and the adagio, tours in the big poses and sur le cou-de-pied can be done not only from a préparation in the basic positions (2nd, 4th, and 5th), but also by various other means: from a step onto demi-pointe, from a tombé, from a coupé, etc.

Several examples are given below, but the variations of tours and poses are numerous.

1. *Tour from a step onto demi-pointe.* a) With the right leg, développé in demi-plié effacé devant at a height of 90°, raising the arms to 1st position. Then, with a step to point 2, transfer the centre of weight onto demi-pointe on the right leg and, taking the pose 1st arabesque, do a tour en dedans.

   b) Développé with the left leg effacé derrière, with the right leg in demi-plié and the arms in 1st position; the body is inclined forward. With a step to point 6, transfer the centre of weight onto demi-pointe on the left leg and, throwing the right leg out to effacé devant at a height of 90°, do a tour en dehors; the arms, from 1st position, open to the side; then the left arm, providing the force, is raised to 3rd position, while the right remains in 2nd.

2. *Tours from tombé.* a) Développé to the side at 90° with the right leg. Then rise to demi-pointe on the left leg and fall beyond the tip of the toe onto the right leg in demi-plié (tombé). Immediately spring onto demi-pointe, throwing the left leg out at a height of 90° to the side, and do a tour en dedans.

   b) Begin in the pose croisée devant, the right leg raised to 90°. Rise to demi-pointe and fall forward beyond the tip of the toe onto the right leg in demi-plié (tombé), then immediately spring up onto demi-pointe on the right leg and, throwing the left leg out croisé derrière, do a tour en dehors in the pose 3rd arabesque. The left arm, which, in the pose croisée, is in 3rd position, is lowered to 1st on the tombé, and, together with the right arm, takes on the arabesque position.

3. *Tours from coupé.* a) Demi-plié on the right leg, with the left bent sur le cou-de-pied derrière. Then put the left foot down onto demi-pointe in back (a coupé) and throw the stretched right leg out écarté derrière to a height of 90°; simultaneously, opening the arms through 1st position (the right going to 3rd and the left to 2nd), do a tour en dehors in the pose écartée derrière.

   b) From the same kind of coupé, one can also do a tour en dehors in the pose effacée devant, etc.

   All tours from a step onto demi-pointe, from tombé, and from coupé are also done on pointe in exactly the same manner.

Tours Sissonne-Tombée

Tours "sissonne tombée" (fallen tours) are executed in various directions: in a straight line forward from point 5 to point 1, on the diagonal from point 6 to point 2 or from point 4 to point 8.

At first, these tours must be studied at a slow tempo, 2/4 each; then they are executed at a moderate tempo, 1/4 each; and finally, in their finished form, they are done at a quick tempo, 1/4 or 1/8 each.

It is recommended that tours sissonne-tombée, like tours-chaînés, should be studied at first in a straight line forward facing the mirror, because this will help to keep the shoulders and hips level and parallel to each other, which is essential for their execution. Then pass on to the study of these tours on the diagonal.

Elementary study in a straight line forward from point 5 to point 1. 4/4 time. Begin in 5th position with épaulement croisé, right foot front.

On the upbeat, demi-plié and do a small jump without leaving the floor; at the time of the jump, the right leg slightly bends in the knee, and the foot, with stretched instep and toes, makes a small opening forward, but through a considerably lower position sur le cou-de-pied than is customary for ordinary sissonnes tombées.

On the first quarter, by falling (tombé) into a plié in a very narrow 4th position en face, the weight of the body is transferred onto the right leg. The accent on the tombé is emphasised by the right leg, which is in front. At the same time, the arms, from preparatory position, are raised and opened at half height, the right to 1st position and the left to 2nd. The shoulders are level, and the head is en face.

On the second quarter, the position is held. Between the second and third quarters, lightly jump en tournant to the right with a minimum take-off from the floor, at which time the legs stretch, joining in a tight fifth position, the left leg behind the right. The left arm provides force for the turn and through preparatory position joins the right in 1st position at half height.

The head (and eyes), as in all tours, for a moment turns across the left shoulder toward the mirror and, at the conclusion of the tour, quickly returns to point 1.

On the third quarter, the jump finishes in a narrow 4th position en face in demi-plié, emphasising the accent of the tombé on the right leg. The left arm opens to 2nd position at half height, and the right arm remains in 1st position.

On the fourth quarter, the position is held. Then repeat the sequence for the following tours.

In studying tours sissonne-tombée, it is recommended that no fewer than eight be practised in one direction at a time. If they are practised turning to the right and the right leg is carelessly put down a little to the right of a straight line forward, they will inevitably lose their "spot" and begin to deviate to the right.

In their final form, at a quick tempo (as also at a moderate tempo), it is essential to bear in mind that, after the tour, the foot should fall forward in demi-plié with an accent precisely opposite the foot that is in back, the toe of one opposite the heel of the other, i. e., opposite 5th position.

The shoulders must be absolutely level. During the tour to the right, the left shoulder must in no case lag behind. During the tour to the left side, the right shoulder in the same way must be kept in alignment with the left.

The thigh and buttocks muscles are pulled up throughout.

These rules will assist in the rapid development of a virtuoso execution of tours sissonne-tombée.

Tours sur le Cou-de-pied from a Grand Plié

Tours en dehors and en dedans from a grand plié are done from 1st, 2nd, 5th and 4th positions. At first, one tour is done, then two.

In the grand plié, before the tours, the heels remain on the floor as long as possible (in 2nd position, of course, the heels at no time leave the floor). At the last moment, when the heels are already off the floor, without pausing, quickly rise onto high demi-pointe on the leg on which the tour is to be done. Here the rule for the evenness of the plié is broken: the lowering takes place in two quarters, but the quick rise upward and the tour are done between the second and third quarters.

Before beginning the plié, throw the arms slightly upward, hold them high for a bit, then, lowering the arms, bring them together, from below, to 1st position for the execution of the turn. The arms must be brought together without delay at the moment the leg is stretched for the tour. In the men's class, use is often made of a method in which, during the plié, one arm is brought to 1st position through preparatory position while the other remains in 2nd; the arms are brought together in the tour. From 1st and 2nd positions, tours are done en face, but from 5th and 4th positions, with épaulement.

Tours from Grand Plié in the Big Poses

From the lowest point of the grand plié in 1st, 2nd, 4th, or 5th position, do one or two tours en dehors or en dedans. Rising from the grand plié onto demi-pointe on one leg, throw the other leg out, simultaneously, with a grand battement, to whatever big pose is required for the tour. The arms, first opened to 2nd position, are lowered during the plié and then open through 1st position to the given pose, simultaneously with the movement of the working leg.

These tours can be done in all the big poses, without exception, from 1st, 2nd, 4th, and 5th positions. Tours à la seconde, however, are done only from 1st and 2nd positions.

Tours Chaînés

A series of turns executed on two legs on high demi-pointe or on pointe are called tours chaînés ("linked").

"A suddenly whirling chain of little tours" is the phrase used by A. Y. Vaganova in her book, *Basic Principles of Classical Ballet,* to define chaînés. It is senseless to do one tour chaîné. At the beginning, the minimum number of these little tours is four; later, they can be done in series of eight, sixteen, or more. They are done on a diagonal from upstage traveling downstage, and in a circle.

It is useful to begin the study of chaînés traveling in a straight line down toward the mirror from upstage (from point 5 to point 1). In this way, the student learns not to deviate from the projected line, and he can control his execution by use of the mirror. The tours are then practised on a diagonal. For the first few days, the tours should be done slowly, in two quarters each, in order to establish the position of the legs, shoulders, and head, and to feel the rigidly pulled-up back, thighs, and knees. Then the tours are gradually accelerated, since a quick, dynamic tempo is essential to chaînés. Each little tour is done in one quarter, then in one eighth, and, finally, in one sixteenth.

Tours chaînés to the right. 2/4 time. The movement is along a straight line toward the mirror from point 5 to point 1. Standing in 5th position en face with the right foot in front, on the upbeat, demi-plié and slide the right leg forward, with the toe to the floor; at the same time, extend the right arm in front of oneself and the left arm to the side, opposite the left shoulder; the palms are turned down; and the body and the head face front. On the first quarter, step onto demi-pointe on the right leg, and make a half tour to the right (en dedans); the arms are brought together in a low 1st position, the left arm providing a little force. The body is turned with the left shoulder to point 1; and the head remains turned toward the mirror, looking over the left shoulder. On the second quarter, the left leg is placed next to the right without a space between (both legs are on high demi-pointe, side by side, in an unturned-out 1st position); and from here, the second half of the tour is done on the left leg (turning to the right); as the body turns, the right shoulder is brought toward the mirror, and the head turns to the right. For the second tour chaîné, remain on demi-pointe and take only a barely noticeable step forward; the arms again open slightly and close during the tour. As the tempo is accelerated the arm movements become smaller; eventually, only the hands move. At a quick tempo, doing a large number of chaînés, the arms, having provided force for the first turn, remain in 1st position at half height and only the elastically rounded elbows help the tour.

Thus, in the first half of the tour, the body is in profile to the mirror, with the left side forward. The second half of the tour also finishes in profile to the mirror, but with the right side forward. In the execution of chaînés on a diagonal from point 6 to point 2, beginning with the right leg, the first half of the tour will finish with the left shoulder to point 2 (the head turned toward the left shoulder); and the second half of the tour will finish with the right shoulder to point 2 (the head toward the right shoulder).

For chaînés to be swift and precise it is very important to turn equally on both legs. If, in the early study, the tour is done completely on one leg, with the second leg merely being placed next to it, the chaînés will end up being unrhythmical and jerky. It is no less important to "feel" the tours in the shoulders and thighs (for example, turning to the right: when on the right leg, the left shoulder is taken forward; when on the left leg, the right shoulder is taken back).

The legs must be side by side at all times. If they separate, the stability of the body will be disturbed and it will be difficult to travel in a straight line, thus depriving the movement of its aesthetic quality.

All of the pirouettes and tours described in this chapter, of course, also are practised equally to the left.

XI. Turning Movements Used in Adagio

In the adagios in the centre of the room, various other turning movements are used: tours lents, renversés, grands fouettés en face and en tournant, and tours fouettés en dehors and en dedans.

Tours Lents

Tours lents are slow turns on the whole foot en dehors or en dedans in the big poses, done by shifting the heel of the supporting leg forward or backward along the floor.

The pose in which the tour lent begins is held until the end of the tour. The movement of the heel must be virtually imperceptible, creating the impression of a motionless figurine slowly rotating on a pedestal.

Tours lents develop the stability of the body and the strength of the leg that is raised at 90°. They are used in the small and the big adagio and also in the centre exercise. In pas de deux, the woman, with the support of the man, does tours lents on pointe (promenade).

The following s t u d y s e q u e n c e is useful: tours lents à la seconde en dehors and en dedans, then in attitude croisée and effacée, then in the pose croisée devant and 1st arabesque, then in 3rd arabesque and the pose effacée devant and then in 2nd arabesque. The most difficult poses, écartées derrière and devant and 4th arabesque, are studied last.

In the beginning, tour lent should be done with half a tour, pausing at each point of the room, then with a whole tour pausing at each point, and, in its final form, smoothly connecting each shift of the heel along the floor in the tour.

Tour lent à la seconde en dehors. Elementary study. 4/4 time, four measures. With the right leg, développé to 2nd position at 90° on the introduction, opening the arms to 2nd position.

First measure. On the first and second quarters, turn on the supporting leg to the right to point 2; on the third and fourth quarters, hold the position.

Second measure. On the first and second quarters, turn to point 3; on the third and fourth quarters, hold the position.

Third measure. In the same manner, turn to point 4.

Fourth measure. Turn to point 5, and, closing the arms in preparatory position, lower the right leg to 5th position back.

Tour lent with a complete turn. 4/4 time, four measures. The movements are distributed in the following manner: turn on one quarter; and pause on the following quarter.

Then tour lent is done in two measures of 4/4, with a pause of 1/8 at each point; then it is done in one measure, pausing only at points 3, 5, 7, and 1. In its final form, one complete tour is executed smoothly, without pauses, in 4/4.

In subsequent tours in other poses, it is no longer necessary to adhere to such an exhausting sequence; the leg that is raised to 90° has acquired sufficient strength so that tour lent in attitude croisée and other poses can be done, pausing at each point for 1/8, in two measures of 4/4, then in one and finally in its legato form.

Tours Lents from Pose to Pose Involving Movements of the Torso. In the adagios of the 5th class, tours lents from one pose to another begin to be given in which the torso inclines a little away from the working leg, raised to 90°, before or during the tour. For example, standing on the left leg in the pose attitude croisée, the right leg is in back, the right arm is in 3rd position and the left in 2nd. On the first quarter, incline the

torso strongly forward; at the same time, the right leg stretches
and the right arm is lowered directly to 1st position. On the
second quarter, begin the tour lent en dehors (i. e., to the
right); and continue the tour during the third quarter; the right
arm gradually opens to 2nd position; the head and eyes remain
toward the mirror as long as possible. When, during the tour,
the leg, which is stretched in back, finds itself toward point 8;
the torso, strongly using the back, straightens; the left arm,
helping the tour, goes from 2nd to 3rd position. And, on the
4th quarter, the body faces point 8; simultaneously, the leg,
continuously preserving the turn-out, finishes in the pose
croisée devànt; the head is to the right.

   In the same way, a tour lent from the poses 3rd and 4th
arabesques can be executed, finishing in the pose croisée
devant. During the inclination of the torso forward, at the
beginning of such a tour lent en dehors, the working leg must
be strongly raised in back; consequently, the muscles of the
lower back must be very strongly held.

   Turn en dedans from the pose croisée devant, on the first
and second quarters, do tour lent en dedans from the
preceding pose (facing point 8) to the back corner (point 6);
then lean the torso slightly back; the head remains to the
mirror. On the third and fourth quarters, with the heel of the
supporting leg strongly turning forward (en dedans), the left
arm opens to 2nd position and the right is raised from 2nd
position to 3rd; the right leg remains toward point 6 and bends
to attitude croisée only at the final moment of the tour; the
head finishes to the left. This tour lent may also finish in the
poses 3rd or 4th arabesque.

   An example of a short adagio utilising these tours lents.

   Eight measures of 4/4, very slow. On the first measure, grand
plié in 5th position (with the right leg in front) and, from grand
plié, tour en dedans in the pose attitude effacée. On the second
measure, tour lent en dedans to the pose attitude croisée
épaulée in the following manner. At the beginning of the tour,

slightly bend the torso back and open the left arm to 2nd position. When concluding the tour, lower the right arm to preparatory position and raise it through 1st position to 3rd; the torso is in the same position as in 4th arabesque (left shoulder taken back, right arm to point 8, elbow forward, head to the right, eyes directed beyond the arm). On the third measure, bend forward in the torso, at the same time stretching the working leg, and do a half turn en dehors to face point 5, opening the arms to 2nd position; the position is à la seconde; plié and step onto the left leg toward point 3 to the pose 1st arabesque. On the fourth measure, turning en dedans, simultaneously do a grand rond de jambe en dedans to the pose croisée devant. On the fifth measure, relevé and tombé forward and do a grand port de bras (6th), finishing in a préparation in 4th position for a tour en dehors. On the sixth measure, tour en dehors in the pose attitude croisée with both arms in 3rd position. On the seventh measure, opening the right arm to 2nd position, turn en dehors as described above, but finish in the pose effacée devant, with a rise to demi-pointe at the end. On the eighth measure, tombé forward effacé and chassé, finishing in 4th position effacée in a préparation for a tour en dedans; then do two tours en dedans en tire-bouchon, with the arms in 3rd position; pause at the conclusion of the tours on demi-pointe before closing 5th position front.

Renversé

In translation from the French, "renversé" has several meanings, including "overturned", "moved elsewhere", "spilled", etc.

In our terminology, however, renversé indicates throwing back of the upper body. This complicated pas is learned in advanced classes and has many variants. During recent years, renversé has begun to lose its virtuosity and beautiful form.

Vulgarised, it resembles a simple pas de bourrée en tournant, combined with port de bras.

But renversé should be a strong throwing back and turn of the upper body, in which the movements of the arms and legs are but an accompaniment to the movement of the body and therefore play only a secondary role. Examples of the most common renversés are described below.

Renversé en Dehors from Attitude Croisée. 4/4 time. Rise to demi-pointe on the left leg to the pose attitude croisée, raising the right arm to 3rd and the left arm to 2nd position. On the upbeat, demi-plié, inclining the body and head slightly forward, and maintaining the right arm in 3rd position. On the first quarter, straighten the body, bend back slightly and, simultaneously, rise to demi-pointe on the left leg; the hands, at the moment the body straightens, extend slightly and then again curve; bending further back, turn the body to the right (en dehors). On the second quarter, the right leg, from attitude, is placed on demi-pointe close to the left in back, and the left is raised to the high conditional position sur le cou-de-pied devant; the body increases the bend and is almost a half turn away from the mirror (approximately to point 4); the head and eyes remain directed toward the mirror; the left arm, from 2nd position, bends to 1st; and the right remains in 3rd; the shoulders are level, for the body bends only back and not sideways.

Having stayed in the pose as long as possible, on the third quarter, at the last moment (as if in haste), finish the turn of the body (en dehors) toward the mirror, stepping over onto demi-pointe on the left leg and bringing the right leg up to the high position sur le cou-de-pied devant. The arms meet in 1st position, the right arm being lowered to 1st position from above, directly from 3rd. Completing the turn, prolong the bend of the body and only at the last moment, when the right leg lowers to 5th position front in demi-plié, come erect. The arms open slightly in 1st position and the head turns to the right. On the fourth quarter, pause.

Renversé en Dehors from Attitude Croisée. 2/4 time.

Begin with the right leg in attitude croisée. On the upbeat, demi-plié on the left leg. On the first quarter, rise onto demi-pointe and bend the body with the turn. Between the first and second quarters, step over onto the right leg and turn the body. At the end of the second eighth (as if in haste), step over onto the left leg, and, on the second quarter, finish the movement in 5th position in demi-plié, having executed renversé as described above.

This renversé can also be done from the pose 3rd arabesque or from the pose à la seconde at 90°. For example, having taken the leg out to 2nd position at 90°, incline the head forward, demi-plié on the supporting leg, at the same time taking the leg back to attitude croisée; then rise to demi-pointe and execute the renversé.

Renversé en Dedans from the Pose Croisée Devant. 4/4

time. The left leg is raised croisé devant at 90°, with the right arm in 3rd and the left in 2nd position. On the upbeat, demi-plié, inclining the body and head slightly forward, maintaining the right arm in 3rd position. Straighten the body and, on the first quarter, bend back, rising to demi-pointe; the hands extend and, during the bend, curve again. Turning the body to the right (en dedans), on the second quarter, place the left leg onto demi-pointe close to the right leg in front, raising the right sur le cou-de-pied derrière; the body is almost a half turn away from the mirror; increase the bend of the body, with the head and eyes directed toward the mirror; the left arm is in 1st and the right is in 3rd position; linger slightly in the pose before finishing the turn to the right toward the mirror, stepping over onto demi-pointe on the right leg and bringing the left foot sur le cou-de-pied derrière; the arms come together in 1st position. On the third quarter, come down in 5th position in demi-plié with the left leg in back, and open the arms slightly from 1st.

Renversé en dedans in 2/4 is done as indicated in the description of renversé en dehors in 2/4.

Renversé en dedans can also be done from 2nd position at 90°.

Renversé en Dedans from the Pose Croisée Devant Through the Pose Écartée Devant. Begin in the pose croisée devant with the left leg at 90°; the right arm is in 3rd and the left in 2nd position. Demi-plié with a slight inclination of the body and head forward. Rise to demi-pointe on the right leg, joining the arms for a moment in 1st position (the left moves through preparatory position and the right lowers from 3rd position). Bend the body back and turn to the right (en dedans) with the left shoulder to point 2; the left leg, from the position croisée devant, is taken écarté devant at 90°; the arms open from 1st position (the left to 3rd and the right to 2nd position); and the head, in the pose écartée devant, is directed to point 2. Then bring the left leg in front of the right, stepping over onto it on demi-pointe and raising the right foot sur le cou-de-pied derrière. Increase the bend of the body and open the arms to 2nd position, with the left shoulder, head, and eyes directed to point 2. Finish the turn of the body, stepping over onto demi-pointe on the right leg and raising the left foot sur le cou-de-pied derrière. Lower the arms quickly to 1st position. Come down in demi-plié in 5th position, left leg back, opening the arms slightly. The distribution of musical counts is the same as in the previous example.

Renversé from attitude croisée and from the pose croisée devant is also done in allegro as jeté renversé and sissonne renversée; and, in the women's class, renversé is also done on pointe.

RULES FOR THE EXECUTION OF RENVERSÉ. Renversé is always done in a legato manner. The bend of the body increases during the turn. There is a small bend at the moment of the rise to demi-pointe. The bend increases in the half turn and, in the concluding pas de bourrée, it is prolonged.

It is inadmissible to bend the body sideways; the body bends only backward. The thighs must be well pulled-up.

The main thing in renversé is the turn of the torso. The legs in the pas de bourrée must be subordinated to this movement of the upper body.

The arms change their positions softly and without sharply fixing them. They do not assist the turn, but only help in giving design to the pas.

The head and eyes are directed toward the mirror until the last moment of the turn; and only at the end of the renversé, in 5th position with épaulement croisé, do they again return to the mirror.

For a steady execution of renversé in one place, it is necessary to put one leg onto demi-pointe in the place of the other. A step backward, to the side, or forward upsets the stability of the body and can lead the performer in the most unexpected direction.

Renversé with Grand Rond de Jambe Développé en Dehors. 4/4 time. The préparation is with the left leg croisé derrière, the toe to the floor; the arms are in the preparatory position. On the upbeat, demi-plié on the right leg, bending the left sur le cou-de-pied derrière and opening the arms slightly to the side. Then lower them and coupé, stepping onto the left leg on demi-pointe and raising the right foot sur le cou-de-pied devant. On the first quarter, come down from demi-pointe in demi-plié, taking the half-bent right leg croisé devant at 45°. The body and head bend forward slightly and to the left; and the eyes are directed at the hands, which are raised to 1st position. Between the first and second quarters, the left leg rises to demi-pointe and the right, stretching, does a grand rond de jambe développé en dehors. Simultaneously, the body comes erect; the head and eyes follow the arms, which are raised to 3rd position. On the second quarter, open the arms to 2nd position and come down in demi-plié with épaulement croisé; the right leg bends backward at 90°, and the body also bends back. Between the second and third quarters, bring the right leg to the left, step onto it on demi-pointe and do a pas de bourrée en tournant en dehors (to the right). The arms are lowered and come together in 1st position. Increase the bend of the body before the renversé. On the third quarter, finish in 5th position in demi-plié, right leg front. On the fourth quarter, pause.

The movements of the body, head, and arms are co-ordinated with the rond de jambe on demi-pointe.

Renversé en dedans is done in the same way. This renversé can be done in allegro, beginning it with a small sissonne simple croisée, and, with the next jump, doing the rond de jambe with renversé. It is also done on pointe.

Renversé en Écarté from 4th Arabesque. "Flip over a glass of water without spilling a drop"—thus is this renversé sometimes jestfully (but aptly) explained in the classroom.

Done correctly, it has the appearance of a brilliantly performed trick. In its design, everything is terse and sharp. It is done in one quarter, beginning on the upbeat; and there is a pause on the second quarter in the final pose.

Stand on the right leg in 4th arabesque and establish the body well on a turned-out supporting leg. Then place the shoulders in one straight line so that the left arm is open to the side, opposite the left shoulder. Firmly securing the back, strongly bend the body to the left and slightly forward, simultaneously bending the left leg at a height of 90° toward the knee of the supporting leg. With a resilient movement of the arms, bring them together in the preparatory position, inclining the head to the left, and rising to demi-pointe on the supporting leg. Then quickly turn the body, which is inclined to the left, en dedans (to the right), and, with a bend back, pause in the pose écartée derrière, sharply placing the heel of the supporting leg on the floor, with the left leg opened to point 6; with a strong movement, simultaneously raise the arms from the preparatory position to 3rd position.

Here there are no intermediate positions: the first figure is an inclination of the body toward the leg that is bent at 90°, and the second is the final pose écartée.

As in all renversés, only the body does the turn here; the supporting leg rises to demi-pointe; and, at the end of the turn, the heel is placed on the floor. One must not do a tour on demi-pointe.

This renversé can be repeated from the final pose écartée; and it can also be done en dehors, beginning from the pose croisée devant and finishing in the pose écartée devant.

Grand Fouetté Effacé en Face

Elementary study. In the execution of grand fouetté effacé, the body is transferred from one diagonal to the other; that is, if the grand fouetté is begun with the right leg, facing the diagonal of points 2-6, then it finishes on the diagonal of points 8-4; or, if it is begun with the left leg, facing the diagonal of points 8-4, then it finishes on the diagonal of points 2-6.

Study Sequence

1. *En dehors.* 4/4 time. Begin with the left leg croisé derrière, toe to the floor. On the upbeat, demi-plié on the right leg, bending the left sur le cou-de-pied derrière and opening the arms slightly to the side. Lower the arms, coupé, stepping onto the left leg on demi-pointe and raising the right foot sur le cou-de-pied devant. Turning effacé to

point 2, come down, on the first quarter, in demi-plié and bring the half-bent right leg effacé devant at 45°, at the same time bending the body strongly to the right; the shoulders are level, the right arm is in 2nd and the left is in 1st position; the head and eyes are turned toward the tip of the toe of the right leg. On the second quarter, straightening the body and raising the left arm, which accompanies the turn of the head and eyes, to 3rd position, rise to demi-pointe and, stretching the right leg, take it to the side at 90° and turn the body en face. On the third quarter, further turn on demi-pointe and open the left arm to 2nd position, simultaneously bringing the right arm to 3rd; at this time, the right leg is taken effacé derrière at 90° to point 4 and the body turns to point 8. On the fourth quarter, come down in demi-plié in the pose attitude effacée, bending the body forward slightly more than is conventional for this attitude.

2.   Final form. 2/4 time. On the upbeat, coupé. On the first quarter, demi-plié on the supporting leg, bending the body sideways. Between the first and second quarters, grand rond de jambe on demi-pointe. On the second quarter, finish the fouetté in demi-plié in the pose attitude effacée.

The entire movement is done fluently, without a pause in 2nd position. The turn of the body is co-ordinated with the grand rond de jambe and with the movements of the head and arms, in which the left arm actively helps the straightening of the body from the initial inclined position, and the right arm assists the turn of the body to the final pose. The shoulders turn in accordance with the movements of the arms. In the execution of these fouettés with a jump and on pointe, the arms also actively take part in the movement.

En dedans. The préparation is with the left leg croisé devant with the toe to the floor. Coupé; then demi-plié on the left leg, turning the body effacé to point 8 and bending it back; the right leg is half-bent effacé derrière at 45°; the right arm is in 1st, the left in 2nd position, and the head is thrown back across the right shoulder, the eyes directed to the tip of the toe of the right leg.

Stretching the right leg back (at 45°) and lowering the right arm to preparatory position, rise to demi-pointe and turn the body en face, bringing the leg to 2nd position at 90°. Simultaneously, open the arms to 2nd position. Finish the grand rond de jambe en dedans, bringing the leg effacé devant at 90° and at the same time turning the body effacé to point 2. Come down in demi-plié and bend the body back; the right arm remains in 2nd position, the left is raised from 2nd to 3rd, and the shoulders are level.

In executing the movement in 2/4, on the first quarter, plié on the supporting leg. Between the first and second quarters, rond de jambe en dedans on demi-pointe. On the second quarter, finish the fouetté in demi-plié in the pose effacé devant.

This fouetté begins and ends with a bend of the body backward, which must be preserved when executing it with a jump and on pointe.

Fouetté effacé on demi-pointe and on pointe can also begin from 5th position: demi-plié and, on the upbeat, with the left leg, which is in 5th position back (for fouetté en dehors with the right leg), take a step onto demi-pointe toward point 8, opening the arms to the side; turn the body effacé to point 2 and simultaneously raise the right foot sur le cou-de-pied devant. After this, come down in demi-plié, bend the body, and do the fouetté en dehors. For fouetté en dedans, the step onto demi-pointe is done with the leg that is in 5th position front.

Grand Fouetté Italien

This fouetté, which derives from the Italian school, is done entirely en face, en dehors and en dedans.

En dehors. Stand on the right leg with épaulement croisé; the left is stretched backward, toe to the floor. On the upbeat, demi-plié on the right leg and bring the left foot sur le cou-de-pied derrière; the arms open slightly to the side; then, step onto the left foot on demi-pointe (with the right foot sur le cou-de-pied devant), at the same time returning the arms to preparatory position (a form of coupé dessous). Then, on the first quarter, demi-plié on the left leg and take the right leg forward en face, slightly bent in the knee, well turned-out and at 45°; the left arm is in 1st position and the right in 2nd; the eyes look over the left arm at the toe of the right leg; the torso is slightly inclined forward. Between the first and second quarters, do the fouetté en dehors in the following manner: rising to demi-pointe on the left leg, the right is stretched forward and taken around to the back (through 2nd position) at 90°; during this, the left arm is raised to 3rd position and lowered to 2nd position; and the right arm is raised to 3rd position (as the left is lowering to 2nd) and lowered to 1st position. The fouetté finishes on the second quarter in demi-plié, maintaining the height of the right leg at 90° and turning both palms down (as in 3rd arabesque).

En dedans. Stand on the right leg with the left stretched croisé forward, toe to the floor. On the upbeat, demi-plié on the right leg, bringing the left foot to the position sur le cou-de-pied devant; the arms are a little open to the side; then step onto the left leg on demi-pointe (right foot sur le cou-de-pied derrière) and lower the arms to preparatory position (coupé dessus). On the first quarter, demi-plié on the left leg; the right leg is bent in back at 45°; the left arm is in 1st position and the right is in 2nd; the head and body are en face. Between the first and second quarters, do the fouetté en dedans in the following manner: rising to demi-pointe on the left leg, the right is stretched in back and taken around through 2nd position at 90° and forward (preserving the height of 90°); during this, the left arm is raised directly to 3rd position and opened to 2nd and the right arm is raised from 2nd to 3rd position. Finish the fouetté, on the second quarter, in demi-plié; the left arm is in 2nd position and the right in 3rd; the head is turned to the right arm, looking up past the elbow.

These fouettés are also executed on pointe and with a jump.

Grand Fouetté en Tournant

Grand fouetté en tournant on demi-pointe, on pointe, and with a jump is done mainly en dedans to the poses attitude croisée and effacée, and to 1st, 2nd, 3rd and 4th arabesques. En dehors, it is done only to the pose croisée devant.

Grand fouetté en tournant en dedans to the pose 3rd arabesque (turning to the right). 2/4 time is generally used for all grands fouettés en tournant.

The préparation is done with the right leg croisé devant, toe to the floor. On the upbeat, demi-plié on the right leg and, rising onto demi-pointe, throw the left leg, with a grand battement jeté, to the side at 90°, turning the body en face and opening the arms from below to 2nd position. On the first quarter, turning (en dedans) to the right to face point 4, throw the left leg through 1st position in demi-plié forward at 90° to point 4; simultaneously, rise to demi-pointe on the right leg; turn the hands palms down, lowering the arms at the moment of the passé through 1st position, and 'with a strong movement, together with the battement, raise the arms to 3rd position; the body bends back, and the head is straight forward. Having fixed the pose for a moment, quickly finish the tour en dedans on the second quarter, toward the mirror, in 3rd arabesque in demi-plié.

The arms are lowered directly from 3rd position, the left arm forward, the right to the side. The left leg remains to point 4 at the same height.

RULES FOR THE EXECUTION OF GRAND FOUET-
TÉ EN TOURNANT. In the execution of fouetté to the right, the
force provided by the left arm and an active turning forward of
the heel of the supporting right leg in the first half of the
fouetté and at the end of the tour help the turn of the body.
This fouetté is done in two sharp counts, without smoothly
flowing through the intermediate positions.

Fouetté to the right to attitude croisée or 4th arabesque is
done in exactly the same way. To attitude effacée, the turn of
the body and the throw of the leg forward at 90° will be to
point 6, and the end of the turn will be to point 2.

In fouetté to 1st or 2nd arabesque, the throw of the leg
forward at 90° is done to point 6; then the body finishes the
turn en face toward the mirror (to point 1), and the leg swings
around to 2nd position at 90°, after which, the pose 1st or 2nd
arabesque to point 3 in demi-plié is taken. The arms, as in all
fouettés en dedans, are raised sharply from below to 3rd
position, and at the last moment open to the pose.

Grand fouetté en tournant en dehors (turning to the right). 2/4
time.

The préparation is with the left leg croisé derrière, toe to the
floor. On the upbeat, demi-plié and rise to demi-pointe on the
left leg. Simultaneously, the right leg is thrown, with a grand
battement jeté, to the side to a height of 90°; the body turns en
face; and the arms open from below to 2nd position. On the
first quarter, throw the right leg through 1st position in
demi-plié to 3rd arabesque, rising to demi-pointe on the left
leg; the arms are brought to 3rd arabesque through preparatory position. Having fixed the pose, turn on demi-pointe en
dehors toward the mirror to the pose croisée devant at 90°.
Come down in demi-plié on the second quarter.

At the moment of the tour, the head is directed toward the
mirror across the left shoulder, and, at the end, it turns to the
right. The right arm is brought to 2nd position from the pose

3rd arabesque, curving at the end; the left arm assists the tour and is raised to 3rd position.

During the tour, the right leg bends just noticeably, with the feeling that the bend is not from the knee, but as if from the toe. This detail softens the line of the leg. However, in the final pose croisée, it is completely stretched.

Grand fouetté en tournant from 2nd position (à la seconde). This is done on pointe en dehors and en dedans from a preliminary demi-plié with a throw of the leg to 2nd position at 90°. During this, the arms open to 2nd position, and the supporting leg rises to pointe by means of a relevé. This is followed by a short demi-plié and the tour, during which (if the tour is en dehors) the leg that was thrown out to 90° bends behind the knee and is quickly brought forward. In a fouetté en dedans, the thrown-out leg will be brought in front of the knee first, then quickly taken back. This fouetté is a variety of the well-known tours fouettés at 45°.

The arms in grand fouetté can come together in a low 1st position, can be raised from 2nd position to 3rd, or one can be in 3rd while the other remains in 2nd.

Tour Fouetté

This is done from a big pose to the same pose. At the barre, it is executed on the whole foot and on demi-pointe; and, in the centre of the room, it is done on the whole foot.

Being already in a pose (for example, attitude effacée), quickly (in one quarter) turn en dedans, moving forward the heel of the supporting leg; simultaneously bend the working leg at a height of 90° toward the knee of the supporting leg and instantly open it again to attitude. The arms help the tour by coming together in 1st position with a strong and resilient movement and sharply opening to the initial pose at the end.

XII. Pointe Work

Dancing on pointe is one of the main components of feminine dance (solo and duet). Its lightness, plasticity, dynamism, and expressiveness are essential for the dancer.

The first movements on pointe are introduced only after the legs (and especially the feet) have been sufficiently strengthened by the barre and centre exercise.

In order that the student be able to stand on pointe correctly and with stability, it is necessary to prepare the legs by exercises on demi-pointe (relevé in 1st, 2nd, 5th, and 4th positions). These are done in the first half year of the first class.

In the position of the foot, standing on a turned-out demi-pointe, the body's weight (with the heel forward) should, as nearly as possible, be evenly distributed onto all five toes; in other words, the foot must not be inclined toward the joint of the big toe.

Standing on pointe, the position of the foot also demands a full turn-out; but the weight is borne by the first, second, and third toes, or by only the first and second, depending on the structure of the foot and the length of the toes. An extremely long first toe and short remaining ones make work on pointe difficult; but, in the presence of general good qualities, this is not seriously detrimental to the study of classical dance.

In the middle of the first year, the simplest pointe exercises on both legs are practised: relevés in 1st, 2nd, and 5th positions, facing the barre (for not more than three or four lessons), and in the centre of the room. Later, the student studies échappé, glissade, pas de bourrée changé in the manner in which it is done on demi-pointe (see "Pas de Bourrée"), and pas de bourrée suivi in 5th and 1st positions (pas couru, a small run on the toes).

In the following years, all kinds of pas de bourrée, en face and en tournant, are learned, as well as movements onto one leg in the small and big poses, such as sissonnes and jetés, tours, various kinds of fouettés (explained in Chapter XI, "Turning Movements Used in Adagio"), and jumps on both legs as well as on one.

In the elementary and intermediate classes, the lesson on pointe is given (after the barre and centre exercise) twice a week; but in the advanced classes, it must be given every other day.

Below we describe only the basic pas of the dance on pointe.

Relevé

Study Sequence

1. *Relevé in all positions, facing the barre* (elementary study). Two measures of 4/4 time. On the first quarter, demi-plié. On the second quarter, push off from the floor with the heels and spring onto pointe, strongly stretching the knees and the insteps. On the third and fourth quarters, stand on pointe, checking the correctness of the position of the feet. On the first and second quarters of the second measure, come down through the instep onto the whole foot in a resilient demi-plié. On the third and fourth quarters, stretch the knees. The exercise is repeated from four to eight times in 1st, 2nd, and 5th positions.

   In the very first exercises, it is necessary to demand a rise onto the toes directly from demi-plié, without gradually passing through demi-pointe; but somewhat later, the student should push off from the floor with the heels and lightly spring onto the toes. In 1st, 2nd, and 4th positions, there is no displacement of the toes on the floor. From 5th position both toes must actively be brought together on pointe and just as actively be returned to 5th position in demi-plié.

Stretched knees, taut leg muscles, and a pulled-up body and thighs greatly assist stability on pointe. It is necessary to come down from pointe into demi-plié resiliently and with control. A sharp falling into demi-plié is inadmissible.

2. *Relevé in all positions at the barre and in the centre of the room.* One measure of 4/4 time. On the first quarter, demi-plié. On the second quarter, spring onto pointe. On the third quarter, come down into demi-plié. On the fourth, stretch the knees.

3. One measure of 2/4 time. On the upbeat, demi-plié. On the first quarter, spring onto pointe. On the second quarter, come down into demi-plié, etc.

4. 1/4. The demi-plié and relevé onto pointe are done on the upbeat, and the lowering from pointe to demi-plié takes place on each quarter.

Échappé

Study Sequence

1. *Échappé to 2nd position* (elementary study). 4/4 time. On the first quarter, demi-plié in 5th position. On the second quarter, spring onto pointe and, sliding the toes along the floor, open the legs equally to 2nd position. On the third quarter, come down, changing the feet, in 5th position in demi-plié. On the fourth quarter, straighten the knees.

It is also possible to do échappé in 2nd position without changing the feet.

Échappé to 4th position croisée and effacée is studied in exactly the same way.

2. *Échappé in* 2/4. Start in 5th position with épaulement croisé. On the upbeat, demi-plié. On the first quarter, turning en face, spring onto pointe in 2nd position. On the second quarter, come down, changing the feet, in 5th position in demi-plié with épaulement croisé, etc.

3. *Échappé in* 1/4. The demi-plié and the spring onto pointe take place on the upbeat, and the completion of the échappé in demi-plié takes place on the quarter. In the execution of several échappés in succession, the spring onto pointe will thus always be on the upbeat and the demi-plié on the quarter.

    The arms can be in preparatory position or open slightly to the side in a half-2nd position.

    Échappé may be executed en tournant (with eighth or quarter turns), with a relevé in the open position (double échappé) and also finishing on one leg (with the other foot sur le cou-de-pied).

Example of a combination of various échappés. Eight measures of 4/4 time. Begin in 5th position with épaulement croisé, right leg front. Four échappés in 2nd position, changing the feet, in 2/4 each. In 4/4, one double échappé, finishing on one leg (the right foot sur le cou-de-pied derrière) and, in 4/4, two pas de bourrées changés en dehors (the second finishing in 5th position). In 4/4, one double échappé finishing on one leg (the right foot sur le cou-de-pied devant) and, in 4/4, two pas de bourrées changés en dedans (the second finishing in 5th position). Four échappés in 2nd position en tournant, with quarter turns, turning to the right, in 2/4 each.

Glissade

Study Sequence

1. *Glissade to the side* (elementary study). 4/4 time. Begin in 5th position with the right leg in front. On the first quarter, demi-plié. Between the first and the second quarters, slide

the right leg along the floor to 2nd position. On the second quarter, transfer the weight of the body onto the toe of the right leg and quickly bring the left leg up to the right in 5th position on pointe. On the third quarter, come down in demi-plié. On the fourth quarter, stretch the knees.

2. *Glissade in* 2/4 (final form). Begin in 5th position with épaulement croisé. On the upbeat, demi-plié and extend the leg to the side. On the first quarter, step onto pointe and join the legs in 5th position. On the second quarter, come down in demi-plié.

Glissade is first studied to the side with and without changing the feet, then in all directions and poses with the arms in the small and large poses (see also p. 423. "Tours en dedans on both legs"). Temps lié on pointe consists of one glissade croisé and one to the side, changing the feet, etc. (see Chapter V).

Jeté

Jeté on pointe is a step onto the toes of one leg from demi-plié.

It is divided into petits and grands jetés, and both kinds are done in all directions and poses.

Doing the step from the preparatory demi-plié in 5th position, it is necessary to transfer the centre of the body's weight onto the toe of the working leg and instantly pull up the thigh, which will further the stability of the pose on pointe. The steps must be wide, traveling in one direction or another.

In a petit jeté, after stepping onto one leg on pointe, immediately bend the other in the position sur le cou-de-pied devant or derrière. Raise the arms to a half height in 1st and 2nd positions, or to a pose with the arms in 3rd and 2nd positions, in 1st and 3rd, or with both arms in 3rd position.

It is possible to come down from pointe to 5th position in demi-plié or to demi-plié on the foot that is sur le cou-de-pied.

If the latter is the case, then the leg that was standing on pointe bends to the position sur le cou-de-pied, softly opens, and again does a jeté onto pointe.

In the grands jetés, having done a demi-plié in 5th position, open the leg to 45°, the centre of weight remaining on the supporting leg. Then take a wide step beyond the tip of the toe onto pointe, immediately transferring onto that foot the centre of the body's weight. Simultaneously, the other leg is raised to 90° and the arms assume the given pose.

The movement can be finished on two legs in 5th position in demi-plié, but the following procedure is the most useful: maintaining the pose, come down in demi-plié on the leg that was on pointe softly and with control, holding the other leg at 90°. Then the movement can be finished with a simple pas de bourrée, changing the feet.

In grands jetés in the poses attitude croisée and attitude effacée and the 1st, 2nd, 3rd, and 4th arabesques, the leg is immediately raised to 90°; in the poses croisée devant and effacée devant and écartée devant and écartée derrière, the leg is quickly drawn out by means of a développé. Grands jetés on pointe are done at a smooth, moderate tempo. The arms immediately assume the given pose and aid the stability on pointe.

Jeté-Fondu (A Soft Step)

This flowing step on pointe is executed en diagonale, forward and backward. The very name, fondu ("melted"), indicates the softness and elasticity of the plié characteristic of this step.

Jeté-fondu forward. 2/4 time. Begin in 5th position with épaulement croisé, left leg front. Traveling en diagonale, from point 6 to point 2, on the upbeat, demi-plié; the right foot is softly taken forward effacé at 45°. On the first quarter, step forward onto pointe on the right leg, immediately transferring onto it the body's weight; at the same time, the left leg, bending in the knee and preserving the turn-out, is softly taken forward croisé at 45°. On the second quarter, in a controlled manner come down through the foot on the right leg in demi-plié. The lowering in demi-plié must exactly coincide with the moment the left leg is completely stretched. The following jeté is done immediately: jeté-fondu on the left leg, while the right is taken forward effacé at 45°, etc. During its initial study, not fewer than eight jetés-fondus in a series should be executed.

Stepping onto pointe, one should not leave the leg stretched out in back but must immediately take it forward. It is also impermissible to come down from pointe with a sharp spring into plié.

The flowing cantilena of the movement of the leg that is characteristic of this particular pas must be reflected in the movements of the arms, which may be found in any number of possible positions: gradually opening to the side through 1st position or gradually raising one arm to 3rd position and opening the other to the side. The torso may be bent forward a little on the first jeté and then, after gradually straightening itself, bend back a little. Corresponding to the movements of the torso, the position of the head is changed.

Jeté-fondu backward is executed in the same way. Stepping onto pointe backward onto one leg, one should not pause with the other forward but must immediately take it softly backward in the direction effacée or croisée, in turn.

Jeté-fondu may also be executed to a waltz at a slow tempo, stepping onto pointe on the first quarter of each measure.

Sissonne

A sissonne is a spring onto pointe from two feet to one. The elementary classes learn sissonne simple sur le cou-de-pied and sissonne ouverte in all the small poses. The succeeding classes learn grande sissonne ouverte in all directions and in the big poses.

Sissonne Simple

Study Sequence

1. Sissonne simple (elementary study). 4/4 time. On the first quarter, demi-plié in 5th position. On the second quarter, push off from the floor with the heels and spring onto pointe on one leg, the other being brought sur le cou-de-pied devant or derrière. On the third quarter, come down in 5th position in demi-plié. On the fourth quarter, stretch the knees.

2. Sissonne simple (final form). 2/4 time. On the upbeat, demi-plié in 5th position. On the first quarter, spring onto pointe on one leg. On the second quarter, come down in 5th position in demi-plié, etc. The musical accent is thus on pointe.

   Sissonne simple is also done in 1/4. The spring onto pointe will be on the preceding eighth and the demi-plié in 5th position on the quarter. The musical accent is thus on demi-plié.

   The arms remain in preparatory position or, according to what is given, may open to 1st and 2nd positions, 2nd and 3rd, 3rd and 1st, etc.

   Example of a combination of sissonnes simples. Sixteen measures of 2/4. Four sissonnes with the right and left legs alternately, putting the working foot down in 5th position back each time. Four sissonnes simples on the left leg, taking the right leg first back, then front, then once more back and front; for these four sissonnes, the torso leans a little to the right, with the right arm in 1st position and the left in 2nd. Each sissonne is done in 2/4. Repeat the combination once before executing it with the left leg.

Petite Sissonne Ouverte. Start in 5th position in demi-plié. Then spring onto pointe on one leg, simultaneously opening the other leg through the position sur le cou-de-pied (devant or derrière) to 2nd position at 45° or to a position croisée, effacée, or écartée devant or derrière, and finish the movement in 5th position in demi-plié.

From the demi-plié, one must push off from the floor equally with both legs, in no case neglecting to push with the leg that will be opening at 45°. In the poses devant, the centre of weight (in the rise onto pointe) is transferred slightly back onto the supporting leg; in the poses derrière, the weight is transferred slightly forward onto the supporting leg; in the execution of the movement to 2nd position, the body inclines to the side opposite the leg that is opened at 45°. The pose is clearly fixed by a pause, and the leg that is open at 45° is immobile. One must come down into demi-plié in 5th position on both legs simultaneously, not coming down on the supporting leg ahead of time.

The study sequence is the same as for sissonne simple: 4/4, 2/4, and 1/4.

Example of a combination of various sissonnes. Sixteen measures of 3/4 (waltz). In eight measures, four sissonnes simples en tournant, with quarter turns to the right, to points 3, 5, 7 and 1. The first sissonne is on the right leg, with the left foot sur le cou-de-pied derrière; the left arm is in 3rd position and the right in 2nd; the torso is bent to the right. The second sissonne is on the left leg, with the right foot sur le cou-de-pied devant; the right arm is in 3rd position and the left in 2nd; the torso is bent to the left. The third and fourth sissonnes are analogous to the first and second. Each sissonne is done to two measures. Sissonne ouverte to the small pose 2nd arabesque, with the right and with the left legs, in two measures each, each time putting the working foot down in front. In four measures, sissonne ouverte to the small pose effacée devant, tombé and tour sur le cou-de-pied en dedans. Repeat to the left.

Grande Sissonne Ouverte. This is done à la seconde without traveling, in all the big poses (first also without traveling) and then, in the poses attitude croisée and attitude effacée, 1st, 2nd, 3rd and 4th arabesques, traveling forward (springing out along the floor) and, in the poses croisée and effacée devant and écartée devant and derrière, without traveling.

In the beginning, grandes sissonnes are studied in 4/4 in the following manner: on the first quarter, demi-plié in 5th position. On the second quarter, spring onto pointe on one leg and open the other to 90°; the arms, body, and head simultaneously assume the given pose (in this, the arms, opening to the pose through 1st position, must be resilient and lend the pose not only expressiveness, but also stability). On the third quarter, come down in 5th position in demi-plié. On the fourth quarter, stretch the knees.

As in the big jumps, the execution of sissonne in the big poses requires a deep demi-plié before the beginning of the movement.

In the poses attitude croisée and attitude effacée, and in the four arabesques, the leg is raised to 90° by means of a battement; but in the poses croisée and effacée devant, écartée derrière and devant, and à la seconde, the leg is taken out by means of a développé.

Grande sissonne ouverte (as well as jeté in the big poses) can be done with a plié-relevé in the pose. Take the pose on pointe; demi-plié on the supporting leg, maintaining the pose and leaving securely immobile the leg that has been taken to 90°; then again spring onto pointe. Plié-relevé can be repeated, once the pose has been established, several times in a series in place. In the poses attitude and arabesque, it can also be done traveling forward at the moment of the relevé onto pointe.

Example of a combination of grandes sissonnes ouvertes. Sixteen measures of 3/4 (waltz). In eight measures, with the right leg, grande sissonne ouverte to the pose écartée derrière, putting the foot down in back; then turn on pointe in 5th position; repeat once. On the following eight measures, toward point 2, onto the right leg, grande sissonne ouverte in 1st arabesque; plié in the pose arabesque and pas de bourrée changé en dehors, finishing in 4th position in a préparation for tours sur le cou-de-pied en dehors; two tours en dehors. In the same manner, execute the combination to the other side.

Rond de Jambe en l'Air

Rond de jambe en l'air is executed at 45° en dehors and en dedans. The movement en dehors is done with the leg that is in 5th position front at the beginning, and the movement en dedans is done with the leg that is in 5th position back. When first studying the movement, a single rond de jambe en l'air is done, later, a double rond de jambe.

En dehors. 2/4 time. Begin in 5th position with épaulement croisé, right leg front. On the first quarter, spring onto pointe on the left leg, simultaneously opening the right leg, with a sliding movement along the floor, to the side in 2nd position at 45°, and quickly execute the rond de jambe en dehors; the arms open to 2nd position through 1st and the head turns to the left; for stability on pointe, the body inclines a little to the side of the supporting left leg. Clearly fix the conclusion of the rond de jambe en l'air at 45° before coming down, on the second quarter, in 5th position in demi-plié with the right leg in back; at the same time, lower the arms to preparatory position.

When executing rond de jambe en l'air en dedans, in order to establish stability on pointe, the body must also incline a little toward the supporting leg; but the head turns toward the working leg which executes and fixes the conclusion of the rond de jambe en l'air en dedans before closing in 5th position front. The arms open through 1st position to 2nd with the opening of the leg to the side and are lowered to preparatory position together with the lowering of the leg.

The demi-plié in 5th position must be done with both legs simultaneously, on no account springing off pointe earlier on the supporting leg.

Coupé-Ballonné

2/4 time. As a préparation, stand on the right leg with the left stretched backward croisé, toe to the floor. On the upbeat, after opening the arms a little to the side, lower them to preparatory position; at the same time, demi-plié and bend the left foot sur le cou-de-pied derrière. On the first quarter, coupé, stepping onto the left foot on pointe behind the right; the right leg is raised to the side at 45° by means of a battement; the body turns en face; and the arms, directly from preparatory position, open to 2nd position. On the second quarter, in a softly controlled manner, come down on the left leg in demi-plié and bring the right foot sur le cou-de-pied derrière; at the same time, the torso bends to the left; the right arm is raised to 1st position through preparatory position; the left stays in 2nd position; the head turns to the left; the whole figure turns to épaulement croisé.

The following ballonné is done from this position: coupé on pointe onto the right leg; the left leg is raised to the side; the torso turns en face; the right arm from 1st position opens to 2nd, etc.

Coupé-ballonné may be executed in the same way but with the arms going alternately to 3rd position. At the moment of the coupé onto pointe, the arms, as in the first instance, open to 2nd position; then, while coming down in demi-plié, the arm corresponding to the working leg is raised to 3rd position; the other arm holds 2nd position; the torso bends to the side of the supporting leg. On the following coupé, the arm, from 3rd position, opens to 2nd position, etc.

Coupé-ballonné may be executed in the same way but with the arms going alternately to 3rd position. At the moment of the coupé onto pointe, the arms, as in the first instance, open to 2nd position; then, while coming down in demi-plié, the arm corresponding to the working leg is raised to 3rd position; the other arm holds 2nd position; the torso bends to the side of the supporting leg. On the following coupé, the arm, from 3rd position, opens to 2nd position, etc.

Coupé-ballonné is studied moving in the opposite direction (downstage) from a préparation croisée devant. After the coupé onto pointe in front of the supporting leg, the working leg opens to the side at 45°. During the demi-plié on the supporting leg, it is bent sur le cou-de-pied devant. The arm corresponding to the supporting leg bends in 1st position. Instead of bending to the side, the torso bends only a little backward in épaulement croisé.

During its initial study, coupé-ballonné is executed, at a moderate tempo, not fewer than eight times in a row, in one measure of 2/4 or two measures of 3/4 (waltz) for each coupé-ballonné.

Pas Ballonné

Pas ballonné on pointe is executed traveling forward and backward in the small poses croisées, effacées and écartées.

An example of ballonné forward in the pose effacée. 2/4 time. Begin in 5th position with épaulement croisé, right leg front. On the upbeat, do a short demi-plié on the left leg, raising the right foot sur le cou-de-pied devant (a kind of coupé); the torso turns to épaulement effacé. On the first quarter, spring onto pointe on the left leg and, at the same time, throw the right leg forward effacé at 45°; while springing onto pointe, move forward beyond the toe of the right foot; the left arm is in 1st position, the right in 2nd; the head is turned to the left. On the second quarter, come down in demi-plié on the left leg and, at the same time, bend the right foot sur le cou-de-pied devant.

From this position, the following ballonnés are executed, traveling forward (from two to four, or more, ballonnés in a series). The arms, torso and head preserve the position taken on the first ballonné. The last ballonné finishes in 5th position croisée, with the right foot in back and the arms lowered to preparatory position.

During the execution of several ballonnés in a series, one may also raise the left arm gradually to 3rd position, the right remaining in 2nd position.

Ballonné backward is also done traveling, but in the opposite direction.

Pas ballonné may be executed in 2/4 or in 1/4 each (in which case, the plié takes place on the quarter). The movement forward or backward on pointe is aided by a pulled-up lower back, level shoulders and hips, and also by the correct resiliency of the position of the arm in 2nd position.

Pas de Bourrée Suivi

Suivi means "continuous, connected". Thus, an unbroken series of pas de bourrées in 1st or 5th position, traveling in any direction, in a straight line to the side, along a diagonal, in a small or a big circle, at a slow, medium, or quick tempo, is called pas de bourrée suivi. This is the most essential part of dance on pointe.

Pas de Bourrée Suivi in 1st Position (Pas Couru)

Study Sequence

1. Pas de bourrée suivi in 1st position (elementary study). 2/4 time. Standing in 1st position, demi-plié and spring onto pointe, joining the legs in an unturned-out 1st position.

    On the first quarter, lift the toe of the right leg from the floor and slightly throw the leg forward (but not high from the floor) in an unturned-out position; then quickly bring it back beside the left leg. On the second quarter, do the same thing with the left leg, etc. Practise the movement in place many times consecutively. Then speed up the movement, throwing the legs out alternately, in 1/8 each.

2. Pas de bourrée suivi in 1st position with movement forward and backward. The beginning is the same as in No. 1. Then, slightly throwing out the legs in front, each time take a small step forward, maintaining the unturned-out position of the foot in 1st position and transferring the weight of the body onto the toe of the working leg.

   After having traveled thus in a straight line from point 5 to point 1, without coming down off pointe and continuing to throw the legs forward slightly, travel backward, with the back to point 5.

3. Final form. Start in 5th position, with épaulement croisé and the right foot in front. On the upbeat, demi-plié, opening the right leg forward slightly to 45°. Step onto pointe on the right unturned-out leg and run forward on pointe in an unturned-out 1st position. Having reached the selected point, run backward on pointe in 1st position, all the time facing the mirror. The legs are side by side throughout.

   As the tempo is accelerated, the legs are thrown out less and less and the steps forward are made smaller and smaller, becoming almost imperceptible to the eye. But precisely this mode of practice, employed in the elementary study, will give clarity to the run on pointe later on.

   This pas de bourrée can be done forward or backward facing point 1, along a diagonal, or in a straight line across the room, moving in profile to the mirror.

   Moreover, each step can be done in 1/16 at a quick or slow tempo.

   The positions of the arms and the head vary according to what the teacher assigns. In elementary execution, however, it is recommended that, when moving forward, the arms be gradually raised to 1st position and slightly opened, and, in moving backward, they be gradually lowered to preparatory position.

Pas de Bourrée Suivi in 5th Position

Study Sequence

1. Elementary execution. Start in 5th position with épaulement croisé and the right foot in front. Demi-plié and spring onto pointe in a well-crossed and firm 5th position, strongly pulling up the thighs and back. Take the toe of the right leg slightly off the floor and, with a clear accent, lightly return it to 5th position. Immediately raise the toe of the left leg slightly and, with an accent, lightly return it to 5th position. Repeat this movement in place no fewer than sixteen times.

   Each time, make the accent with the toe to the floor on the quarter, rhythmically taking the foot from the floor. On raising the toe from the floor, the knee of the working leg bends only slightly; and, on lowering the foot onto the toe, it is necessary to feel instantly a complete stretch of the knee.

   Sometimes, in an inexperienced or poor execution of pas de bourrée suivi, the dancer moves on the toes with slightly bent knees ("sits on the legs"), which produces an impression of heaviness and awkwardness in the run on pointe.

2. Pas de bourrée suivi in 5th position traveling to the side. Start in 5th position with the right foot in front. Demi-plié and spring onto pointe in 5th position with épaulement croisé (right shoulder slightly forward); raise the right arm to 3rd and the left to 2nd position; incline the head slightly to look up from under the elbow of the right arm.

Lift the toe of the right leg from the floor and take a small step to the side; then, immediately take the left leg from the floor and place it in a deep (slightly over-crossed) 5th position in back; again take a small step with the right leg to the side and place the left in the same kind of 5th position back, etc.

Travel thus in a straight line to the right for the course of a musical phrase of no less than eight measures of 2/4. In the beginning, the steps of the right and left legs are done in 1/4 each, then in 1/8, and, finally, in 1/16. The tempo of pas de bourrée suivi is accelerated as the student becomes more accomplished.

The movement is repeated with the left leg, traveling to the left; and then it is studied moving along the diagonal with the right leg in front from point 6 to point 2, and with the left leg from point 4 to point 8. During the movement, the arms can remain in the pose assumed at the beginning, or they may change their position.

In its final form, pas de bourrée suivi begins directly from 5th position demi-plié, opening the leg slightly and taking a step onto pointe in the direction of the given pas de bourrée: to the side, croisé devant, écarté, etc. The first step is wide, the body's weight immediately being transferred onto the toe; and the step with the other leg follows without an instant's delay.

RULES FOR THE EXECUTION OF PAS DE BOURRÉE SUIVI. In pas de bourrée suivi the toes are slightly raised from the floor. The faster the tempo, the less the toes come off the floor; however, the movements of the legs must always remain clear.

Moving to the side, on a diagonal, or in a circle, the steps must be small and imperceptible. The second leg must instantly come up to the first leg in 5th position in order to avoid the appearance of 2nd position.

Moving in the directions croisée and effacée devant and derrière (that is, taking steps forward and backward), it is necessary to keep the legs crossed in 5th position in order to avoid the appearance of 4th position.

A common mistake in the execution of pas de bourrée suivi is a sluggish closing of the second leg. The leg that is taking the step is active; but the other leg, which joins it, must be just as active.

Pas de bourrée suivi is done with strongly pulled-up thighs, and the knees are completely stretched after each little step.

Jumps on Both Legs (Changement de Pieds)

In the third and fourth years, the study of changement de pieds on pointe is begun. In the beginning it is taught with a jump in place, then traveling forward or backward in a direction croisée (along a diagonal), and turning in place (en tournant).

Study Sequence

1. Elementary study. Begin in 5th position. Demi-plié and spring onto pointe in 5th position; remaining on pointe, again demi-plié, opening the knees in a turned-out position with taut leg and buttocks muscles and a pulled-up back. The foot contracts slightly in the instep (especially in feet with a high instep), and the muscles of the foot are also taut. The jump upward is only a moderate one but must be high enough for the knees, the instep and toes to be completely stretched in the air. Land from the jump on the toes, again slightly contracting the instep and opening the knees to the side in demi-plié. Having thus done four jumps (in 1/4 each), finish the last one in 5th position in demi-plié on the whole foot. Then the number of changements de pieds on pointe may gradually be increased.

2. Final form. From 5th position, demi-plié and changement, finishing in 5th position on pointe in demi-plié. From here, continue with all the following changements de pieds, finishing the last jump on the whole foot in 5th position demi-plié.

In the beginning, the arms are held in preparatory position. Later, they are gradually raised to 1st or 3rd position, then open to 2nd position and are lowered. Variations of the positions of the arms and turns of the head can be most diverse.

Changements de pieds are done in 1/4 and 1/8 each.

As the tempo is accelerated, the height of the jump decreases; but, even then, the knees, instep, and toes must quickly stretch in the air.

When changement de pieds is studied traveling, it is necessary to consider that the movement forward or backward takes place at the moment of breaking contact with the floor.

Jumps on One Leg

These jumps can be done in any small pose, in place, or traveling forward. The foot is placed on pointe from above after a preliminary demi-plié. The other leg is raised to the position sur le cou-de-pied or to a small pose (at 45°) in a stretched or half-bent position. The positions of the arms, body, and head are varied according to what the teacher requires. These jumps have an absolutely par terre character, for there is no apparent break from the floor. The knee of the supporting leg must be resilient and strong in plié and remains slightly bent in the jump. The instep must be held absolutely taut.

Jumps traveling forward on a diagonal are done with ballonné or with rond de jambe en l'air en dehors; the position of the body, arms, and head corresponds to the pose effacée or écartée devant. In the jumps, the arms can be in 1st and 2nd, in

2nd and 3rd, in 1st and 3rd positions, can gradually be raised, opened, lowered, or raised again, changing the poses.

These jumps are usually preceded by a coupé onto pointe, which is done on the upbeat from 5th position or from a préparation croisée derrière with the toe to the floor. For example, if one begins with the right leg in front in 5th position, demi-plié, bending the left leg sur le cou-de-pied derrière. Then, with a short movement, place the left leg onto pointe (behind the right foot), transferring onto it the centre of weight, and, with a jump, execute the ballonné or the rond de jambe en l'air with the right leg.

Jumps on one leg traveling forward also can be done in the pose arabesque at 90°. They demand enormous tautness of the foot of the supporting leg and are done on a slightly bent knee, which robs them of any special aesthetic value. The more usual plié-relevé, with movement forward in the arabesque poses, is more expressive, more airy, and more pleasant to the eye.

Tours

In Chapter X, "Tours on the Floor and in the Air", versions of tours done both on demi-pointe and on pointe are enumerated. Here we consider tours done only on pointe.

Tours en Dehors from a Dégagé (turning to the right and traveling on the diagonal from point 6 to point 2). 2/4 time. Begin in 5th position with épaulement croisé, right foot front. On the upbeat, demi-plié and softly open the left leg to the side at 45° (dégagé); at the same time, turn the whole body to face point 2 and open the arms to 2nd position. On the first quarter, step onto the left foot on pointe in front of the right leg and do a tour en dehors on the left leg, immediately bringing the right foot sur le cou-de-pied devant; the arms come together in a low 1st position (the left arm providing the force for the tours); the head and eyes for a moment remain directed across the left shoulder to point 2; and the tour finishes facing point 2. On the second quarter, the right foot leaves the position sur le cou-de-pied and falls forward the distance of a short step, coming down in demi-plié; at the same time, the left leg softly opens to the side at 45° (dégagé) and the arms open to 2nd position. The movement is then repeated the necessary number of times. These tours are also done in 1/4.

During the tours, the arms can also be raised to 3rd position. And another useful variant of the position of the arms (turning to the right) is the following: at the beginning of the tour, the left arm, from 2nd position, closes to 1st, the right remaining in 2nd; and, at the end of the tour, the right arm is quickly brought to 1st position and the left thrown out to 2nd; with the dégagé, both arms again open to 2nd position.

Tours en Dehors from a Dégagé, Finishing in a Big Pose. These tours are executed traveling on the diagonal, in two quarters and one quarter each, as described above, but finishing in a big pose écartée, effacée or croisée devant at 90°.

Tours Finishing in the Big Pose Écartée Devant (turning to the right and traveling downstage from point 6 to point 2). Begin in 5th position with épaulement croisé. Dégagé, and execute a tour en dehors on the left leg and finish it by quickly opening the right leg with a développé to the pose écartée devant at 90°; simultaneously, open the right arm to 3rd position and the left to 2nd; the torso is inclined to the side of the supporting leg (in this case, the left); the eyes are directed toward the right hand. For stability on pointe at the end of the tour, the arms must be held in the pose firmly and without the slightest movement. The left arm, which is in 2nd position, is slightly forward of its normal position. The stomach and lower back are well pulled up. During the tour itself, the right foot is sur le cou-de-pied devant and only at the concluding moment does the leg quickly open to point 2. The precise timing of this opening of the leg exactly to point 2, without an instant of anticipation, also helps achieve stability in the final pose on pointe.

To execute the following tour, widely fall forward onto the right leg in demi-plié and, with the left leg, do a dégagé at 45° to point 6; during this, the body remains in the preceding position (right shoulder to point 2 and the left to point 6); the arms open to 2nd position. The next tour is done from this position.

If the tours are done to the big pose effacée devant, then the fall forward in demi-plié is done facing point 2. If the tours are done to the big pose croisée devant (turning to the right), the tours must be executed on the diagonal from point 4 to point 8. The tours en dehors from a dégagé finishing in these poses must also be done quickly and neatly and the design of the big pose on pointe fixed with a pause.

Tours en Dedans on Both Legs (Glissade en Tournant) (turning to the right and traveling on the diagonal from point 6 to point 2). 2/4 time. Begin in 5th position, the right foot in front, with épaulement croisé. On the upbeat, with a passing movement, turn effacé so that the body faces point 2 and, from a demi-plié, take a sliding step forward onto pointe on the right leg; the right arm is forward and the left arm to the side; the hands are in arabesque position. Having transferred the weight onto the right leg, immediately bring the left leg on pointe to 5th position in front of the right; and, simultaneously, with force provided by the left arm, bring the arms together in a low 1st position and turn the body, so that the left shoulder is directed to point 2 and the right to point 6, the head and eyes being directed across the left shoulder. Then, without a pause, on the first quarter, finish the tour facing point 2. At the end of the tour, the right leg is in 5th position front. Thus, these tours begin and end in the position effacée. On the second quarter, come down in 5th position in demi-plié, taking the left arm to 2nd position and leaving the right in 1st. To repeat the movement, again take a step to point 2, taking the right arm forward and turning the hands to the arabesque position.

As at the beginning of the tour, so at its end, the shoulders must be completely level. The step is taken in the direction of the right hand, as if the hand were indicating the direction of the step along the diagonal; and the same is true later on, when the tours are done in a circle. During the tour, the legs must be tightly pulled together in 5th position (for it is not without reason that these tours are also known as tours soutenus, "upheld"). This becomes particularly important when the tempo is accelerated, as well as when the tours are done in 1/4 each. Tightness of the muscles of the legs, quick turns of the head and shoulders, and pulled-up thighs give the tours their swift virtuosity.

Pas Emboîté en Tournant (Tours Emboîtés). Pas emboîté en tournant on pointe may be put in the category of tours executed en diagonale and in a circle. As with all tours, they are done, by themselves as well as in connection with other tours, always at a quick tempo, one quarter or one eighth for each half turn.

(Turning to the right and traveling en diagonale from point 6 to point 2) 2/4 time. Start in 5th position with épaulement croisé, right foot forward. On the upbeat, demi-plié and open the right foot to the side at 45° (dégagé) in the direction of point 2. On the first quarter, step onto pointe on the right leg and do a half turn, quickly taking the left foot sur le cou-de-pied devant; simultaneously, the left arm bends in 1st position, the right remaining in 2nd; the body is turned so that the left shoulder is to point 2 and the right to point 6; the head and eyes are directed past the elbow toward point 2. On the second quarter, without traveling, put the left foot down on pointe in 5th position, at the same time turning another half turn, and quickly bring the right foot sur le cou-de-pied devant; the body is turned so that the right shoulder is to point 2 and the left to point 6; the head and eyes are directed past the right elbow to point 2; at the conclusion of the second half turn, the left arm opens to 2nd position and the right bends in 1st position. It is not recommended to open the left arm to 2nd position earlier than the conclusion of the turn on the left leg, for this will hinder the precise position of the body and the movement forward in the given direction.

For the following tours, the right foot is put down onto pointe with a small step to the side in the direction of point 2. In the same manner, travel forward only on the first half turn; the second half turn is done in place. The precise turns of the head and exact relationship of the shoulders to the diagonal, the correct and quick change of the arm positions, pulled-up hips and sharp rhythmic movements of the legs—all assist the execution of these tours at a quick tempo.

Tours en Dedans with Coupé (done on a diagonal and in a circle)

Study Sequence

1. Elementary study. 2/4 time (turning to the right and traveling on the diagonal from point 6 to point 2). As in tours en dedans on both legs, on the upbeat, turn the body effacé and open the right arm forward and the left to the side. On the first quarter, step forward onto pointe on the right leg in the direction of the right hand, taking the left foot sur le cou-de-pied devant; simultaneously, transfer the weight forward onto the right leg with a strongly pulled-up torso; and, providing force with the left arm, bring the arms together in 1st position and do a tour en dedans, precisely turning on the pointe of the right leg; the head and eyes remain directed across the left shoulder to point 2 for as long as possible; and, at the end of the tour, the head and the whole body face point 2. On the second quarter, coupé; that is, demi-plié on the left leg, having placed it in

back of the right, and bend the right leg so that the foot is sur le cou-de-pied devant (the whole body is in the position effacé). From here, the movement is repeated.

2. Final form. During the tour, the working leg is bent sur le cou-de-pied derrière (instead of devant) on the supporting leg in a turned-out position and securely held. After the tour, coupé as described above.

These tours are also called tours piqués ("pricked", "dived"), which completely corresponds to the character of their execution; for it is necessary to place the leg down sharply, slightly from above, as if diving to the floor, then quickly turn on pointe, before again, with a big, dynamic step forward, doing the next tour.

All tours on a diagonal or in a circle in one quarter each are done on the strong musical beat on the quarter. The demi-plié before each tour is done on the weak beat, i.e. between the quarters.

Tours-Fouettés at 45°

Study Sequence

1. First form. En dehors, 2/4 time. Start in 5th position, right leg front. On the upbeat, demi-plié en face, opening the right leg to the side at 45°; simultaneously, open the arms to the side in 2nd position. On the first quarter, spring onto demi-pointe on the left leg; the right leg, with a quick, whipping movement, bends, taking the toe behind the calf of the supporting leg and then, instantly, in front of the shin; at the same time, the arms, with a strong movement, come together in a low 1st position. On the second quarter, the left leg comes down in demi-plié; and the right leg and the arms open to 2nd position. Then the movement is repeated from eight to sixteen times.

Tours-fouettés en dedans are executed in the same manner, but the working leg, with a whipping movement, bends in front of the shin of the supporting leg and is taken behind the calf before opening to the side at 45°.

2. Second form. Start in 4th position en face, left leg front, in a préparation for pirouettes en dehors. On the upbeat, pirouette en dehors, turning to the right, and finish on the first quarter in demi-plié on the left leg; simultaneously, the right leg and the arms open to 2nd position. Between the first and second quarters, execute the fouetté at 45° en face, without a tour, and finish it on the second quarter. The following fouettés are executed in the same way in one quarter each, in a group of seven or fifteen, and finish in 4th position, with épaulement croisé, right leg back. Each time the demi-plié takes place on the quarter.

Then fouetté at 45° without a tour is studied on pointe. It is recommended that only after this should one proceed to the study of tours-fouettés at 45° (en tournant), practising at the beginning four tours, then eight, twelve, sixteen, etc.

During the study of fouetté without a tour, one must carefully observe all the rules for its execution en tournant. The lower half of the working leg must bend to the supporting leg precisely in a straight line, keeping the thigh motionless and absolutely turned-out. When the leg stretches to the side at the end of each fouetté, it must go each time to exactly the same height, in no case lowering it from the height taken on the first fouetté. During the whipping movement, the toe must be transferred from behind the calf of the supporting leg in front of the shin (in the case of fouetté en dehors) without the slightest delay. Precisely this moment must be established during the study of fouetté without a tour and, later, in the execution of tours-fouettés, for it is the culmination of the movement, in spite of the fact that the musical accent always takes place at the moment of the demi-plié on the supporting leg (on the quarter) and that the fouetté itself takes place between the quarters. In this way, the accent of the fouetté must always be felt *up* on pointe and the musical accent *down* in demi-plié. The demi-plié between the fouettés must be executed as a short movement, very precisely, pushing away from the floor with the heel of the supporting leg. During a tour en dehors, to the right, the force is provided by the left arm, and for a tour to the left, by the right arm. It is necessary to note that, while there are experienced executants who provide force for a tour to the right with the right arm, leaving the left motionless in preparatory position, such an individual peculiarity does not disturb the academic form of these fouettés. For the secure execution of tours-fouettés at 45°, the eyes provide aid by being each time directed to a definite point of the room, turning the head sharply ("spotting") as in all forms of pirouettes.

A Sample Lesson for the Senior Class

(All combinations are to be executed starting with the right foot and then with the left.)

Barre Exercise

1. Grand plié twice in 1st, 2nd, 4th, and 5th positions, 4/4 each.
2. Battement tendu and battement tendu jeté, 32 measures of 2/4.

Eight forward, 1/4 each, and demi-plié on the eighth; eight backward with the left leg; two to the side with the right leg, lowering the heel, 4/4 each, closing in front on the first one (four times stretching the foot); seven battements tendus jetés to the side, 1/8 each; repeat the jetés one more time.

The whole combination is to be done again in the opposite direction, starting with the right leg in back.

3. Rond de jambe par terre and grand rond de jambe jeté, 8 measures of 4/4.

En dehors: four ronds de jambe par terre, 1/4 each; three, 1/8 each; two grands ronds de jambe jetés, 1/4 each; seven par terre, 1/8 each; and four grands ronds de jambe jétes, 1/4 each. Repeat all en dedans. Then, to four measures of 4/4, take the leg around (rond de jambe par terre) en dedans and en dehors and execute the 3rd port de bras in demi-plié, with the leg stretched out in the back.

4. Battement fondu and frappé, 24 measures of 2/4.

Fondu forward at 45°, in 2/4; plié-relevé, in 2/4; fondu double forward, in 2/4; plié-relevé, in 2/4. Repeat fondu in the same manner to the side, backward, and to the side again.

Frappé: seven to the side, and then seven more, 1/8 each; four doubles frappés, 1/4 each, and seven, 1/8 each.

5. Rond de jambe en l'air, 8 measures of 4/4.

Two ronds de jambe, 1/4 each, ending each in demi-plié; three, 1/8 each, the last one ending in demi-plié. Repeat. Two tours en dehors sur le cou-de-pied from 45°, and finish by opening the leg to the side at 45°, in 2/4; flic-flac en tournant en dehors and finish to the side at 90°, in 2/4; two tours en dehors temps relevé, and finish to the side at 45°, in 2/4; three ronds de jambe, 1/8 each, and five ronds de jambe, 1/16 each. Repeat all en dedans.

6. Petit battement sur le cou-de-pied, 16 measures of 4/4.

Six petits battements, 1/8 beat each, and, to finish, développé at 90° in the pose effacée devant; repeat petits battements, and finish with a développé at 90° in the pose écartée derrière. Twelve petits battements, 1/8 beat each; tombé in place (in front of the supporting leg) onto the right leg in demi-plié, bending the left sur le cou-de-pied derrière; and do a half turn toward the barre with a rise to demi-pointe (concluding the turn with the left foot sur le cou-de-pied devant). From here, execute the combination with the left foot, and then repeat all in the opposite direction with the right and with the left foot.

7. Battement développé, 8 measures of 4/4 or 32 measures of waltz.

1st measure. Développé ballotté forward at 90°, in 1/4; passé on demi-pointe at 90°, in 1/4; développé ballotté backward, in 1/4; passé on demi-pointe at 90°, in 1/4.

2nd measure. Rond de jambe développé en dehors at 90°

with a demi-plié on the supporting leg, in 3/4; in 1/4, passé at 90° on demi-pointe.

3rd measure. Développé to the side in 2nd position, in 1/4; demi-plié in 1/4 and tour en dehors en tire-bouchon, finishing in the pose écartée derrière at 90°.

4th measure. From écarté, bend the leg to attitude effacée allongée in 1/4; développé tombé backward, and finish in the pose attitude effacée on demi-pointe.

Repeat the combination in the reverse direction.

8. Grand battement jeté pointé, 16 measures of 2/4. Two forward, 1/4 each, and then three, 1/8 each, closing in 5th position on the last one. Repeat. To the side, do eight, 1/4 each. Then execute all in the opposite direction.

   Centre Exercise

1. Short adagio with battement tendu. 8 measures of 4/4.

   1st measure. Grand plié in 5th position croisée (right foot front) and, from the deep plié, tour en dehors in the big pose effacée devant.

   2nd measure. Tour lent en dehors in the pose effacée.

   3rd measure. On demi-pointe, take the right leg to 3rd arabesque and come down in demi-plié; then, with a rise to demi-pointe, turn en dehors with passé at 90°, finishing in the pose croisée devant at 90° on the whole foot.

   4th measure. Renversé en dedans, finishing in 4th position croisée in a préparation en dehors, and do one tour en dehors in the pose effacée devant, on the right leg.

   On the following four measures (after lowering the left leg to 5th position back), execute all in the opposite direction: that is, from the grand plié in 5th position, tour en dedans in attitude effacée (on the right leg); tour lent en dedans; take the leg, on demi-pointe, croisé devant, coming down in demi-plié; then, turn en dedans with passé at 90° on demi-pointe, finishing on the whole foot in attitude croisée; renversé en dehors, finishing in 4th position croisée in a préparation en dedans, and do one tour en dedans in the pose attitude effacée.

Battement tendu. 4 measures of 4/4.

With the right leg, two battements tendus and three jetés in the small pose croisée devant; do the same with the left leg backward; with the right, four battements tendus to the side (closing front first) and seven jetés en tournant en dedans. All battements tendus are executed in 1/4 and the jetés in 1/8. Then, to an additional four measures of 4/4, do the following:

Tours sur le cou-de-pied en dehors: with the right leg, dégagé to 2nd, from a demi-plié in 2nd position, one, two, and three tours, finishing in 4th position in a préparation en dehors; then, one and two tours, from 4th position, finishing the last in 5th position, right leg back. Turn in 5th position on demi-pointe, and tombé to a préparation en dedans, in 4th position and do two tours en dedans.

2. Battement fondu. 8 measures of 2/4.

Fondu at 45° in the pose effacée devant, in 2/4; demi-plié and, with a relevé to demi-pointe, take the leg around to effacé derrière (arms in 2nd arabesque), in 2/4. Having done a petit battement, repeat, taking the leg forward for the execution of the fondu.

Then, fondu to the side, in 2/4; demi-plié and, on the following 2/4, do two tours en dehors sur le cou-de-pied, opening the leg to the side at 45° at the end and remaining on demi-pointe: on the next two measures of 2/4, do seven ronds de jambe en l'air en dehors, 1/8 each. Repeat with the other leg, and then execute all en dedans.

3. Grand battement jeté pointé (1/8 each). 8 measures of 2/4.

With the right leg, in the pose effacée devant, two pointés, and a third closing in 5th position. Repeat. Do the same thing with the left leg in 1st arabesque toward point 2. Do the same thing with the right leg in the pose écartée derrière (closing first in front and then in back). With the

left leg, développé on demi-pointe in the pose croisée
devant at 90°; tombé-coupé and pas de ciseaux coming
down in 1st arabesque in demi-plié to point 2.

4. Big adagio. 8 measures of 4/4.

   1st measure. Grand plié in 2nd position with port de
bras; and, from the deep plié, tour en dedans on the right
leg in the pose 2nd arabesque.

   2nd measure. Passé at 90° with a turn of the body to the
pose écartée devant, left shoulder to point 2, then turn the
body (en dedans) toward the mirror to 4th arabesque.

   3rd measure. Renversé en écarté, and repeat the
renversé (from the previous pose écartée derrière).

   4th measure. Rise on demi-pointe in the pose écartée
derrière and execute a pas chassé en diagonale toward
point 6, finishing in 5th position. Développé on demi-
pointe in the pose effacée devant with the right leg and pas
chassé en diagonale to point 2, finishing in 4th position in a
préparation effacée for tours en dedans.

   5th measure. Two tours en dedans in 1st arabesque (on
the right leg) and grand fouetté en tournant en dedans to
the pose 3rd arabesque.

   6th measure. Turn en dehors to the pose croisée devant
on the whole foot, rise to demi-pointe and come down in
4th position in a préparation en dedans.

   7th measure. Two tours à la seconde en dedans (on the
left leg); then, without lowering the right leg, demi-plié and
two tours en tire-bouchon en dedans, finishing in the pose
croisée devant at 90°.

   8th measure. Renversé en dedans (second form, through
écarté devant) and soubresaut from 5th position to 5th
position.

5. A small combination of tours in waltz tempo. 16 measures.

   4 measures: with the right leg, petite sissonne tombée to
the side and pas de bourrée changé, finishing in 4th
position in a préparation en dehors; two tours en dehors

sur le cou-de-pied, finishing in 4th position croisée (left leg front).

4 measures: two and a half tours sur le cou-de-pied en dedans, transferring the weight (a kind of tombé) onto the right leg, which is in 4th position back, and finish in a préparation en dedans in 4th position, left leg front; then, two tours en dedans sur le cou-de-pied (on the left leg), finishing in a big préparation en dehors, with the right leg in front.

4 measures: two tours en dehors in the pose attitude croisée; and, without lowering the leg, plié, and tour en dehors in the pose 3rd arabesque, coming down in 5th position at the end.

4 measures: starting with the right foot, tours chaînés, on the diagonal to point 2, finishing in 4th position in a préparation en dehors, left leg front; and three tours en dehors sur le cou-de-pied (to the right), finishing in the pose attitude croisée.

Allegro

1. 8 measures of 2/4.

    Two assemblés battus to the side in 2nd position (with the right and then the left leg); échappé battu to 2nd position changing the legs. Repeat, starting with the other leg. With the right leg, double assemblé battu, and petit échappé to 4th position croisée. Repeat, starting with the other leg. Then, execute it all in the opposite direction (to 8 more measures).

2. 8 measures of 2/4.

    5th position, right leg back. With the right leg, petit jeté battu, temps levé, assemblé (croisé derrière), and royale. Execute this three times. Then, grande sissonne ouverte en tournant en dehors to the pose croisée devant, assemblé, sissonne fermée battue in a small pose croisée derrière, royale. Repeat with the other leg (8 measures); and then execute it all in the opposite direction (to 16 more measures).

3. 4 measures of 4/4.

Two grands échappés en tournant to 2nd position without changing the legs, one half turn each; pas de basque en avant, cabriole in the pose 4th arabesque, pas de bourrée en tournant and entrechat-quatre. Repeat the two grands échappés en tournant, grande sissonne ouverte en tournant en dehors (for the men's class, with two turns in the air) finishing in 2nd position, assemblé back, petite sissonne tombée croisée devant and cabriole fermée in the pose 4th arabesque. Repeat with the other leg.

4. Waltz, 16 measures.

With the right leg in back, glissade sans changé. Petite cabriole fermée to the side in 2nd position, closing in front. Repeat with the other leg. With the right leg, sissonne tombée forward to point 2 and grande cabriole in 1st arabesque; and, on the diagonal from point 2 to point 6, two jetés entrelacés to 1st arabesque with chassé; step backward and soutenu en tournant en dedans in 5th position on demi-pointe, finishing with the left foot in front (arms in 3rd position); with the right leg, on the diagonal to point 2, sissonne tombée, coupé, grand jeté en tournant in attitude effacée, coupé, grand jeté en tournant, coupé and grand jeté en tournant in attitude effacée. In the women's class, for the last two grands jetés en tournant, substitute two jetés par terre, in a small attitude effacée while in the air.

5. Waltz, 16 measures.

On the diagonal from point 6 to point 2, two sauts de basque with chassé, tours chaînés, finishing in 1st arabesque in demi-plié on the right leg. On the diagonal upstage, chassé and grand fouetté sauté en tournant en dedans to attitude effacée; failli, coupé, grand jeté in attitude croisée, assemblé, two tours en l'air (for the women's class, two tours from 5th position en dehors en tire-bouchon), and sissonne soubresaut to the pose effacée derrière, finishing on the left leg in demi-plié.

6. 4 measures of 6/8.

Grande sissonne ouverte to the pose effacée devant with the right leg; with a temps levé sauté, swing the right leg around to 3rd arabesque, and assemblé. Repeat the same with the left leg, and again with the right. With the right leg, toward point 2, glissade, grande cabriole effacée devant, and finish with an assemblé in 5th position, right foot back. Then continue, starting with the other leg. On repeating the combination, the cabriole may be done with two beats.

7. 8 measures of 2/4.

Eight entrechats-six, 1/4 each, and sixteen petits changements de pieds, 1/8 each.

8. Slow waltz.

Port de bras, bending the body forward, backward, and to the side. The feet are in 1st position.

Sample Pointe Exercise

1. 16 measures of 2/4. Right foot front. Four échappés to 2nd position, changing the legs; échappé to one leg and two times plié-relevé (right foot sur le cou-de-pied derrière), 1/4 for each movement; finish in 5th position. Two échappés in 2nd position, 1/4 each; and three échappés, 1/8 each. Préparation from 5th position to 5th, and three times do a tour en dehors sur le cou-de-pied, from 5th position, evenly, 1/4 each. Finish in 5th position, right leg back, and continue the combination with the other leg.

2. 24 measures of 3/8.

1st measure. 5th position, right leg front. Demi-plié and, 2/8, after a step onto pointe with the left leg forward to point 2 and, after turning the body with the left shoulder also to point 2, do pas de bourrée suivi in 5th position; the left arm goes forward, and the right goes to the side. On the third eighth, with a half turn to the right, step over with the right foot to 5th position front; the right shoulder is toward point 2; the right arm is in 1st, the left in 2nd position; the hands are turned palms down.

2nd measure. Pas de bourrée suivi in 5th position toward point 2.

3rd and 4th measures. Without coming down off pointe, repeat the first two measures; and, on the last eighth, come down on the right foot in demi-plié.

5th measure. Step forward (croisé) on to the left leg in attitude croisée (the left arm is in 3rd, the right in 2nd position).

6th measure. Plié-relevé.

7th measure. Renversé en dehors.

8th measure. Double rond de jambe en l'air en dehors with the right leg in the direction effacée devant, finishing in 5th position, right foot back.

On the next eight measures, repeat everything with the left leg, in the direction of point 8.

The last eight measures are as follows:

1st and 2nd measures. Dégagé to point 8 with the left leg, toe to the floor, with a demi-plié on the right leg and pas de bourrée suivi in 5th position on the diagonal (moving upstage); the left leg in front; the left arm is in 1st position, and the right in 2nd; the hands are turned palms down. On the last eighth, demi-plié on the left leg and dégagé to point 2 with the right leg, toe to the floor.

3rd and 4th measures. Pas de bourrée suivi in 5th position on the diagonal moving upstage toward point 6, right leg front. On the last eighth, coupé on the left leg.

5th-8th measures. Pas couru on pointe in 1st position forward in a direction between points 8 and 1; and pas de chat en avant, finishing on the right leg, the left—croisé derrière.

3.   Slow waltz, 16 measures. Right leg front.

1st measure. Pas de bourrée suivi in 5th position in a straight line to the right toward point 3; the right arm opens from below to 3rd, the left to 2nd position.

2nd and 3rd measures. Coupé on the right leg and grande sissonne ouverte to 2nd position at 90° with the left leg raised (the arms are in 2nd position); plié and relevé with a turn to 1st arabesque to point 3 and demi-plié.

4th measure. Stepping onto pointe on the left leg, two tours en dehors sur le cou-de-pied, with the arms in 3rd position. Finish in demi-plié on the left leg, with the right leg croisé devant, the toe to the floor; the body is inclined forward; the arms also are lowered from 3rd position (épaulement croisé).

5th-8th measures. Repeat.

9th-12th measures. Repeat, but finish the tours en dehors in 5th position in demi-plié, right foot back; then, quickly do a whole tour (to the right) on pointe in 5th position, finishing with épaulement croisé, right foot front; the right arm is in 1st, the left in 2nd position; the head is turned to the right.

13th-16th measures. On the diagonal to point 2, on the left leg, tour en dehors sur le cou-de-pied, with a dégagé, finishing (without coming down off pointe) in the big pose écartée devant; the right arm is in 3rd, the left in 2nd position. Repeat this tour. Then do a double tour sur le cou-de-pied en dehors with a dégagé, finishing in 5th position, right foot back, and grande sissonne ouverte forward onto the left leg to the pose attitude croisée; the arms are in 3rd and 2nd positions allongées.

4.   4 measures of 4/4 (or a waltz of 16 measures).

Préparation. The right leg is croisé derrière with the toe to the floor. On the upbeat, demi-plié and step forward onto pointes with the right leg, toward point 2, opening the arms to the side, and turning the body so that the right shoulder also is to point 2.

1st measure. On the first quarter, demi-plié and fouetté effacé en dehors en face, finishing on the second quarter in demi-plié; between the second and third quarters, relevé onto pointe (without changing the pose); on the third and fourth quarters, grand fouetté en tournant en dedans to 3rd arabesque.

2nd measure. On the first quarter, relevé in attitude croisée, the eyes directed toward the left hand; on the second quarter, come down in 4th position in a préparation for tour en dehors; on the third and fourth quarters, do two tours en dehors sur le cou-de-pied (on the right leg), finishing in 5th position, left foot back.

3rd measure. From the right leg, pas de bourrée suivi in 5th position to the right in a small circle, finishing it to face the mirror; on the last quarter, demi-plié on the right leg, and spring up onto pointe, throwing the left out à la seconde.

4th measure. Grand fouetté en tournant en dedans to 1st arabesque, pas de bourrée changing the legs to a préparation en dedans in 4th position, and do two tours sur le cou-de-pied en dedans on the left leg, finishing in 5th position, right leg front.

5. 4 measures of 4/4.

The pose is croisée derrière, standing on the right leg.

1st measure. Grand port de bras, finishing in 4th position in a préparation en dedans.

2nd measure. Two tours à la seconde en dedans (on the right leg), the arms are in 3rd position; without lowering the left leg, demi-plié on the right and pas de bourrée dessus en tournant; step back off pointe onto the left leg, and stretch the right leg croisé devant with the toe to the floor.

3rd measure. Slide the right leg, toe to the floor, toward

point 3, transferring the weight onto it in demi-plié, and do a half tour en dedans in 1st arabesque; demi-plié, again do a half tour en dedans in 1st arabesque; demi-plié, do a whole tour en dedans in 1st arabesque; and passé, through 1st position, to 4th position croisée, finishing with the left leg in front in demi-plié, the right leg in back with the toe to the floor.

4th measure. Coupé with the right leg, and slide the left leg toward point 7; half tour in 1st arabesque on the left leg, demi-plié, again a half tour; demi-plié and two tours en dedans en tire-bouchon. Finish in 5th position, right leg front.

6. 4 measures of 4/4.

On a diagonal from point 6 to point 2.

Préparation. The left leg is croisé derrière with the toe to the floor; the right arm is in 1st, the left in 2nd position; the head is to the right. On the upbeat, demi-plié and turn the body to point 2, opening the left leg to the side at 45° and the arms to 2nd position, and pas de bourrée dessus en tournant.

1st measure. On the first quarter, demi-plié on the left leg, opening the right leg to the side at 45°, and do a fouetté en dehors. On the second quarter, demi-plié on the right leg, opening the left leg to the side at 45°, and do a fouetté en dedans. On the third quarter, demi-plié on the left leg, and again do a fouetté en dehors. On the fourth quarter, demi-plié on the right leg, and pas de bourrée dessus en tournant.

2nd and 3rd measures. Repeat the fouetté combination two more times. In conclusion, do a fouetté en dedans on the right leg with a double tour, finishing in demi-plié on the left leg with the right foot sur le cou-de-pied devant.

4th measure. Chaînés tours to the right, finishing in 4th position croisée, left leg front in demi-plié, left arm is in 3rd, right is in 2nd position.

Four Sample Big Adagios

1. 4 measures of 4/4 or a waltz of 16 measures.

    1st measure. Grand plié in 5th position (right foot front) and, from the grand plié, two tours en dehors sur le cou-de-pied. Finish by stepping onto the right leg in the direction of point 4 in the pose 3rd arabesque with the left arm raised to the height of 3rd position.

    2nd measure. Incline the body forward and slowly turn to the right, taking the left leg to the pose écartée derrière at 90° to point 6.

    3rd measure. Plié on the supporting right leg and tour en dehors in the pose 4th arabesque; incline the body slightly forward and, turning en dehors (a half turn), take the left leg out to the side at 90° (stopping with the back to the mirror).

    4th measure. Plié on the supporting right leg and, having risen onto demi-pointe on the left leg, do one and a half tours en dedans in the pose attitude effacée. Finish in plié in the pose allongée. Quick passé forward, through 1st position, step-coupé, and entrechat-six de volé in the pose écartée devant to point 8.

2. 4 measures of 4/4.

    1st measure. Beginning with the right leg in front, grand échappé to 2nd position and (from 2nd position) two tours à la seconde en dehors on the left leg, finishing in 5th position, right leg front.

    2nd measure. Grand échappé to 4th position croisée and two tours en dedans to the pose 1st arabesque on the right leg.

    3rd measure. Grand fouetté en tournant en dedans to the pose 1st arabesque and a second fouetté to the pose attitude croisée.

    4th measure. Coupé with the left leg onto demi-pointe, raising the right foot sur le cou-de-pied; then, demi-plié and, with a rise to demi-pointe, renversé en dehors (doing a rond de jambe développé and a pas de bourrée en tournant en dehors); finish in 4th position in a préparation en dedans, right leg front; and do three tours sur le cou-de-pied en dedans, finishing in the pose croisée devant at 90°, the arms are in 3rd position.

3. 4 measures of 4/4.

1st measure. Beginning with the right leg in front, do a short pas failli, finishing in 4th position croisée, left leg front, in a préparation en dehors, and follow this with two tours en dehors sur le cou-de-pied. Finish by opening the right leg to the side at 90°. Then do a short plié on the supporting left leg and grand jeté onto the right leg. With the left leg, passé at 90° to the pose croisée devant; and then do a quick passé en arrière with the left leg, through 1st position, to the pose 1st arabesque on the diagonal to point 2.

2nd measure. Tour lent en dedans in the pose arabesque, to point 2, and rise onto demi-pointe.

3rd measure. Tombé back onto the left leg and do two tours en dehors in the pose effacée devant, raising the right arm to 3rd and the left to 1st position (with the palms turned outward); and finish in 5th position, right leg back.

4th measure. With the left leg, développé to the pose écartée devant with a rise to demi-pointe, tombé, and pas chassé to point 8. Finish by transferring onto the left leg to the pose attitude effacée and doing a tour-fouetté en dedans to the pose attitude effacée.

4. 8 measures of 4/4.

1st measure. The préparation is with the left leg croisé derrière, the toe to the floor. On the upbeat, demi-plié and dégagé with the left leg to the side at 45°; pas de bourrée dessus en tournant, finishing on the first quarter. Then pas de bourrée dessous en tournant, finishing on the second quarter; and, from 5th position, do two tours en dehors sur le cou-de-pied, stopping in the pose 4th arabesque, on the left leg.

2nd measure. Incline the body forward in the pose arabesque (penché) and come back to the initial position.

3rd measure. Demi-plié on the supporting left leg and, taking the right leg through 2nd position at 90°, do two tours en dedans in the pose croisée devant and renversé en dedans.

4th measure. On the upbeat, do a quick développé with the left leg to the side on demi-pointe and a grand fouetté en tournant en dehors to the pose croisée devant; then, with a rise to demi-pointe, take the left leg to attitude effacée.

5th measure. Tombé back onto the left leg and do two tours en dehors in the pose 3rd arabesque and a renversé en dehors (attitude). Finish on the right leg, in the pose croisée derrière, with the toe to the floor.

6th measure. Grand port de bras (sixth).

7th measure. On the first quarter, do the first part of the grand port de bras (stretching out in demi-plié, with an inclination of the body forward); on the second quarter, quickly transfer the weight onto the left leg, with a turn en dedans to the pose 3rd arabesque at 90°; on the third and fourth quarters, on demi-pointe, take the right leg around to écarté devant to point 2.

8th measure. Tombé onto the right leg in 1st arabesque in demi-plié to point 2 and do two tours en dedans with the left leg sur le cou-de-pied, raising the left arm to 3rd and the right to 1st position; finish in 5th position, left leg front.

First Year Class

The elementary exercises for the mastery of the basic stance of the body and the positions of the feet, arms, and head used in classical dance. The development of elementary habits of movement co-ordination.

Barre Exercise

To make their correct execution easier, the exercises are learned, at first, facing the barre. After mastery, their study continues holding the barre with one hand. For the more correct adaption of turn-out, the series of exercises is studied, at first, to the side, later, forward and backward.

1. The basic stance.
2. The positions of the feet:
   1st position
   2nd position
   3rd position
   5th position
   4th position (this position, as being the most difficult, is studied last).
   Musical accompaniment: Stand in each position four measures of 4/4 or eight measures of 3/4.
3. The positions of the arms:
   Preparatory position
   1st position

3rd position

2nd position (this position, as being the most difficult, is studied last).

The positions of the arms are studied, in the beginning, in the centre of the room, without attempting to observe the positions of the feet. Musical accompaniment: four measures of 4/4 or eight measures of 3/4.

4. Demi-plié in 1st, 2nd, 3rd, 5th, and 4th positions. Musical accompaniment: two measures of 4/4; in the second half of the year, one measure of 4/4.

5. Battement tendu in 1st position, to the side, forward and backward.

    Musical accompaniment: two measures of 4/4, later, one measure of 4/4; in the second half of the year, one measure of 2/4 (the movement being executed in 1/4).

6. Battement tendu with demi-plié in 1st position, to the side, forward and backward.

    Musical accompaniment: two measures of 4/4 (on the first measure, battement tendu, on the second measure, demi-plié), later, one measure of 4/4; in the second half of the year, one measure of 2/4.

7. Passé par terre through 1st position forward and backward.

    Musical accompaniment: two measures of 4/4, later, one measure of 4/4.

8. Rond de jambe par terre by quarters of a circle.

    Musical accompaniment: two measures of 4/4, later, one measure of 4/4; by the end of the second half of the year, one measure of 2/4.

9. Battement tendu in 5th position, to the side, forward and backward.

    Musical accompaniment: two measures of 4/4, later, one measure of 4/4; in the second half of the year, one measure of 2/4 (the movement executed in 1/4).

10. Battement tendu with demi-plié in 5th position, to the side, forward and backward.

Musical accompaniment: two measures of 4/4, (on the first measure of 4/4, battement tendu, on the second measure of 4/4, demi-plié). Later, one measure of 4/4, in the second half of the year, one measure of 2/4.

11. Rond de jambe par terre en dehors and en dedans (first explaining the concepts en dehors and en dedans). Musical accompaniment: two measures of 4/4, later, one measure of 4/4; by the end of the second half of the year, one measure of 2/4.

12. Battement tendu jeté in 1st and 5th positions, to the side, forward and backward.
Musical accompaniment: two measures of 2/4, later, one measure of 2/4.

13. Battement tendu jeté with demi-plié in 1st and 5th positions, to the side, forward and backward.
Musical accompaniment: two measures of 4/4, later, one measure of 4/4.

14. Battement tendu pour le pied in 1st and 5th positions
    a) with a lowering of the heel in 2nd position (double tendu),
    b) with a lowering of the heel in 2nd position in demi-plié, second half of the year (double tendu with demi-plié).
    Musical accompaniment: two measures of 4/4, later, one measure of 4/4.

15. Relevé lent at 45° to the side, forward and backward.
Musical accompaniment: two measures of 4/4.

16. Battement tendu jeté piqué in 1st and 5th positions, to the side, forward and backward.
Musical accompaniment: one measure of 4/4. Piqué in 1/4, later, in 1/8.

17. Battement tendu jeté flexing the instep of the working leg at 25° to the side, forward and backward.
Musical accompaniment: one measure of 4/4.

18. The position of the foot sur le cou-de-pied devant (basic position) and derrière.

At first, it is studied from a position in which the leg is opened to the side, toe to the floor, and, after mastering this, from a position in front and in back.
Musical accompaniment: two measures of 4/4.

19. Battement frappé to the side, forward and backward (first learned with the toe to the floor, in the second half of the year, at 45°).
Musical accompaniment: one measure of 4/4, later, one measure of 2/4.

20. Relevé to demi-pointe in 1st, 2nd, and 5th positions. Musical accompaniment: one measure of 4/4, two measures of 2/4, or four measures of 3/4.

21. Grand plié in 1st, 2nd, 3rd, 5th, and 4th positions. Musical accompaniment: two measures of 4/4.

22. The conditional position sur le cou-de-pied (studied from a position in which the leg is opened to the side, toe to the floor, then from 5th position).

23. Battement fondu to the side, forward and backward. (In the beginning, studied with the toe to the floor, in the second half of the year, at 45°.)
Musical accompaniment: two measures of 4/4, later, one measure of 4/4.

24. Battement soutenu to the side, forward and backward, toe to the floor (studied through the position sur le cou-de-pied in front and in back). First studied with the whole foot on the floor, in the second half of the year, with a rise to demi-pointe in 5th position.
Musical accompaniment: two measures of 4/4, later, one measure of 4/4.

25. Petit battement sur le cou-de-pied. (Transferring the foot evenly.)
Musical accompaniment: one measure of 4/4, later, one measure of 2/4.

26. Battements doubles frappés to the side, forward and

backward (first learned with the toe to the floor, in the second half of the year, at 45°).
Musical accompaniment: two measures of 4/4, later, one measure of 4/4.

27. The préparation for rond de jambe par terre, en dehors and en dedans.
Musical accompaniment: one measure of 4/4.

28. Battement relevé lent at 90° from 1st and 5th positions, to the side, forward and backward. (The movement to the side and backward is first learned facing the barre. The movement forward is learned holding the barre with one hand.)
Musical accompaniment: two measures of 4/4.

29. Grand battement jeté from 1st and 5th positions, to the side, forward and backward. (The movement to the side and backward is first learned facing the barre. The movement forward is learned holding the barre with one hand.)
Musical accompaniment: one measure of 2/4, later, each movement in 1/4 and pause for 1/4 in 5th position.

30. Rond de jambe en l'air en dehors and en dedans. (The study is introduced by a simple bending and stretching of the leg to the side at 45°.)
Musical accompaniment: one measure of 4/4, later, one measure of 2/4.

31. Battement retiré.
Musical accompaniment: one measure of 4/4.

32. Battement développé to the side, forward and backward. (The movement to the side and backward is first learned facing the barre. The movement forward is studied with one hand holding the barre.)
Musical accompaniment: two measures of 4/4.

33. Grand battement jeté pointé in 1st and 5th positions, to the side, forward and backward (studied in the second half of the year).

Musical accompaniment: one measure of 4/4.

34. Battement développé passé (studied in the second half of the year).

Musical accompaniment: two measures of 4/4.

35. Rond de jambe par terre in plié en dehors and en dedans, as a conclusion for the rond de jambe par terre exercise.

Musical accompaniment: two measures of 4/4.

36. 1st and 3rd ports de bras combined with various exercises. 3rd port de bras executed as a conclusion for rond de jambe par terre, taking the leg around, backward and forward, toe to the floor.

Musical accompaniment: two measures of 4/4.

37. Pas de bourrée changé, en dehors and en dedans (studied facing the barre).

Musical accompaniment: one measure of 4/4, later, one measure of 3/4, still later, one measure of 2/4.

38. Pas de bourrée suivi on demi-pointe, in 5th position.

Musical accompaniment: two measures of 4/4 or two measures of 3/4. 1/8 for each movement.

39. A bend of the body backward and to the side, facing the barre in 1st position (studied at the end of the barre exercise).

Musical accompaniment: two measures of 4/4, or four measures of 3/4.

40. Half turns in 5th position changing the legs, on demi-pointe, without plié, and with demi-plié.

Musical accompaniment: one measure of 4/4.

Centre Exercise

The exercises are the same as at the barre, with the addition of the following:

1. Épaulement croisé and effacé in 5th and 4th positions (first explaining the concept of épaulement).

2. 1st, 2nd and 3rd ports de bras.

Musical accompaniment: two measures of 4/4, or four measures of 3/4.

3. The poses croisées, effacées, and écartées, devant and derrière, with the arms in the big and small poses.

   1st, 2nd and 3rd arabesques (studied with the toe to the floor).

4. Temps lié par terre.

   Musical accompaniment: four measures of 4/4, or eight measures of 3/4.

5. Relevé on demi-pointe in 1st, 2nd and 5th positions with stretched legs and from demi-plié.

   Musical accompaniment: four measures of 3/4 and two measures of 2/4.

6. Pas de bourrée changé, finishing with épaulement, en dehors and en dedans.

   Musical accompaniment: one measure of 2/4.

7. Turns on demi-pointe around oneself in place in 5th position (pas de bourrée suivi en tournant).

   Musical accompaniment: each step in 1/8.

Allegro

The jumps are first studied facing the barre.

1. Temps levé in 1st, 2nd and 5th positions.

   Musical accompaniment: one measure of 4/4, later, one measure of 2/4.

2. Changement de pieds.

   Musical accompaniment: one measure of 4/4, later, two to three jumps, 1/4 each.

3. Échappé in 2nd position.

   Musical accompaniment: two measures of 4/4, later, one measure of 4/4.

4. Assemblé (in this class, studied throwing the leg only to the side).

   Musical accompaniment: one measure of 4/4. First learned broken down as follows: on the first quarter, plié; on the second quarter, slide the toe of the leg to the side in 2nd position; on the third quarter, jump, joining the legs in 5th position in the air and finish in demi-plié in 5th position; on the fourth quarter, stretch the legs in 5th position.

Later, as follows: on the first quarter, demi-plié, on the second quarter, finish the jump with a landing in demi-plié, on the third quarter, stretch the legs; on the fourth quarter, pause.

5. Balancé.
   Musical accompaniment: slow 3/4.
6. Sissonne simple.
   Musical accompaniment: one measure of 4/4.
7. Jeté (studied only to the side).
   Musical accompaniment: one measure of 4/4.
   On the first quarter, plié; on the second quarter, slide the toe of the leg to the side in 2nd position; on the third quarter, jump off the left leg and finish on the right leg in demi-plié, the left foot sur le cou-de-pied; on the fourth quarter, stretch the legs in 5th position.
8. Glissade (studied only to the side).
   Musical accompaniment: one measure of 4/4.
9. Pas de basque (stage form).
10. Pas de polka.
    Musical accompaniment: 2/4.
11. Trampoline-like jumps (as on a springboard) in 1st position.
    Musical accompaniment: each jump in 1/4.

Pointe Work

(Studied in the second half of the year)

In the beginning, the movements are studied facing the barre. With mastery, their study is transferred to the centre.

1. Relevé in 1st, 2nd and 5th positions.
    Musical accompaniment: one measure of 4/4.
2. Échappé from 1st and 5th positions.
    Musical accompaniment: one measure of 4/4.
3. Assemblé soutenu.
    Musical accompaniment: one measure of 4/4.
4. Pas de bourrée changé.
    Musical accompaniment: one measure of 2/4 or one
    measure of 3/4.
5. Pas couru in 1st position, forward and backward.
    Musical accompaniment: each movement in 1/16.
6. Pas de bourrée suivi in 5th position, traveling.
    Musical accompaniment: each movement in 1/16.
7. Turn in place in 5th position (pas de bourrée suivi en
    tournant).
    Musical accompaniment: each movement in 1/16.

Second Year Class

A repetition of the exercises already learned, in a greater quantity and at a faster tempo. The development of strength of the foot and the instep by means of alternating movements on the whole foot and on demi-pointe and the execution of the exercise on pointe.

Barre Exercise

The repetition of the exercises of the first class in combinations of movements on the whole foot and on demi-pointe, with the addition of épaulement.

1. Battement tendu in the small poses: croisées, effacées, and écartées.
   Musical time: one measure of 4/4.
2. Battement tendu jeté in the small poses: croisées, effacées, and écartées.
   Musical time: one measure of 4/4.
3. Half turn in 5th position on demi-pointe toward and away from the barre, with stretched legs and from a demi-plié.
   Musical time: 4/4.
4. The small poses croisées, effacées, and écartées, toe to the floor, on a stretched supporting leg and in plié, devant and derrière. At the discretion of the teacher, the poses can be introduced as a conclusion to certain exercises.
5. The 3rd port de bras.
   Studied with a plié on the supporting leg (in a lunge) and with the working leg stretched out forward or backward

with the toe to the floor. The movement is executed at the conclusion of rond de jambe par terre and also combined with other movements.

Musical time: two measures of 4/4. On the first measure, bend forward and come up; on the second, bend back and recover.

6. Tombé and coupé onto demi-pointe (executed after battement frappé and petit battement).

Musical time: one measure of 4/4.

7. Battement soutenu with a rise to demi-pointe, executed in all directions en face and in the poses croisées, effacées, and écartées. At first, studied with the toe to the floor; and later at 45°.

Musical time: one measure of 4/4.

8. Battement frappé in all directions. In the beginning of the year, alternate the movement on the whole foot and on demi-pointe. At the end of the first half-year it is done entirely on demi-pointe.

Musical time: 2/4; later, each movement in 1/4.

9. Battement double frappé in all directions. At the beginning of the year, the movement is alternately done on the whole foot and on demi-pointe, at the end of the first half of the year, it is done entirely on demi-pointe.

Musical time: each movement in 1/4.

10. Petit battement sur le cou-de-pied. At the beginning of the year, the movement is alternately done on the whole foot and on demi-pointe; by the end of the first half of the year, it is done entirely on demi-pointe. At first, it is executed evenly, later, with an accent in front or in back.

Musical time: 2/4, each movement in 1/4.

11. Battement fondu in all directions. At the beginning of the year, the movement is alternately done on the whole foot and on demi-pointe; by the end of the first half of the year, it is done entirely on demi-pointe. At the beginning of the second half of the year, it is executed in the small poses.

Musical time: one measure of 2/4.

a) battement fondu with plié-relevé on the whole foot; later, on demi-pointe.

Musical time: one measure of 4/4.

b) battement fondu with plié-relevé with demi-rond de jambe on the whole foot; later, on demi-pointe.

Musical time: one measure of 4/4.

12. Temps relevé at 45° en dehors and en dedans on the whole foot; at the end of the first half of the year, on demi-pointe.

Musical time: one measure of 4/4; later, in one measure of 2/4.

13. Rond de jambe en l'air en dehors and en dedans on the whole foot; by the end of the first half of the year, on demi-pointe.

Musical time: the movement is executed in 2/4 and 1/4.

14. Battement relevé lent at 90° in all directions and in the big poses croisées, effacées, and ecartées, devant and derrière, attitudes croisée and effacée, and in 2nd arabesque.

Musical time: two measures of 4/4.

15. Battement développé in all directions and all the big poses croisées, effacées, and écartees, devant and derrière, attitudes croisée and effacée, and in 2nd arabesque.

Musical time: two measures of 4/4.

16. Battement développé passé (bending the leg to the knee) in all directions and going from pose to pose.

Musical time: four measures of 4/4 or eight measures of 3/4.

17. Demi-rond de jambe développé at 90° en dehors and en dedans.

Musical time: two measures of 4/4.

18. Grand rond de jambe développé en dehors and en dedans (studied in the second half of the year).

Musical time: four measures of 4/4.

19. Grand battement jeté in all directions and in all the big poses croisées, effacées, and ecartées, devant and derrière, and 2nd arabesque.

Musical time: 2/4. One movement in 1/4 and pause 1/4.

20. Grand battement jeté pointé in all directions and in the big poses croisées, effacées, and écartées, devant and derrière, and 2nd arabesque.
Musical time: one measure of 2/4. One movement in 1/4 and pause 1/4.

Centre Exercise

The same exercises as at the barre, en face and with épaulement, without using demi-pointe.

1. Battement tendu in the small and big poses croisées, effacées, and écartées, devant and derrière, and in 1st,2nd, 3rd, and 4th arabesques (in 4th arabesque, only after the study of the 4th port de bras).
Musical time: each movement in 1/4.

2. Battement tendu jeté, in the small and big poses croisées, effacées, and écartées, devant and derrière.
Musical time: each movement in 1/4.

3. Relevé to demi-pointe in 4th position croisée and effacée, with straight legs and from demi-plié.
Musical time: two measures of 4/4 and one measure of 4/4.

4. Battement relevé lent at 90° forward, to the side and backward and in the poses croisées, effacées, and écartées, devant and derrière, attitudes croisée and effacée, and in 3rd, 1st and 2nd arabesques. 4th arabesque is studied in the second half of the year.
Musical time: two measures of 4/4 or four measures of 3/4.

5. Grand battement jeté forward, to the side and backward, and in the poses croisées, effacées, and écartées, devant and derrière, and in 1st, 2nd and 3rd arabesques.
Musical time: one measure of 2/4.

6. Battement développé forward, to the side and backward and in the poses croisées, effacées, and écartées, devant and derrière, and in 1st, 2nd and 3rd arabesques. 4th arabesque is studied in the second half of the year.

Musical time: two measures of 4/4 or four measures of 3/4.
7. Elementary adagio constructed of the poses already learned: attitude, arabesque, battement développé at 90°, and relevé lent (done in the second half of the year). Musical time: 16 measures or more of 4/4.
8. Temps lié par terre with cambrés. Musical time: four measures of 4/4 or eight measures of 3/4.
9. 4th and 5th ports de bras. Musical time: two measures of 4/4 or four measures of 3/4.
10. Pas de bourrée sans changé, traveling from side to side and forward and backward with the toe to the floor, later at 45°. Musical time: one measure of 2/4 or one measure of 3/4.
11. Pas de bourrée-ballotté croisé and effacé traveling forward and backward. At first studied with a pause, toe to the floor; in the second half of the year, at 45°. Musical time: one measure of 4/4.

Allegro

1. Glissade forward and backward en face and in the small poses croisées, effacées, and écartées, devant and derrière (glissade in the poses is studied in the second half of the year). Musical time: one measure of 4/4.
2. Double assemblé. Musical time: one measure of 4/4.
3. Assemblé forward and backward (at first studied en face; in the second half of the year, in the small poses croisées and effacées). Musical time: one measure of 2/4.
4. Grand changement de pieds. Musical time: one measure of 4/4.
5. Échappé to 2nd position, returning on one leg, with the other sur le cou-de-pied devant or derrière.

Musical time: two measures of 4/4; later, one measure of 4/4.

6. Grand échappé to 2nd position.
   Musical time: one measure of 4/4 and one measure of 2/4.
7. Grand and petit échappé en face to 4th position and in the small poses croisées and effacées.
   Musical time: one measure of 4/4 and one measure of 2/4.
8. Petit changement de pieds.
   Musical time: one measure of 2/4.
9. Jeté to the side, finishing in the small pose croisée, devant and derrière, and en face.
   Musical time: one measure of 4/4 and one measure of 2/4.
10. Pas de basque forward and backward.
    Musical time: two measures of 3/4; by the end of the year, in one measure of 3/4 and in one measure of 2/4.
11. Sissonne ouverte to the side, forward and backward, en face and in the poses croisées and effacées, finishing the movement with the toe to the floor; in the second half of the year, finishing with the working leg at 45°.
    Musical time: one measure of 4/4.
12. Sissonne fermée forward, to the side and backward.
    Musical time: one measure of 4/4. The movement is in 2/4, then straighten the legs from demi-plié in 2/4.
13. Sissonne in the poses 1st and 2nd arabesques en diagonale, the preparation for the jump and the jump itself are in the stage form.
    Musical time: one measure of 4/4 or one measure of 3/4.
14. Pas de chat, stage form. Studied in combination with sissonne in 1st arabesque.
    Musical time: one measure of 2/4 or one measure of 3/4.
15. Balancé and pas de basque with quarter turns in the stage form. (In the musical accompaniment, use should be made of the standard dance literature.)
16. Temps levé sauté in 4th position.
    Musical time: one measure of 4/4.

Pointe Work

1. Relevé in 4th position en face, croisée and effacée.
   Musical time: one measure of 4/4.
2. Échappé in 4th position croisée and effacée.
   Musical time: one measure of 4/4.
3. Échappé, coming down from 2nd position on one leg with
   the other sur le cou-de-pied devant or derrière.
   Musical time: one measure of 4/4.
4. Pas de bourrée changé en dehors and en dedans, finishing
   in a small pose croisée.
   Musical time: one measure of 2/4 or one measure of 3/4.
5. Pas de bourrée sans changé, from side to side, toe to the
   floor; by the end of the first half of the year, executed at
   45°.
   Musical time: one measure of 4/4 or one measure of 3/4.
6. Pas de bourrée ballotté forward and backward, finishing
   the movement with the toe to the floor croisé or effacé.
   Musical time: one measure of 4/4.
7. Assemblé soutenu, finishing in the small poses.
   Musical time: one measure of 4/4.
8. Glissade forward, backward and to the side and in the small
   poses croisées, effacées, and écartées.
   Musical time: one measure of 4/4 and one measure of 2/4.
9. Pas suivi and pas couru (studied en diagonale).
   Musical time: the movements are done in 1/16 each.
10. Sissonne simple, en face and with épaulement.
    Musical time: one measure of 4/4.
11. Turn in 5th position (pas de bourrée suivi en tournant).
    Musical time: one measure of 4/4.
12. Pas suivi en tournant.
    Musical time: the movements are in 1/16 each.
13. Sus-sous forward and backward.
    Musical time: one measure of 2/4.

Third Year Class

The beginning of the study of centre exercises on demi-pointe. The elementary study of the easiest movements en tournant. The beginning of the study of tours sur le cou-de-pied and beats. Some acceleration of tempo in comparison with the second class.

Barre Exercise

The repetition and development of the exercises of the second class on demi-pointe. Rond de jambe par terre, battement frappé and petit battement, executed up to now in 1/4, may be alternated with the movements executed in 1/8 each, for example, two movements in 1/4 each and three movements in 1/8 each.

1. Whole turn on both legs on demi-pointe, toward and away from the barre.
   Musical time: one measure of 4/4; by the end of the year, one measure of 2/4.

2. Battement frappé in the poses croisées, effacées, and écartées, devant and derrière.
   Musical time: the movement is done in 1/4.

3. Battement double frappé in the poses croisées, effacées, and écartées, devant and derrière.
   Musical time: 2/4.

4. Battement fondu with plié-relevé and demi rond de jambe in all directions and in all poses, forward and backward.

Musical time: two measures of 2/4. Battement fondu in 2/4 and plié-relevé with demi-rond de jambe in 2/4.

5. Battement fondu tombé to the side, forward and backward. Musical time: two measures of 2/4.

6. Battement double fondu in all directions and poses, forward and backward (in the second half of the year, executed with demi-rond de jambe in all directions and poses).
Musical time: double fondu, one measure of 2/4; demi-rond de jambe, one measure of 2/4.

7. Battement relevé lent at 90° and développé in all directions and the poses croisées, effacées, and écartées, attitude croisée and effacée, and in 2nd arabesque, with a rise to demi-pointe.
Musical time: two measures of 4/4 or eight measures of 3/4. Later, one measure of 4/4 or four measures of 3/4.

8. Battement soutenu at 90° in all directions (in the second half of the year, executed in the poses).
Musical time: one measure of 4/4; later, one measure of 2/4.

9. Grand rond de jambe développé, en dehors and en dedans (in the second half of the year, demi-rond de jambe executed on demi-pointe).
Musical time: two measures of 4/4 or eight measures of 3/4.

10. Half turn on one leg with the other raised, en dehors and en dedans, on the whole foot and with a rise to demi-pointe.
Musical time: two measures of 2/4. Half turn in 2/4 and pause for 2/4.

11. Tombé with a half turn changing the position of the foot sur le cou-de-pied, en dehors and en dedans.
Musical time: two measures of 2/4, half turn in 2/4 and pause for 2/4 (combined with other exercises).

12. Préparation and tour from 5th position.
Musical time: one measure of 4/4.

13. Préparation and tour from 2nd position (only for the men's class).
Musical time: one measure of 4/4.

Centre Exercise

The study of the barre exercise with a rise to demi-pointe and on demi-pointe.

1. Battement tendu and battement tendu jeté en tournant, en dehors and en dedans with 1/8 turns (executed in the second half of the year).
   Musical time: 2/4.

2. Battement relevé lent at 90° in all directions and poses with a rise to demi-pointe (with the exception of the poses écartées and 4th arabesque).
   Musical time: two measures of 4/4 or four measures of 3/4.

3. Battement développé in all directions and poses with a rise to demi-pointe (with the exception of the poses écartées and 4th arabesque).
   Musical time: two measures of 4/4 or eight measures of 3/4.

4. 6th port de bras.
   Musical time: two measures of 4/4 or eight measures of 3/4; later, one measure of 4/4.

5. Grand rond de jambe développé, en dehors and en dedans, concluding with a rise to demi-pointe.
   Musical time: two measures of 4/4 or eight measures of 3/4; later, one measure of 4/4.

6. Adagios made up of the poses previously learned, combined with turns on both legs in 5th position, pas de bourrée and other movements.
   Musical time: 4/4, 3/4 or 6/8.

7. Rond de jambe par terre en tournant with 1/8 turns (studied in the second half of the year).
   Musical time: each turn in 1/4.

8. Demi-rond de jambe at 90° from pose to pose.
   Musical time: two measures of 4/4 or eight measures of 3/4.

9. Préparation for tours from 5th, 2nd and 4th positions, en dehors and en dedans.
   Musical time: from 2nd and 4th positions, two measures of 4/4; from 5th position, one measure of 4/4.

10. One tour sur le cou-de-pied from 2nd and 5th positions, en dehors and en dedans.
    Musical time: the same as for the préparation (studied in the second half of the year).

11. Pas de bourrée dessus-dessous.
    Musical time: two measures of 2/4 or one measure of 3/4.

12. Coupé used in combinations.
    Musical time: the movement is executed in 1/8.

13. Glissade en tournant (at first studied with half turns; in the second half of the year, with whole turns).
    Musical time: two measures of 2/4 and later, one measure of 2/4.

Allegro

1. Temps levé on one leg.
   Musical time: 2/4. Each jump is executed in 1/4.

2. Sissonne ouverte in the poses croisées, effacées, and écartées at 45°.
   Musical time: 4/4. In the beginning, the movement is executed in one measure with a pause; and later, without a pause in 2/4.

3. Jeté traveling in all directions and poses (jéte porté).
   Musical time: 4/4; later, 2/4.

4. Sissonne fermée in all directions and in the small poses.
   Musical time: one measure of 2/4.

5. Sissonne tombée in all directions and in the small poses.
   Musical time: one measure of 4/4 or one measure of 2/4.

6. Ballonné in all directions and in the small poses forward and backward (at first, executed in place; in the second half of the year, traveling).
Musical time: one measure of 4/4, later, one measure of 2/4 or 3/4.

7. Petit pas de chat, both versions (throwing the legs out backward or forward).
Musical time: one measure of 4/4, later in one measure of 2/4.

8. Temps lié sauté, forward and backward.
Musical time: one measure of 4/4 or four measures of 3/4.

9. Changement de pieds en tournant with 1/4 and 1/2 turns.
Musical time: one measure of 4/4; later, one measure of 2/4; subsequently, each jump in 1/4.

10. Tour en l'air, for the men's class (executed in the second half of the year, at the discretion of the teacher).

11. Échappé battu in 2nd position.
Musical time: one measure of 4/4; later, one measure of 2/4.

12. Royale.

13. Entrechat-quatre.

14. The stage form of sissonne in 1st arabesque with pas couru.

Pointe Work

1. Pas de bourrée dessus-dessous.
Musical time: two measures of 2/4 or one measure of 3/4.

2. Jeté without traveling and also traveling in all directions.
Musical time: one measure of 2/4 or one measure of 3/4.

3. Pas de polka.
Musical time: 2/4.

4. Échappé in 2nd position en tournant with 1/4 turns.
Musical time: one measure of 2/4.

5. Jeté fondu (stepping en diagonale forward and backward).
Musical time: one measure of 2/4 or 3/4.

6. Glissade en tournant (first studied with half turns; in the second half of the year, with a whole turn).
Musical time: one measure of 2/4 or two measures of 3/4.

7. Préparation and tour from 5th position.
Musical time: two measures of 2/4.

8. Pas de bourrée suivi at a quicker tempo.

9. Sissonne simple en tournant with 1/4 turns on one leg turning in a single direction.

10. Changement de pieds.

Fourth Year Class

The strengthening of stability (aplomb) in various turning movements in the exercise on demi-pointe and on pointe. The development of plasticity of the arms and torso.

Barre Exercise

More complicated combinations of exercises. Half turns on one leg. Rond de jambe en l'air is executed in 1/4 and 1/8.

1. Flic-flac (without a turn).
2. Half turn with the leg stretched forward or backward at 45°, en dehors and en dedans.
3. Half turn with plié-relevé on demi-pointe, with the leg stretched forward or backward at 45°, en dehors and en dedans.
4. Battement fondu at 90°.
5. Grand rond de jambe développé on demi-pointe, en face and from pose to pose, en dehors and en dedans.
6. Développé with plié-relevé in all directions and in big poses.
7. Développé with plié-relevé, with demi-rond de jambe, en face and from pose to pose.
8. Développé-ballotté.
9. Développé with a slow turn, en dehors and en dedans, with the leg stretched forward or backward.
10. Tour from 5th position sur le cou-de-pied en dehors and en dedans, in combination with various exercises.

11. Préparation for tours with temps relevé, en dehors and en dedans.

12. Soft battement on the whole foot.

Centre Exercise

1. Battement tendu and battement tendu jeté en tournant (with quarter turns), en dehors and en dedans.

2. Rond de jambe par terre en tournant, en dehors and en dedans (with quarter turns).

3. Jeté en tournant, traveling to the side with half turns, and in the reverse direction.

4. Préparation from 2nd and 4th positions for tours, à la seconde and in the big poses, en dehors and en dedans, and préparation from 4th position for tours en tire-bouchon.

5. Tour lent in the big poses (executed at first with half turns).

6. 6th port de bras, finishing in a grande préparation in 4th position for tours in the big poses, en dehors and en dedans.

7. One tour sur le cou-de-pied from 4th and 5th positions.

8. Two tours from 2nd position (men's class); for the girls, at the discretion of the teacher.

9. Grand temps lié (going onto the whole foot), forward and backward.

10. Grand rond de jambe développé on demi-pointe, en face and from pose to pose, en dehors and en dedans.

11. Pas de bourrée-ballotté en tournant in the poses croisées and effacées, with quarter turns.

12. Pas de bourrée changé en tournant, en dehors and en dedans.

13. Pas de bourrée dessus-dessous en tournant.

14. Tour lent with passé at 90° from pose to pose, en dehors and en dedans.

15. Pas couru used in combinations.

16. Assemblé soutenu en tournant to the side with half turns and whole turns, en dehors and en dedans.

Allegro

1. Pas chassé in all directions and poses (executed from a preparatory sissonne tombée or développé tombé).
2. Pas emboîté en face at 45°, traveling in a straight line to the side and en diagonale forward and backward (first studied in place).
3. Grande sissonne ouverte in place, in all directions and poses.
4. Grand changement de pieds and petit échappé en tournant with quarter turns and, at the discretion of the teacher, with half turns.
5. Assemblé at 45° traveling in all directions (assemblé porté), preparatory to grand assemblé.
6. Tours en l'air for the men's class.

Batterie

1. Échappé battu with a compound beat.
2. Échappé battu finishing on one leg.
3. Entrechat-trois.
4. Entrechat-cinq.
5. Assemblé battu.

Exercise on Pointe

1. Pas de bourrée en tournant, all versions.
2. Coupé-ballonné to the side.
3. Échappé in 4th position en tournant with quarter turns, in 2nd position with half turns.
4. Sissonne ouverte at 45° in all directions and poses (in place).
5. Jeté in the big poses and plié in the same pose.

6. Changement de pieds en tournant.
7. Assemblé soutenu en tournant to the side with half turns, en dehors and en dedans; in the second half of the year, whole turns.
8. Sissonne simple en tournant with quarter turns; at the end of the year, with half turns.
9. Préparation for tours sur le cou-de-pied from 4th position, en dehors and en dedans.
10. One tour sur le cou-de-pied from 4th position, en dehors and en dedans, studied in the second half of the year.
11. Grande sissonne ouverte in all directions and poses, in place.

Fifth Year Class

Mastery of the technique of beats, tours from various preparatory movements. The beginning of the study of tours in the big poses. The development of plasticity and suppleness in turns from one pose to another. The beginning of the development of elevation in the big jumps.

Barre Exercise

Tours from 5th position with temps relevé and from 2nd position at 45° are combined with various exercises.

1. One tour temps relevé, en dehors and en dedans.
2. One tour from 2nd position at 45° en dehors and en dedans.
3. Développé with a quick (vertical) balancé in all directions and poses.
4. Développé with plié-relevé, turning toward the barre and away from the barre.
5. Grand rond de jambe jeté en dehors and en dedans in 4/4, then 2/4, and by the end of the year, in 1/4.
6. Grand temps relevé, en dehors and en dedans, in 4/4; by the end of the year, in 2/4.
7. Flic-flac en tournant, en dehors and en dedans, finishing at 45°.
8. Battement battu forward and backward with épaulement effacé and croisé.
9. Grand battement jeté balancé forward and backward.

10. Grand battement jeté with a quick développé (soft battement) in all directions and poses and with a rise to demi-pointe.
11. Développé tombe in all directions.

Centre Exercise

The following exercises are executed en tournant: frappé, double frappé, soutenu at 45°, petits battements.
1. Temps lié at 90°, stepping onto demi-pointe.
2. Flic-flac en face, en dehors and en dedans, finishing in a pose at 45° en face (i.e. without a turn).
3. Slow turns from one pose to another, en dehors and en dedans, involving movements of the torso.
4. Battement divisé en quart (with quarter turns) forward and backward, en dehors and en dedans.
5. Tour sur le cou-de-pied by various means: tombé, dégagé, temps relevé, and others, en dehors and en dedans.
6. Two tours sur le cou-de-pied from 2nd, 4th, and 5th positions, en dehors and en dedans.
7. Temps lié par terre with one tour sur le cou-de-pied, en dehors and en dedans, 2 measures of 4/4.
8. One tour sur le cou-de-pied and en tire-bouchon from a grand plié in 1st, 2nd, and 5th positions, en dehors and en dedans.
9. Préparation for tour in the big poses from grand plié in 1st, 2nd, and 5th positions, en dehors and en dedans, followed by a tour lent in the big pose.
10. Grand temps relevé en face, en dehors and en dedans.
11. Tour à la seconde from 2nd position.
12. Tour in the big poses, en tire-bouchon and à la seconde, en dehors and en dedans, from 4th position effacée and croisée.
13. Grand fouetté effacé en dehors and en dedans (first

studied in 4/4, later in 3/4, and by the end of the year, in 2/4).

14. Grand fouetté en face italien, en dehors and en dedans.

Allegro

Échappé in 4th position and assemblé are executed en tournant with quarter turns.

1. Double assemblé in 1/4 (each assemblé in 1/8).
2. Double assemblé battu.
3. Jeté battu.
4. Ballonné battu to the side, in place and traveling.
5. Brisé forward and backward.
6. Rond de jambe en l'air sauté, en dehors and en dedans with a preparatory sissonne ouverte to the side and from 5th position.
7. Grande sissonne ouverte traveling in all directions.
8. Grand temps levé in the big poses effacées, devant and derrière.
9. Sissonne fondue at 90° in all directions and poses.
10. Jeté fermé at 45° to the side and in all poses.
11. Pas failli forward and backward.
12. Grande sissonne tombée in all directions and poses (combined with a pas de bourrée traveling en diagonale and in a straight line to the side).
13. Grand temps lié sauté.
14. Jeté fondu at 90°.
15. Grand assemblé preceded by various preparatory movements: step-coupé, glissade, sissonne tombée, développé-tombé croisé devant at 90°.
16. Grand jeté in attitude croisée and 3rd arabesque from a step-coupé; in attitude effacée and 1st and 2nd arabesques directly from 5th position and from a coupé.
17. Grands emboîtés.
18. Sissonne en tournant simple and ouverte (for the men's class).

19. Cabriole at 45° (for the men's class).
20. Fouetté at 45°, 4-8 times.

Pointe Exercise

1. Rond de jambe en l'air en dehors and en dedans (single).
2. Jeté en tournant traveling to the side with half turns (in a straight line to the side and en diagonale and in the reverse direction).
3. Grande sissonne ouverte traveling in all directions and poses.
4. One tour sur le cou-de-pied from 4th position and from various preceding movements, en dehors and en dedans (at the discretion of the teacher, two tours).
5. Ballonné croisé and effacé, traveling forward and backward.
6. Tour glissade en tournant, in a straight line to the side and en diagonale.
7. Grand battement in all directions and poses.
8. Consecutive tours sur le cou-de-pied from 5th position (from 4 to 8 tours), en dehors and en dedans.
9. Pas de bourrée suivi in all directions and around the room.
10. Two tours from 5th position (at the discretion of the teacher).
11. Fouetté at 45°, four times.
12. Petit changement de pieds en tournant and traveling en diagonale.

Sixth Year Class

The study of jumps preceded by various preparatory movements and the development of ballon in the big jumps. More complicated combinations of beats at a quick tempo.

Barre Exercise

To the exercise of the preceding year are added two tours from 5th position and from 2nd position with temps relevé, finishing in a big pose. Rond de jambe en l'air is executed in 1/4, 1/8 and 1/16. Petit battement in 1/8 and 1/16. Grand battement jeté in 1/4 and 1/8.
1. Grand battement jeté passé at 90°, forward and backward.
2. Développé balancé with a quick demi-rond (d'ici-delà).
3. Port de bras with the leg raised at 90°, forward and backward, on demi-pointe.
4. Flic-flac en tournant from one big pose to another (at first without a turn), en dehors and en dedans.
(Exercises to be executed en tournant: frappé, double frappé, fondu and soutenu, petit battement and rond de jambe en l'air.)

Centre Exercise

1. Flic-flac en tournant, en dehors and en dedans, finishing in the small poses.
2. Battement fondu en tournant at 45° with quarter turns.
3. Battement battu, forward and backward.

4. Grand battement balancé in 2nd position, traveling forward and backward.
5. Grand battement balancé, forward and backward (at the discretion of the teacher).
6. Rond de jambe en l'air en tournant, en dehors and en dedans.
7. Grand temps lié at 90° with two tours from 5th position, en dehors and en dedans, and stepping to the side, with a tour à la seconde on a tour en tire-bouchon.
8. Two tours sur le cou-de-pied from a jump, from all positions (e.g., assemblé, échappé).
9. Tour à la seconde, en tire-bouchon and in all the big poses from 2nd, 4th, and 5th positions.
10. One tour sur le cou-de-pied from a grand plié in 2nd position, en dehors and en dedans.
11. Two tours sur le cou-de-pied from a grand plié in 1st and 5th positions, en dehors and en dedans.
12. One tour in the big poses from a grand plié in 1st, 2nd, 4th, and 5th positions, en dehors and en dedans.
13. Grand temps relevé with tours, en dehors and en dedans (studied in the second half of the year).
14. Battement divisé à demi with half turns and with full turns, en dehors and en dedans.
15. Grand fouetté from a step forward croisé to the poses attitude effacée, 1st and 2nd arabesques; and fouetté from a step backward croisé to the pose effacée devant.
16. Tilt forward and recover the body in 1st and 3rd arabesques (penché).
17. Développé tombé in all directions and poses.
18. Quatre pirouettes with grand port de bras—préparation and one tour en dedans in the big poses (e.g. tire-bouchon, à la seconde, and 1st arabesque), and two tours sur le cou-de-pied en dedans.
19. Two tours sur le cou-de-pied finishing in a big pose.

20. One tour in all the big poses from a coupé and from a step onto a stretched leg, en dehors and en dedans.
21. Temps lié par terre with two tours.
22. Italian adagio with passé and tour-fouetté en effacé.

Allegro

1. Sissonne simple en tournant, en dehors and en dedans.
2. Sissonne ouverte en tournant in all directions and in all small poses, en dehors and en dedans.
3. Sissonne tombée en tournant in all directions and in all small poses, en dehors and en dedans.
4. Temps lié sauté en tournant, en dehors and en dedans.
5. Double rond de jambe en l'air sauté, en dehors and en dedans.
6. Gargouillade (rond de jambe double), en dehors and en dedans.
7. Cabriole at 45° in all directions and in all the small poses (for the men's class, at 90°, by the end of the year; for the women's class, at 90° only in back).
8. Brisé dessus-dessous.
9. Pas ballotté (at first studied forward and backward with a pause after each movement, toe to the floor; later, at 45°).
10. Emboîté en tournant traveling to the side with half turns, in a straight line to the side and en diagonale (at first studied with a pause after each one).
11. Jeté en tournant traveling to the side with half turns, in a straight line to the side and en diagonale and in the reverse direction (first studied with a pause after each one).
12. Grand pas de chat, throwing the legs out backward and forward.
13. Pas soubresaut forward and backward (first studied without a bend backward in the torso).
14. Grand jeté from a preparatory pas couru, glissade, pas de bourrée or sissonne tombée-coupée.

15. Jeté passé croisé and effacé at 45° and 90° from a preparatory step, sissonne tombée or pas couru forward and backward.
16. Grand assemblé en tournant to the side from a step-coupé (in the second half of the year, en diagonale forward and en diagonale backward from a step-coupé effacé).
17. Ballonné en tournant from a step by half turns.
18. Grande sissonne ouverte in the big poses with half turns and traveling in one direction or another, en dehors and en dedans.
19. Grand fouetté sauté italien.
20. Grand fouetté with a step forward croisé to the poses attitude effacée, 1st and 2nd arabesques and, in reverse, to the pose effacée devant.
21. Entrechat-six (first studied facing the barre).
22. Tours sissonne-tombée "blinchiki" (first studied without turns).
23. Tours chaînés, in a series of eight.
24. Échappé en tournant, with a half turn and with a full turn.
25. Double tour en l'air (men's class).
26. Hopping en diagonale forward and backward in the pose 1st arabesque (temps glissé).

Pointe Exercise

All movements of the preceding classes in complicated and dancy combinations.

1. Double rond de jambe en l'air from 5th position and from a sissonne ouverte.
2. Consecutive tours en dehors from a degagé, en diagonale forward en effacé.
3. Consecutive tours en dedans from a step-coupé, en diagonale forward en effacé.
4. Two tours sur le cou-de-pied from various preparatory

movements (e.g., from coupé, stepping onto a stretched leg, from tombé, en dehors and en dedans).

5. Grand fouetté effacé, en dehors and en dedans.
6. Grand fouetté with a step forward croisé to attitude effacée, to 1st and 2nd arabesques and, in reverse, to the pose effacée devant.
7. Consecutive fouetté italien en face.
8. Consecutive tours from 5th position en dehors, traveling en diagonale.
9. Fouetté at 45°, with eight tours.
10. Tours chaînés en diagonale and in a straight line to the side, in a series of eight tours.

Note: Beats and various pas de bourrée on pointe are more frequently included in the combinations of the sixth class. According to the basic programme of the class, extracts from the standard dance repertoire are studied with consideration of the programme for the current productions in the theatre.

Seventh Year Class

The perfection and polishing of the programme for the preceding classes, including the mastery of all the basic movements of classical dance.

Barre Exercise

In comparison with the preceding classes, the tempo is accelerated.
1. Rond de jambe en l'air at 90°, en dehors and en dedans.
2. Grand fouetté en tournant from one pose to another, en dehors and en dedans (tour-fouetté) on the whole foot, then on demi-pointe.

Centre Exercise

The inclusion of jumps in the big adagio, two tours in the big poses and two tours sur le cou-de-pied from all the big poses, en dehors and en dedans.
1. Port de bras in the big poses.
2. Tours in all the big poses from an échappé sauté to a préparation in 2nd or 4th position and from a sissonne-tombée to 4th position, en dehors and en dedans.
3. Fouetté at 45°, sixteen tours en dehors and en dedans.
4. Flic-flac en tournant from one big pose to another, en dehors and en dedans.
5. Two tours in all the big poses from 2nd and 4th positions, en dehors and en dedans.

6. Grand fouetté en tournant, en dehors and en dedans.
7. Tours in the big poses from grand plié in 1st, 2nd, 4th, and 5th positions, en dehors and en dedans.
8. Renversé croisé, en dehors and en dedans.
9. Quatre pirouettes, with two tours in the big poses.
10. Grande pirouette with relevé, eight tours (for the men's class).
11. Italian adagio with the 4th port de bras.

Allegro

1. Jeté battu en tournant, traveling to the side with half turns.
2. Grand ballotté.
3. Grande sissonne soubresaut in all poses.
4. Grande sissonne ouverte en tournant, en dehors and en dedans.
5. Grand fouetté effacé, en dehors and en dedans.
6. Grand rond de jambe en l'air sauté (single).
7. Grand cabriole in all poses forward and backward (first studied from a step-coupé, then from a sissonne-tombée, glissade, and grande sissonne ouverte).
8. Grand pas de basque forward and backward.
9. Saut de basque from a step-coupé in a straight line to the side (and with a turn in the reverse direction (in the second half of the year, in a straight line to the side and en diagonale, with chassé and with pas de bourrée).
10. Grand jeté passé to the side, finishing in attitude croisée or in the poses croisée and effacée devant.
11. Grande sissonne renversée, en dehors and en dedans.
12. Grand jeté renversé, en dehors and en dedans.
13. Jeté passé battu.
14. Sissonne ouverte battue (with compound beats) in the men's class.
15. Gabriole fermée at 45° and 90° in all directions and in all poses.

16. Jeté entrelacé en diagonale effacé and croisé and in a straight line to the side (first studied with a step, afterward with pas chassé and pas de bourrée).
17. Sissonne fermée battue in all directions and in all poses.
18. Sissonne fondue battue at 45° in all directions and poses.
19. Grand assemblé entrechat-six de volé.
20. Grand temps lié sauté en tournant (at 90°), en dehors and en dedans.
21. Tours chaînés en diagonale, effacé and croisé.
22. Tours sissonnes-tombées ("blinchiki") en diagonale, effacé and croisé.
23. Sissonne en tournant with two tours (men's class).
24. Grand jeté pas de chat.
25. Grand fouetté from the pose à la seconde to attitude effacée, and 1st and 2nd arabesques.

Exercises on Pointe

1. Two tours sur le cou-de-pied from a dégagé, step-coupé and tombé, en dehors and en dedans.
2. Fouetté at 45°, sixteen tours, en dehors and en dedans.
3. Tours chaînés en diagonale, effacé and croisé.
4. Tours en dehors with dégagé en diagonale croisé.
5. Tours en dedans en diagonale croisé.
6. Sauté on one leg in the small poses, in place and traveling en diagonale, with arms in various positions (in the second half of the year, en tournant, at the discretion of the teacher).
7. Consecutive tours from 5th position en dehors, traveling forward en diagonale, sixteen turns.

Note: Beats and pas de bourrée suivi are more frequently employed in combinations of a dancy character. On the basis of the programme for the class which already has been passed and with regard to the programme for stage practice, excerpts from the standard literature are studied.

Eighth Year Class

Further perfection of the movements and the polishing of them for the stage. The creation of dancy combinations in adagio, allegro, and on pointe, as well as the selection of more complicated musical material. Development of performing artistry and virtuosity. Special work with the most gifted students.

Barre Exercise

Fouetté at 45° and grand fouetté en tournant are included in the exercise.

Centre Exercise

1. Grand fouetté en tournant from one pose to another, en dehors and en dedans (tour-fouetté).
2. Three tours sur le cou-de-pied from 2nd, 4th, and 5th positions, en dehors and en dedans.
3. Renversé en écarté en dehors from 4th arabesque and en dedans from the pose croisée devant.
4. Grand temps relevé with two tours.
5. Grande pirouette in the big poses with relevé (for the women's class, four tours).

Allegro

1. Pas ciseaux.
2. Grand rond de jambe en l'air sauté (double), en dehors and en dedans.
3. Grande cabriole in all the big poses several times consecutively (men's class).
4. Grande sissonne ouverte battue in all the poses devant and derrière (for the men's class, with compound beats).
5. Sissonne fondue battue at 90° in all directions and poses.
6. Grande cabriole fouettée to 1st and 2nd arabesques and attitude effacée.
7. Grande cabriole fermée forward and backward.
8. Jeté par terre en tournant and jeté en tournant executed en diagonale and in a circle.
9. Grand jeté en tournant in attitude croisée and attitude effacée from a sissonne tombée-coupée, in croisé and effacé from a sissonne-coupée dessous.
10. Pas de basque (tours pas de basque with pas de bourrée, en diagonale).
11. Brisé en tournant in a circle with 1/8 and 1/4 turns.
12. Tours sissonne-tombée en tournant en diagonale croisé and effacé.
13. Révoltade finishing in 3rd arabesque (men's class).
14. Grande sissonne à la seconde de volé en tournant en dedans by means of coupé, a step to the side, pas de bourrée, and pas chassé forward, in a straight line and en diagonale.
15. Saut de basque in a circle and finishing in a big pose by means of a step-coupé, pas de bourrée suivi, and pas chassé.
16. Jeté entrelacé in a circle from a step, pas de bourrée and pas chassé.
17. Jeté entrelacé with beats in all directions finishing in various poses (men's class).

18. Grand assemblé en tournant with beats.
19. Double grand assemblé en tournant without beats (men's class).
20. Grande cabriole double (men's class).
21. Grande sissonne en tournant with a double turn to a big pose (men's class).

Movements studied according to the individual capabilities of the students:

1. Grand jeté en tournant, in a circle (men's class).
2. Entrechat-sept and entrechat-huit (men's class).
3. Grande pirouette, 16 turns in the men's class, 4 turns in the women's class.
4. Révoltade finishing in 1st arabesque (men's class).

Exercises on Pointe

1. Renversé en croisé, en dehors and en dedans.
2. Two tours à la seconde and in all big poses from 4th position, from a coupé, by stepping onto a stretched leg, by a relevé tombé, etc.
3. Grand fouetté en tournant en dedans to 1st, 3rd, and 4th arabesques, and attitude effacée; en dehors, to the big poses croisée and effacée devant.
4. Tours glissade en tournant in a circle (16 tours).
5. Tours en dehors with dégagé en diagonale en effacé in the big poses effacée and écartée devant; en diagonale en croisé in the pose croisée devant.
6. Rond de jambe en l'air with hops on one leg, traveling en diagonale (4 to 8 times).
7. Ballonné with hops on one leg and traveling en diagonale effacé and croisé in the small poses.
8. Tours sur le cou-de-pied without putting the foot down in 5th position (16 tours).

**Movements studied
according to the individual capabilities
of the students (women's class):**

1. Various tours in combination in a circle; for example, tours en dedans chaînés with glissade en tournant.
2. Fouetté at 45° (32 tours).
    Note: According to the abilities of the class, selections are studied from the standard dance literature and from the current repertory.

From the Translator

It is now over ten years since the appearance of this book, during which it has established itself as an authoritative reference work and is used throughout the world by teachers, ballet masters, dancers and writers.

The following errata should be noted:

Page 166 - the first paragraph should read as follows:

The Small Pose Écartée Devant. The left leg is stretched forward, toe to the floor or at 45°. 1. The left arm may be in 1st position, the right in 2nd, the head and torso as in the big pose. 2. The arms may be opened from preparatory position directly to the side at a half-height (45°), palms turned down; the elbows are softly bent and the fingers outstretched.

Page 166 - add the following before *General Remarks*:

The Small Pose Écartée Derrière. The right leg is stretched backward, toe to the floor or at 45°. 1. The left arm may be in 2nd position, the right in 1st, the head to the left. 2. The arms may be opened from preparatory position directly to the side at a half-height (45°), the head and torso as in the big pose.

Page 413 - delete the next to the last paragraph (lines 26 through 33) which is redundant.

Page 415 - add the following paragraph before **Pas de Bourrée Suivi in 1st Position (Pas Couru)**:

Beginning with the first year, it is necessary to perfect this movement gradually in all the succeeding years, developing quickness, lightness and a filigree-like execution.

Page 430 - lines 15 and 16 should read as follows:

45°; in 2/4, five ronds de jambe, 1/16 each.   Repeat all en dedans.

Page 478 - line 7 should read as follows:

7.   Fouetté italien en face.

Furthermore, I wish to acknowledge my indebtedness for aid in the preparation of this translation to the following persons:

To Natalia Roslavleva-René, for bringing the book to my attention at the time of its publication; for writing the foreword; and for finding the energy at a most difficult time to read through the entire manuscript.

To Vera Kostrovitskaya, for authorizing and vigorously supporting my work; for writing many additional sections at my request; for taking the time to answer a great many questions; and for her faith in my ability.

To the many students who have passed through my hands during the course of my work on this book, thus enabling me to perfect my practical grasp of its contents - especially,

To Joyce Horvath, for the extensive help she gave me in the preparation of the first draft and

To Ann Sembower and Howard Epstein, for much help in proof-reading.

To my friend James Fugati, for cheerfully typing the complete manuscript in each of its several drafts and for much encouragement during the entire undertaking.

To Nancy Reynolds, for calling my attention to numerous places needing some sort of clarification for the Western reader.

It is my hope that the reader will find herein the information necessary for establishing the solid foundation upon which the future creative growth of classical dance depends.

SUSAN MARSDEN
ANNE-MARIE BRUNNER ABDER HOLDEN
MADISON, WI.
608-255-8876